Católicos

Resistance and Affirmation in
Chicano Catholic History

MARIO T. GARCÍA

UNIVERSITY OF TEXAS PRESS, AUSTIN

Requests for permission to reproduce
material from this work should be
sent to:
    Permissions
    University of Texas Press
    P.O. Box 7819
    Austin, TX 78713-7819
    www.utexas.edu/utpress/about/
    bpermission.html

♾ The paper used in this book meets
the minimum requirements of ANSI/
NISO Z39.48-1992 (R1997) (Permanence
of Paper).

Library of Congress Cataloging-in-
Publication Data

García, Mario T.
    Católicos : resistance and affirmation
in Chicano Catholic history / Mario T.
García. — 1st ed.
        p.   cm.
    Includes bibliographical references
and index.
    ISBN 978-0-292-71841-8
    ISBN 0-292-71841-1
    1. Mexican American Catholics—
History—20th century. 2. Mexican
Americans—Religion. 3. Mexican
Americans—History—20th century.
I. Title.
    BX1407.M48G37 2008
    282'.730896872—dc22
                    2008000379

To my mother, Alma García Araiza,

who taught me the meaning of right and wrong

In memory of Father Luis Quihuis, S.J. (1951–2007)

CONTENTS

I WANT TO particularly thank Theresa May of the University of Texas Press for her enthusiastic support of my project and her professional advice. I want to also thank the staff at the press that worked on different aspects of the book. The University of Texas Press is to be congratulated for its commitment to Chicano history, and I am honored to be publishing my second book with the press.

Thanks also to those who read the manuscript for the press, including Richard Griswold del Castillo, a pioneering historian of the Chicano experience. I appreciate their professional and constructive comments.

There are many others who in one way or another inspired, advised, or assisted me in imagining, plotting, researching, and organizing this book. They include, in no particular order, Gaston Espinosa, Luis León, Darryl Caterine, Richard Hecht, Jim Viegh, Magdalena Torres, Tom Chávez, Orlando Romero, Tomás Jaehn, Hazel Romero, César Caballero, Salvador Guerena, Ed Fields, Gilda Baeza, Mary Sarbor, Carmen Sacomani, Gerald Poyo, Brother Ed, Fr. Luis Quihuis, Camilo Cruz, Fr. Mike Kennedy, SJ, Henry Olivares and the Olivares family, Lydia López, Fr. Richard Estrada, CMF, Patricia Krommer, Mary Brent Wehrli, Mario Rivas, Arturo López, Fr. Virgilio Elizondo, Tim Matovina, Raul Ruiz, Pedro Arias, Fr. Juan Romero, Fr. Steve Niskanen, CMF, the students in Fr. Virgilio Elizondo's classes at UCSB, Corine García, Monica García, Colleen Ho, Simon Elliott, Randy Lamb, and Maura Jess.

I want to acknowledge in addition the influence of Fr. Virgilio Elizondo, who encouraged me to pursue research in Chicano Catholic history. His friendship over the years has been a great comfort and joy.

As I do in my introduction but wish to do here as well, I want to thank Professor Gaston Espinosa, who as a graduate student at UCSB working with me provided the spark that moved me in the direction of researching the role of religion in the Chicano experience.

I want to also express my gratitude to funding sources that assisted me in my research. These include the University of California, Santa Barbara (UCSB) Academic Senate, UC Mexus, and the Center for Chicano Studies at UCSB.

Research facilities that aided me include the Fray Angélico Chávez History Library of the Museum of New Mexico; the Southwest Collection at the El Paso Public Library; Special Collections at the University of Texas at El Paso; the Benson Latin American Library at the University of Texas at Austin; the Catholic Archives of the Archdiocese of San Antonio; the Department of Archives and Manuscripts of The Catholic University of America; Special Collections at the UCSB Davidson Library; Special Collections in the Charles E. Young Research Library at UCLA.

As always, I thank my wife and companion, Professor Ellen McCracken, for her love and support. Her discovery of the work of Fray Angélico Chávez influenced my work on him and helped inspire my imagination of this larger project.

Of course, I want to acknowledge my two children, Giuliana and Carlo, who for years lived with their parents' research and, in particular, their various research trips, especially to Santa Fe. I hope they learned something from this experience about their parents' work and how these family excursions helped bind us together as a family. I hope they never forget these memories.

Finally, I dedicate this book to my mother, Alma García Araiza. She has influenced and encouraged me since birth. Like Pop, Nama, and Tanaca, my mother will always be in my heart and soul.

Católicos

In Search of Chicano Catholic History

> *While Hispanics [Chicanos] were the first Catholic . . . inhabitants to establish settlements in territories now under U.S. control, for much of U.S. history Hispanics have constituted a relatively . . . overlooked group within U.S. Catholicism.*
>
> —TIMOTHY MATOVINA AND GERALD POYO

> *They can take away everything else from me but not my faith.*
>
> —FATHER VIRGILIO ELIZONDO

Becoming a Chicano Catholic

AS A STUDENT at the University of Texas at El Paso (then named Texas Western College) in the early to mid-1960s, I drove my grandmother Nama to 6:30 Mass every Sunday morning. These years coincided with Vatican Council II, but its liturgical reforms had not yet become evident. The council (1962–1965) had been called by Pope John XXIII to revitalize and breathe some fresh air into the Catholic Church. The Mass I took Nama to was a quiet one, with few in attendance, always the same people. Every Sunday we sat in the same pew at St. Patrick's Cathedral on Arizona Avenue, about a mile from our rented house on the same street on Golden Hill with its sweeping vista of El Paso and Ciudad Juárez to the south. I could see the border and south to Mexico, where Nama had come from many years before during the Mexican Revolution of 1910.

At Mass only the drone of the priest's prayers in Latin could be heard. No homily was preached, so we were out by 7 A.M. We would walk to the car—my mother's, not mine—but before driving home we always stopped at the Mexican bakery, or *panadería*, on Nevada Street, just a couple of blocks from the church. Invariably we ordered the same Mexican breads with colorful names that I, an acculturated Mexican American, never learned. The teenage girl behind the counter, whom I had a crush on, was the daughter of the owner, and she would give us an extra piece of bread, a *pilón*, as Nama called it. We then drove home, where my aunt, Tanaca, had breakfast ready while my mother and siblings still slept. Breakfast consisted of fresh flour tortillas that Nama and Tanaca had prepared early in the morning before Mass. Hot tortillas with butter, eggs over easy, a beef patty, hot coffee, and an orange drink called Tang, a powder that you mixed with water, was my big Sunday breakfast. Then, in the cool of the morning in summertime or the bright glare of the winter sun, I would retire to devour the Sunday *El Paso Times*.

Religion, specifically Catholicism, was always a part of my life. Not a day passed that I wasn't aware of this. It was a Catholicism first planted in the Southwest by Spanish Franciscan friars and over time influenced by both Mexicans and Anglo-Americans (mostly Irish Americans) in a border context. But I wasn't yet aware of all of these historical influences. Awareness would come later, and my education continues to this day.

My family was Catholic but not in a showy, exaggerated way. That wouldn't have been fitting for the Araizas, my mother's family, which saw itself as *gente decente*, or people properly brought up, and from the better classes that had escaped the Mexican Revolution. My great-grandfather Araiza was a well-to-do landowner in northern Chihuahua and partner to American mining companies. His fate was sealed as a supporter of Francisco Madero, the "Apostle" of Mexican democracy, who raised his banner against the long-standing dictator Porfirio Díaz. My great-grandfather was executed, and his family fled to the border and crossed into El Paso. They left everything but their honor and middle-class Catholic values behind.

We were Catholics, but not barrio Catholics. We weren't part of the barrio experience. My mother, born and raised in El Paso, didn't grow up in the big immigrant barrio, El Segundo Barrio, of south El Paso. Her family rented homes in west and central El Paso. Here, the middle-class political refugees from Mexico settled and lived apart from the lower-class immigrants and workers. The refugees built the Catholic church of La Sagrada Familia, or Holy Family Church, in the Sunset Heights area on the west side, where my mother married my father, who came from the state of Durango, thus bridging the Mexican American experience with the mexicano.

But we were always on the move north of the tracks, where the more aspiring Mexican Americans resided. First on Missouri Street, where I was born, then Yandell Boulevard, then Wyoming Street, and then finally to Arizona Avenue, all in the central part of El Paso.

As a kid, I don't remember particular Catholic images in our various homes. We must have had a crucifix and some holy pictures, but I can't remember any. I think it's because we didn't have too many of these images. My family was religious, but not like the poorer Mexican immigrants with their home icons and popular religious traditions. I think this was how my mother preferred it. She was proud of her ethnic heritage, but as a bicultural and bilingual Mexican American, she also desired American mobility. Appearance was important to her, and she probably didn't want a household that was too Mexican or Catholic Mexican.

I remember, however, the elaborate home altar at the home of my friend and classmate Frank de la Torre. I don't remember if this was Frank's house on Yandell or his grandmother's, but I do remember being there with several other neighborhood kids and being awed by the elaborate nature of the home altar. I don't remember specific images, just the clutter of items on it. It was like having a chapel in the house. I now am more aware that home altars, or *altarcitos,* big and small, elaborate and simple, are very much a part of Mexican Catholic culture along the border and in the Southwest. Some installation artists such as Amalia Mesa-Bains today have elevated home altars to artistic heights.

I also connected border Catholic culture with older women wearing black. Nama and Tanaca didn't wear black, or at least not often, nor did my mother, but I recall many other women, especially in El Segundo Barrio and around the Catholic churches there such as El Sagrado Corazón, or Sacred Heart Church, always wearing black, including black shawls, and always carrying rosaries in their hands. This darkness mystified me and made those south-side churches with their ornate icons, including darker and more bloody crucified Jesus figures, scary and even threatening to me.

Border and southwestern Catholic culture also prescribed that I attend parochial schools. My mother insisted on it. She had gone to public schools, but she believed, and correctly so, at that time anyway, that the parochial schools provided a better education. So my siblings and I were enrolled in St. Patrick's Elementary School. I remember the images of the Sisters of Loretto who operated and taught in the school. With one or two exceptions, nuns in classic black habits taught every class. Only a small amount of white garment around the rim of the head habit and a bit in the bodice challenged the blackness of the rest of the outfit. The habits seemed heavy and hot, especially for the El Paso climate, which, with the exception of some bitter cold winter weeks, was warm. I can still smell the odor of the habits, noticeable when I drew near one of the nuns. I don't know whether it was the habit or the nun herself, but it smelled of old cloth or an old gunnysack.

I don't recall whether any of these nuns—sisters they're now called—was Mexican American. Perhaps one or two were. The rest were Anglos. I remember some of their names: Sister Charatina, Sister Eugene Marie. They seemed old to me but probably were not. A few looked young and even pretty, though we couldn't see much of their faces.

It was a good education as far as I knew at the time. There was a good spirit about the school. It was a mixed school. Many of us were Mexican Americans, but there were also a good number of Anglos (again, probably Irish Americans). This was the usual pattern in the parochial schools north of the tracks. The schools in south El Paso and east El Paso parishes like Sacred Heart, St. Ignatius, and Guardian Angel had all Mexican Americans.

The other Mexican American kids and I knew mostly Spanish when we entered kindergarten, but we very quickly picked up English. There was no bilingual education at St. Patrick's in the 1950s when I attended, but, unlike the public schools, you were not punished or made to feel bad about speaking Spanish. The sisters were quite strict, but they seemed to care about us.

St. Patrick's under Monsignor Caffrey, with his full head of white hair, was not a "Mexican" parish even though many Mexican Americans attended the church. It was also the official church of Bishop Sidney Metzger, who seemed to reign for years and years. St. Patrick's and the Catholic churches north of the tracks were different from the "Mexican" churches south of the tracks. Our church was more "Anglo." It seemed more airy and roomier than Sacred Heart, for example, which seemed crowded and stifling. Our homilies were in English, while those at Sacred Heart were in Spanish. St. Patrick's was more middle class while Sacred Heart was poor and immigrant.

Yet our whole culture while growing up was very much Catholic. Our education was Catholic, our friends were Catholic, our sports activities were all centered on the Catholic Youth Organization (CYO), our social events, such as dances, were all connected to our Catholic school. We lived in a border and southwestern Catholic culture. The metaphor of the border is very appropriate because, like real borders, different influences intersected in what some postcolonial theorists refer to as "contact zones."[1] At St. Patrick's, it was an intersection of our family, Mexican American culture with what I now recognize as largely Irish American culture. St. Patrick may have been an Irish saint, but he was our saint as well and not as San Patricio but as St. Patrick. We proudly wore the green and white of our school athletic uniforms.

When I attended the local Catholic high school, Cathedral High School, just up the street from St. Patrick's, I identified with the school's nickname, the "Irish." Our colors were blue and gold, patterned after the University of Notre Dame, and our school song was the Notre Dame fight song. I'll never forget attending, as a member of the school basketball team, the Texas Catholic High School Basketball Tournament in San Antonio in 1961. Before one of our games, an older Anglo gentleman came up to us and asked us why we called ourselves Irish since we were all Mexican Americans. We didn't know what to say. This was before the Chicano movement. "It's our team name," we told him.

Catholic high school only added to my Catholic experience. The boys—the majority Mexican Americans—attended Cathedral, run by the Christian Brothers, while the girls, including, later, my own sister, attended Loretto High School, run by the Sisters of Loretto. The kids from south El Paso at Cathedral introduced me to Chicano barrio culture, which made me more aware of ethnicity. It wasn't that ethnic identity was not part of our growing up. It was. We knew we were Mexicans. How couldn't we? I spoke only Spanish to Nama and Tanaca, who knew little or no English. They didn't really need to because El Paso was such a predominantly Spanish-speaking city, with even more Mexicans across the border in Juárez. But we saw ourselves as middle-class Mexican Americans.

At Cathedral I learned more about barrio culture from my south El Paso classmates. I first heard the term *Chicano*, which the barrio students used as a term of identity. I didn't identify fully with Chicano, but the swagger and what seemed to be pride in identifying as Chicano fascinated me. I was impressed by the Elvis-style ducktail hair the Chicanos wore almost like a crown. I tried to comb a ducktail but with little success, probably because my hair was shorter than theirs. My cowlick always bounced back despite the large amount of hair gel I put on. I liked these kids, although I didn't run around with them. They were more barrio and working-class kids, while I was used to more middle-class friends. However, I played sports with some of them. I think this connection, fascination even, with the barrio students because they were different left an unconscious base for my later work as a historian, such as my history of Mexican immigrant El Paso, which focused on the south side and described the ancestors of many of the Chicanos I went to school with at Cathedral. By later studying and writing about this history, I came to appreciate what I didn't know as a middle-class Mexican American high school student from the "right side of the tracks."

Catholicism in El Paso was not just part of family and school life; it also had a public face. I particularly recall the large procession on the feast day of Corpus Christi each June. Because the temperature at this time of the year approaches one hundred degrees during the hottest time of day, the procession began at 5 P.M., when it had cooled off somewhat. I marched in one while in high school. We gathered at the front of St. Patrick's, people covering the front steps and spilling onto Arizona Avenue and Mesa Boulevard. I remember the richly colored robes of the clergy, including those of the bishop. Especially attractive were the elaborate outfits of the Knights of Columbus with their white-plumed hats and their black and red capes. It was, as the kids say now, awesome. We marched down Mesa into the downtown area, stopping to pray at decorated temporary Stations of the Cross or makeshift altars. People came from all of the parishes; some recited the rosary in English and some in Spanish. The procession through the streets of the city stopped all traffic. The later antiwar marches of the 1960s reminded me of these processions. The procession snaked its way into south El Paso, where it seemed to take on an even more Mexican character. It finally ended at Sacred Heart in El Segundo Barrio. By now it was evening, and this gave the ceremony within the already-somber church an even darker appearance. Everything was in Spanish now and more of a Mexican ritual.

I remember going a few times with my family, including my father, to Cristo Rey, a high hill overlooking the El Paso Smelter on one side and Juárez on the other side of the Rio Grande. At the top of the hill was a large cross of the crucified Jesus dedicated to Christ the King, or Cristo Rey. At different times of the year, but I mostly remember summertime, people made pilgrimages up the hill. It was a winding road, and mostly dark-shawled Mexican women prayed the rosary as they went up the hill. Like the Corpus Christi procession, this impressed me probably because of the spectacle of it all.

Visits to the Evergreen Cemetery, going over the bridge to Juárez to visit the cathedral on that side of the border, accompanying Nama when she took my little sister, Alma María, to offer flowers to the Virgin Mary at a small church on the edge of the barrio, all of these and more remain memories of what Catholicism meant to me growing up in El Paso, along the U.S.-Mexican border, and in the Southwest.

My Catholic faith was very much a part of a particular region. It had a southwestern touch. I now appreciate this more, but in a way my earlier work as a historian of the Chicano experience was already leading me in this direction.

Chicanismo and Catholicism

By the time I was in graduate school in the early 1970s at the University of California, San Diego, I wasn't as Catholic as I was when growing up in El Paso. By now I had become a Chicano owing to my involvement with the Chicano movement when I came to California in 1969. "Chicanismo" replaced Catholicism as my faith. It seemed more relevant to my life then. But I was still culturally a Catholic. I couldn't escape my Catholic upbringing.

As I look back on this highly politicized period in my life, I think my concern for issues of social justice, civil rights, human rights, and respect for people of all backgrounds had its origins in my Catholic background. I didn't become a Chicano out of thin air. My progressive political views were tied in part to my Catholic faith, taught to me by the sisters and brothers. I can't pinpoint any specific doctrine or biblical teachings that constitute this influence. It was just a general sense that we were all people of God and that God did not support such things as racism and discrimination. Growing up during the civil rights era, I sensed in my high school years that what that movement stood for was the right thing and that as Catholics we should support it.

I remember watching on television as a sophomore in college Martin Luther King's "I Have a Dream" speech at the March on Washington in 1963 and being moved by his stirring words. I think my reaction had to do with my own ethnic background as a Mexican American. In the early 1960s, I certainly wasn't politically conscious in ethnic terms, but I believe that part of my positive response to the black civil rights movement had to do with identifying with the underdogs. In my town, Mexican Americans were the underdogs. Growing up along the border, you couldn't help but distinguish between Anglos and Mexican Americans. Even though we had a Mexican American mayor, Raymond Telles, whose biography I would later write, most of the faces in the newspapers and on television, especially those representing business, civic, and social circles, were predominantly Anglos. The annual Sun Carnival Pageant over the Christmas holidays always had an Anglo queen and mostly Anglo princesses, the exception being the representative from Juárez across the border. I always thought this a bit strange since Anglos were a minority in El Paso.

I think that whatever political and even intellectual ideas I had then were shaped by my Catholicism and by being Mexican American in a border context. The Mexican part was intuitive and emotional, the Catholic, cerebral and intellectual. These two characteristics gave me the foundation on which I built my later conscious politics when I became part of the Chicano movement in the late 1960s and after I moved from El Paso to California.

This move influenced my ethnic identity as a Chicano—a term that I now embraced. I rethought my identity and took on a more radical, militant attitude concerning ethnic identity and prejudice. But my conversion to Chicanismo wasn't as big a leap as I might have considered it at the time. During much of the 1960s, I saw myself as a liberal Democrat. I supported not only civil rights, but also liberal reforms such as the War on Poverty, and gradually became more skeptical of the Vietnam War. In retrospect, I don't think it was such a huge change to go from liberalism to radical Chicano movement politics that stood for Chicanos not being ashamed of their ethnic background and for pushing more militantly for civil rights and equal opportunities.

As I became a Chicano radical, however, I also became less of a practicing Catholic. Chicanismo, or what was called cultural nationalism, absorbed my intensity and interest. I remember in the fall of 1969, shortly after arriving in California as an instructor of history at San Jose State College (later University), attending Mass in a downtown San Jose church and thinking how irrelevant the priest's homily was now that I had been stirred by movement rhetoric and the excitement of participating in marches and demonstrations. My public Catholicism began to wane. During the next two decades, I attended Mass and other religious services only occasionally. These were my radical Marxist years, when I combined being a Chicano—in a political sense—with being a Marxist and joining the Trotskyite Socialist Workers Party.

I wasn't a public Catholic, but I believe my earlier Catholic ideals still complemented my new secular ones. From a certain cultural and psychological perspective, my Catholic school formation was still very much a part of me. This included a sense of discipline, respect for others, and a certain proper behavior (which often conflicted with radical politics). I didn't completely abandon the Church. I suppose if asked then what my religion was, I would have still answered, "Catholic." I was a "cultural Catholic," to use Andrew Greeley's term.[2] When I got married in 1979, I knew I wanted a Catholic ceremony. My wife, whom I met in graduate school, is also Catholic, although of Irish-Italian background. It's possible that we found much in common because of our similar Catholic upbringing, including attending parochial schools. In fact, my wife had done me one better. She had attended a Catholic college, graduating from Santa Clara University, a Jesuit institution. Because of her Santa Clara affiliation, we were married in the beautiful Santa Clara Mission. I had no problem with this. I was still a Catholic.

History and Liberation Theology

But what does all of this have to do with my career as a historian? Historians and other scholars bring to their disciplines a whole baggage of cultural, social, political, ideological formation. What they choose to study is more than an intellectual and scholarly interest. They study in part based on who they are. Writing history is also autobiographical. "The storyteller is often as important as the story being told," the historian Michael P. Carroll observes.[3] This doesn't mean that as a historian of Catholic background, I chose to work only on Catholic subjects, although, in my case, I am now doing so. But it does mean that one's personal experiences have a lot to do with one's research choices. The historian is a product of his or her own history. I agree with Timothy Matovina, one of the leading scholars of Latino religion, when he writes, "Every attempt at scholarly analysis is filtered through the lens of the interpreter's bias and social location."[4]

In my case, I think the combination of my Catholic liberalism, which included accepting the new progressive winds of change brought on by Vatican II, and my political radicalism as a result of my involvement in the Chicano movement affected my research and intellectual interests. I chose to work on Chicano history, but it was a history that, in retrospect, was a liberating history. I was not conscious of liberation theology as it was developing in Latin America in the 1960s and 1970s. Liberation theology endorsed social change, even revolutionary change, and called on the Church to have a "preferential option for the poor."[5] However, when I began my dissertation research, which in 1981 became my book *Desert Immigrants: The Mexicans of El Paso, 1880–1920*, I chose to focus on poor Mexican immigrant workers.[6] This was, in a way, accepting a preferential option for the poor. It is a history that in a scholarly sense is aimed at uncovering the role of Chicanos in U.S. history, but at another level is also aimed at showing how the discovery or rediscovery of that history (I was in fact rediscovering my own history in El Paso) could likewise be liberating for Chicanos. A significant part of Chicanismo was knowing oneself through a rediscovering of one's roots in pre-Columbian history, in Mexico, and as a Chicano. The truth, or in this case history, would set us free. It would free us from what Carlos Fuentes calls "mental colonization."[7] Chicano history and those of us who researched and wrote it were both scholars and, in a sense, "theologians." Our history had a dual purpose, although it was certainly written in a professional academic style. Still, the histories that my colleagues and I wrote were not written solely for a professional audience, but also for the movement, for Chicanos, our communities, and for advocating La Causa—the cause of freedom and social justice.[8]

This theological involvement with history—this liberating aspect to my writing of Chicano history—was not only, I believe, the result of secular politics. It was part of my Catholic soul. It was my unconscious reflection on the Passion, the crucifixion of Jesus, carrying my cross, and the resurrection that would follow. I may have come from a middle-class Mexican American Catholic background, but my Catholic sensibility and imagination along with my ethnic border position and my later radical politics did not divorce me from the oppression of the poor. Indeed, it made me sympathetic to researching not only the Mexican immigrant poor, but also the Mexican American middle class (see my *Mexican Americans: Leadership, Ideology and Identity, 1930–1960*) because I knew, having been raised in a struggling middle-class household, that to be middle class and Mexican American also meant experiencing degrees of discrimination, injustice, exclusion, and being treated as a "stranger."[9] When I chose to write about the civil rights and labor rights struggles of what I call the Mexican American Generation between the 1930s and 1960s, I again was continuing that liberationist tendency. To be a Catholic, a Chicano Catholic, along the U.S.-Mexico border and in the Southwest is to be an underdog—what the great novelist of the Mexican Revolution of 1910, Mariano Azuela, referred to as "los de abajo."

This emphasis on liberation extends to some of my other works. In my oral history, or *testimonio*, of Bert Corona, a major Chicano labor and civil rights leader (*Memories of Chicano History: The Life and Narrative of Bert Corona*), I focused on Corona's long history of giving his life, almost in a sacrificial way, to empowering poor and oppressed Chicanos. In my edited volume on Ruben Salazar, a leading Mexican American journalist who championed the rights of Mexican Americans (*Ruben Salazar, Border Correspondent: Selected Writings, 1955–1970*), I stressed not only Salazar's writings on the impact of discrimination and exclusion on Mexican Americans, but how Salazar supported the Chicano movement for liberation. And in the coming-of-age story I coauthored with Frances Esquibel Tywoniak—the tale of a young Mexican American girl in the 1940s in the San Joaquin Valley (*Migrant Daughter: Com-*

ing of Age as Mexican American Woman)—we highlighted a daughter of migrant parents who struggled to make something of herself through education and who went on to dedicate herself, almost in a missionary sense, to teach the children of poor Latino families.[10]

All of these texts have to do with the concept of liberation. They do not ostensibly focus on Catholic themes; however, they are guided, in my opinion, by my ingrained Catholic faith and sensitivity to the marginalized. Not all of this has to do, of course, with just Catholicism. The Chicano movement resonates in my research as well. But the liberationist character of these studies is the product of more than sectarian political influences. I believe there is also a certain spirituality to them that speaks to my own faith background.

Yes, I know some will say, "He's really straining here to make the Catholic connection, and he's reading back what might have not been there at all." This is a reasonable response. I am reading back. But in so doing, I truly believe there is a religious and certainly moral influence in my early work as a historian that in part has to do with my Catholic background.

Chicano Catholic History

My previous work, which I now interpret as a form of liberation theology and of my personal changes, including my rediscovery of my Chicano Catholic background, has brought me to this current work on Chicano Catholic history—my first effort at researching and conceptualizing this field of study. Like most things in life, however, change is rooted in a particular context. For me, this context involved my work in the mid-1990s with a small group of graduate students interested in Chicano/Latino religious subjects. One of these students, Gaston Espinosa, came specifically to UCSB to work with me and to develop a dissertation on early Latino Pentecostal movements in the United States. Luis León and Darryl Caterine, both graduate students in religious studies, asked me to be a member of their examination and dissertation committees and to work with them in the area of Chicano history with some emphasis on religion. I was most happy to assist them and am proud that all three completed their degrees and have gone on to academic and professional careers.

This work with the students stimulated my interest in Chicano religious history. In addition, and of great consequence for me, Espinosa approached me about organizing a conference—one of the first of its kind—on Chicano religions. This was to be an interdisciplinary conference that would include

inviting a number of scholars from diverse disciplines working on various facets of what we called Chicano religions, which included not only Catholicism
but Protestantism and Pentecostalism as well. Espinosa and I coorganized
the conference in 1995, and it was, we believed, very successful. This experience not only moved me further in the direction of religious studies, but also
specifically led to my initial research in Chicano Catholic history. Wanting
to participate fully in the conference by reading a paper in addition to helping organize it, I decided to write a paper on Católicos Por La Raza, a Chicano Catholic group associated with the militant Chicano movement of the
late 1960s and early 1970s. As a student of Chicano history and of the Chicano
movement, I was aware of the role of Católicos and of their struggle to make
the Catholic Church in Los Angeles more relevant to the Chicano community.
The conference, however, gave me the opportunity to research Católicos more
extensively. No study of the group, which emerged in 1969, had been done. I
spent the months leading up to the conference preparing my paper and then
delivering it.

Encouraged by the positive response to my Católicos paper and stimulated
by our conference, I began to think of doing additional research in Chicano
Catholic history. I began to conceptualize a project that would provide a sense
of the evolution of this historical experience over the course of the twentieth century, when Chicanos become a major ethnic group within the United
States. This would not be an overview, but specific case studies of the role of
Catholicism in Chicano life. I also knew that not every period in that century
could be covered, but I hoped to unravel enough research sources to provide
sufficient coverage of this time frame. On the basis of my knowledge of Chicano history and my previous research, I was fortunate to discover various
archival collections along with the ethnographic employment of oral histories
I compiled to put together a panorama of Chicano Catholic history based on
case studies. Some of this research I presented at various religious studies conferences in California and elsewhere in order to get feedback and suggestions
for revisions. This book is the result of my several years of research.

This work was also motivated by my recognition of the dearth of research
in Chicano Catholic history. This remains a very underexplored area in an
otherwise booming field of Chicano history.[11] This is not just my assessment,
but also that of various other historians and scholars. Roberto Treviño astutely
observes, "The religious history of Mexican Americans remains understudied
despite their long association with Catholicism and their growing importance
in the American Catholic Church today."[12] The number of monographs, and
even articles, on religion and the Chicano historical experience is still quite

scant. The same is true of the larger field of Chicano and Latino studies. I agree with Anthony Stevens-Arroyo and Ana María Díaz-Stevens when they write, "Although we admire the many university-based Latino and Latina scholars engaged in Chicano, Puerto Rican, and Cuban American Studies who have greatly enriched the knowledge of Latino experiences, we note with disappointment that most of them have afforded only limited and superficial importance to religion."[13] David Badillo in his recent study of Latino religions also brings attention to this gap: "Religion's primacy has often been ignored in academic writing and other studies on modern Latinos."[14] Luis León expands on this neglect when he writes, "Lamentably, religious thought and practice throughout the borderlands remain largely 'undocumented' in primary texts."[15]

Recognizing this historical vacuum, I hoped I could contribute to fill it to some extent. As Bishop Ricardo Ramírez of Las Cruces, New Mexico, notes in regard to the importance of Chicano Catholic history: "History can be a powerful tool in the clarification of a people's identity and in the unification of its various components."[16]

How does one explain that the field of Chicano Catholic history has been little explored? It cannot be because Catholicism is not a major influence on Chicanos as well as other Latinos. There is no question that religion, specifically, Catholicism, in both its institutional and popular religious forms, has been a central factor in the history of Chicanos in the United States, as it is, of course, in Mexico also.

In my estimation, the neglect of Chicano Catholic history is related to the development of Chicano studies as a field of study beginning in the late 1960s. Chicano studies is a product of the Chicano movement. It helped to institutionalize the intellectual and philosophical tenets of the movement. This included Chicanismo, the ideological grab bag that was rooted in what the movement referred to as cultural nationalism.[17] This stressed a renewed sense of pride in being Chicano and of rediscovering the historical roots of the Chicano, especially the pre-European indigenous background. This emphasis, in turn, led to the further discovery and embrace of the concept of Aztlán, the mythic homeland of the Aztecs that Chicanos conveniently located in the Southwest. Aztlán became the historical birthplace of Chicanos, who eschewed the suggestion that Chicanos were immigrants like many other Americans.[18]

However, the historical homeland also became the lost land as a result of the U.S.–Mexico War of 1846–1848, which led to the taking of Mexico's northern territory, what became the American Southwest, by Yankees under the sway of Manifest Destiny. The conquest of Aztlán imposed U.S. racial attitudes and practices that relegated the newly formed Mexican American population to second-class citizenship and led to the rejection and subjugation of Mexican American cultural traditions and practices.[19] Chicanismo embodied these historical insights and imaginations as well as other views that together formed a new Chicano cognizant of his and her history, emboldened by a new consciousness, identity, and collective personality prepared to wage a struggle for liberation.[20]

Chicanismo and the Chicano movement were largely articulated in secular terms. While it was certainly not devoid of religious influences, for example, César Chávez's farmworkers' struggle and Católicos Por La Raza, for the most part the movement saw itself as a secular one. Indeed, because of its opposition to establishment institutions, the movement, as in the case of Católicos, considered the Catholic Church part of an oppressive system. In fact, as León correctly observes, Catholicism has always represented a dialectic among Mexicans on both sides of the border. While, on the one hand, especially in its institutional form, it has served as an ideology of domination, at another level, especially as León further notes, within popular religiosity it has functioned as a means of resistance. "In short," León asserts, "religion—broadly and personally defined—in addition to serving power as an ideological mechanism of social control, exploitation, and domination, is also effectively deployed in attempts to destabilize those very same forces by people who have access to only the bare resources that constitute conventional power."[21] I agree with León. Although I challenge some of the stress on the secularism of the movement as more religious influences are discovered, still the lingering impression then and even now in Chicano studies circles is that religion played little role in the movement. Gaston Espinosa, Virgilio Elizondo, and Jesse Miranda observe that this misconception "contributed to the long-standing perception that religion has not had an important role in Latino political, civic, and social action."[22] Chicano studies integrated this impression in the form of intellectual "constraints," to use Foucault's term, that did not allow other ways of thinking about the role of religion.[23] As a result, the field's curriculum and research emphasis, for the most part, excluded religious themes or relegated them, as Matovina and Poyo note, to a "peripheral topic."[24] Today, almost forty years after the founding of the first Chicano studies programs, it is still difficult to find many courses that specifically focus on Chicano religion. As noted, this has also had an impact on the lack of research and publications in this area as well.

Yet, despite this omission, there has been a gradual emergence since the late 1980s of what can be called Latino religious studies. Many of these studies are theological in nature or what Andrés Guerrero calls a "Chicano theology of liberation."[25] As the Latino population in the country has exploded in the past thirty years or so and now, numbering over forty million, is the largest minority, this has had an impact on churches such as the Catholic Church given the large number of Latino Catholics. Estimates suggest that Latinos now compose between 40 and 50 percent of all Catholics in the United States. Beginning in the late 1960s, as part of the Chicano movement but likewise influenced by the reforms of Vatican Council II, Chicano/Latino Catholic priests, sisters, and laypeople organized to bring about a new sensibility within the Church to this demographic revolution. This development can be considered the "browning of the Catholic Church" or its "Latinization" or what Díaz-Stevens and Stevens-Arroyo call the "Latino resurgence in U.S. religion."[26]

Led by key theologians/scholars such as Virgilio Elizondo, Roberto Goizueta, Allan Figueroa Deck, Orlando Espin, Ada María Isasi-Díaz, Ana María Pineda, and various others, there has emerged a growing Latino theological response to these changes and challenges related to Latinos in the Church. Some similar work by Latino Protestant theologians has also surfaced. Latino theology in general stresses the particular religious traditions and practices of Latino Catholics, for example, especially those rooted in popular religiosity or the way people practice their faith on a daily basis, as opposed to the role of the institutional Church, which has actually in too many cases been hostile to Latino Catholics and to their popular religious traditions. Latino theology, moreover, in the age of academic multiculturalism, stresses a more pluralistic approach to religion and to the role of ethnicity and culture in the practice of religion. It reflects what the Protestant theologian Justo González refers to as "reading the Bible in Spanish," a metaphor for the inclusion of Latino theological insights in interpreting or reinterpreting the Bible.[27] There is no question that Chicano/Latino theologians have, in turn, helped to stimulate academic scholarship in this area as well.[28]

As a result, more academic studies, primarily in the social sciences but also in the humanistic wing of religious studies, have likewise been produced in the past few years as part of Latino religious studies.[29] However, the one area still less researched is history. This is not to say that history has been entirely neglected. Indeed, in the academic studies as well as in the theological ones, most writers pay some attention to history, although without recurring to actual primary research in historical sources. The few specific historical studies fall into two categories. The first are overviews employing mostly secondary sources, although with some use of primary archival ones. These would include important introductory texts such as Moises Sandoval's *On the Move: A History of the Hispanic Church in the United States.*[30] One groundbreaking text in the area of Chicano Catholic history that bridges secondary research with primary research is the coedited volume by Jay Dolan and Gilberto Hinojosa *Mexican Americans and the Catholic Church, 1900–1965.*[31] This book focuses on the history of Mexican American Catholics in the Southwest, California, and the Midwest and on the importance of religion, in this case Catholicism, to the Chicano experience. In my estimation, this text is the best general historical study to date on Chicano Catholic history. At the same time, it represents an overview of this history.

Second, there is a small but growing body of historical work grounded in archival and oral history sources and on specific topics (as opposed to overviews) that is beginning to discover the significant role of religion, faith, and spirituality in the lives of Chicano Catholics. Of these, I would mention the work of Matovina, who has examined the nineteenth-century roots of Chicano Catholic popular religiosity in San Antonio, as well as his more recent and excellent study of the role that the adoration of Our Lady of Guadalupe has played in the history of San Antonio's Mexican American Catholics.[32] More recently, two significant studies dealing with the Chicano movement period have been published. Lara Medina's fine work on Las Hermanas, the organization of Chicana Catholic sisters in the early 1970s, is a significant contribution to revising the impression, as noted, that the Chicano movement was largely bereft of religious influences.[33] Likewise, Richard Edward Martínez's study of PADRES, the organization of Chicano Catholic priests in the late 1960s that strove to improve the status of Chicano priests and to sensitize the Church to Chicano/Latino needs and religious traditions, challenges these earlier misconceptions about the role of religion in the movement.[34] Other historical studies include Félix D. Almaráz's sweeping biography of the Mexican American Catholic historian Carlos Eduardo Castañeda.[35] In light of his older studies of the Church in Texas, Castañeda in some respects could be considered the father of Mexican American Catholic history. What distinguishes Castañeda's work from the new literature is that his studies focused primarily on institutions rather than concentrating on Mexican American Catholics as a people. By contrast, perhaps the best study of a Mexican American Catholic community is Roberto R. Treviño's recent book on Houston. A comparative history of Latino Catholics, including Chicanos, is David A. Badillo's *Latinos and the New Immigrant Church*. There are also some monographs that while not specifically focused on Catholicism include the role of religion. An excellent example is Anthony Quiroz's study of the history of Mexican Americans in Victoria, Texas, which includes a fine chapter on the relationship of Mexican Americans to the Church. Still another is Linda Gordon's outstanding study of Mexican American miners in early twentieth-century Arizona and the controversy over what she calls "the great Arizona orphan abduction." These studies, along with some journal articles and dissertations, are laying the foundation for the field of Chicano/Latino Catholic history.[36] My book, which is based exclusively on primary sources, contributes to this developing field.

But if Chicano studies has neglected Chicano religions, so too has the larger field of U.S. religious studies, especially Catholic studies. With few exceptions, such as the work of Jay Dolan at Notre Dame, most historians of U.S. Catholicism seem totally ignorant or blasé about the role of Chicanos/Latinos in the history of the U.S. Church. "While Hispanics were the first Catholic . . . inhabitants to establish settlements in territories now under U.S. control," write Matovina and Poyo, "for much of U.S. history Hispanics have constituted a relatively small and frequently overlooked group within U.S. Catholicism."[37] This gap represents part of what Juan Hurtado calls the "social distance" between Chicanos and the Catholic Church.[38] What little does exist, according to Lawrence Mosqueda, "is limited and primarily impressionistic."[39] Hence, the importance of Chicano Catholic history transcends Chicano studies and, hopefully, these studies will lead U.S. Catholic studies to integrate Chicano/Latino Catholic studies and "re-map," to use Matovina's and Gary Riebe-Estrella's term, Catholic studies as a whole in this country.[40] As Sandoval critically observes about the neglect of Chicano/Latino Catholics by U.S. Catholic historians in the Southwest,

> Church historians in the United States have given little attention to Hispanics. Though the Catholic Church had been firmly rooted in the Southwest for 250 years when the United States seized that region from Mexico in 1846, most historians imply that the church was really established by the non-Hispanic bishops and clergy who came after the conquest. Whenever Hispanics are mentioned in those histories, their religious expression is often demeaned; whenever there is controversy,

their point of view is left out. Parish histories, even in places where
Hispanics are now the majority, seldom mention them. It is as if they
did not exist.[41]

Resistance and Affirmation

This book reflects two dominant themes that have emerged in both Latino
theology and Latino religious studies: resistance and affirmation. Indeed, resistance and affirmation are central expressions in Chicano studies.[42] I borrow
the theme from a landmark exhibit at UCLA in 1990 entitled "Chicano Art:
Resistance and Affirmation, 1965–1985" (the CARA Exhibit). "Chicano art is
the modern, ongoing expression of the long-term cultural, economic, and political struggle of the Mexicano people within the United States," reads the
founding statement of the CARA National Advisory Committee. "It is an affirmation of the complex identity and vitality of the Chicano people."[43] If Chicano art is an example of Chicano ethnic and cultural resistance and affirmation, so too, I maintain, is Chicano Catholicism. Discussing my thesis here is
not an afterthought. I believe I had to first position my personal context in
coming to this study and, second, to address the historiographical vacuum
that my study seeks to help fill. Having done so, I now want to discuss my
overall thesis. This is particularly important because, unlike a more traditional historical text focused on a single topic, my book encompasses a variety
of topics in a case study format. It is an anthology except that I have written all
of the chapters myself.[44] Because of this, however, it is important to connect
the different case studies. My thesis flows from my reflection of what these
chapters have in common.

By *resistance* I mean that Chicanos over time have resisted attempts to
deprive them of their religious identity and of their religious traditions and
practices, especially those associated with popular religiosity—the religion
of the people that is not always linked to the institutional church. Resistance
by Mexican Americans to what Díaz-Stevens and Stevens-Arroyo term "pious colonialism" and what Guerrero refers to as "spiritual colonization" imposed by the U.S. Catholic Church after the American conquest of Mexico's
northern territory in 1848 often took a religious form. "We think," Díaz-
Stevens and Stevens-Arroyo note, "that religious traditions serve as a collective memory for the colonized, preserving a cultural identity that cannot be
easily destroyed even by military conquest."[45] Although affected by the forces
of Anglo-Catholic acculturation, what Matovina and Riebe-Estrella term the

"Segundo Mestizaje," Chicanos and other Latinos have struggled—personally and collectively—to retain their identity as Mexican/Chicano/Latino Catholics.[46] This can be interpreted as both a religious and political response and as what Treviño refers to as "ethno-Catholicism" and Gina Marie Pitti calls "ethno-religious identity."[47] This was their way, as Dolan and Hinojosa stress, of understanding the Church as community.[48] Thomas Steele further notes that religion "protected the culture . . . from the worst of all failures: the loss of the people's confidence in their way of life."[49] Resistance has included remembering and passing on traditions and practices associated with weddings, baptisms, *quinceañeras*, feast days, blessings, home altars, pilgrimages, and key religious holidays, such as the feast day of Our Lady of Guadalupe on December 12. Such remembering was a way, Treviño observes, of fostering self-respect and confidence among Mexican American Catholics.[50] Matovina, in his history of Guadalupe celebrations and rituals at the historic San Fernando Cathedral in San Antonio, links these events to Mexican American ethnic resistance: "Guadalupe celebrations at San Fernando have often ritually counteracted the hostility and disdain that ethnic Mexicans have endured in San Antonio, dramatically positing an alternative worldview that reinforces their sense of dignity and personhood and enables them to combat prejudicial views and the expectation that they become 'Americanized.'"[51] Linking the popular religiosity of Chicanos to that of the workers and peasants of Latin America, the theologian Alan Figueroa Deck writes, "For popular religiosity is one of the more powerful forms of *cultural resistance* that exists in Latin America."[52] Hinojosa adds, "Traditional Catholic devotions energized their [Mexican Americans'] spirituality and complemented their religiosity, assisting the faith community to survive exploitation and change."[53] The one corrective I would add here, based on my research, is that not all Chicano Catholic resistance, as additional critics such as Luis León argue, has been based solely on popular religiosity, as the above quotations suggest. Chicano Catholic resistance has also been asserted in more public political venues, as several of my chapters reveal. That is, resistance has also come in the form of overt political struggles that are faith-based and that, while undoubtedly influenced to an extent by popular religion, go beyond that in more public displays of Chicano Catholic political movements. As León astutely observes, "Religions are shaped and reshaped in the struggle for political power."[54]

But the other side of resistance is affirmation. Indeed, they are two sides of the same coin. To resist is to affirm. As Bishop Ricardo Ramírez, a leading exponent of liberation theology among Chicanos, stresses, "The struggle of

Hispanic Americans to maintain their cultural-religious character has gone hand in hand with the social-economic-political struggle."[55] By struggling to maintain, adapt, and pass on particular ethnic religious traditions, Chicanos likewise have affirmed their identity and religious culture. Father Elizondo notes about Chicano Catholics, "They can take away everything else from me but not my faith."[56] The interrelated themes of resistance and affirmation, at the same time, coincide with the broader historical experiences of Chicanos in the United States as they resist discrimination and exploitation and affirm their ethnic and cultural identity. Indeed, in my own work in Chicano history, these themes are manifest in my focus on such issues as civil rights and labor struggles, political representation, community leadership, and personal efforts to construct Chicano identity.

Yet, the twin themes of resistance and affirmation—whether in a religious, cultural, or political context—do not, and should not, convey a static, monolithic process. Religious identity and culture, like political identity and culture, are evolutionary. Different historical and social conditions impact this change. Moreover, within Chicano Catholicism there is a range of evolving differences that relate to the historical, cultural, and political diversity of Chicanos. These differences include immigration status, the U.S.-born populations, class context, regional location, cultural and language variables, political identifications, gender, and, of course, religious diversity. My case studies suggest such evolving differences.

These differences likewise include terminology. I understand that the term *Chicano* remains a debatable one. Not every person of Mexican descent employs it or relates to it. This is self-evident. I am using the term *Chicano* in my main title and as an umbrella reference term because it is used by my fellow historians to encompass their studies concerning Mexican American history. There is a field called Chicano history just as there is a discipline called Chicano studies. My book, and hence my use of *Chicano* in the title, deliberately engage these fields. My study is in dialogue with Chicano history and Chicano studies. This dialogue is similar to that of Treviño in his book on Mexican American Catholicism in Houston. Although Trevino does not use the term *Chicano* in his title, he acknowledges in his introduction that his work aims at a "recovery of Chicano religious history."[57] Having said that, I also acknowledge that historically outside the academy people of Mexican descent in the United States use various terms. As a result, the chapters will reference certain regional and historical terms, for example, *Hispano, Mexican American*, and, of course, *Chicano*. At various points, in order to suggest a certain connection with other people of Latin American descent in this country, I will use the term *Latino*. But I use the term *Chicano* because the context of my study is Chicano history.

In resisting discrimination and exploitation and affirming their cultural identity, Chicanos likewise address the issue of poverty. Chicanos have historically been a poor people, working as cheap labor in agriculture, mining, railroads, construction as well as urban industries and services, including domestic work. As a result, Chicano theologians and scholars further emphasize the importance of writing a Chicano Catholic history from the perspective of the poor. They encourage others to adopt in their studies a preferential option for the poor. Sandoval, for example, urges "a new kind of church history emphasizing the religious experience of the poor."[58] I accept this challenge and have written this book largely from that perspective and in the hope of influencing the "critical consciousness" advocated by Figueroa Deck in his writings.[59]

Hence, resistance and affirmation characterize the chapters in my book. Although each chapter stands on its own as an individual slice of Chicano Catholic history, the chapters are tied together, in one form or another, by the expression of resistance and affirmation. This is what holds them together collectively.

In Chapter One, I interpret the work of Fray Angélico Chávez, a Franciscan friar and one of the most significant historians of Hispano Catholicism in New Mexico in the twentieth century, as a form of resistance and affirmation history. *Hispano* as well as *Spanish-American* were the terms that people of Spanish/Mexican descent in New Mexico employed following the U.S.-Mexico war and to distinguish themselves from the incoming Anglo-Americans.[60] Reflecting the political, social, and cultural tensions between Hispanos and Anglos in that state, Fray Angélico, through his various histories of Hispano-Catholicism, challenged dominant notions of history in New Mexico after 1848 and the U.S. conquest. By affirming that the history of nonindigenous New Mexico commenced with the Spanish settlements in the seventeenth century, including the major role of the Franciscan missionaries, Fray Angélico brought attention to the Hispano contributions to the history of his native state. In all of his work, he strongly observed the pervasive influence of Hispano-Catholicism in the history and culture of New Mexico. Years before the Chicano movement elaborated its concept of a counterhistory, Fray Angélico, beginning in the 1940s, was proposing his version of an oppositional history to an Anglo-inspired version that marginalized Hispanos/Chicanos.

Resistance and affirmation can likewise be seen in the Chicano civil rights efforts inspired by Catholic social doctrine. This is the thesis laid out in Chapter Two, which concerns the leadership of two vital Mexican American

Catholic leaders in Texas from the 1930s to the 1950s: Cleofas Calleros of El Paso and Alonso Perales of San Antonio. In their efforts to deal with racial discrimination against Mexican Americans, both were influenced by Catholic social doctrine. It is their Catholic faith in large part, I argue, that provides their sense of right and wrong and that influences their civil rights leadership. Catholic doctrine and civic culture come together in the work of Calleros and Perales. Their Catholicism provides much of the basis for their resistance to racism and also affirms their sense of the dignity of Mexican Americans as children of God and as citizens of the United States. Calleros and Perales belonged to what I term the Mexican American Generation of that period, who attempted to connect their Mexican cultural background and identity with their position as U.S. citizens—the "third space" that both David Gutiérrez and Gina Marie Pitti employ to suggest the ethnic space occupied by Chicanos. Calleros and Perales represent Hinojosa's observation of this generation, that it "attempted to define not only what it meant to be Mexican American, but also what it meant to be a Mexican-American Catholic." [61]

The significance and value of Catholic popular religious practices to a sense of identity and community is the theme of Chapter Three. It examines the work of Hispano Works Progress Administration (WPA) personnel as part of the New Deal's Federal Writers' Project in the 1930s. This work led to major efforts to record and help preserve the Hispano village culture of northern New Mexico, including religious traditions and practices. Such forms of popular Catholicism had been the central basis of village culture for generations, much of it passed on by oral traditions. It represents what Harvey Cox calls the "people's religion" and what Figueroa Deck refers to as the "Catholic wisdom of the common people." [62] Deprived of access to priests in these sparsely populated and isolated areas, Hispano villagers relied on themselves to maintain their Catholic faith and develop their various rituals, beliefs, and practices, including the observation of the feast days of each village named after a particular saint. This represented what Sandoval calls a "parallel church" or "non-institutional religion." [63] The WPA set out through oral history and observation to record this popular religiosity as a way of validating it and preserving it for future generations. The extensive WPA records for New Mexico are a gold mine for the study of Hispano-Catholic popular religion that, on the one hand, served to resist Americanization at the expense of Hispano culture and, on the other, to affirm those traditions.

By World War II the Catholic Church hierarchy recognized that Mexican American Catholic culture, including the Spanish language, was of vital importance in maintaining the faith among Mexican Americans. Based on the records of the National Catholic Welfare Conference, Chapter Four reflects the resistance, affirmation, and vitality of Mexican-origin Catholic faith in the Southwest at a time when efforts by the Anglo-Catholic Church sought to undermine this faith and impose an Americanized Catholicism on Mexican Americans. Too many Anglo clerics incorrectly regarded Chicano Catholic rituals as a "scandal" and as "superstition." [64] "To preserve the faith of 'Americans,'" Jeffrey Burns observes, "these practices had to be prohibited. Nonetheless, with or without approval, they persisted, reflecting the authentic faith experience on the part of the Mexican/Mexican-American people." [65] The failure of this effort by the period of the war forced the Church to understand that the best way to reach out to Mexican Americans was to utilize Mexican American Catholic traditions, including the use of Spanish. This change of attitude was the result, as the chapter notes, of two key factors. The first is the perceived need by the Church to integrate Mexican Americans into the national effort in support of the war. The war was a test of ethnic Catholics' loyalty to the United States, and in the Southwest this meant including the large numbers of Mexican American Catholics in the effort. The second reason, and perhaps the more important one, had to do with the Church's concern over inroads made by Spanish-speaking Protestant and Pentecostal groups into Mexican American communities. Fearing the loss of more Mexican Americans to rival religions, the Church fell back on a more conscious outreach to this community through the validation of various Mexican American faith practices as well as the greater use of Spanish by its clerics. The Church's transformation, or at least partial transformation, prior to the changes of Vatican Council II in the 1960s, which encouraged multiculturalism in the Church through the process of inculturation, in my opinion, speaks to the resistance and affirmation by Mexican American Catholics in the pre–Vatican II years and the pre–Chicano movement era.

The Chicano movement, however, introduced new expressions of resistance and affirmation, as exemplified by the case of Católicos Por La Raza, the focus of Chapter Five. Although displaying new and more militant ideologies and tactics, the movement, as Sandoval notes, was "really part of the same struggle that has characterized the dealings of the Hispanic people with their oppressors ever since the occupation of the Southwest in 1836 and 1848." [66] Organized in 1969 in Los Angeles by young Chicano Catholics who identified with the movement, Católicos challenged the Catholic archdiocese of Los Angeles for not doing enough for Chicanos, who formed a sizeable percentage of all Catholics in the archdioceses. Espousing a Chicano version of liberation theology, the group called on the Church to return to its roots as a Church for the poor and oppressed rather than continue to be the billion-dollar institution that Católicos charged it with being. Displaying the militancy and confrontational politics of the movement and of 1960s politics, Católicos publicly protested against the Church and, in particular, Cardinal Francis McIntyre, its head in Los Angeles. Its most celebrated demonstration involved a Christmas Eve confrontation at the newly built three-million-dollar St. Basil's Church on Wilshire Boulevard prior to the cardinal's midnight Mass. After holding its own counter-Mass, members of Católicos attempted to enter the church to address their demands to the cardinal, only to be met by undercover police posing as ushers. Confusion and conflict ensued, leading ultimately to the arrest and trial of twenty-one Católicos members. However, their tactics brought attention to their issues and forced the Church, especially after Cardinal McIntyre's resignation following the St. Basil's protest, to address more concretely the conditions of its Mexican American adherents. As noted, Católicos was an example not only of the role played by religion, specifically Catholicism, in the Chicano movement, but also of a new generation of Chicano Catholics who resisted second-class citizenship within their own Church and affirmed through their protests their right to the resources of the Church and to their identity as Chicano Catholics.

Influenced by Católicos and by the Chicano movement, some Chicano Catholic priests, beginning in the 1970s, took up the struggle to link Catholic values to civic life, in particular to advance the conditions of Chicanos/Latinos. Working within the Church but influenced by protest politics, such priests mobilized as community priests engaged in "civil religion."[67] By community priests, I mean those who use the Church as a foundation to reach out to link the Church to civil and human rights struggles affecting the Chicano/Latino communities. They represent the influential roles that parish priests can and do play in community movements. This is where the people are, and some Chicano priests understand this. This is the focus of Chapter Six, which concerns Fathers Juan Romero, Luis Quihuis, and Virgilio Elizondo. Each in his own way displays various characteristics of the meaning of community priest, such as community activist, community organizer, and cultural worker.

In the 1980s a new Chicano/Latino Catholic movement surfaced, one that, although still influenced by the politics of the 1960s, adapted it to changing conditions, specifically, around the issue of providing sanctuary for the thousands of Central American refugees flocking into Los Angeles. This was the sanctuary movement at La Placita Church (Our Lady Queen of Angeles) in downtown Los Angeles led by Father Luis Olivares, the charismatic and dedicated pastor of the church. Olivares and his movement are the subject of Chapter Seven. Fleeing the civil wars in Central America, the refugees were regrettably refused safe haven in the United States. The Reagan administration insisted that the refugees from countries such as El Salvador were not legitimate political refugees but rather undocumented immigrants illegally entering in search of jobs. Rejecting this argument on moral grounds, churches and synagogues in the United States opened their doors to the refugees to shelter them and assist them in their efforts to avoid deportation. In Los Angeles, La Placita led this movement through the leadership of Father Olivares. Father Luis and his supporters, both Latinos and Anglos, resisted efforts to deny the Central Americans safe refuge, insisting that they were obeying a higher law, God's law. They affirmed that human life was above legal technicalities and that sanctuary was more than anything else a moral issue.

Finally, Chapter Eight underscores the continued importance of religion and spirituality, especially popular religiosity, to contemporary Chicano/ Latino Catholics. Based on oral history projects conducted by students at the University of California, Santa Barbara in the late 1990s, the chapter explores the resiliency of such popular religious traditions as the role of women in preserving religious practices in the home, what some theologians refer to as "abuelita theology" or "mujerista theology"; blessings; pilgrimages; home altars; celebrating El Día de los Muertos and Our Lady of Guadalupe; and sundry other practices.[68] Interviews with a diverse group of both older and younger Chicanos/Latinos reveal the significance of Catholic rituals in providing a sense of comfort and community in sometimes hostile environments in the United States and of the need for a particular Chicano/Latino Catholic identity.

These eight chapters, in turn, also reflect three important subthemes. One involves the role of Catholic intellectuals in Mexican American communities who have expressed a particular Chicano Catholic perspective through their writings. This includes the work of Fray Angélico Chávez in his many historical texts as well as journal and magazine articles. In addition, Cleofas Calleros and Alonso Perales, besides their community work, likewise served as public intellectuals through their long-standing newspaper columns as well as books. Both are the precursors of contemporary Chicano Catholic journalists like Richard Rodríguez and Rubén Martínez.[69] Also a public intellectual, Fa-

ther Juan Romero, in his many essays, published and unpublished, added to a
Chicano Catholic worldview. Finally, Father Virgilio Elizondo, in addition to
carrying out his pastoral mission as a community priest, emerged in the 1980s
as the leading Chicano Catholic theologian whose many treatises have helped
shape contemporary Chicano Catholic thought.

If the role of intellectuals forms one aspect of this study, still another is
the key role of Chicano popular religiosity. The WPA project, in recording
and preserving Hispano popular religious traditions and practices among
the villagers of New Mexico, speaks to the resiliency of this religious culture
centered on the people themselves and outside the Church's control. In turn,
the continued importance of Chicano Catholic practices, including the use
of Spanish, forced the institutional Church by World War II to incorporate
some of these practices in order to insure the loyalty of Chicano Catholics and
to ward off competing Spanish-speaking Protestant and Pentecostal rivals.
The strength and continuity of Chicano Catholic popular religion are further
seen in the oral history projects conducted by UCSB students in the late 1990s.
These reveal the persistence of popular forms of religiosity well into the late
twentieth century and the new millennium.

Finally, an additional theme concerns the linking of religion to public life
among Chicano Catholics. Here the work of Calleros and Perales in the civil
rights struggles of what I call the Mexican American Generation is suggestive.
Influenced, as noted, by Catholic social doctrine, both consciously brought
together their Catholic faith and their civil rights struggles. If the Mexican
American Generation laid the foundation for the civil rights movement among
Mexican Americans, the Chicano Generation of the 1960s and 1970s furthered
this effort in a more militant and challenging way. Católicos Por La Raza, the
work of the community priests, and the sanctuary movement led by Father
Olivares, all expressed a new and more militant culture of protest influenced
by the Chicano movement and the continued linking of religion to public life.

Approaching these themes under the rubric of resistance and affirmation,
my book will bring greater attention to the importance of Chicano Catholic
history in a reevaluation not only of Chicano historiography but also of Chicano studies as a whole and of U.S. Catholic history and Catholic studies. One
cannot fully understand Chicanos, or any ethnic group for that matter, without taking into consideration the significant role played by religion in shaping
community. In turn, one cannot do justice to the history of U.S. Catholicism
without integrating the history of Chicano/Latino Catholics. This is part of
the dialogue that Figueroa Deck calls for between mainstream U.S. Catholi-

cism and Hispanic Catholicism, a dialogue that is essential to "shaping the future as well as recalling the past." [70] I hope that studies such as mine will lead to this appreciation and to concrete changes, such as new and more courses in Chicano studies and religious studies on Chicano/Latino religions as well as increased research projects on Chicano Catholicism and other manifestations of religious practices. Such revision is important not only on an intellectual and academic level, but also on a demographic level as the Chicano/Latino population continues to grow and attain importance in the United States. Chicanos/Latinos will transform the contours of this country in the twenty-first century, not least its religious culture. Of this change, Father Elizondo asserts, "The Hispanics are not only entering the U.S. Catholic Church, but we are enriching it by bringing in everything which is distinctive to our expressions of faith: music, colors, dance, ritual and tradition." [71]

Religion in the United States, certainly Catholicism, will become very much a Chicano/Latino-influenced one. While Chicanos and Latinos will continue to acculturate and be influenced by other ethnic cultures and a more generic U.S. culture, they will, at the same time, maintain and adapt their culture, including their religious culture, to this society. Yet such changes are not something to be feared or to be threatened by, but rather to be welcomed because, as Father Elizondo stresses, they will enrich us all. The strong religious values of Chicano/Latino Catholics exemplified in my book suggest that we can only profit by this strength. At a time of increasing concern over eroding values and morals in U.S. society, we should welcome this infusion of strong religious traditions and practices that characterize much of the Chicano/Latino communities.

ONE

Fray Angélico Chávez, Religiosity, and New Mexican Oppositional Historical Narrative

We Hispanic New Mexicans are all Penitentes in some way, through blood origins and landscape and a long history of suffering.

—FRAY ANGÉLICO CHÁVEZ

I WANT TO begin my exploration of Chicano Catholic history by focusing on a remarkable Catholic priest and intellectual whose work encompasses most of the twentieth century: Fray Angélico Chávez of New Mexico. Moreover, by beginning with Fray Angélico I am able to introduce the concept of oppositional historical narrative, which, while not directly employed in the other chapters, encompasses the entire text. Indeed, an oppositional historical narrative reflects resistance and affirmation and, in Fray Angélico's case, Hispano Catholic resistance and affirmation. Commencing with a New Mexico figure is additionally appropriate because this area is one of the foundational locations of the beginning of what is called Chicano history. This, of course, is where the use of particular terms becomes complicated. The term *Chicano* is a twentieth-century invention and hence is unknown in earlier periods. At the same time, the definition of what constitutes Chicano history is currently seen in an expansive perspective that covers the Spanish colonial period of the Southwest to the present.

Fray Angélico's oppositional historical narrative can be better understood by recognizing that since the 1960s the master historical narrative of the

United States has been significantly challenged. This narrative, which we all learned in school, proposes an America largely based on what can be termed the Anglo-American, eastern-based ethnic experience. From this perspective, northern European, predominantly Protestant peoples in North America are given center stage, especially in the formative years of the colonial era and early years of the republic.

It is this narrative that over the past three decades has been countered by oppositional narratives. These alternative stories decenter the master narrative and permit other historical experiences and voices access into a reconstructed U.S. historical identity stressing not one major ethnic community but multiple ones. Oppositional historical narratives depicting the roles of Native Americans, African Americans, Spanish/Mexican Americans (Chicanos) as well as Euro-American women and Euro-American working-class peoples have affected the way we are redefining American history. Such narratives are not or should not be intended to eliminate the Anglo-American role, but to put it into perspective by recognizing the heterogeneous nature of the American experience.

In the Southwest, this challenge as well as to its regional counterpart, likewise extolling the contributions of Anglo-Americans at the expense of those of other ethnic groups in the region, has come significantly from the development of Chicano historiography. Since the 1960s and the emergence of the militant, nationalist Chicano movement, historians, most of whom are of Chicano descent and identify with the movement's stress on ethnic awareness, have rewritten southwestern history by calling attention to the major roles played by Chicanos—people of Mexican descent—in this area. Consequently, themes such as communities and cultures that antedate the arrival of the United States, U.S. expansion and conquest, internal colonialism, Mexican immigration, the establishment of a southwestern race and class system, the role of Mexican Americans in civil rights activities in the region, and the importance of multiculturalism in the Southwest have all been advanced by Chicano historians.

Although not often recognized, this influence on and inspiration for the rewriting of southwestern and western history gave rise, directly and indirectly, to the so-called new western history. Building on Chicano oppositional historiography such as Rodolfo Acuña's theme of internal colonialism in his classic text, *Occupied America* (1972), the new western history has called attention to other omissions and contradictions in earlier western historiography. Such early work was heavily based on the influence of Frederick Jackson

Turner and his dubious concept of the evolution of American democracy into the western frontier.[1]

Chicano oppositional historical narratives can be divided into the following general themes. First, Chicano historiography problematizes the origins of southwestern history. By noting the Native American/Spanish colonial roots of Chicano history, this revisionist perspective encourages us to rethink the issue of time and space in the history of the Southwest. Time is reconfigured to the extent that southwestern history is pushed back to encompass the earlier Indian/Spanish communities and encounters prior to the American conquest of the region in the 1840s. Space is rethought in that Chicano historiography stresses not the usual east to west movement of peoples found in the master historical narrative, but a south to north perspective. *El norte* becomes the precursor of the Southwest. In this sense, the concept of the Southwest becomes a specific Anglo-American invention.

A second characteristic of Chicano historiography is the emphasis on multiple identities in the Southwest. Just as there is no such thing as *the* American experience, there is no such thing as *the* southwestern experience. Despite the essentialist Chicano identity promoted by the Chicano movement (which has since been significantly revised), Chicano historiography, by paying attention to Spanish/Mexicans in the region, has helped to diversify the concept of a southwestern regional identity. It has helped to complicate in a positive fashion the issue of identity with respect to race, ethnicity, class, gender, and even sexuality. Who and what is a southwesterner, just as who and what is an American, is not as easy to define as a result of post-1960s historiography. It is out of this poststructural/postmodernist revisionist perspective on historical identity that a new and constantly evolving synthesis of both southwestern and American identity is hopefully emerging.

Finally, Chicano historiography has provided a revised way of thinking about who makes history. It has challenged the general notion of what I call historical agency. Chicanos now revise the idea that it has been largely Anglo-Americans who have made southwestern history. Chicano historiography has countered the stereotype of Chicanos as being either simply victims of history or, worse, invisible in history by seeing Chicanos in a postcolonial fashion as the makers of history and as struggling to control their own destinies. Through their families, communities, churches, popular religious practices, and organized leadership, Chicanos have shaped the contours of southwestern history and of American history.

Roots of Chicano Oppositional History

While much of this oppositional historical revision has come in the wake of the Chicano movement of the late 1960s and early 1970s, there are important precursors to Chicano historiography. Chicano historiography does not exist in a vacuum. It has a genealogy that while not as evident during the glory years of the movement is now, in what I call the post–Chicano movement period, becoming more appreciated. Further removed from the militant ethnic nationalism of the movement that stressed the radical roots of Chicano history, postmovement writers, including historians, are now recognizing the diversity of the Chicano experience in contrast to the unified subject offered by the movement. This emphasis on diversity has led to a greater sensitivity and acknowledgment of premovement writers and intellectuals, who in their own historical periods produced what can be interpreted as oppositional narratives as a way of countering, sometimes subtly and covertly, the master southwestern narrative that excluded, marginalized, or exoticized the Spanish/Mexican experience.[2]

Genaro Padilla and Rosaura Sánchez, for example, have recently rediscovered the oppositional quality of the post-1848 oral and written narratives of Californio men and women. The Californios, by stressing a romantic nostalgia for the pre-1848 rancho experience, were, according to Padilla, affirming their identity as Californios in the U.S. period and critiquing what they considered to be the destructive consequences of the American conquest and annexation. In the case of New Mexico, Padilla, in his revised interpretation of such figures as Rafael Chacón, notes that the assertion of New Mexican popular culture, including regional cuisine, was a form of opposition to the Americanization movement that became even more prominent into the twentieth century.[3]

In my own recent work on what I call the Mexican American Generation of the 1930s, 1940s, and 1950s, I have proposed that earlier Mexican American intellectuals like Carlos E. Castañeda, George Sánchez, and Arthur Campa represent oppositional writers. Castañeda, for example, in his role as a historian of the Spanish colonial period in Texas, challenged the notion that Texas history was primarily an Anglo-American Protestant affair that commenced at the Alamo. He proposed a dual way of interpreting Texas history that did not neglect or marginalize the Spanish/Mexican roles. More challenging than Castañeda, Sánchez advanced a view of southwestern history as one centered on conquest, in particular the U.S. conquest, that he believed laid the foundation for the marginalization of Mexican Americans in the Southwest or what he called the "forgotten people" in the case of New Mexico. And in the folk-lorist Campa, I discovered a scholar who, building on the work of an even earlier Hispano scholar, Aurelio Espiñosa, focused on the viability of a native New Mexican popular culture that in its evolution and adaptation into the twentieth century had helped to maintain a sense of historical identity for Hispanos, especially in rural New Mexico.[4]

One can also note other important premovement writers and intellectuals, such as Jovita Gonzáles, Josefina Niggli, Ernesto Galarza, Américo Paredes, Luis Leal, and José Villareal, to name a few who in their own way and under more difficult and hostile racialized conditions still managed to assert a counterhegemonic and revisionist perspective on southwestern life and culture.[5]

Fray Angélico Chávez, Catholicism, and Hispano Identity

It is with this background in mind that I wish to interpret the historical writings of Fray Angélico Chávez (1910–1996), one of the most significant but in some ways least acknowledged historical critics in this country. This lack of recognition, unfortunately, extends to the area of Chicano studies, even though much of his work complements this field.

A true renaissance man, Chávez, in a writing career spanning six decades, produced some twenty-three published books, including history, fiction, and poetry as well as numerous articles, essays, and reviews. In addition, Chávez as a self-taught artist produced a range of religious and artistic images.[6]

It is important to understand, however, the historical context of New Mexico to appreciate Fray Angélico's work. I do not intend to write a thesis here on the history of this area, but only to summarize some key aspects. First of all, it is in New Mexico where the original Spanish settlements in what later became the Southwest of the United States were founded. Beginning with the *entrada,* or entry, of Juan de Oñate into New Mexico in 1598, a permanent Spanish colony began to develop. This involved the conquest of the so-called Pueblo Indians and their incorporation, albeit as second-class citizens, into Spanish society. The role of the Franciscan missionaries in the religious conversion of the Indians, such as it was, was critical in this colonizing enterprise. Despite these efforts, Spanish rule proved to be tentative. In the Pueblo Revolt of 1680, the Indians of northern New Mexico rebelled and drove the Spanish out and into exile in the El Paso region until the reconquest of 1693. The next century and more witnessed a relatively limited and partially isolated Spanish frontier society characterized by the continued mixing of cultures, or *mestizaje,* to develop a particular Spanish/Mexican presence surrounded by hostile, un-conquered Indians such as the Apaches. Historians like Ramón Gutiérrez and James Brooks have superbly analyzed this narrative.[7]

This long history—over two centuries—of what I refer to as Spanish/Mexicans in New Mexico provides the context of the native Hispanic New Mexicans' sense of roots. One can quibble about what term to use for these people, but whatever term one uses it is still a history of strong identity with the land of their ancestors. John M. Nieto-Philips, in his insightful text on Spanish-American identity in New Mexico, notes the various terms of ethnic identification used by Hispanos—a term utilized by Fray Angélico. These have included *la raza, manitos, mejicanos, neomejicanos, nuevomexicanos, hispanoamericanos*, and Spanish Americans.[8] The Hispanos of this region are among the first American colonists in the history of the United States. Over this time a particular sense of being, of place, and of spirit developed among these people—Fray Angélico's people.

At the same time, this history is one of conflict and conquest, especially with an expanding United States in the mid-nineteenth century. Emboldened by the spirit of Manifest Destiny and by the need to acquire new territories for economic growth, the United States, first in Texas in 1836 and then with the commencement of the U.S.-Mexico War in 1846, pursued a policy of en-croachment on the northern frontier of Mexico after its independence in 1821. The U.S. victory resulted in the transference of Mexico's northern frontier, el Norte, including New Mexico, to the United States. In turn, the Treaty of Guadalupe Hidalgo (1848) that ended the conflict gave citizenship to the Mexican population north of the new border. New Mexicans, or Nuevo Mexicanos, became American citizens overnight.[9]

The annexation of New Mexico into the United States introduced a new chapter in the history of Hispanos in that area. Although not overwhelmed initially by an influx of Anglo-Americans, Hispanos in time and certainly by the end of the nineteenth century faced challenges to their landowning system, their political status, and their cultural integrity. They became "strangers in their own land." [10]

Yet, as Nieto-Philips correctly observes, Hispanos were not passive on-lookers to these changes. Not only did they organize political and economic countermovements to their increased subaltern position, but also they asserted new political identities for themselves. They used history to propose that they descended from a proud and rich past as Spanish Americans, a term they invented to counter the new and negative stereotypic images of them introduced and circulated by some of the Anglo-Americans. These stereotypes build on previous pre–Mexican War ones by early Anglo travelers in New Mexico that suggested that Hispanos were lazy, corrupt, immoral, and un-Christian in their Catholic practices—attitudes themselves based on the famous Black Legend invented by England in the colonial era to portray rival Spain as an uncivilized people.[11] As more Anglo-Americans arrived by the end of the nineteenth century and early twentieth century, including writers, they not only maintained such negative images of Hispanos, they added to them and increased their circulation. Others, such as Charles Lummis, went to the other extreme and heavily romanticized Hispano history and culture. Such views, certainly the negative ones, created a version of the "clash of civilizations" between Anglos and Hispanos in New Mexico and indeed throughout the Southwest that affected ethnic relations. It was these stereotypes, in particular the negative ones, that many Hispanos rejected and challenged.[12]

The juxtaposition of a decline in social status as a result of the U.S. conquest and a counterassertion to this decline marked ethnic relations in New Mexico into the twentieth century, Fray Angélico's century. This backdrop helps us understand this Hispano-Franciscan priest/historian and his role as a proponent of an oppositional historical narrative.

What I wish to concentrate on here is the nature of Fray Angélico's historical work, especially on the role of Hispano Catholics, and to suggest that Chávez's focus on religion was a way of asserting ethnic identity and opposing a growing Anglo-American historical narrative that was pushing Chávez's subjects to the margins.

To understand Fray Angélico's stress on history and religion is to also understand the historian himself. His writing of history contains a hidden and, at times, not so hidden autobiographical self. Born Manuel Chávez in Wagon Mound, New Mexico, on April 10, 1910, Chávez descended from a long family line in New Mexico. Besides his Hispano family traditions, he was also shaped by his strong Catholic socialization, which in fact originated within his family. Beginning with his elementary schooling in Mora, conducted by the Sisters of Loretto, Chávez's entire education was at the hands of the Church. At age fourteen he "discovered" that he possessed a vocation and in 1924 commenced a long educational and training period in the Midwest; he became an ordained member of the Franciscan order in 1937.

Because he displayed some talent in painting, he was given the religious name of Fray Angélico after Fra Angelico, a medieval Dominican painter. His joining the Franciscans was in fact a form of identity with New Mexico's Spanish past, owing to the important role of the Franciscans in that history.

FIGURE 1.1 Fray Angélico Chávez, circa 1940s. Courtesy the Archives of the Franciscan Province of St. John Baptist of Cincinnati.

"Everything I read about New Mexico," he would later tell an interviewer, "emphasized the Franciscans and their contributions to the country. I became attracted to them even though I had never seen one." [13]

Beginning in the 1940s, Fray Angélico systematically researched the roots of the Hispano presence in New Mexico. Although not an academically trained

historian, Chávez brought a rigorous and meticulous quality to his historical investigations. Not as readable as his nonhistorical writings, his historical
narratives, with the possible exception of *My Penitente Land*, are somewhat
ponderous. Yet what these narratives lack in style, they more than make up in
precise details. Chávez himself recognized differences between fictional and
historical writing, or at least how he differentiated between these two genres.
"People more and more want to rush into print," he noted in a 1970 review,

> taking authorship *per se* as a status symbol maybe, or craving immor-
> tality thereby. If it's a book of poems, whether good or bad—a novel or
> a collection of short stories, whether tops or lousy—there is no harm
> done by inferior products. But when it's history, that's another matter;
> the would-be historian must research, sort out and weigh every possible
> source material on his chosen subject, or else risk disseminating wrong
> or at least faulty history.[14]

Accepting responsibility for historical accuracy, Chávez sought to understand and to educate himself as well as others about the non-Anglo-Hispano
roots of New Mexico's history. Not learning about this history either at home
or in school, Chávez felt—and believed that others, whom he called native
New Mexicans, did also—a certain historical vacuum or ambivalence at a
time of increased Anglo-American influence in the post–World War II era.

Chávez approached the excavation of his and that of other Hispanos' historical roots with a fervor and discipline that conveyed his own religious commitment as a Franciscan. In a sense, he became a historical missionary not
only to himself but to others as well. History, especially the role of the Hispano
Church, would bring new spiritual and cultural nourishment to his people. It
would be good for his soul and that of others.

As a result, Chávez's historical pilgrimage became a personal as well as a
collective endeavor. Of this connection between the personal and the collective in his work, Thomas Steele has written the following about *My Penitente
Land*, Fray Angélico's most autobiographical historical text: "Chávez's book
embodies *Chávez's* New Mexico, '*my* penitente land': his personally appropri-
ated New Mexico, the New Mexico that formed him into the man he is, the
New Mexico that is profoundly and vastly more *his* than it is anybody else's."[15]

Chávez himself acknowledged his personal identification with the Hispano
roots of New Mexico: "I myself was born when those first Spanish settlers
were preparing to enter New Mexico, their land and mine. A goodly number
of them are my own proven direct ancestors, some by several lines."[16]

If history was a way to understand one's personal genealogy, it was also a way of providing a collective identity. For example, in his important work on tracing the origins and genealogy of New Mexican Hispano families, *Origins of New Mexico Families: A Genealogy of the Spanish Colonial Period* (1954), Fray Angélico provided not only a sense of roots but also, perhaps more important, of subjectivity—of being somebody. Chávez believed that Hispanos and non-Hispanos needed to know the origins of Spanish surnames of Hispano families as well as the place-names, which derived from Spanish names.

For both autobiographical and community purposes, Fray Angélico traced the roots of his own surname. "Chaves or Chávez," he observed, represented the "old Spanish-Galician and Portuguese word for 'keys.'" Locating the name in Portugal and in Estremadura in Spain, Fray Angélico noted that the name was transferred to the Americas in the sixteenth century. Don Pedro Durán de Chávez, a member of the Oñate expedition that led to the initial Spanish conquest and settlement of New Mexico, then brought it into New Mexico. The Chávez family over time gave their name to a variety of place-names in the region. With his penchant for historical accuracy, Fray Angélico concluded that the "almost universal spelling of the name in New Mexico is *Chávez*, but this is not correct." [17]

Origins of New Mexico Families represents a form of "collective biography" through its attention to the stories of the various Hispano family lines from the seventeenth century to the mid-nineteenth century. This includes families such as the Armijos, the Vigils, and the Vargases. Chávez, never fully accepting what Carey McWilliams called the "Spanish Fantasy," noted that while many of these initial families had migrated to New Mexico in hopes of achieving social status as hidalgos, most were of modest military and pastoral backgrounds: "good folks in the main, who were neither peons nor convicts." [18] He further understood that most of these settlers were not "authentic" Spaniards, but rather mixed people, or mestizos. The fact that they would later adopt such terms as *Hispano* and *Spanish American* had more to do with culture than with race. [19]

But what particularly impressed Fray Angélico was how closely knit all of these families were. In effect, colonial Hispano settlements represented family or at least extended family. He especially illustrated this by literally reproducing, through the use of graphs, his own family line, which showed the close ties between the early families such as the Montoyas, Bacas, Lunas, Padillas, Romeros, Tafoyas, and Roybals. "The most important feature brought out here," Fray Angélico concluded, "is the inter-relation of all New Mexicans in one big family, at least as far as the first two centuries are concerned."[20]

Part of Fray Angélico's search for personal as well as collective historical roots involved countering the view from Anglo-America of native New Mexicans, both Indians and Hispanos, as being foreigners, as being the "other," of not truly being American and of possessing a culture, including religious practices, that did not conform to an Anglo-American standard. Chávez opposed these biased and even racist opinions by stressing the deep roots of Hispanos in an area that became part of the United States.

Fray Angélico believed in an inclusive rather than an exclusive American history. He ascribed to this inclusion by quoting from Ecclesiastes 9:11, which was also a favorite quote of Padre Antonio Martínez, the nineteenth-century controversial priest/leader whom Fray Angélico admired. "I returned and saw under the sun," the biblical quotation reads, "that the race is not to the swift, nor the battle to the strong . . . but time and chance happeneth to them all."[21] This "all" Fray Angélico believed included Hispanos.

Chávez observed with a touch of humor that New Mexico itself was often mistaken for another country by people from other parts of the United States, who inquired whether one needed to pay export duties to conduct commerce in New Mexico or if one needed to have a visa to enter it. "One would expect that anyone who had any geography in school," he responded, "would readily recall that on our national map New Mexico, wedged between Arizona and the Texas Panhandle, is most graphically an integral part of the United States."[22]

By focusing on the pioneering work of the early Hispano settlers, including the missionaries, Fray Angélico likewise hoped to counter what he believed to be common prejudices and stereotypes of local Hispano customs, including those of the Church. These false views extended to the belief that the early Church charged exorbitant fees for its services. Fray Angélico attempted to correct such misimpressions through his research on what he believed to be the more complicated role of the Church, including its own poverty.[23]

Displaying what Herbert Eugene Bolton called the concept of "Greater America," Fray Angélico, at the risk of uncritically examining the role of the initial Spanish expeditions into New Mexico, nevertheless used these *entradas*, including that of Coronado in 1540, to emphasize the long-standing Hispanic presence in the region. This was looking at American history from a south-to-north perspective and opposing the standard narrative that American history begins with the thirteen original colonies. Chávez revised or attempted to revise this interpretation by integrating into this narrative the Spanish colonies in future U.S. territory, which antedated the first English settlements. In this revised version Coronado is just as American as John Smith. "For on the whole," Fray Angélico observed,

> the expedition of Francisco Vásquez Coronado of 1540–1542, no matter what the human drawbacks in its operations and the fantastic dream which made it a failure from the start, remains one of the most colorful and admirable feats of derring-do in the history of North America. It was a distinct triumph of man's spirit braving the unknown in search of a dream whether for gold or glory, or both, and no matter whether either of them were attained or not. The same counts in greater measure for the Franciscans who accompanied it on the particular quest of each single one for a different kind of gold, a more lasting glory.[24]

It was this Hispanic foundational history in New Mexico, especially its Catholic nature, Fray Angélico believed, that the later U.S. conquest of the area had attempted to negate. Although hardly a radical, Chávez, like George Sánchez and later Chicano historians, viewed the Anglo-American entrance into New Mexico, and what at that time was northern Mexico, as a colonizing venture. For Fray Angélico, the Santa Fe Trail was less a corridor of commerce than an instance of Manifest Destiny. What particularly offended Fray Angélico was the tendency of Anglo-Americans then, and in his own time, to see themselves as the true Christians while discounting the Spanish Catholic missionaries who had engaged in Christianizing New Mexico centuries before the arrival of the Anglos.[25] Like Castañeda in his writing about Texas, Fray Angélico attempted to problematize the concept of being an American and to propose a more inclusive multicultural interpretation of American history.[26]

In seeking the historical roots of New Mexico especially from the perspective of religion, Fray Angélico further asserted the Hispano character of the area by ascribing sacredness to it. Chicano movement activists linked the concept of Aztlán (the mythical pre-Columbian roots of the Southwest) with that of sacred space, and Chávez in his own ethnic fashion interpreted Hispano–New Mexico in a similar vein. Comparing New Mexico to other parts of the United States, Fray Angélico wrote, "But the New Mexican landscape has something that they all lack. It is Holy Land." The Rio Grande in Chávez's narrative became the River Jordan.[27] While Michael P. Carroll has challenged just how religious the early Spanish colonists in New Mexico were, the fact remains that for Fray Angélico religion or sacredness permeated New Mexico.[28]

Fray Angélico noted that many towns and geographic sites possessed religious names. In his work on New Mexican religious place-names, he countered the tendency by Anglos to dehistoricize the landscape pertaining to the
pre-American period. In his listing of the various religious place-names, which
represent mininarratives, Chávez, for example, educated his readers about the
background of the Sangre de Cristo Mountains. He noted that the name in
English was "the Blood of Christ":

> This name is applied to the southernmost section of the Rockies proper
> extending from southern Colorado to Santa Fe and Pecos. As late as
> 1790 these mountains bore the name of "Sierra Madre." The present
> name, undoubtedly, took its start at the beginning of the nineteenth
> century with the birth of the Penitentes and these mountain folks'
> accentuated devotion to the Passion and Death of the Savior.[29]

Fray Angélico believed this religiosity or sacredness to be at the heart of
New Mexico's early Hispanic past. It not only reinforced his own personal
devotion to the Church, but it gave this history its special quality and value.
Hence in his research Chávez stressed the role of the Church and that of the
Franciscan missionaries as the true and original American pioneers.

Through his research in early Church documents and in his impressive
annotation of the archives of the archdiocese of Santa Fe from 1678 to 1900,
Chávez documented the origins of American history in New Mexico. He proposed that New Mexico and its native Hispano population possessed a history
because they could document it. Here the role of the Church as the guardian
of historical identity was crucial. "Although the documents of the Mission Period contain hardly any papers of major historical importance," he observed,
"they do as a whole, and in numberless little items and asides, even the baptismal and other registers, contribute immensely to early southwestern history
by either supplementing or complementing other sources with heretofore unknown and unsuspected data." [30]

The religious nature of this history validated for Fray Angélico the Hispano
experience. Here religion becomes synonymous with ethnicity at a time (the
1940s and 1950s, what some called the "Age of Consensus") when it was not
particularly acceptable to be "ethnic" or to assert in any oppositional manner
one's ethnic identity.[31] This is not to say that Fray Angélico was simply using
religion to discuss ethnicity, but rather that for him religion and ethnicity in
the case of New Mexico's colonial history were one and the same. Sacredness
encompassed the two. "One can only feel the highest admiration for the ma-

jority of the padres," he concluded, "who kept the missions going in the face of either poverty and loneliness, and for the Hispanic folk who for generations had survived among perils and hardship that might have driven other people to desertion, if not extinction."[32]

Fray Angélico's search for historical roots, of course, was not without its contradictions. While acknowledging that the Spanish did not treat the Indians well in all cases and that, in fact, conquest, bloodshed, and cruelty also characterized the establishment of Spanish outposts and missions, still Chávez regrettably downplayed these episodes. Despite the meticulousness of his research, he could not easily confront the subjugation of the Indians. He either chose not to dwell on it or else, viewing most of the Indians as passive subjects, to regard it as a fairly benign experience. Even later, more radical Chicano historians have not adequately confronted this aspect of history. They have totally condemned the Spanish conquest of the Indians and substituted the Indians/mestizos as the true southwestern ancestors of Chicanos, while relegating the *gauchupines* [Spaniards] to the margins. Yet none of these treatments and interpretations, it seems to me, is satisfying in that they fail to synthesize the full range of differences and experiences that encompass Chicano history.

At least one can say on behalf of Fray Angélico that his view of New Mexico's colonial history is a complicated one. Rather than claiming ethnic unity existed in the region or adopting a them vs. us approach, he observed the various ethnic/race gradations. However, his concern was not with those who identified as Indians or as *genízaros* (the Christianized, acculturated Indian slaves and the mestizos), but with native New Mexicans or Hispanos, whether they were racially mixed or not. Fray Angélico chose to study this dominant group because he believed it was they who had provided New Mexico with its particular regional ethnic, cultural, and religious identity.

In this search for roots, Fray Angélico clearly did not believe that the clock could be moved back. As in other native New Mexican writers there is in Chávez's writings a touch of nostalgia, but there is also a realistic awareness that well into the twentieth century many new changes had taken place. "We can't turn history back," he noted, "no matter how many efforts are now being made to remedy old injustices."[33] Indeed, it was precisely these changes, for example, the greater acculturation of Hispanos, that served as the motivating force for Fray Angélico's search for history. He sensed a loss of historical identity for himself and other Hispanos, and he lamented the loss. Lack of identity disempowered Hispanos in a land that bore so much of their imprint.

To empower Hispanos, Fray Angélico embarked on his personal and collective crusade to regain this identity, that of the Hispano-Catholic. This was not nostalgia but a struggle to combat prejudice and the loss of religious fervor among native New Mexicans. Historical identity, for Chávez, was the way to achieve equality and regain one's soul.

Historical Agency and Hispano Clergy

A second major theme in Fray Angélico's historical writings concerns what I refer to as historical agency. That is, Mexican Americans, or in this case Hispanos, have not just been the victims of history, but the makers of history. Of course, in his writings on the colonial Spanish missions and settlements, Chávez was attesting to the historical agency of these ancestors. But the theme of historical agency is even better expressed in his writings on the nineteenth century, in particular his works on Padre Antonio José Martínez and Padre José Manuel Gallegos.

These texts, which are also texts on religious Catholic leadership, were to a large degree Chávez's response to the racism expressed toward Hispanos, including the clergy, in the initial American period of New Mexico. Early Anglo writers such as W. W. H. Davis, Josiah Gregg, Susan Shelby Magoffin, and others portrayed Hispanos as immoral, unscrupulous, and without honor or virtue. They particularly criticized them for their predilections for gambling, drinking, and immoral sexual behavior.[34]

This critique extended to the clergy, especially to leaders such as Martínez and Gallegos. The general portrayal of Martínez, for example, was one of an immoral priest who was disloyal to the new American church hierarchy as well as to the United States. Perhaps the most influential impression of Martínez is Willa Cather's characterization of the Hispano priest in her classic *Death Comes for the Archbishop*. In her fictional account of events in New Mexico following the U.S. takeover, Cather sets up Bishop Lamy, the new head of the Church in New Mexico, as the hero and Padre Martínez as the villain. Lamy found little of merit in the Hispano population and despite his French/Latin background, according to Fray Angélico, was more comfortable with the Anglos than with the Hispanos.[35]

Such portrayals of Hispanos, especially of the clergy, disturbed Chávez. He saw these criticisms, which he felt continued to his own day, as inaccurate and stereotypical, causing much damage to ethnic relations and to Hispano self-image. Fray Angélico sought to revise such views. Unfortunately referring to Cather as a spinster, he admired her talent as a writer but dismissed her as a historian by observing that her characterization of Padre Martínez was more legendary than historical. "Cather's version reflects the cynical view which had come down from the padre's foes," he proposed.[36] Cather, according to Chávez, was simply repeating the same biased views toward Martínez and other Hispano clergy that had been expressed in the 1850s with the arrival of the new French priests such as Bishop Lamy and his right-hand man, Father Machebeuf.

In Chávez's view, the chief opponent of the Hispano clergy was Machebeuf, who had been influenced by anti-Mexican, anti-Hispano sentiments expressed to him by some of the Anglo-Texas Catholic clergy. This influence, transferred by Machebeuf and Lamy to New Mexico, centered on the alleged sexual immorality of the Hispano clergy, who were accused of violating their vows of chastity. Fray Angélico conceded that this might have applied in some cases but considered this charge part of a larger indictment and condemnation of the Hispano clergy and community that were biased and ethnocentric.

In his defense of Martínez and the other Hispano clergy, Chávez unfortunately allowed his own strong feelings on this matter to get somewhat out of hand. For example, he accused Machebeuf not only of being anti-Hispano, but of suffering from a repressed homosexuality, or what Chávez referred to as Machebeuf's "latent homosexual inclination." Fray Angélico linked this characterization with what he called the French priest's "unusual affection" for his friend and compatriot Bishop Lamy.[37]

Machebeuf's views and that of other newcomers, then and later, Chávez believed, were the result of a Puritan mentality and what he referred to as "Puritan history." This perspective suggested that whereas non-Hispanics were moral and virtuous, Hispanos were not.[38] Chávez criticized such an irrational division as representing a double standard. He observed that the Hispano clergy, for example, did not possess a monopoly on improper behavior. In fact, such behavior had a long history in France and Europe, one that obviously Machebeuf had conveniently not addressed. "What unabashed chauvinism, one is forced to explain," Fray Angélico wrote of Machebeuf, at the same time psychoanalyzing the French priest: "Had he forgotten about such worldly and ambitious fellows as Richelieu and Talleyrand, both of them high churchmen of his native soil? Or had he suppressed history in his mind, just as he had those other subtler things which tormented his juvenile soul?"[39]

Chávez believed that what was really involved in the ethnic tensions that resulted from the American takeover was that the newcomers lacked a knowledge of Hispano culture and an unwillingness to learn.[40] This clash of cultures resulted in misunderstanding and unfortunate biased views on the part of the Anglos and other non–New Mexicans. Chávez observed that part of what Lamy, Machebeuf, Cather, and other later critics of Hispano culture did not understand was that New Mexico, like the rest of Spanish America, had never been effectively influenced by the Reformation and the Counter-Reformation. These areas of the Americas were largely untouched by the Puritan worldview that had affected the United States. Not understanding this, Anglo-Americans and other strangers to New Mexico unfairly attempted to impose their own "puritanical" views and values on a people and a culture that was less repressed about God and life. "As opposed to the Puritan, the Latin mind saw those things in a different light," Fray Angélico noted:

> To the Latin there was nothing in the law of nature, or in the Scriptures, that labeled tobacco, liquor, or gambling, as sins in themselves. Neither nature nor nature's God decreed that getting something for nothing was a sin; on the contrary, man got much of what he has from God and nature strictly for nothing. These activities were pleasant forms of recreation and relaxation, and of social well-being.[41]

Chávez further countered the new "Puritan history," what he also called the "Aryan history," of the Anglo-American era by his revisionist studies of Padres Martínez and Gallegos. Besides discharging their clerical duties, the two priests participated in political activities before and after the U.S. conquest. Bishop Lamy excommunicated both. Yet rather than seeing them as rogue priests, Chávez revised their images by portraying them in more complicated terms. Martínez and Gallegos represent not villains but Catholic leaders and heroes to the Hispano population. To Fray Angélico they stood as role models.

Chávez especially valued Padre Martínez, in whom he found a variety of admirable qualities. Like Carroll in his own revisionist interpretation of Martínez, Chávez saw him as an agent of Catholic reform.[42] This included Martínez's political liberalism, which he took from his own admiration of Padre Miguel Hidalgo and the movement for Mexican independence. "Whatever Padre Martínez afterward proposed or tried to carry out as a self-designated priest-politician in his own homeland can be traced directly to his unbounded admiration for the man," Fray Angélico observed of Martínez's affinity for Hidalgo. A republican liberal, Martínez, according to Chávez, also represented a tolerant man, one who supported freedom of religion for every group, not just Catholics. Furthermore, Martínez supported "los de abajo"—the underdogs—of his society, such as the often-repressed Penitente cults and the *santeros* (religious woodcarvers), both of whom the Mexican hierarchy and the later American one frowned upon. Chávez further admired Martínez for his enlightened educational views. He noted that Padre Martínez operated one of the early printing presses in New Mexico and that he used the press to publish both religious and educational texts, including the first book ever printed in New Mexico, his *Cuaderno de Ortografía* (1835), a Castilian speller. Chávez likewise attributed Martínez's enlightened views to his collective consciousness and support for the Hispano community as well as to his personal aspirations, "for, like those of farming and stockraising which he had learned from boyhood, the fruits were plowed back into the overall single grand venture of helping his fellowman—even if all this was also meant to promote his dream of personal greatness." [43]

Martínez was, in addition, a supporter of human rights and a humanist. Although a strong defender of Mexico's independence and of the new republic, Martínez, according to Chávez, gave greater weight to "the equal rights of all men without distinction under their Common creator." [44]

No doubt seeing much of himself in Martínez, Chávez observed that Martínez was a conflicted individual, one who contained contradictions. Still, Fray Angélico revised the Cather-inspired view of Martínez as a disloyal priest and rebel by documenting that in fact Martínez, despite his differences with the new French priests after the U.S. takeover, never repudiated Lamy's authority or participated in rebellious action against American rule. [45] Chávez noted that Martínez was not anti-American and that in addition to learning English he welcomed Anglo-Americans into his church in Taos. "All this might surprise those who have always held up the Padre of Taos as the staunchest of Mexican patriots," Fray Angélico stressed. "But the fact is that his nature and ideals went beyond mere national patriotism. He was first and foremost a humanist and humanitarian, not a chauvinist in its narrow sense." [46]

At the same time, Padre Martínez, like Fray Angélico himself, believed in reinforcing a native New Mexican identity, especially in reaction to new and hostile forces after the American annexation. Chávez praised both Martínez and Gallegos for "cherishing the Castilian pride of their own heritage." [47] It was Anglo-American racism, according to Chávez, that created the grounds for the invention of a Hispano ethnic identity as a form of self-protection. "But it was this Iberian proudful consciousness," he wrote of Martínez and Gallegos, "which lay behind what some have called the stubbornness or recalcitrance when confronted later on with challenges which they considered unjust by their very nature."[48]

Padre Martínez, Chávez concluded, was a "major genius in his own century as well as those before and after his time."[49] Denied their heroic nature and their subjectivity in history in the American period, including in Chávez's own time, the Hispanos of New Mexico needed to know that they possessed a genealogy of leadership and agency and that it included the clergy. No doubt through his writings and art, Fray Angélico believed that in his own way he was following in the footsteps of Martínez and Gallegos, who practiced a form of nineteenth-century theology of liberation.

A Native Soul

The third major theme in Fray Angélico's historical writings concerns his stress on a particular New Mexican Hispano regional identity. His research in colonial records had led him to the conclusion that despite military, commercial, and religious connections between New Mexico and the rest of New Spain for the most part, owing to its remote location and hostile topography, New Mexico remained isolated and out of the mainstream. This allowed a regional culture and identity to develop and evolve over several centuries. It was this identity that Fray Angélico believed was in his own time being lost and confused.

In large part the threat to the native New Mexican's identity was the result of a century of Anglo-American racism and denigration of native customs. Rather than understanding the unique regional aspects of Hispano culture, most Anglos lumped this way of life under the category of Mexican, thereby homogenizing the culture rather than appreciating the differentiation between New Mexican and Mexican cultures. "For the English-speaking American," Fray Angélico observed, "it was then easy in the extreme to begin and continue making New Mexico more and more his own, and in his philistine image. Whatever was 'mexican,' as he termed the entire regional tradition . . . had no place in the new scheme of things."[50] Chávez abhorred what he termed "the Nordic notion of superman" that Anglo-Americans had introduced into New Mexico and that had marginalized, except for tourist purposes, Hispano culture and identity.[51]

This marginalization had produced ambivalence and a loss of historical memory among Hispanos. Yet, as Fray Angélico noted, enough of a way of life, of a way of looking at the world and at God had survived to remind Hispanos that they were distinct, that they possessed a particular New Mexican Catholic identity. In his quasi-autobiographical *My Penitente Land,* Fray Angélico poignantly referred to both the ambivalence and the memory:

> This matter of antiquity, the very vagueness of it, played havoc with my young mind. I also remember asking my mother more than once why we were not exactly the same in speech and demeanor as the priest from Spain who was our assistant pastor at the time, and why we differed in the same way from a family from Mexico living up the street from us. She would flush with impatience—at her own inability to explain, I am sure—merely saying that our forebears had come from Spain a very long time ago. But she didn't know when or how. All this made the double puzzle of Penitentes and ancestral origins merge most confusedly inside my inquisitive young head.[52]

The sense that Hispanos had lived a certain experience drove Fray Angélico to rediscover it and to champion it. This became part of his mission. He pursued what he called the "native soul."[53]

This soul, however, had suffered much in attempting to know itself. Indeed, for Chávez, one of the characteristics of being a native New Mexican was suffering and doing penance. Due to their isolation, their lack of material comforts, and the threats to their communities from the outside, Hispanos since the colonial era had been *penitentes.* Fray Angélico described the evolution of certain Catholic penitente groups but suggested that in a spiritual sense all Hispanos were penitentes. "After all," he wrote, "we Hispanic New Mexicans are all Penitentes in some way, through blood origins and landscape and a long history of suffering. Hence this is far less a treatise on the Penitentes, who are a late feature in New Mexico's long story, than a sort of 'scripture' about a penitential New Mexico wrestling with her God upon a Bethel landscape made to order."[54]

Part of the Hispanos' penance, Fray Angélico suggested, was not being accepted as native to New Mexico and instead being stereotyped and marginalized as "Mexicans" by Anglos, implying that Hispanos were immigrants and foreigners. "And yet they do not wish to be identified as Mexicans," Chávez pointed out,

> but correctly as long-term Americans by birth and nationality. Their not being accepted as such in the national picture of the United States has been part of their continuing penance. While being classified as

Mexicans, which should be no stigma at all, they do know, if more with the heart than with the head, that their own ancestry, language, and traditions are distinct from the Mexican, or perhaps that a difference exists like the one between a horse and a jackass without their knowing which is which—sometimes afraid that they might be the latter.[55]

Part of the confusion with respect to Hispano identity were the very terms *New Mexico* and *Mexico*. Such place-names, Fray Angélico believed, made it appear as if the Hispanos were simply an extension of Mexico, a view he disputed. In fact, as he observed, the designation New Mexico had been first applied to the northern Spanish frontier centuries before New Spain became Mexico at independence. Chávez lamented that an independent Mexico had not chosen another name, such as Azteca or Aztlán, the mythical homeland of the Aztecs. Chávez even suggested that a good name for Mexico might have been Guadalupe, after the Virgin of Guadalupe. "Then our present New Mexico with her old historic name," he emphasized, "would stand free with her own clear identity in the eyes of the outsider. Her own distinctive landscape and heritage, however poor the latter may be, would not be aligned or confused with the Mexican."[56] Fray Angélico reflected no bias against Mexicans—immigrants or Mexican Americans in other parts of the Southwest— but instead asserted that the Hispanos of northern New Mexico possessed their own particular ethnic and cultural identity.

Yet what helped Hispanos to protect their regional identity was the very mountainous topography of New Mexico that sheltered them and their traditions. The "Spanish New Mexicans," he concluded, "know that they are not aliens, but natives of their very own landscape for almost four hundred years."[57]

As a way of educating Anglos to the particular cultural traditions of the Hispano, Fray Angélico wrote numerous popular essays, especially for the *New Mexico Magazine*, on the origins of such things as the adobe, *sopaipillas* (fried pastry), *buñuelos* (Mexican doughnuts), and *luminarias* (paper-bag lights). Of the chile, Chávez traced its transcultural origins in an essay that gave a voice to the chile: "I am Spanish and Pueblo New Mexican, to be more exact, as I keep on warming the cockler of the heat with princely flavor and adorning the home with necklaces or coral."[58]

In discovering a regional Hispano identity, Fray Angélico confronted McWilliams's "Spanish Fantasy," the idea that Mexican Americans in the Southwest, or at least some of them, believed or asserted that they were pure

FIGURE 1.2 Fray Angélico Chávez, 1979. Courtesy Palace of the Governors
(MNM/DCA), Santa Fe, #164116.

Spaniards, not mestizos. Chávez addressed this issue, although perhaps never
in a fully decisive way. Yet he did problematize the issue of ethnic identity by
recognizing that the ancestors of contemporary Hispanos were neither a pure
Spanish breed nor of noble origins. "Amerindian genes interlock complicat-
edly through many a New Mexican family strain," he wrote, "and throughout
all of Spanish America for that matter. Nor is it anything to be ashamed of." [59]
Chávez criticized those Hispanos who, after the U.S. conquest, published vanity biographies alleging that their lineage came directly from Spain. "It was
a handy way of disassociating themselves from their less fortunate cousins
bearing the same surnames," he commented.[60]

What was distinctive about Hispanos, according to Chávez, was not racial
but cultural. It was a way of life and a worldview that had evolved for centuries
in relative isolation until the Anglo-American intervention as well as, later,
increased immigration from Mexico.

Stressing a regional approach to Mexican American history, Chávez in the
1970s felt the need to comment, if only briefly, on the emergence of Chicano
identity as the result of the Chicano movement. While it appears that Fray Angélico sympathized with the civil and human rights goals of the movement, he

resisted what he believed was a tendency by the movement to impose a monolithic, essentialist Chicano identity on all Mexican Americans, including Hispanos in New Mexico. Chávez rejected this effort and instead suggested that
the movement had more to do with Mexican immigrants and their offspring
and even with Indians than it had to do with native New Mexicans. In reviewing, for example, Joan Moore's and Alfredo Cuellar's text *Mexican Americans*
(1970), Fray Angélico wrote, "This work is one more sociological study trying
to put all Mexican Americans into one broad classification, as if all had one
identical background."[61] And in reviewing Rudolfo Anaya's fictional *Bless Me,
Ultima* (1972), Chávez, while praising Anaya's writing style and comparing it
to William Faulkner's, nevertheless opposed the idea that Anaya accurately
captured the Hispano culture of New Mexico. Perhaps because of his ties to
the Church, Fray Angélico criticized Anaya's focus on what Chávez called
witchcraft and the occult, which he believed better depicted what he called a
"Mexican mental background . . . than a New Mexican one."[62]

One of the differences between Hispano culture and Chicano culture,
Chávez further noted, concerned the Hispano's ability to retain the use of
Spanish, despite Anglo-American acculturation pressures, and, according to
Fray Angélico, to speak it correctly, as opposed to Chicanos, who he felt had
lost the language and did not speak it properly. In reviewing in 1976 a book
by Benedicto Cuestas entitled *El Paisano*, written in Spanish, Chávez praised
the author's use of correct "New Mexico Spanish." "Hence," he added, "it is
strongly recommended to both 'Anglos' and 'Chicanos' who are interested in
bettering their own knowledge and use of the language."[63]

But more than anything, Fray Angélico stressed the importance of Catholicism in the formation of a regional Hispano identity. For Chávez, Catholicism
was Hispano identity. By Catholicism he did not necessarily mean primarily institutionalized religion since this had fallen largely under the control of
non-Hispanics after the American annexation. Instead, Fray Angélico emphasized the importance of the continuities of popular or folk religious practices
and confraternities, many of which could be traced to the colonial past. Here
his work over the years in researching and writing about the cult around La
Conquistadora, the image of the Virgin Mary that had been used in the reconquest of New Mexico in 1693 following the Pueblo Revolt of 1680, is especially
important. Fray Angélico's family was involved in organizing the annual processions honoring La Conquistadora in Santa Fe, and he noted the importance
of this veneration in maintaining a sense of community among Hispanos.

La Conquistadora, whom he called *paisana* (compatriot), was not only a religious symbol, but also an ethnic one. "Our ancestors have been witness to her glory," he wrote, "and she in turn bears witness to our parentage."[64]

Fray Angélico observed that many efforts had been made by non-Hispano Catholics to eliminate or destroy these popular Hispano-Catholic traditions, including the cult of the Penitentes, but that they had failed. For Chávez, these forms of religious practice more than anything else kept alive the Hispano soul.

Revising U.S. History

Besides observing the contributions to southwestern and American history by a remarkable writer and scholar, I, in my interpretation of Fray Angélico Chávez's historical work, have also suggested that his historical texts represent a form of Catholic oppositional narrative. The nature of this opposition is based on countering racial and stereotypical images of Hispanos in New Mexico and their marginalization in the region. By stressing the long, rich historical roots of Hispanos, their leadership in making history, and their development of a regional ethnic identity heavily influenced by their religious practices, Fray Angélico sought not only to combat prejudice but to provide testimony to his and his people's being and self-worth. These contributions by a major Catholic historian in the twentieth century need to be acknowledged, and his work integrated by those of us who desire to revise U.S. history in the hope of making this country a more hospitable one for all who have contributed and continue to contribute to it.

TWO

Catholic Social Doctrine and Mexican American Political Thought

Ours must be a war against prejudice, ignorance, injustice, and poverty. We must teach fair play, brotherhood of man, love of One's neighbors, and unselfishness. We must teach and practice the doctrine of Jesus Christ having as its theme love and tolerance.

—ALONSO PERALES

The real reason that they [Mexicans] live in deplorable conditions is due to the fact that the majority are not paid a living wage, and that is our fault. How can we expect them to live with all the thrills and frills of our "standard of living" if we do not pay them a living wage.

—CLEOFAS CALLEROS

IF HISPANOS IN New Mexico into the twentieth century attempted to rethink their ethnic identity and history as a way of responding to their relations with incoming Anglo-Americans—as exemplified by the work of Fray Angélico Chávez—so too were Mexican Americans in other southwestern locations. Revisionist thinking was certainly occurring in Texas, where ethnic and race relations were even more intense than in New Mexico. Texas, of course, possessed a long history of animosities between Mexicans and Anglos, one going back to the Texas Revolution (1836), the Alamo, and the U.S.-Mexico War of the 1840s.[1] Although in the southern border areas of Texas following the conflict with Mexico, Anglos and Mexicans initially developed a cooperative relationship based on economic (ranching) arrangements, as David Montejano documents, by the turn of the twentieth century, with the conversion of this area as well as others in Texas into agribusiness enterprises, this relationship soured. Mexican American farmers and ranchers could not compete with the new capitalist system. They became migrants on their own lands. Their labor, in turn, was supplemented by large-scale Mexican immigration.[2]

As Montejano further notes, it is at this point in history where Mexicans are more intensely racialized to suggest inferiority and to justify their subaltern class status as cheap labor.[3] Racialization included discrimination in other areas: education, housing, social services, and public accommodations. Signs reading "No Mexicans or Dogs Allowed" were commonplace throughout the state.[4]

Faced with this assault on their dignity as a people, many Mexican American and Mexican immigrants found solace in their faith. Mexican American communities along the border and in urban areas like San Antonio and El Paso had a long history of Catholic popular religious traditions within the home and in the community. Some of these were Church-sponsored, but many were at the behest of the people themselves, especially in rural locations, where the availability of priests was limited. Similar conditions, of course, prevailed in Mexico. The practices included celebrating popular feast days such as that of Our Lady of Guadalupe, as Matovina documents in San Antonio.[5] Religious associations of various kinds also afforded a sense of community and leadership.[6] Moreover, folk healers like Don Pedrito Jaramillo in the Rio Grande Valley of Texas and Teresa Urrea in southern Arizona and El Paso, who were informally linked to Catholicism, added to this religious support system.[7] In these manifestations, religion, specifically Mexican American Catholicism, became a form of resistance and affirmation to growing Anglo racism. Religion became a way of organizing defense mechanisms as well as of asserting a sense of dignity and community.

Partly within this context Mexican Americans, by the early part of the twentieth century, had begun to react to racial discrimination in more public ways, including civil rights protests. For some, faith buttressed these movements and affected Mexican American political thought and identity.[8]

Political identity in Chicano history has been one of my central research concerns. To this end, I have employed a generational approach concerning the changing character of the Mexican communities in the United States.[9] Yet one area of political identity that others and I have as yet not well researched involves the impact of religious beliefs, especially Catholic ones, on Chicano political consciousness and praxis. It seems to me that political and ethnic identity and consciousness in the Mexican American context have been directly and indirectly influenced by religious beliefs. This has certainly not been the only influence, as Chicanos and other Latinos have experienced their own particular process of acculturation or transculturation within the United States. Certainly secular American political and cultural influences—

themselves not fully devoid of religious influences—have had a profound impact on the "Americanization" of Latinos. The formation of a political and ethnic consciousness is a complicated process, one that is constantly being reinvented between and even within political generations. In this reinvention, I suggest, religion plays an important role.

In this chapter I examine the religious influences manifested in Mexican American political thought in one crucial period in Chicano history. This is what others and I refer to as the period of the Mexican American Generation.[10] This was the generation of Mexican Americans, many, but not all, the children of the first great wave of Mexican immigrants to the United States in the early twentieth century, who came of political age prior to or during the Great Depression and World War II and who struggled with dual identities: Mexican and American. The struggle with ethnic and political identity was made even more difficult because most Mexicans in the United States were relegated to the subaltern position of pools of cheap labor; employment restrictions were reinforced by severe forms of racial discrimination and segregation, especially in the Southwest, where the majority of Mexicans lived and worked. One result of this generation's struggle with identity and social status was the emergence of new ethnic leadership through such organizations as the League of United Latin American Citizens (LULAC), the Mexican American Movement, the Spanish-Speaking Congress, the Unity Leagues, the American G.I. Forum, the Community Service Organization (CSO), the Asociación Nacional México-Americana (ANMA) as well as in key CIO unions in the Southwest. This leadership in turn commenced the first significant civil rights struggles by Mexican Americans in this century, predating the later Chicano movement.[11]

In these civil and human rights efforts from the 1930s through the 1950s— the key period of the Mexican American Generation—it appears that some areas of Mexican American political thought were influenced by Catholic social doctrine or what some refer to as Catholic social teaching or the social question. Catholic social doctrine recognizes the human dimension of people— the incarnational—and, as such, further recognizes the social and political in human beings. According to Charles Curran, it stresses human dignity, truth, justice, charity, freedom, and civil and political as well as social and economic human rights.[12] While much work needs to be done to explore these relationships in all of their dimensions, I want to at least suggest the influence of Catholic social doctrine, what Mueller further calls "social Catholicism." This does not mean, however, that Mexican American political thought that reflected

Catholic social principles was influenced solely by the outside introduction of Catholic social doctrine. As observed earlier, there had already existed Mexican American Catholic social and community concerns aimed in part at deflecting racial discrimination. This influence combined with the added one of Catholic social doctrine as pronounced by the Church to produce a Mexican American interpretation of Catholic social doctrine based on Mexican American experiences. The key word here is "interpretation," meaning that Mexican Americans did not automatically accept this doctrine wholesale or without filtering it through their own ethnic consciousness and experiences. In certain instances, one sees a direct convergence, and in others a parallel one. To explore this relationship, I examine here two Catholic political figures whose views helped to shape Mexican American political thought during this period through their roles not as professional politicians or professional intellectuals, but as community leaders and community intellectuals. I am referring to Alonso Perales of San Antonio and Cleofas Calleros of El Paso, contemporaries of Fray Angélico.[13]

Alonso Perales and Cleofas Calleros

Alonso Perales and Cleofas Calleros represent two strands of Mexican ethnic and political evolution. Perales represents that smaller body of Mexican Americans whose origins within the United States have nothing to do with mass immigration from Mexico. Rather, Perales descended from those Mexican Americans in locations such as south Texas, northern New Mexico, southern Arizona, and parts of California whose roots emanated from the early Spanish colonizing efforts in the northern frontier of New Spain and the subsequent Spanish/Mexican settlements in this borderland. These Mexican Americans—such as Fray Angélico—saw themselves as natives to the Southwest and the Anglos as the strangers and intruders.[14]

Yet despite their native roots, these Mexican Americans constituted what I call the conquered generation in Chicano history. Their central political experience involved the U.S. conquest of what became the Southwest and their subsequent dispossession and disempowerment in the new American social order.

Perales's family came out of this colonized experience. Perales was born in Alice, Texas, in 1898. His experience paralleled that of a small but influential group of middle-class Mexican Americans who, despite the new Anglo ruling economic order, were able to retain some political and economic status in still

FIGURE 2.1 Alonso S. Perales, 1937. *En Defensa de mi Raza*
(San Antonio: Artes Gráficas, 1937).

predominantly Mexican south Texas as merchants, politicians, teachers, and attorneys. Perales attended college in Washington, D.C., served in World War I, and on his return to Texas became a lawyer. He also became one of the leading Mexican American community leaders in San Antonio and south Texas. He helped found LULAC in 1929, an organization that became the predominant civil rights group for Mexican Americans in Texas. He likewise served as a diplomat, being asked by both Republican and Democratic administrations to participate in diplomatic missions to Central America. Perales's views on

FIGURE 2.2 Cleofas Calleros, 1957. Courtesy Cleofas Calleros Papers, MS 231, Special Collections, University of Texas at El Paso Library.

Mexican American issues were promoted through his numerous essays beginning in the 1930s, which were published in the leading Spanish-language newspaper of Texas, *La Prensa* of San Antonio. These essays included a weekly column, "Arquitecto," which ran from the late 1940s to the late 1950s.[15]

Cleofas Calleros, on the other hand, represented another strand among Mexicans in the United States. This was the large-scale immigrant population flowing out of Mexico by the turn of the century and increasing during the period of the Mexican Revolution of 1910. Calleros's immigrant parents belonged to what I further call the immigrant generation in Chicano history. While there have obviously been subsequent generations of immigrant Mexicans, the initial mass one between 1900 and 1930 stands as the only one that, with a few exceptions, dominated the Mexican-based experience on this side of the border. In no other period in Chicano history have immigrants played such a dominant role as in the early part of the twentieth century. They, for the most part, with exceptions such as northern New Mexico and parts of south Texas, overwhelmed the Mexican American population of nineteenth-century origin. Earlier Mexican American communities in San Antonio and Los Angeles were transformed into immigrant communities.[16]

Calleros was born in a small town in Chihuahua in 1896, two years earlier than Perales. He came to El Paso in 1902 with his parents. There, along the border, Calleros grew up and became Mexican American. Calleros's early socialization, unlike that of Perales, is clearly of Catholic origins. He attended Sacred Heart Catholic elementary school in south El Paso, the major immigrant barrio. Calleros's education was limited to the eight grades available at Sacred Heart. Nevertheless, Calleros became a self-taught community intellectual and local historian of the early Spanish/Mexican experience in the El Paso area and, like Perales, a regular newspaper columnist, although in an English-language paper, the *El Paso Times*. Calleros served in World War I, returned to his hometown, and became a major community leader, especially through his many years as the representative of the Bureau of Immigration of the National Catholic Welfare Conference.[17]

Catholic Social Doctrine and Mexican Americans

Although Perales and Calleros were undoubtedly influenced in their political thinking by their Mexican American experiences, their Mexican American Catholic practices, and the liberal social thought that came to be concretized in the New Deal, they also appear to have been influenced to one extent or another by Catholic social doctrine and by their understanding of the social nature of human beings.[18] This latter influence was centered on certain papal encyclicals, such as Pope Leo XIII's classic *Rerum Novarum* (1891) and Pope Pius XI's *Quadragesimo Anno* (1931), issued on the fortieth anniversary of *Rerum Novarum*. Both of these encyclicals proposed social ethical views of humanity and society that Perales and Calleros reflected in their own writings, columns, and reports. The key influences, especially of *Rerum Novarum*, involved the encyclicals' proclamation that all humans are equal in the eyes of God and that despite social and class differences in a new industrial order all men and women must be treated with dignity and justice. "To ignore the right to freedom of other people is to ignore human dignity," Archbishop Robert E. Lucey of San Antonio and a friend of both Perales and Calleros asserted in 1943 in a statement that both Calleros and Perales would agree with.[19] In the case of working people, certainly the majority of Mexicans in the United States, this meant, as Pope Leo XIII stressed, that workers, besides being treated humanely by their employers, were entitled to a just wage for their labor. "[Their] great and principal obligation," Leo XIII said of employers, "is to give to every one that which is just . . . to defraud anyone of wages that are his due is a crime which cries to the avenging angel of Heaven."[20]

In addition to *Rerum Novarum*'s insistence on justice for working people, the other significant part of the encyclical that resonated in the works of both Perales and Calleros is its stress on the priority of the collective good over individual attainment. *Rerum Novarum* is hardly a socialist text and, indeed, both *Rerum Novarum* and *Quadragesimo Anno* were written to combat socialism and communism. However, to do so, both Leo XIII and Pius XI understood that the excesses of what they called "liberalism" or capitalism had to be curtailed. This meant that while both pontiffs accepted the acquisition of private property as a natural right, they also recognized that such a right carried obligations. Both employers and workers had to always keep in mind the social good of the community as opposed to the jungle of uncontrolled individualism. "But if the question be asked," inquired Leo XIII, "How [should] one's possessions be used? The Church replies without hesitation in the words of the same holy doctor: 'man should not consider his outward possessions as his own, but as common to all, so as to share them without difficulty when others are in need.'"[21]

Perales and Calleros were both staunch Catholic laymen. They represented what Archbishop Lucey referred to as the "priesthood of the laity."[22] The historian and the two men's fellow Catholic Carlos E. Castañeda referred to Perales as possessing "una visión de profeta" (a vision of a prophet).[23] Calleros was often called the "apostle of the border."[24] He, of course, had attended a Catholic elementary school. Both men were members of the Knights of Columbus, a Catholic men's fraternal association, and both were products of a Mexican American Catholic upbringing. In his resume, Perales is listed in 1952 as being the president of the Holy Name Society of San Fernando Cathedral; a member of the advisory board of the National Catholic Community Service of San Antonio; and a charter member of the San Fernando Post of the Catholic War Veterans of America.[25]

Both men were close to Catholic religious leaders such as Archbishop Lucey of San Antonio, who in his own teachings, writings, and ministry, especially to his large Mexican constituency, expressed and practiced Catholic social doctrine emanating from *Rerum Novarum* and *Quadragesimo Anno*. As the archbishop of a largely Mexican American church in San Antonio, Lucey was undoubtedly influenced by Mexican American Catholic devotion and its stress on respect and dignity. Both Calleros and Perales, for example, would have agreed with Archbishop Lucey's call in 1949 that "Spanish-speaking leaders who have a measure of property not . . . abandon the brethren of their own race." [26] And they would have concurred with Archbishop Lucey's 1954 statement that "in the field of morality and particularly in the field of social justice and social charity Catholics should lead, not follow." [27] Calleros and Perales alike reflected what Pope Pius XI referred to as "Catholic Action." [28] Indeed, Catholic Action was premised on the assertion of lay Catholic leadership. [29]

In Perales's case, the direct influence of the encyclicals is less evident. However, his identification with Catholic social doctrine indirectly appears in some of his writings and statements. Perales consistently stressed the inalienable rights of Mexicans in the United States, whether native-born or of immigrant background. Clearly, these were views inspired by Jeffersonian principles as well as by the Mexican American experience, but given Perales's strong Catholic attachments and relationships, this stress on natural rights and human dignity also drew consciously and unconsciously from Catholic social teachings. [30] Moreover, Perales was not reluctant to state that there was no inconsistency between holding strong religious views and being American. In a 1933 column in *La Prensa*, he agreed, for example, with John Valls, the district attorney of Laredo, Texas, who noted "the community that recognizes God and the dictates of one's conscience and the rights of man, possess[es] the spirit of true Americanism." Perales further agreed with Valls that the real patriots were those who held the Constitution of the United States in one hand and the Bible in the other. [31]

Perales never directly referred to the encyclicals in his writings, although the closest he came to doing so was by liberally quoting in one of his columns from a speech made by Father John J. Birch, the executive secretary of the Bishop's Committee for the Spanish-Speaking of the Southwest. The speech was delivered to the 1947 convention of the National Catholic Women's Conference in El Paso, which Perales attended. In the speech, Father Birch echoed a theme that Perales had been articulating for many years: the dignity of every human being as a creation and mirror of God and hence deserving of being treated as such. One could not be Christian and Catholic and practice discrimination toward fellow humans. "One can understand a pagan and an atheist behaving like this and of even treating a person like an animal," Father Birch stated, and Perales agreed, "but it is difficult to understand a Catholic who recognized his neighbor as a brother in Christ and treating that person as anything but as a child of God." [32]

Where he specifically addressed the issue of religion, Perales not only encouraged Mexican Americans to practice their religion especially as Catholics, but he applied the theme of Catholic social doctrine with respect to perfecting the human condition here on earth and not just waiting for salvation and justice in heaven. This theme, of course, would be elaborated even more explicitly by liberation theology in the 1960s and beyond. Perales in a 1945 column noted that while in the end one's destiny was controlled by God, one nevertheless had an obligation as a Christian to struggle in this life to achieve one's God-given rights, including social justice.[33] He reiterated this two years later when he wrote, "We have to understand how to help ourselves. That is, with the help of God, our progress depends in large part on ourselves."[34]

The impact of Catholic social doctrine on Calleros's political views is much more direct. This was the result of his involvement not only with Church lay organizations such as the Knights of Columbus, the Catholic Welfare Association of El Paso, and the Diocesan Council of Catholic Men, but more significantly of his long-term association, beginning in 1926, with the National Catholic Welfare Conference (NCWC) as head of its Immigration Bureau in El Paso. The NCWC, which was organized in the United States in 1919, was a direct outgrowth of Catholic social doctrine beginning with *Rerum Novarum*. The conference's specific mandate, when approved by Pope Benedict XV, was for the purpose of "unifying, coordinating, and organizing the Catholic people of the United States in works of education, social welfare, immigration aid, and other activities."[35] Part of the charge of the NCWC, especially through its Department of Social Action, was "to promote the social teaching of the Church and to integrate, under the guidance of the Bishop, the application of this teaching to the complex social problems of the country."[36] The Department of Social Action focused on what it called the "industrial question" by "making known, exploring, and trying to show the application to America of Leo XIII's great Encyclical 'The Condition of Labor' (*Rerum Novarum*); of the incomparable Encyclical of Pius XI, 'Reconstructing the Social Order' (*Quadragesimo Anno*)."[37]

As a result of Calleros's work with local relief and recovery programs during the depths of the Great Depression in El Paso, he requested copies of *Rerum Novarum* from the director of the Bureau of Immigration of the NCWC in Washington, D.C. He received copies not only of *Rerum Novarum* but also of *Quadragesimo Anno*.[38]

As a way of specifically applying Catholic social doctrine to Mexicans in the United States, the NCWC in 1943 sponsored, with the support of Archbishop Lucey, the Conference on the Spanish-Speaking People of the Southwest in San Antonio, which Calleros was invited to attend. It is not known whether Perales, who was a friend of Calleros, also attended. However, Archbishop Lucey appreciated Perales's work with Mexican Americans and closely collaborated with him to extend the Church's outreach to Mexican Americans in San Antonio.[39]

Coming in the wake of the zoot-suit riots in Los Angeles a month earlier, when armed forces personnel indiscriminately attacked Mexican Americans in the streets of Los Angeles, the conference aimed at coming up with strategies to deal with issues of poverty and discrimination facing Mexicans, both native-born and immigrants, in the Southwest. In his opening address, Archbishop Lucey made it very clear that the conference and the work of its delegates was inspired by Catholic social thought as applied to the Mexican American condition: "If I were asked to mention one outstanding problem that weighs most heavily upon our Mexican people I would say that it is the burden of undeserved poverty." Lucey added, in words that Calleros and Perales undoubtedly agreed with,

> These people are our people. They are the most numerous body of
> Catholics in the whole Southwest. They are God's children created
> to His image and likeness. All of us, English and Spanish-speaking
> Catholics, have been blessed with the same heritage of Christian faith.
> We receive with them the same sacraments, at the baptismal font, at the
> altar, in the tribunal of repentance and the last anointing on our bed of
> death. With them we believe, we pray, we are governed. With them, we
> strive for salvation in a blessed immortality.[40]

Whether apparent, as in the case of Calleros, or more indirect, as in that of Perales, Catholic social doctrine appears to have been part of the "intellectual baggage" that both Mexican American leaders brought to their views on Mexican American issues. Not the whole baggage, for they were too multidimensional for that, but an important part that needs to be appreciated.

Labor and Immigration

In their capacities as community leaders, Perales and Calleros spoke out on a range of issues that intersected or paralleled the Church's social doctrines. First and foremost was concern over the treatment of labor in the case of Mexican workers in the United States, both native-born and immigrants. Catholic social thought, beginning with *Rerum Novarum*, of course, stressed the need for employers to treat workers humanely, including the distribution of just wages and a living wage. Both Perales and Calleros echoed this theme with respect to Mexican workers. They agreed that Mexican workers did not receive a just or a living wage. At a two-day regional meeting of the Catholic Conference on Industrial Problems in Los Angeles in 1930, Calleros, in his address to the group, observed that employers considered the Mexican laborer as an asset, but that the full importance of his work was not appreciated and hence not paid a fair return.[41] Perales, quoting Father Birch's talk in 1947, seconded this critique. "One of the sins that cries out for God's vengeance," Father Birch had exclaimed, "is the denial to the worker of a just wage and our pontiffs have stressed that a just wage is one that makes it possible for a man to live in reasonable comfort and frugality with his family."[42]

A just wage made it feasible for workers, including Mexicans, to achieve a higher standard of living. A just wage would include not only a living wage but also what Mueller calls a "saving wage" that would go beyond subsistence and allow workers to plan for their futures.[43] But unfortunately Mexican workers did not enjoy such a level of remuneration. In 1931 Calleros noted that he was in the process of conducting a survey in El Paso to determine how many contractors paid their workers, predominantly Mexicans, less than two dollars a day, which Calleros did not regard as a living wage.[44] "There is no doubt but what the Mexican is exploited"; Calleros told a Texas Conference of Social Welfare in Waco, Texas, in 1938, "He is never paid a living wage. As a matter of fact industry generally considers him so many pounds of flesh performing any given task for the least possible wages."[45] Perales believed that employers should raise salaries for their Mexican workers out of both humanistic as well as economic motives: "In order for the Mexican to educate himself and his children and to live in good and sanitary housing it is absolutely indispensable that he receive for his labor a wage that will permit him to live a normal human life. I firmly believe that if employers who hire Mexican workers would raise their wages that they would be performing not only a humanistic act but that it would benefit the whole community economically."[46] In again quoting from Father Birch, Perales agreed with the priest's encouragement to Catholic women who employed Mexican domestics to raise the wages of their employees. "Pay them an adequate wage," Father Birch exhorted, "even if your neighbor doesn't." He also encouraged Anglo women to organize campaigns in favor of better wages for young Mexican females who worked in five and dime stores, in department stores, and in factories. "Nobody knows how many young single women have been forced into dishonorable work," Father Birch concluded, "due to being unable to gain a living wage."[47]

Perales and Calleros alike acknowledged that employers manipulated the false stereotyping of Mexican workers as lazy and unproductive too often in order to justify paying them low wages. "Of course," Calleros noted in 1938,

> we always hear the cry that he [the Mexican] is paid low wages, because he is naturally lazy. We find lazy workers amongst all racial groups but we seem to capitalize in the poor Mexican's patience, brand him as lazy and offer him low wages, which by necessity, he has to accept. Hundreds of personal interviews with employers and foremen invariably bear out the fact that a Mexican workman is highly competent when shown a given task and is properly instructed in the proper performance and in the way it must be completed. Those who are lazy, or become lazy on their jobs, are forced to become so by the "lazy-low" wages paid for services.[48]

Perales further observed that one of the false arguments used by employers of Mexican women in stores and factories as well as private homes was that by nature they had low standards of living and consequently that it would do no good to raise their wages because they would just squander them.[49] Archbishop Lucey, in his address to the Conference on Spanish-Speaking People, observed and endorsed Calleros's and Perales's critique of such stereotyping to justify low wages:

> One of the myths seriously entertained by some English-speaking Americans is that Mexican workers are lazy, slow and improvident. He would indeed be an optimist who would declare that no Mexican workers deserve that description. But the same is true of all nationals—a few are improvident but the vast majority are normal, hard working people. . . . And right here a thought occurs to me which I believe has validity. How hard would an Irishman work if you paid him twenty cents an hour? How much exuberance, vitality and enthusiasm could any people show, who had been underpaid, undernourished and badly housed for half a century?[50]

Such unjust, non-living wages came to be called Mexican wages. Calleros and Perales noted that these were the lowest wages paid to any workers in the Southwest. Perales observed that when a Mexican was employed he was forced to accept less pay than an Anglo or non-Mexican of equal experience or lack of experience.[51] Calleros remarked in 1930 about the Mexican wage: "The employer believes that because of the mere fact he is a Mexican he is supposed to receive a smaller wage and is expected to live on less." [52]

Calleros's and Perales's views on wages were echoed in 1940 by the U.S. bishops in their pastoral letter "Church and Social Order." The bishops forcefully stated, according to Mueller, that "principles that would hold that wages should provide for nothing more than the subsistence of the worker or that they should be determined solely by supply and demand are both 'anti-social and anti-Christian.'" [53]

Besides bringing attention to the injustice involved in Mexican wages, Perales and Calleros supported public policy, or what David O'Brien refers to as class legislation, to eliminate such an injustice.[54] Both agreed with Catholic social doctrine on the role of the state in bringing about social justice. *Rerum Novarum*, for example, was explicit on the need for the state to intervene to protect workers and the poor. Both were likewise in agreement with the encyclical as well as with other Catholic social teachings that stressed that the end purpose of the state was the common good.[55] Moral law superseded the marketplace.[56] Catholics in general and many Mexican American Catholics supported New Deal social policies. As O'Brien notes of Catholic thought and the New Deal, "The pressures of the Depression reduced minority fears and helped create a climate of opinion receptive to the use of government power to alleviate suffering, end unemployment, restore prosperity, and reform American business practices." [57] Indeed, New Deal rhetoric on social issues came very close to that of Catholic social thought. "The assertion of social values over individual values, the friendly attitude toward labor, the use of government for the protection and promotion of the common good," O'Brien observes, "these were principles which were far closer to the Catholic position than were those of the old order or of the Republican party of 1936." [58]

In a 1937 column Perales encouraged Mexican Americans to support New Deal legislation, such as the Black-Connery Wage and Hour Bill before the Congress, which would have mandated a minimum wage and maximum hours of work and prohibited interstate transportation of goods produced by child labor. All three aspects of this bill, Perales stressed, would improve the Mexican workers' position in the United States. "We Mexican Americans," he wrote, "who truly wish our people to progress should immediately support this legislation. We should realize that as long as our people are paid less than a living wage which would allow them to live as human beings, we cannot progress."[59] At the 1930 Los Angeles Catholic Conference on Industrial Problems, Calleros undoubtedly supported the proposal by Father Thomas J. O'Dwyer, director of the Catholic Welfare Bureau of Los Angeles, who in his address to the conference noted that low wages were the single [most important] cause of poverty and called for legislation to correct this problem. "It is our duty," he said, "to sponsor and support in every way possible legislation that will procure for the workman his fundamental right to a living wage, adequate protection against industrial hazards and an income that will provide properly for old age."[60]

In their call for public policy to address the inequities of wages in the Southwest, both Calleros and Perales echoed Pope Leo XIII's insistence that the state had a moral obligation to intervene on behalf of the poor. "In protecting the rights of private individuals," the pontiff said of the state, "special consideration must be given to the weak and the poor. For the notion, as it were, of the rich is guarded by its own defense and is in less need of governmental protection; whereas the suffering multitude without the means to protect itself, relies especially on the protection of the state. Wherefore, since wage workers are numbered among the great mass of the needy the state must include them under its special care and foresight."[61]

Regrettably, several years later, in 1962, Calleros observed that the practice of paying Mexican wages to Mexican workers still was occurring in the Southwest with the consequence of continued underdevelopment for the Mexican. In reacting to an article that blamed Mexicans for their lack of progress, Calleros angrily responded, "The real reason that they live in deplorable conditions is due to the fact that the majority are not paid a living wage, and that is our fault. How can we expect them to live with all the thrills and frills of our 'standard of living' if we do not pay them a living wage?"[62]

Mexican wages and the lack of a living wage in turn were symptomatic of the fact that Mexican workers were also relegated to what were called Mexican jobs. These were the lowest and most menial unskilled jobs in the Southwest. Mexican jobs were justified, as were Mexican wages, by the stereotyping of Mexicans as incapable of more skilled labor and as being, like blacks, more physically suited than Anglos to perform menial labor. Perales and Calleros consistently called attention to job discrimination against Mexicans and encouraged the upgrading of job opportunities for them. Mexicans were not only initially hired in these Mexican jobs, but even after acquiring work experience and some education, they, in most cases, were still denied job mobility. "There is no such thing as promotion," Calleros noted of Mexican workers. "It is for that reason that he cannot adjust his ways because he is not given the means to adjust his life to the American way of life."[63]

Calleros further observed in 1930 that in a recent survey, which he had made in El Paso, he had discovered that Mexicans who had acquired some education were still denied better jobs. Moreover, in a visit to Kansas City, he observed that some Mexican female high school graduates were discriminated against in job opportunities and were forced to take unskilled jobs in factory work. Such discrimination discouraged many Mexicans from acquiring more education either for themselves or for their children.[64] In a speech before a convention of teachers of adult night schools, Perales, for his part, noted that such night schools needed to train Mexicans for better skilled jobs and that this training had to be linked with equal employment opportunities. "I am one who believes," Perales told his audience, "that my community is deserving of the opportunity to learn the same knowledge and skills and to acquire the same jobs and professions as are available to those of Anglo background."[65]

Perales further believed that job-training programs for Mexican Americans should not be segregated but integrated with those of Anglo-Americans to insure equal treatment and equal opportunity. In 1935, he and Professor Castañeda of the University of Texas at Austin wrote a strong protest to Lyndon B. Johnson, at that time the director of the National Youth Administration (NYA) in Texas, one of the New Deal agencies. Castañeda, himself a devout Catholic, in his historical work focused heavily on the history of the Catholic Church in Texas. Johnson had proposed the establishment of two youth camps in San Antonio where young women between the ages of sixteen and twenty-five would be trained in vocational work. However, the reason for the dual camps was that one would be reserved for whites and the other for Mexicans. Perales agreed with Castañeda's assertion that "any plan that will segregate Mexican women in the proposed camp . . . will have a far reaching effect in establishing the admission of the inferiority of our people."[66] Perales, in turn, added, "I would very much rather see one camp where the Mexican and Anglo-American girls would have the opportunity to mingle with each other freely than two camps where, whether intended or not, one group would be segregated from the other."[67]

As a result of Castañeda's and Perales's protest, as well as that of other Mexican American leaders, Johnson, who, of course, would later become president of the United States, backed down on his idea of segregating the camps, although he retaliated by accepting fewer women of both backgrounds.[68]

In addition to supporting livable wages and better jobs for Mexicans, neither Calleros nor Perales appears to have made any distinction between

Mexican Americans and Mexican nationals in the United States. Both men believed that neither group should be discriminated against in employment or education or public facilities. Both groups, they thought, in keeping with Catholic social doctrine, deserved social justice and dignity as working people. Calleros, in particular, owing to his position as head of the Bureau of Immigration of the NCWC, paid attention to the rights of immigrants. Perales, in turn, consistently spoke out against discrimination against Mexicans of any background, including immigrants. The positions the two men took contradict recent indictments of Mexican American leaders of this period, such as Perales and Calleros, for not supporting immigrant rights. This indictment, most prominently by David Gutiérrez and Benjamin Márquez, is largely based on the premise that the acculturation and the stress on integration by Mexican American middle-class leaders prevented them from forming coalitions with Mexican immigrants. This is an indictment I have challenged in my earlier work as not bearing out the actual facts. However, it may be that a key variable that has been overlooked in the relationship of Mexican Americans and Mexican immigrants is their Catholic religious connections, which not only would draw them together, but also, as in the case of Calleros and Perales, would promote a Catholic social responsibility and practice that would further connect Mexican Americans and immigrants in combating discrimination.[69] Gina Marie Pitti, for example, in her work on Sociedades Guadalupanas (in honor of Our Lady of Guadalupe) in the San Francisco Bay area, observes that Catholic affinities among people of Mexican origins transcended national status, class, and gender positions.[70] As president of the Education Committee of LULAC in the 1930s, Perales informed Spanish-speaking Mexicans, including immigrants, of the availability of classes for them in English, hygiene, health, and civics for naturalization as well as vocational training at the Sidney Lanier High School in the Mexican west side of San Antonio and sponsored by both the federal government and the local school board.[71]

This attention was especially critical during the early years of the Great Depression, when efforts were made in the Southwest and elsewhere to scapegoat Mexican immigrant workers as one of the causes for the depression on the false charge that they were taking jobs away from "real" Americans. The result was large-scale deportations and repatriation drives that forced close to half a million Mexicans out of the country, many of them illegally as they were U.S.-born children of immigrants.[72] From his position in El Paso, Calleros witnessed this tragic story of the *repatriados*, or repatriates. "Words fail to describe the condition of some of these unfortunates reaching the border," Calleros stated in 1932. "They are penniless, hungry, with troubled minds as to their future, as to what to expect in Mexico, and with a feeling that they are being forced out of the United States through racial and other contributing causes."[73]

As head of the NCWC Immigration Bureau in El Paso, Calleros was responsible for most of the U.S.-Mexico border region. His main task with respect to the repatriados was to ensure that they were adequately provided for while they waited to return to Mexico; relief agencies, including federal ones, often refused to help them.[74]

Moreover, Calleros worked to prevent those who were U.S. citizens or who were legal residents from being illegally returned to Mexico. The issue of nationality was not one that U.S. immigration officials concerned themselves with in the process of deporting or repatriating Mexicans. If you were of Mexican descent, it was assumed that you were a noncitizen and thus an "illegal alien." Race and cultural background seemed to be the criteria for determining one's nationality. In an interview with the historian Oscar Martínez in 1972, Calleros expressed his outrage at the lack of discrimination on the part of officials. "A Depression when it comes in any country," Calleros told Martínez,

> the ones who suffer are supposed to be aliens. And very few Americans knew the difference between being a citizen and being a Mexican national. They look at them and say, "Oh, you are a Mexican." The average American does not believe in the constitutional rights for others. As a matter of fact, he doesn't even know what the Constitution says. So the thing was nationally—from El Paso to Vermont and from the Carolinas to California—to get rid of the Mexicans, just like that. And within six months over 400,000 individuals of different ages had been sent to Mexico.[75]

In a 1934 report, Calleros observed that of the Mexican repatriados he had dealt with, more than 80 percent were U.S. citizens. For those, especially children and teenagers, who had grown up on this side of the border, a new life in Mexico proved to be traumatic.[76] Hence, many families and individuals returned to the border crossing areas such as El Paso, where Calleros attempted to secure their entrance back into the United States on the basis that they were American citizens.[77]

Calleros was particularly concerned about families being separated. In some cases, one of the parents who could not prove legal residence in the

United States was deported or "convinced" to repatriate back to Mexico, leaving the rest of their family, including small children, on the north side of the border. Calleros worked to prevent such family separation and to reunite those families by documenting the legal residence of the deported or repatriated parent.[78]

In his work with the repatriados and with Mexican immigrants over the years, Calleros reinforced the Catholic Church's efforts to include immigrants within the fold of Catholic social doctrine. While much of the Church's work in the United States concerned European immigrants, Calleros expanded these services and protection to the U.S.-Mexico border. Calleros's work was recognized as early as 1929, when Father John J. Burke, the general secretary of the NCWC, said of Calleros, "If we could have a few men with the experience and ability and Catholic spirit of Mr. Calleros, going through the Country, both speaking to the Mexicans directly and interesting Catholic native Americans in the importance and pressing nature of this problem."[79]

Racial Justice

Calleros's and Perales's reaction to the so-called Mexican problem included one of the important additions that both men made directly and indirectly to Catholic social thought. That is, while encyclicals such as *Rerum Novarum* and *Quadragesimo Anno* addressed very well the issues of class conflict with respect to industrial workers in Europe and the United States, they did not deal with the additional social injustice of race prejudice. This omission was distinctly noticeable in the United States, where race conflict was as significant as class conflict. Aware of the importance of race in American culture, both Perales and Calleros focused not just on the class injustices suffered by Mexicans in the Southwest, but on the racial ones as well. This is a good example of how their Mexican American experience complemented their awareness of Catholic social doctrine.

Perales, for example, stressed the basic fundamental equality of all people, irrespective of race. Human beings, despite their ethnic differences, were all equal beings. And no group was inferior or superior to another. As Charles Curran notes, "The Catholic tradition in general and Catholic social teaching in particular traditionally have emphasized the basic dignity of the human being, who is an image of God through reason and the power of self-determination."[80] This, argued Perales, certainly applied to Mexican-Anglo relations. "The Mexican people," he wrote, "do not pertain to a fundamental inferior race. The history of our people proves this." Indeed, he stated, "Mexicans are descendants of two great peoples: the indigenous and the Spanish." [81] This reference to the mestizaje, or racial mixing, of Mexican Americans is a significant rebuttal to contemporary scholars who incorrectly suggest that Mexican American middle-class leaders only wanted to assert their "whiteness" as a way of being accepted by U.S. society. [82] Perales noted that being proud of his Mexican background and of his American citizenship only convinced him further of the equality of all peoples. [83] This equality, he added, was linked to Christian principles and, in his case, to Catholic ones. "Ours must be a war against prejudice, ignorance, injustice, and poverty," he stressed in a 1940 speech. "We must teach fair play, brotherhood of man, love of One's neighbors, and unselfishness. We must teach and practice the doctrine of Jesus Christ having as its theme love and tolerance." [84]

The problem in race relations in the United States and specifically in the Southwest, Perales contented, had nothing to do with race per se, but with attitudes. Anglos believed themselves to be superior to Mexicans, even though this was not true. Perales appeared to be arguing that the notion of race represented not a scientific construction, but a social and a political one elaborated in order to allow one group to acquire power and privileges over another. [85] If attitudes created a race problem, then for Perales the solution was to transform not the system that hosted them but the attitudes themselves. In this view, Perales was consistent with Catholic social thought, which in the case of class conflict did not see capitalism per se as at fault, but rather the excesses of capitalism. While Perales certainly understood the economic consequences of the race problem in the Southwest, he seems to have attached a greater weight to race issues as being first and foremost an ideological conflict. Throughout most of his writings, Perales emphasized that race relations would not improve in Texas, for example, until a solid body of Anglos came to the conclusion or were brought to the conclusion that Mexicans were equal human beings and deserving of mutual respect. Furthermore, he believed that what was also needed was for Anglos to provide Mexicans with the opportunities to prove themselves as equal and as capable as any other group. [86]

If Mexicans were equal to others based on natural human rights, they were also equal, Perales argued, on the basis of law and of their contributions to American society. Perales reminded Anglos that under the Constitution of the United States, Mexicans, whether citizens or immigrants, were equal in the eyes of the law. [87] Moreover, during World War II, Perales did not hesitate to point out the loyalty of Mexican Americans to the United States. They were putting their lives on the line for their country and because of this were deserving of being treated as equally as any other American ethnic group. About half a million Mexican Americans were fighting the "good war," and Perales believed they were entitled to come back to a Texas where they would have equal rights and equal opportunities with other Texans.[88] "Our hope," he wrote in 1944, "is that when our brothers return from the warfront that they will find if not a more truly democratic Texas at least a political climate much healthier than when they left to go to war." Perales added that the following slogan needed to apply: "Equal in the trenches, but also equal in the factories, in the stores, in the schools, in the churches, in the restaurants, in the barbershops, in the theaters, and everywhere else."[89]

The most onerous manifestation of racial injustice for Perales and Calleros, as well as for the rest of the Mexican American Generation, consisted of educational discrimination, including school segregation for most Mexican American children. Since the turn of the century, when mass immigration from Mexico commenced, the practice of the public schools in the Southwest was to establish segregated and inferior schools in the barrios and in the countryside for Mexicans. These were the so-called Mexican schools, which despite their designation revealed little if any sensitivity to the cultural backgrounds of the students. Instead, they provided limited educational opportunities stressing vocational education. As segregated schools, they were inherently unequal.[90]

Perales, for example, called for a new educational system that would allow Mexican American children to pursue whatever goals and dreams they desired rather than a system that channeled them only to blue-collar jobs. "In other words," he wrote in 1940, "we want our children to have opportunity to become educators, doctors, engineers, lawyers, merchants, industry leaders, pharmacists, or bakers, mechanics, carpenters, bricklayers, etc. if they feel like it. But we do not want them to become any of these things against their will and inclinations and most certainly we do not want our school systems to so mold their setup that our children cannot become anything but artisans."[91]

Both Perales and Calleros understood this and spoke out against such segregation and inferior education. Perales observed that education in the United States was not a privilege, but a right that was being deprived Mexican American children. This deprivation was particularly troublesome to Perales because he further understood that education was the key avenue for Mexican American mobility. It would not only open doors for better jobs and livable wages—what the encyclicals called for—but would also assist in the social and political integration of Mexican Americans. "Education is the most important factor," Perales stressed in 1928, "since human progress depends on it." [92]

Perales also made it clear that the only explanation for the exclusion of Mexican Americans from equal education with Anglo children was racism. He rejected the often-repeated response by school administrators and school boards throughout the Southwest that the Mexican schools existed only to deal with special pedagogical issues applicable to Mexican American students, such as language difference. Perales conceded that perhaps some initial special instruction had to be provided for those Mexican American children who entered school speaking only Spanish, but that such separation should be limited to the first few years. "With reference to the segregation of our children in Texas schools," Perales wrote as follows: "That segregation which exists beyond the third grade is purely racial. . . . and it is illegal and we also know that school officials always come up with an excuse to skirt the spirit if not the letter of the law." [93] Indignant about such practices in Texas, Perales in 1932 went so far as to declare to the annual LULAC convention that if ever the U.S. Supreme Court were to approve the segregation of Mexican American children in the public schools he would give up his U.S. citizenship in protest. [94]

Calleros further pointed out that the denial of equal educational opportunities and facilities to Mexican Americans represented part of the denial of social justice to Mexicans in the United States. Calleros attacked the practice of the public schools utilizing questionable and biased intelligence tests as applied to Mexican American children in order to justify continued segregation and inferior education. He especially reacted to a 1940 report on such tests in El Paso by a Dr. I. M. Epstein, who concluded that an even lower education standard than the one already being applied in the south side Mexican schools needed to be implemented, in keeping with what Epstein concluded was the lower mental capacities of most of the Mexican American children. According to Epstein, the Mexican American students tested significantly lower than Anglo students in the north side schools, the results suggesting that most of the Mexican American children were mentally retarded, feebleminded, or slow learners. [95]

Calleros, in a letter to the El Paso Times that minced no words, attacked the Epstein report and its conclusions as racist. "The report is unfair and highly colored with racial prejudice," Calleros asserted. "It brands the south side school children as dumbbells and of low mentality." Calleros pointed out what he believed to be the real factors behind the educational underdevelopment of the Mexican American children. This included a disproportionate number of halftime classes, overcrowded classrooms, and inferior school buildings. "To these may be added the following facts which also contribute," Calleros noted:

1. The segregation of children by racial classification.
2. The flagrant racial prejudice of some school officials and teachers.
3. The constant evidence of some officials and teachers in having the so-called "Mexican" child feel that he is inferior to his so-called "white" companion although both are, believe [it] or not, of the white race.[96]

If Epstein's report concluded that the educational practices as applied to the south side schools were a failure, Calleros observed, then that failure had nothing to do with the children and everything to do with the schools themselves. Moreover, this failed system was in the hands of Anglo administrators, who could impose reforms, but such changes would not come about as long "as the system persists in some of their racist tactics and in giving the south side schools the 'leavings or discards.'" Calleros concluded that the problem lay with a fundamental contradiction in the public schools: "The fact is that too much good American citizenship is preached and very little practiced. So-called 'Mexican' children are constantly reminded that they are expected to be good citizens and the same reminders turn right around and deny them the same privileges accorded other human beings."[97]

If educational discrimination represented an affront to the dignity of Mexican Americans, so too did discrimination in public facilities. Both Perales and Calleros protested such discrimination and called for specific measures, including legislation, to eliminate it. According to Perales, discrimination was widespread throughout Texas. One area of segregation was in public medical facilities. In 1939 Perales, as leader of the League of Loyal Americans, which he had founded in the 1930s, protested against the segregation of Mexican Americans along with blacks at the Brackenridge Hospital in Austin. Mexican Americans and blacks were being segregated together apart from Anglos. Perales decried this action, although he focused only on Mexican Americans.[98] The relationship between Mexican Americans and blacks in this period is a relatively unexplored one. It would be too simple to suggest that Mexican Americans were totally influenced by Anglo racism against blacks. It is very conceivable that this had some influence, but other issues, including political strategies as well as the lack of Mexican American-black contacts in the

Southwest owing to a paucity of blacks in many areas of the region, may have also played a role.[99] Moreover, in 1942 Perales supported efforts by both the U.S. and Mexican governments to investigate discrimination against Mexican contract workers in Texas—the *braceros*—but at the same time pointed out that such discrimination, especially in public facilities, had a very long and ugly history. Perales noted that he personally possessed data on at least 150 cities and towns in Texas where at a minimum ten commercial establishments refused services to Mexicans, both citizens and immigrants.[100] In one case, Perales in 1937 protested to the mayor of San Angelo about the segregation of Mexicans along with blacks in the balcony of the municipal auditorium. "I write to energetically protest against the insult to the dignity of Mexicans," Perales wrote, "and to solicit your assistance so that this humiliation not be repeated."[101] Perales further noted that such discrimination also pertained to restaurants, barbershops, and many other establishments.[102]

Calleros, for his part, later recalled how wide and distasteful discrimination was: "There were towns in Texas where Mexicans were actually forced to walk on the street, denying them the privilege of using the sidewalk; services were refused in most restaurants and movie houses."[103]

Perales advocated legislation to outlaw such affronts to Mexicans. In 1941 he wrote to Undersecretary of State Sumner Wells informing him of an incident in New Braunfels, Texas, where a group of Venezuelan air force pilots who were training in San Antonio were told to vacate certain tables in a public park because those were reserved for whites, while some other tables were for Latin Americans. Such an incident harmed the inter-American relations advocated by Franklin Roosevelt's Good Neighbor Policy, and Perales inquired of Wells if the president could ask Congress to pass a law prohibiting such discrimination. He reminded Wells of the large numbers of Mexican Americans serving in World War II.[104] He further informed the secretary of another incident in Lockhart, Texas, where a group of Mexicans were ordered to leave a public Fourth of July dance, being told that this was a celebration only for Americans and for whites.[105]

During the war, Perales supported making the Fair Employment Practice Commission into a permanent arm of the federal government and expanding its work to include investigations of discrimination in public facilities. He also attempted, unsuccessfully, to get the Texas state government to pass antidiscrimination laws concerning public facilities.[106]

Discrimination and segregation, however, knew no religious boundaries. In a revealing letter to his good friend and Mexican American civil rights leader Castañeda, Perales lambasted fellow Catholics—Anglo-Catholics—who discriminated against Mexicans. This included Anglo-Catholic priests who tolerated and even allowed segregation in their churches. "You and I and others," Perales wrote as late as 1952,

> want to help bring our people closer to our Church, but it is an uphill fight with all these petty foolish tactics on the part of some Catholic lay people, and in some instances on the part of some members of the clergy who permit themselves to be swayed by those lay Catholics who are prejudiced and who will stop at nothing to keep our people ostracized. I am getting pretty well fed up and I do not know how much longer I will be able to endure it. We go to conferences and lambaste everybody else for discriminating and segregating our people, but our Catholic friends (some of them) reserve the right to do it themselves and do not wish to be reminded that it is a sin to do so, that [it] is unchristian, undemocratic, etc. . . . I shall not be happy until our Church (those in authority) put an end to this darned foolishness.[107]

Conclusion

On these issues as well as in their efforts to acquire adequate and equal public resources for Mexican residents in Texas communities, Perales and Calleros embodied a consciousness and a commitment to achieving social justice and the common good for Mexicans in the United States. These themes, with respect to labor, wages, education, and the dignity of Mexicans as human beings, complemented and resonated directly and indirectly with Catholic social doctrines. This does not mean that it was only such principles that influenced Perales and Calleros. They, as noted, obviously were motivated by their Mexican American experiences, including the Mexican American Catholic ethos and environment as well as New Deal liberal thought. What this chapter suggests, however, is that another important influence concerned the Church's pronouncements on social justice. As Mexican Americans, the two men exemplified dual influences from both Mexican and non-Mexican sources. As a result, Mexican American political thought during the period of the Mexican American Generation, as exemplified in the writings and praxis of Perales and Calleros, possessed a religious and specifically a Catholic dimension linked to Catholic social doctrine that needs to be acknowledged and examined more closely in other writers and activists of this formative period in Chicano history.

THREE

Recording the Sacred

The Federal Writers' Project and Hispano-Catholic
Traditions in New Mexico, 1935–1939

*The customs and traditions of centuries are tenacious and hard to eradi-
cate entirely. All of the customary fiestas and saints' days are still observed
with the same spirit of reverence mixed with gaiety, and hospitality is
extended just as freely to the stranger or visitor as always. The religious
parts of the celebrations remain the same; no new or jarring note mars
them. Observance of the ritual is still carried out with the same simplicity
and devotion as before.*

—LORIN W. BROWN, WPA WRITER

IF THE LINKAGE between Mexican American Catholicism and the public sphere was made by civil rights leaders such as Calleros and Perales, the
fact remained that for many Mexicans of Catholic background (irrespective
of what terms of ethnic identity they used), popular religious traditions and
practices remained the heart of their faith and of their particular form of resistance and affirmation in a new Anglo-American system. This should not
imply, however, as perhaps the above epigraph may suggest, that such popular
religion is constant and static. It changes or adapts to new circumstances and
conditions while preserving the nucleus of the faith. Reflecting this adaptive
culture, which involves rural to urban movements, economic dislocation, immigration, racial discrimination, educational mobility, and socialization to
Anglo mores and values, people of Spanish/Mexican descent have attempted
to preserve their popular faith and pass it on to later generations in one form of
another. Each generation rediscovers and readapts these traditions (see Chapter Eight). This chapter is about the rediscovery and preservation of popular
religious customs in northern New Mexico during the dislocating period of
the Great Depression. While Latino popular religiosity is an important focus

of recent scholarship, my chapter introduces a previously unacknowledged factor, that is, the efforts of the Works Progress Administration (WPA) in preserving those traditions.[1] Moreover, some of these customs as rediscovered by the WPA are particular to northern New Mexico and not as widely known in the field of Chicano/Latino popular religious studies.

Much of Catholic popular religiosity among Latinos in the United States has, of course, been preserved and transmitted through oral traditions. Religion and memory become intertwined.[2] Rituals, celebrations of feast days, religious stories, hymns, and a myriad other customs have been passed on from generation to generation orally and through practice. These are examples of what some scholars refer to as "lived religion" or what Luis León calls "religious poetics."[3] However, one of the first attempts to record and preserve these traditions was carried out among Hispanos in New Mexico during the 1930s by the Federal Writers' Project. The project, which represented a unique experiment, was part of the Works Progress Administration (WPA) established by President Franklin Roosevelt's New Deal in 1935. The WPA was created to combat the massive unemployment resulting from the Great Depression. While the WPA primarily concentrated on creating federal jobs for blue-collar workers, including the building of libraries, schools, fire stations, federal buildings, roads, dams, and other infrastructure needs, it also reached out to unemployed artists, actors, musicians, and writers. By 1939, this part of the WPA employed some twenty-five thousand people. To assist writers, the Federal Writers Project was formed. The term *writer* was liberally interpreted to include professional writers as well as amateur ones and even aspiring writers. Thousands of writers found jobs with the project. "So began a governmental adventure in cultural collectivism," one former participant later wrote, "the like of which no nation has experienced before or since."[4]

Started in 1935, the project survived until 1939, when its activities were either absorbed by the states or dismantled. Moreover, the U.S. entrance into World War II in 1941 for all practical purposes terminated the WPA and other federal efforts to battle unemployment, as the military and wartime production ended the depression. However, during its short tenure, the project, besides providing employment for many writers and intellectuals, produced various publications, most notably the now-classic WPA guides to the history and culture of the forty-eight states plus the District of Columbia and important cities.[5] Besides producing the guides, the project researched and gathered information on a variety of topics. Some of this material was integrated into the guides and other publications and some went into the archives. This research included historical and geographic data, demographic and economic statistics, and information on social, educational, and cultural customs from a multiethnic perspective, including folklore, music, literature, and art. In less than four years, the project published over three hundred publications.[6]

In New Mexico, the project, with headquarters in Santa Fe, concentrated on researching the diverse ethnic traditions of the "Land of Enchantment," as the state was known: Indians, Hispanos, and Euro-Americans. This effort, along with other New Deal economic and social programs, aimed at countering poverty, illiteracy, and lack of educational opportunities among Hispanos. It represented what Suzanne Forrest refers to as the "Hispanic New Deal."[7] This New Deal, at one level, sought to bring Hispanos into a more modern world, and yet, at another, recognized the importance of preserving and even fostering more traditional, premodern cultural traditions. "Paradoxically," Forrest observes, "while some federal, state, and local officials were striving mightily to relieve the symptoms of Hispanic poverty, and in the process extinguishing, so far as they were able, the remnants of a pre-industrial Hispanic life style, others were striving ever so mightily to record and preserve its dying embers."[8] Some of this preservation had to do with enticing tourists to witness a supposedly primitive Hispano culture, and the tourist trade might possibly offset some of the effects of the Depression. In this sense, such preservation carried with it ideological baggage, including stereotyping of Hispanos and the suggestion that they were an ahistorical people who did not change.[9] Understanding this, I would argue nevertheless that it appears that the writers involved in this project were genuinely motivated by a desire to honor and recognize the historical contributions of Hispano culture. They seemed to recognize that in the retention of their rural cultural traditions, Hispanos, consciously and unconsciously, were asserting their ethnic identity in opposition to the earlier Anglo-American conquest of New Mexico in the 1840s and the subsequent encroachment on their lands and the denigration of their culture. Ideological domination, after all, always involves a dialectic, and the retention of popular religion among Hispanos as a form of ethnic self-defense constituted part of that dialectic. Part of this WPA sensitivity undoubtedly had to do with the fact that several of the writers employed were Hispanos themselves. Hispano writers included such figures as Lorin W. Brown, Aurora Lucero-White, and Reyes Martínez. Brown, a Hispano native of Cordova, alone wrote 150 manuscripts. One hundred and seven people were employed by the WPA in New Mexico, of whom twenty-four had Spanish surnames; among these there were probably some Indians with Hispano surnames.[10]

To capture and preserve Hispano popular culture, these writers primarily focused on the numerous small villages scattered throughout northern New Mexico, historically the major concentration of Hispanos. Some relied on their own memories and observations of growing up in these villages. They also interviewed other Hispanos, especially the elders. Popular family and community traditions, customs, folklore, and music formed the basis of this research.

A central part of these traditions involved religion, especially popular religiosity—the religion practiced by the people and controlled by them rather than by the priests. This was not surprising in that religion—in this case Hispano-Catholicism—and community were heavily interconnected in the villages. Religion, what Badillo refers to as "religión ranchera," permeated almost every aspect of village life.[11] It exemplifies León's assertion that in the Chicano case, culture is religion.[12] The result was a rich collection of popular Hispano-Catholic traditions, including community feast days, religious drama and pageants, religious folklore, the practices of the Penitentes (penitential groups), and the rich tradition of *alabados*, or religious hymns sung in the villages. This tradition of Hispano popular religiosity, as Badillo correctly observes, is part of the heritage of Spanish colonialism in the Americas. The colonizing enterprise introduced the highly ritualistic and medieval forms of popular religion practiced prior to the post-Reformation period initiated by the Council of Trent (1545–1563), which began to encourage movement away from what is referred to as pre-Tridentine Catholicism, more reflective of rural Spain.[13] This form of popular religion, as Treviño notes in his study of what he calls "Tejano ethno-Catholicism," was further influenced by various Mexican indigenous popular religious traditions.[14] The preservation and practice of these traditions in rural New Mexico were especially important in a period of much change brought about by the increased poverty pursuant to the Depression and the exit of younger Hispanos from the rural areas to urban ones. Many left New Mexico altogether, as Sarah Deutsch observes in her study of northern New Mexico.[15] Popular religion in this changing environment offered a sense of continuity, order, security, and community. It required a more personal and informal version of resistance and affirmation as practiced by grassroots Hispanos and Mexican American Catholics.

Despite some cultural erosion by the 1930s due to acculturation and Anglo-American influences, there was still much Hispano cultural continuity, as observed by Brown. "The customs and traditions of centuries are tenacious and hard to eradicate entirely," he wrote. "All of the customary fiestas and saints' days are still observed with the same spirit of reverence mixed with gaiety, and hospitality is extended just as freely to the stranger or visitor as always. The religious parts of the celebrations remain the same; no new or jarring note mars them. Observance of the ritual is still carried out with the same simplicity and devotion as before." [16]

These customs, many of them never before recorded, were written down by the federal writers, translated from Spanish to English, and preserved in a bilingual format, both handwritten and typed, in the WPA archives. Nearly six hundred manuscripts were written. [17] Much of this material has never been published. In fact, much of the information recorded on religious traditions was not used in the writing of the WPA guide to New Mexico. [18] Copies of these records exist in the National Archives, the Library of Congress, the New Mexico State Records Center and Archives in Santa Fe, and in the Fray Angélico Chávez History Library of the Museum of New Mexico in Santa Fe, where I researched them.

Community Feast Days

One area of research involved a variety of Hispano-Catholic community traditions. These included, for example, the custom of community saints. Each Hispano village annually celebrated a particular saint, who represented the patron or patroness of the village. These yearly feasts were called *funciones.* [19] "The veneration of their favorite saints by the rural Spanish-American people of New Mexico has a special quality of intimacy," one writer observed. "Their belief in the power of their saints, both to aid and to punish, is implicit and absolute." [20] One popular saint is San Antonio, who was venerated throughout Hispano New Mexico, but in particular in villages that bore his name. Hence the small mountain village of San Antonio, eighteen miles east of Albuquerque, celebrated the feast day of San Antonio on June 13 each year, as one writer noted, "in exactly the same way as it did when great, primitive *carretas* (ox-carts) creaked slowly all the way to distant Santa Fe on trading expeditions." [21]

This writer noted that the villages possessed an "unbounded faith" in San Antonio and his ability to protect them. Some of the old men, unfortunately expressing historical ethnic tensions between Hispanos and Native Americans, recalled how during the Spanish colonial period bands of hostile

Indians would attack the village, only to be repulsed by the intervention of San Antonio, who "sent a shower of missiles from heaven, causing the invaders to flee."[22]

Days before the fiesta, intense preparations were made, including the baking of bread, whitewashing of houses, purchasing of new clothes, and cutting down of evergreen trees from the hills and planting them along the route of the festival procession. On the morning of the feast, girls in white dresses carried the statue of San Antonio on a platform out of the church and placed it in a prominent place in the town plaza, where he could enjoy the day's festivities. These included performances by the *matachines* (dancers dressed in various costumes depicting the Spanish conquest of the Indians in New Mexico), fiddle music, and a mock bullfight.[23] At dusk, the church bell called the people back into the church, where a visiting priest conducted services. At the conclusion, a procession with the image of San Antonio made its way around the village, lighted along the way by *luminarias*, or lighted posts built from the cut evergreen trees. At intervals, the procession stopped while the priest chanted a prayer and the villagers replied. The procession resumed until the route had been completed, and then San Antonio was returned to the church until the next feast day. "It is an experience," the writer concluded, "one is not likely to forget."[24]

Another popular saint among the Hispanos is San Juan or St. John, whose feast day falls on June 24. In the village of Arroyo Hondo, Reyes Martínez, a native of the hamlet, recorded the special activities organized by the villagers. On the morning of the twenty-fourth, a group gathered at the church and, after saying a few prayers and singing hymns, escorted the images of San Juan and the Virgin Mary out of the church along with statues of other saints. A procession then commenced, stopping at every house along the way. At each location, the woman of the house greeted the procession and enveloped the figure of the Virgin in homemade incense. After kneeling and praying before the statue, the woman picked it up and carried it into her home. Inside, she placed the Virgin on an altar decorated with flowers and lighted candles. The other saints, including San Juan, were also placed on the home altar. Everyone in the procession then entered the abode to recite prayers and sing hymns. The Virgin and the saints were then gathered up and taken out, where the procession commenced again. This ritual was performed at each house along the way.

By late afternoon, the procession reached the central plaza, where that night a *velorio* (vigil or wake), was held in a home in honor of the saints. The velorio lasted until the next morning, when the procession resumed until all of the rest of the homes in the village were visited. The saints were then returned to their proper places in the church. "The strange part of the performance being," Martínez noted, "that Saint John takes second place to the Virgin Mary, throughout the ceremonials." [25]

Yet another popular saint throughout the Hispano villages was (and still is) that of San Ysidro Labrador, the patron saint of farmers, the main occupation of Hispanos in the 1930s. Farmers believed that their crops depended on observing San Ysidro's feast day and honoring him throughout the growing season. Different villages celebrated the feast day on different dates, but irrespective of what day the celebration took place, no one worked on that occasion. [26] One federal writer described the celebration of the feast day of San Ysidro, May 14, in the village of Córdova: "He is the saint to whom the people look for his blessing of their soil, a bountiful harvest, and freedom from drought and pests. There is the touch of the pagan, of sun worship, in the manner in which San Ysidro is honored on his day by these people whose roots are fixed in the soil from which they derive their livelihood." [27]

The evening before the feast day, the villagers participated in vespers or prayers at the church. At the conclusion of the service, the statue of San Ysidro, usually depicted with a top hat and dress coat and accompanied by his yoke of oxen, was carried out of the church on a platform. The procession entered the adjacent fields, the people following San Ysidro and singing hymns dedicated to him. Upon reaching the first farms, the procession halted, and San Ysidro was placed on the ground facing east. "He has been brought here to bless the fields with his presence," the writer pointed out, "and to insure that the seed, which has already been planted, will bear abundantly." [28]

An all-night vigil was then held in the field, the villagers praying and singing alabados around the image of San Ysidro. Not all was serious, as the villagers also enjoyed the socializing that went on. Brown, in observing the feast of San Ysidro in the village of Valdéz, noted that the evening velorio offered "the opportunity for flirtatious interludes" among the younger participants. [29]

At midnight, the women served food. The praying and singing continued until the first rays of the sun touched the face of San Ysidro. The statue was then raised, and the procession resumed through the accompanying fields. It was believed that San Ysidro's presence blessed the fields. The procession continued throughout the day until each farmer's field was blessed. The villagers then returned to the church, where San Ysidro was returned to his proper place. [30] In his report Brown concluded, "It is a tired but happy people, who after ensconcing San Ysidro in his own place in the church, disperse to prepare for the dance that night confident that their fields would yield bounteously this year again." [31]

Other feast days recorded by the Federal Writers' Project in New Mexico included that of San Juan Bautista (St. John the Baptist) on June 24, also in Córdova. On that day all the nearby streams and rivers were blessed, and the villagers bathed in them, believing that on this day the waters possessed curative powers. In this report, the writer noted that it was not unusual for invalids to be immersed in the waters in the hope of being miraculously cured. [32]

Although Hispanos mostly celebrated these feast days on their own, there is one celebration recorded by the WPA that brought together Hispanos and the Pueblo Indians. This consisted of the feast day of Nuestra Señora de Dolores (Our Lady of Sorrows) in the village of El Cañon de Taos, east of Taos proper. In this Hispano village, the people held in their church a small image of Nuestra Señora de Dolores, the patron saint of the community. In Taos Pueblo, the Indians had a much larger and more beautiful statue, or *bulto*, of the same Virgin in their church. For many years the two communities developed a tradition of honoring Nuestra Señora by coming together in the late summer or early fall. On an agreed-upon day, the Hispanos in procession carried their image to Taos Pueblo while singing hymns. When they reached the Indian church, the Pueblos apparently carried their larger image out of the church and lent it to the Hispanos. With both images in hand, the procession of Hispanos moved to a nearby field, where they enshrined both Virgins and conducted a wake or vigil all night. It is not clear if the Pueblos participated. At midnight, a large meal was served. Following the celebration, the Hispanos returned the larger image to the Pueblos until the following year. [33]

One writer noted that throughout the year in northern New Mexico, villagers visited each other to participate in the particular feast days associated with each village. "If one were so inclined," he wrote, "he could spend a giant part of the year going from one village to the other as each saint's day fell due, and his life could be one almost continuous round of feasting and dancing." [34]

Velorios

One of the Hispano Catholic traditions recorded by the federal writers concerned the burial practices of the velorio. According to Lucero-White, the word *velorio* derived from the Spanish word *velar*, meaning to watch over.[35] Martínez wrote about this tradition in his home village of Arroyo Hondo. He noted that velorios, in addition to various other religious customs, helped to maintain a sense of community. Not only the family of the deceased but also villagers participated in a velorio. The tolling of the church bell signaled the demise of one of the villagers. According to Martínez, young villagers, during the day leading up to the evening velorio, would ask each other, "Vas al chilito esta noche?" (are you going to the chile supper tonight?). The chile supper, which was served during the occasion, was a metaphor for the velorio.[36]

After the death of an individual, the body was laid to rest in the home. Throughout the night of the velorio, those who attended said prayers and sang alabados. In some cases, a professional *rezador* was hired to say prayers and sing alabados all night long.[37] If the deceased had been a Penitente, the rezador was a fellow Penitente.[38] The prayers asked for the intercession of various saints for the repose of the departed's soul as well as for those of his or her ancestors as far back as great-great grandparents. Martínez observed that this genealogy was one way younger people learned about their ancestry. Before midnight the rosary was said, and this was followed by the chile supper, a meal consisting usually of traditional Hispano dishes such as chili or posole.[39] The supper, also called the *cena de media noche*, or midnight supper, had a particular gendered order. The men ate first, and when they were finished, the women and children ate.[40]

In the case of a Penitente velorio, the ceremony was more elaborate. When the *hermanos*, or members of the secret brotherhood arrived, everyone else had to leave the room where the body of the deceased lay. The rezador, or *hermano mayor*, then put out all of the candles surrounding the body. The hermanos proceeded to sing alabados. They then called on the dead to join them. "Salgan vivos y difuntos, aquí estamos todos juntos" [come out dead and living, we are here together], they called out while rattling chains and pounding on a drum. Following these rituals, the hermanos carried the body out into the night for a procession attended only by members of the order. This was the *despedida del mundo*, or "taking the dead to bid the world good-bye." Upon returning an hour later, the members placed the body back in the house, and the velorio continued, joined by relatives and friends, until dawn.[41]

Very early the next morning, some of the men went to the cemetery and dug the grave. Brown noted that every able-bodied man and boy volunteered to dig the grave.[42] When this was completed, a funeral procession began, often taking place without a priest, according to Lucero-White, because of the remoteness of many of the villages.[43] Three male *cantadores*, or singers, led the procession and sang alabados all the way to the cemetery, in Martínez's account. During the procession, the contingent stopped at various rest places, or *descansos*, where more praying and singing took place. Eventually the group reached the cemetery, and the body was laid to rest. Throughout this entire affair, there were lamentations, in some cases quite loud and usually voiced by the women. Martínez recorded that attendance at a velorio was virtually a social obligation for all the villagers. "Not to attend a wake and funeral of a person that dies," he wrote, "is considered a mark of disrespect to the memory of the deceased and a lack of friendly feeling toward his or her immediate family and the offense is seldom forgotten during a lifetime."[44]

Brown described the velorio tradition in his hometown of Córdova. He noted both the religious and social aspects of the tradition. "In the remote village of Córdova," he observed, "a wake is next to a dance or a feast day in importance socially. It is a legitimate excuse for a get-together for everybody in the village as well as relatives and friends of the deceased from nearby towns and farms."[45]

Brown provided more details about the velorio tradition. He noted that within the home of the deceased, the body was laid out and occupied a central position in the largest room and was surrounded by lighted candles. "As is the custom," he added, "all looking-glasses in the house have been covered or turned to face the wall. Vanity will have no place in that home until a certain period of mourning is over."[46]

By evening, relatives and other families arrived at the home. The women, who all wore black, knelt around the body and prayed. Next to the body there was a bowl for monetary contributions, to be used to pay for a Mass for the deceased the next time a priest came to Córdova.[47]

The writer Annette Thorp observed that in some cases, for example, in the velorios in the San Pedro Mountains, if the dead person was male only men went to the cemetery to bury him. When the body was lowered into the ground, a cloth was put over his face and a bag of salt placed at his feet. The salt, Thorp recorded, was supposed to keep the body from decaying. Moreover, Thorp noted another burial custom involving the widow. She was not to wash her face or comb her hair for eight days. If she did, people would think that she did not really grieve for her husband.[48]

Velorios were held not only for individuals but for particular saints as well. According to Lucero-White, these were referred to as *Velorios de Santos*, or Wakes of the Saints. These velorios occurred as part of the appeal for special favors from the saint, such as for rain during times of drought. She observed that these velorios represented a community event usually involving all the *santos* or personal religious images in a village. "No one may refuse to lend his or her santo for the occasion," Lucero-White wrote, "including the sacristan who has custody of the church's icons."[49] If the velorio was held at someone's home, all of the santos were placed on a home altar—an *altarcito*—surrounded by vases filled with paper flowers. But before the velorio began, a procession was held outside, where the santos were paraded and the rosary recited. The santos were then returned to the home altar, and the velorio commenced with rituals very similar to those of a *velorio de muerto*, a velorio for a deceased person.[50]

Of these customs, Lucero-White noted that she was not a dispassionate observer. "Customs observed in connection with Velorios (wakes) indicated in this article," she reported,

> are those told to me by my grandmother, now deceased, and personally observed by me since childhood when as her companion I attended many velorios both "de santo" [of saints] and "de difunto" [of individuals]. These velorios were witnessed in San Miguel County, New Mexico, but Santa Feans whom I have interviewed assure me that the same customs prevail here, as well as in the rest of the Northern counties in the state.[51]

Descansos

As noted, one of the unique aspects of a velorio was the descanso associated with the funeral procession. Brown observed that many newcomers to New Mexico mistakenly identified the sites of descansos with the crosses stuck in the ground as the actual burial places. However, the descansos represented "the place where his coffin rested on the earth for the last time before being committed to its depth."[52] A descanso, Brown explained, meant "a short halt or stop for rest hence the name by which these places are known."[53] Owing to the length of the funeral march, the people caring for the coffin or body would stop to rest, and as they did they attached a religious meaning to the

FIGURE 3.1 Hispano woman standing at a descanso, Arroyo Hondo, New Mexico, 1925. Courtesy Bergere Family Photographs, no. 23304, New Mexico State Records Center and Archives.

rest stop as they heard the church bell toll. "Soon however there is a gentler accompaniment to the bell's mournful tones," Brown further described this ritual,

> as the kneeling group join in a prayer for the peace and spiritual welfare of the soul of the deceased. After the prayer the bearers resume their burden but not before some member or friend of the bereaved family has placed a small cross by the roadside marking the site of the halt at the base of which each mourner places a small stone. This cross will have inscribed on it a supplication to the passerby to say a prayer for the rest and peace of the soul of the deceased. If the passerby is heedful he will comply with the request and add his stone to the others supporting the cross. In time several crosses will decorate the same site, for it is the natural resting place, being midway from church to graveyard.[54]

Kenneth Fordyce, a WPA field worker, described a note sent to him by Mabel Shearer of Raton, who referred to the crosses planted at the descansos as "prayer crosses." Shearer observed that the ground leading to the cemetery in some cases would be covered with these crosses. "It is easily understood," she wrote to Fordyce, "that when someone dies who has many friends and a host of relatives that the ground near the cemetery appears literally dotted with little white crosses." [55]

Lucero-White further noted that in addition to descansos there was also the concept of the *parada*. The parada was the actual stopping of the funeral procession, while the descanso was the placement of a cross. She observed that in one case the paradas occurred in front of each of the homes of the deceased's sons, there being four sons. She also witnessed that in villages where there was a resident priest who accompanied the procession, the priest charged for each parada since he was asked to bless the deceased at each stop. "There is a case on record," Lucero-White wrote, "where there were four Paradas and the priest received $50.00 for each, the *difunto* (deceased) being *Muy Rico* (very rich)." [56]

Religious Dramas and Dances

A feature of the Hispano-Catholic tradition in New Mexico recorded by the federal writers consisted of the various religious plays and dances that added to Hispano-Catholic culture. These community-based rituals had their roots in the Spanish colonization of Mexico and New Mexico. Much, if not most, of these activities had been preserved over the years as oral tradition. The federal writers sought to further maintain them by recording them in written form.

The Christmas season served as the nexus for some of these rituals and performances. Nina Otero-Warren, the daughter of a prominent Hispano family, and John Flores, in one of their field reports for the WPA, first summarized the popular practices surrounding Christmas in northern New Mexico. "The Spanish descendants of the Conquistadores in New Mexico," they wrote, "brought with them from Spain ancient religious customs. Christmas, one of the big festivals, is first celebrated with a religious observance." [57] This included the celebration of la Noche Buena, or the Good Night, on Christmas Eve with a midnight Mass called "La Misa de Gallo," or the Mass of the cockcrow since the Mass lasted almost until dawn when the cock crowed. "In small villages," the writers observed, "paper sacks are filled with sand and a lighted candle planted therein [called luminarias] then placed on the flat adobe roof of the little church to illuminate the place of worship, where, too, a crib is placed—perhaps not such an elaborate one, but frequently more devotional. Gifts are brought and placed at the feet of the Infant Child, for it is His birthday—candles, beads, paper flowers, the best people have." [58]

Otero-Warren and Flores further noted that in addition to Christmas, Hispanos celebrated January 6, as the feast of the Three Kings, or Los Reyes Magos. It was on this day, not Christmas day, that children received gifts since it was the occasion when the three kings brought their gifts to the baby Jesus. Of this gift-giving practice, the writers stressed,

On this day the children placed straw in their shoes which were deposited in a conspicuous place. This was food for the camels of [the] Wise Men. In appreciation for this the Wise Men left gifts for the children—candy, small toys, just as now these gifts are placed in the stocking hung over the fireplace. So, our children in New Mexico, descendants of the Spanish conquerors, for many years followed the custom of Spain.[59]

Despite the writers' obvious hispanophilia, they did convey the sense of tradition linked to the Christmas season in New Mexico. Part of this tradition, as they pointed out, was the plays associated not only with Christmas but also with the entire religious calendar. "It is believed that these plays were written by the early missionaries," they emphasized, "who traveled in this region during the time of the early settlers."[60] Here, missionaries, according to Otero-Warren and Flores, took episodes from the life of Jesus and presented them as religious plays to the Indians as a way of converting and teaching them. These plays included El Coloquio [conversation] de San José, Las Posadas, El Coloquio de Los Pastores, El Auto de Los Reyes Magos, and El Niño Perdido.[61]

El Coloquio de San José, for example, was presented each March in the villages of northern New Mexico and was observed by the WPA writers. It depicted the selection of Joseph as Mary's husband. Las Posadas in New Mexico was performed on Christmas Eve, although in earlier years it had started on December 16 and was performed for nine straight days. Las Posadas dramatized the search by Mary and Joseph for shelter in order for Mary to give birth. At each home, they were refused entry until finally one home is opened to them. Inside, a party was given for all of the participants in the pageant until it was time to go to the Misa de Gallo, or the midnight mass.[62]

The next play in the cycle was Los Pastores or La Pastorella. This was the Shepherd's Play, and it also was performed on Christmas Eve. It focused on the birth of Jesus and the visit by the shepherds guided by the star. The writers noted that several versions of Los Pastores were performed in New Mexico. This play was then followed, as previously noted, by that of Los Tres Reyes

Magos, or the Wise Men. This is the story of the three Magi kings in search of the new King of Kings.[63]

The last play performed was El Niño Perdido, presented in March to complete the cycle. Otero-Warren and Flores noted that in the 1930s this play was still being performed in certain rural areas of northern New Mexico.[64] Brown, who observed the play in Taos, where it was presented in the fall, corroborated this account.[65] The theme of this performance is the story of the young Jesus leaving his parents without notice to go to the temple, where he astonished the rabbis with his knowledge and wisdom. This play, like the others, was performed not by professional actors but by community members.[66] Besides recording the existence of these plays, the federal writers wrote down and translated into English the words of the plays as well as the songs connected to feast days such as Christmas.[67]

Brown discovered that there were many versions of the Christmas play Los Pastores. Each community seemed to have a slightly different version. In San Rafael, for example, the people introduced another shepherd, in this case a shepherdess, Dina, who, according to Brown, was not in any other version of the play. He also observed that in Agua Fria there was a version of Los Pastores in which a new character called El Indito, or the Little Indian, was introduced. "This character is a New Mexican addition to the original play," he stressed, "and whoever wrote the lines for the Indian imitated the Spirit of the Indians to perfection and this character adds a distinctly New World touch to the play."[68]

Brown further recorded performances of the play depicting the apparition of our Lady of Guadalupe, or La Aparición de la Virgen Guadalupe. This play, imported from Mexico, was performed on December 12, the feast day of Our Lady of Guadalupe.[69]

A dance-drama with some religious overtones performed in New Mexico was Los Moros y los Cristianos, or The Moors and the Christians. This play originated in Spain and was transferred to Mexico during the Spanish conquest and colonial era. It focuses on the Spanish defeat and expulsion of the Moors from Spain in 1492, the year of Columbus's voyage to the "new world." Lucero-White observed that this performance remained very popular and was performed at many fiestas in the villages and towns of northern New Mexico. In her report on this pageant, she included not only a description of the play but also sketches of the dance choreography associated with the performance.[70] In one of his reports Brown further noted that Los Moros y los Cristianos was performed in the village of Santa Cruz sometimes on the feast of

Our Lady of Carmel on July 16 and sometimes on the feast of Santa Cruz on May 3. He added that the performances were done on horseback.[71]

Still another religious play recorded by the federal writers, in this case Manuel Berg, was La Aurora del Nuevo Día, or The Dawn of a New Day. This was an allegory concerning the victory of St. Michael over Luzbel, or Lucifer, and his devils on the plain of Bethlehem. Berg wrote down the words of the play as well as the stage directions to this short production and translated them from Spanish into English. In the third scene, St. Michael, according to Berg, proclaims with sword in his hand to Luzbel,

> Quail in my presence, accursed ones
> who blaspheme against the Supreme Being
> when you know that you are condemned
> to the Infernal Regions for all eternity;
> From the Empire on high you have been exiled
> For your perfidious and insolent beliefs
> Do you still deny Mary Immaculate
> Who is as pure as the light of day?[72]

Religious Folklore

One of the major activities of the federal writers involved the collection of New Mexico folklore. The WPA files are filled with various kinds of folklore collected throughout the state. One aspect of this collection is folk stories concerning Hispano-Catholicism. Some of these stories go back generations, if not centuries. These oral narratives reemphasize the deep religiosity and spirituality of the Hispano villages.

A story told by Mrs. Enrique Tafoya to Martínez is a rather humorous one set in the territorial period of New Mexico (1848–1912). The setting is Taos, and the narrative concerns the devotion of the people to San Roque, the patron saint of their parish church. Although poor, the villagers always contributed as much as they could every Sunday when the collection was taken. The only exception, curiously enough, was on the feast day of San Roque, when the collection fell dramatically. The parish priest was dumbfounded about this gap and inquired of many parishioners as to why this occurred. They told him that this was a secret they could not reveal. Finally, one woman gave in to the priest's pressure. She revealed that the secret had to do with how many times the priest invoked the name of San Roque in his homily. For every time

San Roque was mentioned, the people at Mass contributed twenty-five cents apiece. However, she pointed out that on the previous feast days of San Roque, the priest rarely mentioned the saint and hence the meager collection. But what the woman did not tell the priest was that hidden under the altar during the feast Mass was a young man who counted the number of times San Roque's name was invoked by cutting a notch on a cornstalk. At collection time, he came out of his cover and gathered the collection until the quarters corresponded to the notches.

On the next feast day of San Roque, the priest was ready: his homily was filled with references to San Roque. "My dear brethren," he began,

> we are gathered here in honor of San Roque, San Roque is our patron saint, San Roque lived a very exemplary life. We should all try to emulate the life of San Roque. The father of the family should take San Roque for a model. The mother of the family should try to emulate the life of San Roque. The children should invoke San Roque. San Roque was very pious. San Roque was very modest, etc., etc., etc.

Every time the priest mentioned San Roque's name, the young man cut a notch on the cornstalk. The priest went on and on until the young man had no more room to cut notches. At that point, he emerged from his hiding place and said to the startled priest, "Wait a while, Father, let me go for another cornstalk."

That day the priest collected the largest contribution in the history of the parish.[73]

In an interview with Frances Lucero in 1936, the federal writer Lester Raines recorded a story concerning the apparition of Our Lady of Guadalupe in the village of El Porvenir in 1900. Lucero recalled that her grandmother had often told her of a vision that her brother, a Mr. Romero, had had in El Porvenir. Romero belonged to the Holy Cross Society, which twice a year, on September 3 and May 3, made a *peregrinación*, or pilgrimage, to a mountaintop called Hermit's Peak. There they would light luminarias and pray the rosary. After spending the night, they observed the Stations of the Cross the next day. The stations consisted of fourteen crosses that were placed from the spring near the top to the summit. On May 3, 1900, some members of the society, including some children, did a peregrinación, and on that occasion Mr. Romero snapped a photo of the group. When he later developed the film in his darkroom, he was astonished to see in the upper right-hand corner of the photo an image of Our Lady of Guadalupe standing on top of a tree and of Jesus blessing the pilgrims. He showed the photo to a man, who verified the sacred images. He further showed it to some Jesuit priests, who concluded that the vision had miraculously appeared. Mr. Romero had always been devoted to Guadalupe, and after the image had appeared in the photo he built a chapel on the mountain in her honor. He had an artist depict the vision above the altar. In time, the image faded in the photo. Strangely, according to Lucero, the children who had been part of the group on the mountain died shortly thereafter, and the man who had first verified the photo became a faithful Catholic. Finally, the tree where Guadalupe appeared in the picture soon died.[74]

Another example of Hispano-Catholic folklore recorded by the federal writers concerned San José, or St. Joseph. Guadalupe Gallegos in 1939 informed the writer Bright Lynn of a story called La Promesa, or The Promise. In this story, a wealthy young man went on an ocean voyage. During the trip a terrible storm arose. Fearing for his life, he prayed to St. Joseph to save him and the others on the ship. He promised that if saved he would one day marry the poorest girl he could find. His prayers were answered, and the storm subsided. Years went by, and the young man forgot about his promise. At the same time, a poor old carpenter devoted to St. Joseph died, leaving behind his daughter, whom in his will the carpenter left in St. Joseph's hands. The daughter was penniless, not having any money to bury her father or to care for herself. However, a stranger came to her door and said he was a friend. He paid for the burial. He then told the girl to wait for him, and he would return the next day. The stranger went to another town, where he visited the wealthy man who had made the promise. He told the man he had been on the ship that stormy day and remembered the promise to St. Joseph the wealthy man had made. He further told him that he knew of such a poor girl and wanted to know if the man would marry her. The wealthy man agreed to do so and returned to the other town with the stranger and married the girl. As Gallegos concluded the story, "They returned to the wealthy man's house to live and during supper a tiny baby descended through the roof of the house. Going straight up to the stranger he [the baby] said, 'Father and mother sent for you. For three days you have remained on earth!' The stranger smiled and turned to the wealthy man and his wife. He gave them his blessing, bade them farewell, and disappeared. The stranger was St. Joseph himself."[75]

The power of the saints through their images constituted still another rich area of religious folklore. In Córdova, Brown interviewed an elderly woman named Guadalupe Martínez, or Tía Lupe, as she was popularly called. Tía

Lupe, a retired domestic who had worked for many years in Santa Fe, kept busy by caring for the village church and cleaning it during the intervals when no priest was available. When a *bulto*, or statue, of Santa Barbara that stood in the church was replaced with a larger one, Tía Lupe took the smaller version home. When Brown visited her in her *casita*, or small house, during a lightning storm, he was astounded to find her engaged in what he considered to be a sacrilegious act. She was mutilating the bulto of Santa Barbara. "Qué tiene, Tía?" he inquired. "What are you doing with poor Santa Barbara? She will punish you for maltreating her so." But she replied, "No, hijo [son], come in and I will show you what I am doing." At that moment, lightning shook the ground, but Tía Lupe reassured Brown that they were safe because Santa Barbara would protect them. She then took the piece of the bulto she had cut off and threw it into the flames of the fire burning in the fireplace. She made the sign of the cross and said a silent prayer. Turning to Brown, she said, "Santa Barbara should be prayed to in time of storms but in the way I have shown you she is more sure protection. For many years I [have] guarded myself and 'casita' in time of storms in the way I have shown you." An impressed Brown concluded, "So that was the explanation I received for that seeming irreverent treatment of the saint's image." [76]

Curanderas

Popular religiosity among Hispanos in New Mexico also involved *curanderas*, or faith healers. Curanderas were important community figures because there were no medical doctors or health facilities in the villages. The curanderas, with their herbal medicines mixed with their Catholic faith, filled a large void. They doctored the sick and helped at births as *parteras*, or midwives. Most, according to the WPA field agent Thorp, were middle-aged or old women whose mothers, grandmothers, or aunts had been curanderas before them. The tradition of *remedios*, or remedies, and the faith was passed on from one generation to another. In her report on curanderas, Thorp observed that they were praised if the sick got well, but if they worsened and died, it was seen as God's will and not the fault of the curandera. Moreover, curanderas never charged for their services but accepted whatever the patient or the patient's family could provide in the form of money or food.[77]

Using remedies based on herbs, the curanderas gathered what they needed in open fields, along rivers and streams, in the hills, and in their gardens. Different herbs or combinations of herbs were used by the curandera to cure various illnesses. Thorp noted some of these remedios. For example, for *calentura*, or fever, the curandera placed elderberry flowers called *flor de sauco* in a jar of water, soaked them for twenty-four hours, then strained them through a cloth; the water or residue was given to the sick person. For deafness or difficulty in hearing, the curandera took a plant called *polvos de coyote* (powder of the coyote), which resembled a tomato bush. It was given this name because it was found in the mesa or hills where the coyotes roamed. Instead of tomatoes, the bush produced a type of green berry that, when dried, turned into a gray powder. The curandera blew this powder into the ears of the *sordo*, or deaf person.[78]

One interesting remedio in Thorp's report had to do with *mal de ojo*, or the evil eye, given to babies. Some people had the power to give the mal de ojo if they looked directly into the baby's eyes. These individuals did not necessarily know they had this power. Unable to relieve the baby's crying and its sickness, the parents called for the curandera. She first asked which person other than the parents and siblings had last seen the baby. This person was then called for, and the curandera instructed him or her to give the baby some water, rub the baby's head with salt, and hold it in his or her arms while the curandera and the family prayed. This would get rid of the mal de ojo. To prevent the evil eye in the first place, the curandera, if asked by the parents, would make a string of coral beads that she placed around the baby's neck. When anyone played with the baby, they were to give the baby a little slap on the head to break the spell in case the baby had mal de ojo.[79]

In the village of Las Placitas, one WPA report noted, the Hispanos passed on from one generation to another the history of Jesusita, a curandera who had been born in 1830. Although the name Jesusita (the diminutive, female version of Jesus) had been banned by the Church in New Mexico, Jesusita the curandera, according to Lou Sage Batchen, who contributed this report, "was a pious, honorable curandera devoted to the saints and her remedios. She had high faith in each of them."[80]

Villagers described Jesusita as a very diminutive person with "graceful hands with which she did half of her talking and much of her healing." She wore many petticoats, and to one of them she fastened a little sack filled with the hair of different species. According to Jesusita, this sack would protect her from witches, as would the piece of *cachana*, an herb, that she wore around her neck. "Jesusita," Batchen wrote, "feared the witches even more than she feared the devil."[81]

Like other curanderas, Jesusita had her particular remedios, which she dispensed always with the prayer "En el nombre de Dios te voy a curar" (In the name of God I am going to cure you). At her house, called La Casa de la Curandera (The House of the Curandera), Jesusita kept all of her medicinal herbs, some hanging from the ceiling and others in containers. She used different herbs for different ailments. *Yerbabuena* (mint), *guaco* (birthwort), and *berraza* (water parsnip), she administered for *dolor de estómago* (stomachache) in the form of a tea. She used *poleo* (pennyroyal) to cure fevers, sometimes adding an egg white and a little salt to it. The concoction was then spread on pieces of cloth covered with paper and placed on the patient's forehead and feet. "So good a remedy was it," Batchen observed, "that it is used to this day."[82]

Still other remedios included *manzanilla* (chamomile) as a tea given to babies for colic. *Yerba del manza*, or chamomile, was used for infections by boiling the herb and adding it to a hot bath. The infected parts of the body were soaked in the bath several times and over several days. "No infection survived those repeated, sustained baths," villagers told Batchen. "To this day it is declared that the doctors of medicine, who came to the Territory of New Mexico in the early days, had no germ destroyer to compare with yerba del manza." For colds, Jesusita had a root called *inmortal*, which induced sneezing and cured the cold. If the cold was more severe, accompanied by chest pains or possibly pneumonia, she prescribed a more complex treatment consisting of a mixture of shredded onions with bear grease in a small cloth sack, which was placed on the chest of the sick person. And to cure hemorrhoids, the curandera dried *anil del muerto* (herb of death), mixed the powder with hot grease, applied the compound to the affected parts, and then covered the application with a very hot cloth. Other remedios Jesusita used to cure smallpox, aching bones and muscles, paralysis, back aches, and headaches.[83]

In a culture often lacking both doctors and clergy, the curanderas and their male counterparts, the curanderos, served as both medical and religious figures, not separating medicine and religion but joining them.

Penitentes

Perhaps one of the largest collections of information gathered by the federal writers concerned the Penitentes, the penitential groups in New Mexico whose roots, some suggest, go back to the colonial period and certainly to the nineteenth century. Fray Angélico Chávez, for example, was quite adamant that the Penitentes emerged in the later period.[84] The literature on the Penitentes is quite extensive, and I have no pretensions about mining a new

FIGURE 3.2 Penitente *morada* (chapel), Northern New Mexico, circa 1920s. Courtesy E. Boyd Collection, no. 35939, photograph by Joe Samuelson, New Mexico State Records Center and Archives.

subject here and hence also will limit this section.[85] What is new in my study is what the WPA itself uncovered through its own research and interviews and what and how they chose to present this material. Moreover, few other scholars, with the exception of Marta Weigle, have made use of the WPA reports on the Penitentes.[86] For one thing, the federal writers noted that in all villages some of the men belonged to these fraternities. They were referred to as *hermanos*. Each village had a *morada*, or prayer chapel, under the control of the hermanos. Only Hispano men could belong, and membership was theoretically secret. "To be a Penitente in New Mexico," one WPA observer wrote, "is to be a man among men, for its initiatory rites are severe, and a weakling cannot take them."[87] Women, according to Lucero-White, could belong to an auxiliary and perform some of the penitential rituals.[88] The hermanos were particularly known for their rites during Holy Week, including sometimes a reenactment of the crucifixion of Jesus. Although outsiders and the media often exaggerated these rituals, the hermanos, as Alberto Pulido has recently documented, were and still are much more than a sacrificial cult. They represent community leadership and mutual support for their members and their families. Their activities reinforce the close connection between religion and community in the New Mexico villages.[89] Forrest seconds this broader view of the Penitentes when she writes, "Beyond the religious purpose, however, the 'Penitentes' served as a benevolent society dedicated to the welfare of the entire community, particularly orphans and widows."[90]

Although at various times censored by the official Church, the Penitentes continued to survive. "But in spite of opposition," the wpa guide for New Mexico noted in 1940, "the Penitente Brotherhood continued to exist, and still exists in the more remote communities of New Mexico, although the severity of their self-imposed penance has been considerably modified."[91]

In her 1936 report on the Penitentes, Lucero-White noted that because of this mutual support the brotherhood was increasing rather than decreasing, despite the fact that most of its rituals were no longer practiced in public. Undoubtedly, the severity of the Great Depression further explains this growth. She provided this definition of a hermano:

> To be a penitente . . . constitutes a haven, a place of refuge. A penitente has rules, he obeys orders. If he becomes an official he improves them. A penitente is a social factor for does he not help create a fund to alleviate the sufferings of his more unfortunate brothers? He is a force in the administration of justice—for does he not, in conjunction with his brothers, lay down laws of conduct, and of punishment for failure to meet these? He is a force in politics—for do not brothers always support each other?[92]

Lucero-White outlined the conditions under which a male Hispano would be selected as an hermano as well as the typical organizational structure and offices that each Penitente group possessed. Moreover, she described some of the rituals characteristic of the hermanos, all centered on the body. For example, she observed that flagellation was a common practice, especially during pilgrimages. As for the Holy Week activities, Lucero-White noted that the hermanos participated in many of the same rituals as nonhermanos. This consisted of reciting the Stations of the Cross every afternoon and praying from the Common Prayer Book. On Good Friday, everyone—hermanos and others—went to the morada and recited *sudarios*, or prayers for the dead. However, as evening descended the hermanos engaged in their own secret rituals, including a procession to the cemetery. Lucero-White explained what she knew of these secret rites:

We know that there is a Crucifixion; that the Christus (the hermano selected to portray Christ) drags the Madero (wooden cross) to the spot sometimes having to have assistance; we know that the Hermano Mayor (the Chief Brother) and two assistants lead the Chosen One to the Cross and lay him down upon it; we know that he is then tied to it with ropes so tightly that they cut into the flesh, and almost stop the circulation; we know that sometimes the Chosen One turns black; we know that the Cross is raised until it falls in a hole made for the purpose and that this is then filled with earth and stones; we know that the Christus is allowed to remain so for 31 minutes; we know that when the Hermano Mayor gives the signal, the cross is taken down and the Chosen One is removed to the Morada where he is brought back to life by the Coadjutor, or where he is given the last rites should His Creator design to call him for his eternal reward. In such a case the Chosen One's shoes are sent to his family and after a year his resting place is divulged.[93]

Besides these religious practices associated with the Penitentes, the federal writers collected a number of examples of Penitente folk stories. One of these, told by a sixty-year-old woman to Martínez, concerned the belief that during Holy Week the souls of deceased hermanos returned and resumed bodily, although ghostly, forms. They would participate in the processions of the Penitentes. In the village of Arroyo Hondo there was a story that one Good Friday a young woman went to the morada and requested to be permitted to take the image of La Sebastiana, or the Hispano wooden skeleton depicting death, in the rosary procession that evening. This was a privilege that the hermanos allowed nonmembers, including women, only during that sacred week. When the woman entered the morada she noticed nine hermanos lining each side of the morada, a total of eighteen. Inside she received the image of La Sebastiana and then exited to await the procession to the church by the hermanos and their *acompañadores*, or followers. At this time, she noticed two more Penitentes in the lines. "The last penitente in each of the two rows," Martínez wrote in his report of the story, "presented to her a strange appearance. He seemed to possess a translucency of the flesh that showed the outline of his skeleton, the ribs specifically."[94]

When the procession reached the church, the group engaged in the ceremony of *Tinieblas* (darkness). This marked the death of Christ on the cross, when darkness fell upon the earth and a great commotion occurred. As part

FIGURE 3.3 Penitente rites, Watrous, New Mexico, 1928. Courtesy E. Boyd Collection, no. 35940, photograph by Will Doll, New Mexico State Records Center and Archives.

of the ceremony all lights were extinguished for several minutes, during which time the people made all kinds of loud noises, chanting, rattling of chains, knocking on benches, blowing on reed whistles, and beating on a *caja*, or small drum. After several minutes a match was lit and the candles inside the church were lit. This ritual was then repeated throughout the night. During one of these periods the young woman carrying La Sebastiana entered the church to fulfill her promise.

After the woman left the church, the procession returned to the morada, where she entered and returned La Sebastiana. Upon leaving, she noted that in the row of hermanos only eighteen remained rather than the twenty she had seen earlier that evening. "Verily, she thought," Martínez concluded the story, "the dead do come to earth, sometimes." [95]

Still another story had to do with the secret membership of the Penitentes. Martínez related a tale told to him by his father, Julián A. Martínez. Set in 1890 in Arroyo Hondo, the tale took place on Good Friday, when the Penitentes, having concluded their procession from their morada, appeared before the entrance to the church to participate in the ritual of the Tinieblas. However, before they entered, the veil of one of the Penitentes fell from his face, exposing his identity. Uncomfortable, the Penitente commenced making various kinds of faces in order to disguise himself. Because only candlelight illuminated the church no one saw what had happened except for Don Julian, the village merchant. He recognized the Penitente as Pablo Pacheco. Not wishing to embarrass Pacheco, Don Julian told one of the acompañadores, or nonveiled followers of the Penitentes, what had happened. The acompañador then helped the Penitente adjust his veil over his face again.

A few days later, Don Julián encountered Pacheco and remarked about the incident that had exposed the Penitente. Pacheco denied that he had been involved or that he was a Penitente. Instead, he told Don Julián, "Don't you know that those (the penitentes) are the dead, come down from the other world to perform these sacrifices?" Penitentes at that time, according to this story, never revealed their identities and kept their membership secret. Martínez concluded by noting the extent to which Penitentes would go to protect their identities: "A penitente never acknowledged that he whipped himself; never exposed his nude back to the gaze of any one not a member (the back of a penitente bears the lengthwise scars, mark of the order). When bathing with others, not members of the cult, he either keeps his undershirt on, or keeps his back away from their gaze. Queer? Yes, but he must have good reasons for doing so." [96]

Alabados

As part of the Penitente tradition, a litany of alabados and other religious songs formed an important part of the Hispano oral and musical culture. The federal writers in New Mexico collected, recorded, and translated many of these alabados, some of which go back to the nineteenth century, if not earlier. [97] "One form of Spanish-American folk song prevalent at that time [Spanish colonial period] and still heard today," the WPA guide for New Mexico informed its readers, "is the alabado, a religious ballad, an outgrowth of Gregorian Chant. This form has little melodic interest, is primitive and monotonous, but very moving when sung by a large number of voices." [98] Some had been previously written down in Spanish and kept in songbooks within individual families. As part of their research, the writers discovered, copied, and translated some of this rich historical material. Still other alabados had never been written down and remained part of oral tradition until recorded by the project. Many of these alabados influenced by the Penitente tradition focus on the Passion and crucifixion of Jesus. Sacrifice, pain, wounds, blood, death, penance, and redemption represent key themes in the hymns. One alabado collected by Martínez is entitled "Cristo Nuestro Redentor," or "Christ Our Redeemer." Some of the stanzas, translated into English by Martínez, illustrate the stress on the Passion:

> You came down to earth
> with ever-increasing love
> And died on the cross
> For the sinner.
>
> To a column you were tied
> And whipped and with blood was
> Sprinkled your body
> And your side.
>
> The nails with which
> Then nailed Him to the cross
> Were my sins
> Which caused all this.
>
> In the five wounds of your body
> I ask, O Lord
> May this sinner
> Find refuge from his faults.[99]

Jesus, especially the suffering and crucified Jesus, is a dominant theme of many of the alabados. This is particularly the case since many of the hymns were associated with the Penitentes. Martínez recorded and translated, for example, an alabado entitled "A Jesús Quiero Acudir," or "I Wish to Have Recourse to Jesus." In part, it stressed,

> I will have recourse to Jesus
> I wish to see Jesus
> I will obey Jesus
> Jesus always serves
>
> Good Jesus of mine listen to me
> Good Jesus have compassion of me

> Good Jesus favor me
> Good Jesus forgive me![100]

In addition to Jesus, Mary, the mother of Christ, is another major theme of many alabados. Like Jesus, the suffering character of the Virgin Mother is especially stressed. Martínez reported one such alabado entitled "A La Madre del Rosario," or "To the Mother of the Rosary," which, according to him, was sung by Penitentes during Lent. Although much of the alabado concerns the crucified and resurrected Jesus, its opening stanza reflects on the Virgin Mary:

> Give me a happy death,
> Man, God Jesus sacred
> Give me a happy death,
> My mother of the rosary.[101]

The figure of the Virgin of Guadalupe also is found in the alabados of New Mexico. One WPA worker filed an alabado called simply "A La Virgen de Guadalupe," or "To the Virgin of Guadalupe." As is typical of prayers to Guadalupe, this alabado focuses on asking for her intervention to help the poor and oppressed and to be a symbol of liberation:

> The needy find aid
> From heaven in Mexico she guides you,
> Hear us, Virgin Mary
> Mother of the forlorn!
>
> Mother full of so great pity
> Touched with compassion
> Leave us not in prison
> As God has given you everything
>
> Hear us, Virgin Mary
> Mother of the forlorn!
>
> Forever, o mother of mine
> Your name "Guadalupano,"
> Shall be revered by the Indians, as so it has

Been decreed.
Hear us, Virgin Mary
Mother of the forlorn!

O chosen gem!
O mother of charity!
You have come to liberate
Forsaken orphans.

Hear us Virgin Mary
Mother of the Forlorn![102]

An interesting and amusing alabado recorded and translated by Brown parodies the Hail Mary prayer of the rosary and instead refers to "La Ave María de los Borrachos," or "The Hail Mary of the Drunkards." This short alabado goes as follows:

Hail Mary! They say
At a party gathered there,
And quite a gathering it is,
The one most tipsy tells the rest:
"Go and pray for us."

There come two more,
Uttering loud ejaculations.
"We are in state of bliss
With all the other drinkers."

Do not talk to me so gruffly,
I think it is improper,
For this bottle
May be full of grace.

It is said that one who drinks is a brute,
And that he is not baptized.
Well, God: "Blessed is the fruit
Of thy womb, Jesus."

When I am having a good time,
They try to catch me
And they want to beat me up,
All the women of the town.

When I am given a drink,
Even though the glass be full,
And even though they beat me up,
I will always say: "Amen." [103]

Other alabados have various additional religious themes, including those involving myriad saints. Recognizing the strong tradition that the alabados have played in the history and culture of Hispanos, the WPA writers performed a significant service by recording these unwritten hymns, translating them from Spanish to English to make them more accessible to an English-language audience while at the same time retaining them in their original language and preserving them for posterity.

Conclusion

Popular religious culture has been the mainstay of much of Latino religiosity and spirituality in the United States. In the case of New Mexico, its roots go back generations. Contemporary immigration from Mexico, Central America, and the Caribbean refresh these traditions and introduce new ones. Popular religion has lasted because unlike too much of institutional religion, it is a more organic and natural part of people's lives. It springs from their personal relationship with God, with their neighbors, and with their environment. This has certainly been the case in the Hispano villages of New Mexico. Yet these traditions are not immune to erosion and decline. While many of them remain, many others are no longer practiced or at least not as much as in the past. As younger generations become more acculturated to other U.S. influences, including urbanization and suburbanization, they begin to move away from or discard altogether this part of their parental culture. The preservation of such customs, as noted, has been largely through oral traditions and practice. As these traditions over the years have faced challenges, the role of the Federal Writers' Project in New Mexico in recording them looms even larger. Without the intervention of the writers, many of these customs might remain only memories or isolated rituals. What the writers did was to preserve in writing our knowledge of this rich Hispano-Catholic culture. It does not matter whether many people were aware of this project or not. Its importance is that the collection exists as a kind of archeology of religious culture to be discovered or rediscovered.

With the contemporary revival of interest in New Mexico religious folk art, such as the *santero* tradition, the federal writers' collection becomes even more valuable. The lesson here is that heritage is not a given or an ever-lasting presence, at least not for minority cultures. It has to be guarded, preserved, adapted, and certainly struggled for so that it can be passed on to later generations. While the federal writers in New Mexico, many of them Hispanos themselves, were perhaps not conscious of participating in this struggle, nevertheless, they represent for their time a cultural vanguard no less important than the later and more publicized cultural activists associated with the Chicano Renaissance of the 1960s and 1970s or the more contemporary Hispano/ Latino arts revival.

FOUR

The U.S. Catholic Church and the Mexican Cultural Question in Wartime America, 1941–1945

The heritage of Catholicity which the Spanish-speaking peoples derived from their forebears has, in large part, been preserved so that today these people constitute the great bulk of the Catholic population in many parts of the Southwest.

—CATHOLIC CONFERENCE ON THE SPANISH SPEAKING
OF THE SOUTHWEST AND WEST, 1943

SINCE THE 1970S, the U.S. Catholic Church as an institution has become much more sensitive and aware of Latino cultural traditions, including religious ones as exemplified by the popular religiosity of Hispanos in northern New Mexico. In many parishes serving predominantly Latinos or at least significant numbers of Latinos, the liturgy employs not only the Spanish language or a bilingual format, but also important and innovative elements of Latino music and dance, along with other cultural expressions. Moreover, important religious holidays associated with Latinos and identified with people of Mexican descent, among them the feast of Our Lady of Guadalupe and El Día de los Muertos, have become part of many church calendars.

Such recognition of Latino culture by the Church is often associated not only with the theological transformations of the Church following Vatican Council II in the 1960s, but perhaps more significantly with the ethnic protest movements in the United States during the late 1960s and early 1970s. Some writers and scholars interpret the Chicano movement, for example, which included both secular and religious protests against the Church, as the major catalyst in forcing the Church to become more attuned to the role of Latinos

within the Church, including becoming more culturally relevant to its Latino members, both laity and clergy. The formation of new Latino advocacy
groups within the Church during this period, such as PADRES, composed of
Latino priests, and Las Hermanas, composed of Latino sisters, proved to be,
according to such critics, indispensable variables in bringing about a multicultural perspective within the Church.[1] At the First National Encuentro of
Latino Church leaders in 1972, delegates expressed the need for the Church to
abandon its earlier strategy of aiding in the assimilation of Latinos to Anglo-
American culture and, instead, to adopt a pluralistic perspective. One scholar,
writing in 1976 about what he called the "social distance" between Mexican
Americans and the Church, proposed that as the Church became more Americanized in the twentieth century it "likewise reflected the biases and prejudices of the dominant white American society against Mexicans and Mexican
Americans."[2]

There is no question that movement protests led to significant changes.
However, these changes did not appear in a historical vacuum. Some of the
awareness of the needs and culture of Latino Catholics possessed an earlier genealogy, as Roberto Treviño and David Badillo have recently noted.[3] The fact
of the matter is that for many years, especially beginning in the early twentieth
century with the first major wave of immigration from Mexico, often linked
to the Mexican Revolution of 1910, many Catholic churches in the Southwest
at the local level incorporated the language and culture of Mexicans. To be
sure, the Church at the same time, unfortunately, also displayed in some locations prejudice and discrimination against Mexicans. It further represented a
U.S. acculturating agency, although not, as Gilberto Hinojosa correctly notes
in his history of the Church in Texas, in the totally insensitive and arrogant
way that later critics would charge. The Church in the Southwest was not
monolithic, and hence in certain areas it promoted a bicultural approach to
Mexican American Catholicism, in the same way it had for European ethnic
groups, where the pattern of national parishes was the norm for many years.
One historian has referred to this approach as "benign Americanization."[4]

What was lacking in this earlier period, however, was a more national or
regional appreciation on the part of the Church to what I call the "Mexican
Cultural Question" and the Church referred to as "the Mexican problem." Yet
such recognition did not come as late as the 1960s or 1970s, as some critics
contend, but in fact by the early 1940s, during World War II.

Why note this earlier validation of Latino culture by the Church? In my
view, because it is a way of going beyond what I refer to as Chicano movement

interpretations of Chicano or Latino history based on reductionist ethnic or cultural viewpoints too often linked to protest struggles such as the Chicano movement. Such interpretations tend to see history in very simple, totalistic, and binary terms—white versus black, white versus brown, assimilation versus cultural nationalism. They continue to reflect the often rigid ideological dogmatism of the protest movements themselves. They also tend in some cases to be self-serving. Such interpretations often disguise more than they reveal. They do not explore what I call the wrinkles, that is, the full complexities of history and the multiple variables that produce historical change.

It is additionally important to observe the earlier effort by the Church to negotiate with Latino culture as a way of fostering more sober and cooperative contemporary approaches to strategies of social change that prioritize inter-ethnic coalitions rather than just one-dimensional ethnic ones. The appreciation of Latino culture within the Church has never been just a Latino agenda, but in fact has emanated—for different reasons—from many sources, both Latino and non-Latino. Such an agenda surfaced in wartime America in the 1940s. The purpose of this chapter is to note this initial institutional exertion on the part of the Church to deal with the Mexican Cultural Question. While the Church hierarchy represents the more visible historical actor in this chapter, it is equally important to recognize that Mexican American agency in resisting U.S. Catholic assimilation and affirming Mexican cultural traditions is likewise very much a part of this story.

Addressing the Mexican Question

It appears that the Church's addressing, in the early 1940s and on a national and regional level, of the cultural issues associated with its Latino and predominantly Mexican parishioners in the Southwest was the result of three conditions. The first, and one which I will address only briefly since I have already discussed it in Chapter Two, concerns the application of Catholic social doctrine to the Mexican context in the United States. The application of key papal encyclicals such as Pope Leo XIII's *Rerum Novarum* (1891) and Pope Pius's XI's *Quadragesimo Anno* (1931), which, among other things, called for the just and humane treatment of working people, led the Church in the Southwest to confront the historic racism, discrimination, prejudice, and labor exploitation faced by Mexicans in the region ever since the U.S. conquest in the 1840s. Continued discrimination against Mexicans into the World War II years moved the Church to address such injustices on the basis of the importance of Catholic social doctrine to the remedy of these problems.[5]

A second and related factor had to do with the war itself. Although the Church had been one of the few American bodies that had attempted to improve the social and economic conditions of Mexicans in the Southwest, where the great majority of them had historically lived or had recently immigrated to from Mexico, some believed that the Church had done little, or at least not enough, along these lines. This included some in the U.S. government. A confidential report in the early 1940s entitled "Spanish-Americans in the Southwest and the War Effort," Confidential Report No. 24, commissioned by the Special Services Division of the Bureau of Intelligence of the Office of War Information and apparently written by such scholars as George I. Sánchez of the University of Texas, Emory S. Bogardus of the University of Southern California, and Paul S. Taylor of the University of California, Berkeley, criticized the Church for not doing a more effective job of organizing Mexicans for the war effort. The report was particularly concerned that the socioeconomic problems of the Mexicans, including the discrimination they encountered, was affecting their full participation in the struggle, undermining their morale, and providing the basis for Axis propaganda against the United States throughout Latin America. "The existence of institutionalized discrimination against several million Latin-Americans in the American Southwest," the report stressed, "is a constant irritant in hemispheric relations, a mockery of the Good Neighbor policy, an open invitation to Axis propagandists to depict us as hypocrites to South and Central America and, above all, a serious waste of potential manpower."[6] The Good Neighbor Policy, which had been instituted by President Franklin Roosevelt in the 1930s, stressed peaceful and diplomatic solutions to issues between the United States and the Latin American countries after the years of military interventions and gunboat diplomacy favored by earlier U.S. administrations.[7]

The report observed that the most important influence on the Mexican population was religion, and that the Church thus carried significant weight within this ethnic community. Although the report conceded that the Church had performed some positive roles among the Mexicans, more could be done, especially in creating leadership and organization among the Mexicans themselves; taking this step could lead to better integration with other Americans in the war effort. "The Church has played the most significant role in the weakness of leadership and organization of Spanish-speaking people," the report concluded, citing as the source of this problem the hierarchical nature of the Church.[8] If such issues were not immediately faced, the report concluded, these problems might exacerbate the protests already visible within the Mexican community. "Their disaffections will be increasingly exploited by Fascist and Falangist," it said of the Mexicans, "and outbreaks have already occurred and more are indicated." [9]

Such criticism was not well received by the Church. Especially disturbed was the National Catholic Welfare Conference (NCWC), which obtained a copy through its congressional contacts. The NCWC, through its Social Action Department, had, since its inception in 1919, dealt with immigrant/ethnic issues, including those pertaining to Mexicans. It disputed the report's assessment of the failures of the Church and believed that such incorrect interpretations would only harm the Church's work and reputation, especially in the Southwest. "Report No. 24 is going to get a lot of publicity in certain sections in the next few weeks," Monsignor Michael J. Ready, the general secretary of the NCWC, wrote to one of his staff, "as the attitude of the [Roosevelt] Administration in many places [is] favorable to Communists. There are too many strange experts and investigators roaming the country making 'confidential' reports which impugn the loyalty of Catholics in general and the Hierarchy and priests in particular." [10]

To assess the impact of the report, a representative of the NCWC, William F. Montavon, met with Senator Dennis Chávez of New Mexico, the sole Hispanic representative in Congress. While apparently more diplomatic than the Bureau of Intelligence, the senator nevertheless agreed with the report's conclusions and suggested that the Church needed to do more. "My impression after the interview with Senator Chávez," Montavon informed Monsignor Ready, "is that the Senator feels that the Church in the United States should make some concerted effort to strengthen the clergy and the work of the Church among the Spanish-speaking peoples in the Southwestern states." [11] Montavon disagreed with Chávez's conclusions, observing that it was unfair for the report to "lay upon the Church the burden of making up the economic deficiencies of these people [the Mexicans], although these deficiencies are the consequence in great measure of injustice against which the Church protests and for which the Church is not responsible." [12] Having said that, NCWC officials apparently understood that because of the report, the Church would have to intensify and further publicize its mission among the Mexican population in the Southwest.

Consequently, it appears that partly as a result of Report No. 24 as well as the advice of Senator Chávez, the NCWC more publicly and from a broader regional and national basis began to address the range of problems affecting Mexicans in the Southwest, especially in light of wartime conditions. This involved the entrance of thousands of Mexican contract workers into different parts of the United States in the wartime program instituted by the Roosevelt administration and the Mexican government, what came to be referred to as the Bracero Program beginning in 1942.[13] The NCWC's labors represented for the Church not only an acceleration of its ongoing work among Mexicans, but a particular contribution to the war effort.

As a way of linking the two, the NCWC, by the spring of 1943, approached the Office of the Coordinator of Inter-American Affairs, a federal agency headed by Nelson Rockefeller that was charged during the war with promoting the Good Neighbor Policy on both sides of the border. It requested the coordinator's office to subsidize a meeting in San Antonio under the auspices of the NCWC for the purpose of bringing attention to the "sociological questions," as Monsignor Ready put it, facing Mexicans in the Southwest. Also proposed for discussion was how best to integrate this ethnic group with other Americans, given the wartime crisis. The four-day conference, to be held in July of that year, "would be the first time that a group of leaders will have come together to know one another and exchange views and programs on the whole range of work that is being done in the Southwest." The meeting would include over fifty religious and lay leaders throughout the region who were involved in efforts among the Mexicans.[14]

Speaking in the wake of the infamous zoot-suit riots in Los Angeles during the first week of June 1943, when racial tensions in that city exploded as U.S. military personnel went on a rampage against Mexicans Americans, especially those attired in zoot suits, Archbishop Robert E. Lucey of San Antonio, a longtime champion of Mexican Americans, opened the San Antonio conference, entitled "The Spanish Speaking of the Southwest and West," on July 20. In his welcoming address, "Are We Good Neighbors?" he reinforced the need for the Church to confront what Lucey called the "undeserved poverty" of the Mexicans and underlined the war's role in motivating the Church to do so. "Can we condemn our Latin-Americans to starvation wages, bad housing and tuberculosis," the prelate asked the delegates to this historic assembly, "and then expect them to be strong, robust soldiers of Uncle Sam? . . . In a word, can we, the greatest nation on earth, assume the moral leadership of the world when race riots and murder, political crimes and economic injustices disgrace the very name of America?"[15]

As a follow-up to the San Antonio conference, the NCWC organized a second one on the Spanish speaking in Denver in October of the next year. Like the San Antonio conference, the Denver one laid out three goals. The first involved the need to integrate Mexican American workers more effectively into the wartime economy. The second aimed at eliminating conditions that caused friction and prevented unity between Anglos and Mexicans. And the third concerned organizing groups, undoubtedly affiliated with the Church or organized by the Church, to assist the Mexican population in the United States.[16] These two regional meetings in turn laid the foundation for the formation in 1945 of the Bishops' Committee for the Spanish-Speaking, the first national organization within the U.S. Catholic Church to specifically focus on the Latino Catholic community.[17] Although the Church had a previous record, uneven as it was, of administering to the Mexican population, there is no question that the urgency of wartime increased this ministry and moved the Church, through the NCWC, to more publicly call attention to the issues involved.

The third major factor, and, in my opinion the key one, that motivated the Church in this direction concerned its perception, indeed fear, of an increased Protestant campaign to convert Mexican Catholics in the Southwest. In fact, at least since the 1910s in various parts of the Southwest, different Protestant churches began to practice outreach to the increasing Mexican immigrant population. "By 1920," Badillo writes of San Antonio, "several Protestant denominations had established footholds in the Mexican Quarter, on streets once dominated by the Catholic Church."[18] Denominations such as the Baptists, Presbyterians, Methodists, Lutherans, and Disciples of Christ all had Spanish-speaking congregations in San Antonio.[19] Treviño discovered the same growing influence of the "aleluyas," as Mexican Catholics referred to Mexican Protestants in Houston.[20] In Los Angeles, as Sánchez notes, Protestant groups had organized a variety of both religious and community self-help programs for Mexicans.[21]

By the 1940s Protestant denominations such as the Presbyterians, Baptists, Methodists, and even early Pentecostals had made inroads, forcing the Church to accelerate its own community-based work among the Mexicans, especially with respect to socioeconomic issues. But it also led to combating the Protestants at the cultural grassroots level on the basis of the Church's correct assessment that the Protestant challenge assumed greater concern because of their ability to recruit Spanish-speaking ministers and hence to relate better to Mexican cultural traditions. The rivalry between Catholics and Protestants, of course, had a long history emanating from the Reformation and Counter-Reformation. Certainly, the Catholic Church in the pre–Vatican II years continued to believe that it represented the one true Church of Christ and that only through the Catholic faith could one be saved. Hence, Protestantism and other religions as well represented threats to the Church's position. "Catholics were convinced," Badillo observes, "that to be Protestant was to be anti-Catholic."[22] Of course, this would change after the reforms of Vatican II, which stressed ecumenism and the acceptance or at least toleration of other Christian denominations and non-Christian faiths.[23]

Archbishop John J. Cantwell of Los Angeles noted the Protestant threat in a rather remarkable document—remarkable for its bluntness about the Protestant competition—in the summer of 1944. His report "Work Among the Mexicans in the United States" was first submitted to the apostolic delegate in Washington, D.C., the Vatican's religious representative to the Catholic Church in the United States, and then to Monsignor Ready at the NCWC for his review.[24] The Los Angeles archbishop warned that with the war turning in favor of the Allies what he called the "Protestant American crusading spirit" would be redirected from Europe and Asia toward immigrant groups in the United States like Mexicans as well as toward Latin America. Moreover, this redirection posed even greater danger, Cantwell feared, owing to a preexisting history of Protestant activity south of the border. "Our enemies are already well entrenched," he alerted others.[25] In detail, Cantwell further underscored this threat:

> They [the Protestants] have the accumulated experience of more than 70 years of missionary work among Latin Americans. Since the first Continental Congress of Panama (1916) some 47 sects have joined their forces under a unified command. Actually, they have developed a splendid organization both at home and in the field. They have built up the following resources: a plentiful supply of well trained missionaries; numerous well equipped seminaries; an excellent press in English, Spanish, Italian, and Portuguese; well appointed schools both educational and technical; numerous clinics and social welfare centers; abundant financial resources. Of set purpose they have endeavored to create, and not without much success, a sympathetic attitude toward their work on the part of public officials here and in Latin America. They have eagerly sought public approval through their work among the youth, the delinquent, the migrant, the sick and through civic organizations.[26]

Cantwell further pointed out that because Catholic priests in the United States were used to working with large congregations they might minimize the potential damage the smaller Protestant groups might cause. He warned against such underestimation, pointing out that the groups were everywhere. They were a national as well as a local threat. "It is only when we see the 'over all' picture of Proselytism within a diocese or on a national scale," he added, "that we realize how extensive the damage really is, which is being done to the Faith." [27] Protestant subversion was real, Cantwell concluded, but it could be combated by the Church paying renewed attention to the social, economic, and cultural needs of its Mexican adherents. "Protestant leaders are not superior," the archbishop exhorted, "quite the contrary, they are very easily discouraged." [28]

Mexican American History and the Church

As a result of these three conditions—the continued application of Catholic social doctrine to the Church's work in the Southwest, the crisis of World War II and the increased need for wartime unity, and the perceived growing Protestant threat—the Church, through such agencies as the NCWC as well as Church leaders like Archbishop Lucey, called greater attention to the suffering of Mexicans and how their marginalization affected war mobilization and the ability of the United States to assert ideological and moral leadership in the struggle against Fascism. At both the San Antonio and Denver conferences as well as in reports and documents generated by the Church's wartime offensive, extensive acknowledgment was made of the dire socioeconomic and educational conditions facing Mexicans as a result of discrimination. While some Mexican Americans had themselves, through civil rights organizations such as LULAC and the Spanish-Speaking Congress as well as through the new militant CIO unions, been attacking these problems, the Church and its predominantly Irish-American leaders represented an important ally in the efforts to democratize and humanize the race/class system of the region. [29]

This movement by the Church during World War II did not neglect the Mexican Cultural Question. But this attention to culture was not, as some critics contend, only in the form of the Church's version of Americanization. The approach was much more complicated and sensitive to the Mexican experience. Through various forums and means of communication, the Church spoke to the need to recognize, validate, and incorporate aspects of Mexican cultural traditions in the Church's work in the Southwest. Undoubtedly, this also involved cultural tensions, cultural misunderstandings, and even a certain patronization by some Church leaders. Nevertheless, what is significant is that particular elements within the Church understood that Church-Mexican relations would best be served not by a dogmatic, rigid, one-way process of Americanization, but by a pragmatic and relevant bicultural process. This had already been the norm, as noted, in many local parishes. What was new in the early 1940s was that for the first time this strategy received national recognition.

One of the first steps in this bicultural orientation was a reassessment of the history of the Southwest. Rather than seeing the Mexicans only or primarily as recent immigrants, some within the Church began to acknowledge the native historical roots of Mexicans in the area. For example, Archbishop Lucey, in his opening address to the San Antonio conference, stressed the prominence of this characteristic in Texas, where Spanish/Mexican settlements preceded Anglo ones by at least a century. As evidence of this earlier presence, Lucey noted that the very names of cities and rivers in what had been Spanish/Mexican territory spoke to this saga. "It is passing strange that we should consider these Spanish-Americans as aliens and foreigners in this great Southwest," he told his audience. "They are native to this land. . . . It was theirs when the Alamo was the center of a community in a circle of missions along the winding river of St. Anthony. . . . They have named our cities Santa Fe, Los Angeles, San Diego, and San Antonio. They have named our rivers Rio Grande, Guadalupe, San Pedro, and Colorado. This is their country." [30]

No doubt inspired by his words, the writer of a report of the San Antonio conference reiterated Lucey's revisionist interpretation of southwestern history by reference to the native roots of Mexicans in the region, a theme later asserted by Chicano historians in the 1960s affiliated with the militant Chicano movement. [31] However, the report went one step further by locating these roots deeper in the pre-Columbian and Indian backgrounds of people of Mexican descent. The report also placed this experience within a broader understanding of the history of the United States. In a statement that mirrors our own contemporary multicultural views of American history, an inclusive approach to this narrative was emphasized. "Many of the Spanish-speaking were in the United States before Columbus," the document observed.

It was their country when Lord Baltimore reached Maryland, when the Puritans arrived in Massachusetts, when the Cavaliers settled Virginia, when the Dutch colonized New York, and the Swedes, Delaware, when the Dutch entered Pennsylvania and spread south and west, when the Irish and North-Irish spread throughout the colonies. They were here long before the great influx of Irish and Germans of Slav, French Canadians and Italian Catholics during the nineteenth and twentieth centuries.[32]

The Spanish Language and the Church

If the Mexicans were native to the Southwest, then so, too, was the Spanish language. Besides the historical foundation of Spanish, its use by the Church was likewise pragmatic. Prior to the 1940s in many local parishes, Anglo-American priests learned Spanish in order to minister to the Mexicans. With the growth of that population, the Church found itself with a scarcity of bilingual priests and hence recognized the importance of filling this need. "We fear," noted the report of the Committee on Migratory Workers at the San Antonio conference, "that a great number of souls are being lost for want of priests who have prepared themselves to speak the language of this sizable group. Wherever these migrants appear, even for a temporary stay, a priest with some knowledge of Spanish should be available; otherwise he can barely be successful among them."[33]

To be effective with the Mexicans, knowledge of Spanish was necessary, not only for priests but also for any layperson employed by the Church in community outreach. In discussing the hiring of laypeople to assist in the work of the Bishops' Committee for the Spanish Speaking, the organizers of the committee observed the importance of bilingual abilities. "The men and women officials [of the committee] should preferably speak some Spanish, know their field of work, be 'simpático' and have the ability to organize both English and Spanish speaking people."[34] Where a priest did not know Spanish, it was recommended that a parish employ, even if only temporarily, the services of a Spanish-speaking visiting priest to hold a mission and to hear confessions.[35]

Priests and lay Catholics who could speak Spanish in the Southwest could also combat the Protestants. The Church saw itself at a disadvantage on the language front since most Protestant ministers were native Spanish speakers. This made it even more imperative for the Church to train bilingual priests. Archbishop Cantwell, for example, pointed out there was only one Spanish-speaking priest for every 3,000 to 5,000 Mexicans compared to one priest for every 750 English-speaking Catholics. By comparison, there was one Spanish-speaking Protestant minister for every 143 churchgoing Hispanic Protestants. "We need a much larger and more assured supply of bi-lingual priests, particularly, following the war," Cantwell concluded. "Five or ten years from now, a more acute shortage of Spanish-speaking priests will be created as those now working, particularly the old, die off." [36]

This disadvantage was compounded by the dearth of vocations among the Mexicans themselves as the result of poverty, lack of education, and the absence of a tradition of native priests both in Mexico and the Southwest. To meet this shortage, Archbishop Cantwell suggested that the Church promote a separate order for Mexican American nuns. In addition, he proposed that the laity might be tapped for missionary work among Mexicans both in the United States and in Latin America. This would be another way to combat Protestantism. "Compared with Protestant Churches," he observed, "we give our lay folk too little to do. Yet many Catholics, who have little taste for parish work, might become veritable apostles if their energies were directed towards the mission field." [37]

To develop bilingual skills among their Anglo priests, some bishops apparently sent some to Mexico to learn Spanish and Mexican customs.[38] Yet it was important to develop this training even earlier. Consequently, as part of their education of future priests seminaries in the Southwest were encouraged and, in some cases apparently instructed by bishops, to integrate Spanish into their curriculums.

The teaching of Spanish in seminaries was stressed at the San Antonio conference. The Committee on Large Populations in Cities and Towns at the meeting made specific recommendations on what it termed "The Language Question." First, it proposed the introduction of Spanish into the curriculum of seminaries where it was not already being taught. Second, it called for making Spanish obligatory for all seminary students who were going to serve in predominantly Spanish-speaking dioceses. The committee based these two recommendations on several reasons, including

(a) Knowledge of their language will help the priest working among Latin-Americans to understand his people; it will be likewise concrete evidence of his sympathy and regard for them.
(b) The continuous immigration, unrestricted by quota, of Mexican people into the southwestern and western United States, means that the need of knowing their language will persist.[39]

A committee of the San Antonio conference dealing with migratory workers advocated the establishment of summer schools for seminarians as well as for priests on a diocesan or provincial basis. Spanish and the specific problems of the Mexicans would be studied during these sessions. "Only Spanish would be spoken during these schools," this committee stressed, "these priests or future priests would gain facility in the language."[40] The committee further emphasized that all seminarians scheduled to be appointed to the Southwest and West should study Spanish for at least two years.[41]

Archbishop Cantwell, in his 1944 report "Work Among the Mexicans," likewise emphasized the importance of Spanish-language training for seminarians, especially with a view toward competing with the Protestants. He observed that Mexican Protestant seminaries very deliberately taught Spanish as well as the history, culture, psychology, geography, and economy of Latin America and specifically of Mexico. "We must not be less well prepared," he argued. "The struggle for the spiritual conquest of the 3,000,000 Mexicans here and the 127,000,000 Latin Americans below the Border will go on for the next 75 years, even though we are ultimately victorious."

Cantwell, who possessed a history of recognizing Mexican religious traditions in Los Angeles such as the celebration of Our Lady of Guadalupe, noted that in the archdiocese of Los Angeles he had already implemented Spanish instruction and cultural training in the seminaries. This included making Spanish a mandatory subject in the junior seminary. At the major seminary, part of the six-year tenure of students was to continue to learn Spanish in its "literary, conversational and ecclesiastical" contexts. In addition, the cultures of Mexico, Latin America, and Spain as well as the contemporary problems facing the Spanish-speaking in the United States, including "Proselytism, Cults, [and] Communism among Mexicans," were part of the curriculum.

If Spanish was important in the seminaries, it was likewise relevant in the instruction of schoolchildren. The Church in the 1940s did not adopt any formal position on bilingual instruction in either Catholic or public schools but did acknowledge the need for such instruction. At the San Antonio conference, one additional recommendation on "The Language Question" involved the importance of Mexican American children learning English, although the practical need to employ Spanish where necessary was also recognized. "Instruction has been found to be more effective," one conference committee report proclaimed, "with the younger generation by using the English language first and following with explanation in Spanish."[42]

The Confraternity of Christian Doctrine (CCD) likewise recommended the employment of a bilingual approach for the religious instruction of Mexican American children, especially in classes provided for public school students.

The San Antonio conference, for example, was of the opinion that it was best to provide such instruction in Spanish to younger children, who would better understand the lessons in their native language. Moreover, it was suggested that the use of Spanish might help get Spanish-speaking parents involved in their children's religious education. On the other hand, English was advised as the language of instruction in CCD classes for the older children, who presumably would be more English-speaking or bilingual.[43] The later Denver conference proposed that in Catholic schools teachers possess a "double culture," that is, become bicultural to better instruct Mexican American children.[44]

The use of Spanish in ministry among Mexicans was likewise seen as important in other venues as well. One of these concerned the need to expand the number of Spanish-language publications available through Church auspices and to take advantage of available religious materials in Spanish, some of them published in Mexico.[45] To distribute this literature efficiently, Archbishop Cantwell suggested that a Spanish book department with branches in all the large southwestern cities be established.[46]

Specific Church publications in Spanish included catechisms and Bibles. Archbishop Cantwell, for example, noted the availability of a new Spanish translation of the Baltimore Catechism, the standard text used in Catholic religious education in the United States, in addition to a Spanish version of Bible stories. He contended that the use of these materials would be of assistance in getting parents involved because it would deal with their English-language difficulty.[47]

One bilingual catechism aimed at preparing children for first communion was entitled "Catecismo de la Primera Comunión," published in 1943 by St. Anthony Guild Press in Paterson, New Jersey.[48] Catechisms in Spanish were made available not only to children, but also apparently to adults. Monsignor Ready, after learning that several hundred Mexican contract workers, or braceros, were laboring on the Pennsylvania Railroad near Harrisburg and York, Pennsylvania, sent them some Spanish-language catechisms as well as other religious materials in Spanish available at the NCWC.[49] For Sunday worship, the Church commissioned an inexpensive Sunday missal in Spanish.[50] Prayer books in Spanish, such as one entitled "Devocionario Popular," were also available through the National Catholic Community Service.[51] During the war fifteen thousand Spanish prayer books along with catechisms in Spanish were sent to Mexican American and other Latino soldiers at the front.[52]

Newspapers—either in Spanish or in bilingual format—were another way of reaching Spanish-speaking Catholics. Archbishop Cantwell noted the existence of many weekly and monthly publications in the United States but also observed that some were better than others. He called for a consolidation of the Catholic Spanish-language press as a way of upgrading its quality and of reaching a larger audience. "The general tone of this Press might be described as 'liberal,'" Cantwell explained, "but not hostile to the Church. The staff is usually Catholic and welcomes our contributions."[53] Other suggestions for the use of the Spanish-language press included the writing of Spanish-language columns in English-language Catholic newspapers.[54]

The Church as a medium of ministry to the Spanish speaking, of course, could not, in the 1940s, overlook radio. The San Antonio conference called attention to the use of radio. It reported that in cities like Los Angeles and Oakland there were already successful Spanish Catholic Hours over local stations, and it recommended that similar programs be broadcast in other parts of the Southwest under the sponsorship of a national Catholic organization.[55] Archbishop Cantwell confirmed the existence of such a broadcast in Los Angeles but at the same time observed the need for improving the programs.[56] Cantwell even suggested that Hollywood might be convinced, or even pressed, to produce films, presumably in Spanish, "in accordance with the best Catholic tradition of Mexico. This is a field where Protestants have nothing to offer."[57]

Cultural Coexistence

However, the use of Spanish, whether in direct ministry or through publications and the radio, by itself was not enough. Language alone would not reach the Spanish speaking. Also needed was the sympathetic and genuine appreciation of Mexican culture in all of its dimensions. That culture was deeply rooted in the Southwest and would not be displaced easily, nor, as some in the Church believed, should it be. "The heritage of Catholicity which the Spanish-speaking peoples derived from their forebears has, in large part, been preserved," the San Antonio conference stressed, "so that today these people constitute the great bulk of the Catholic population in many parts of the Southwest."[58] The participants at the meeting further recognized that acculturation to U.S. ways, while benefiting Mexicans, could likewise endanger their particular identity and "the better elements of their cultural tradition and their religion."[59]

To help preserve and to make use of this culture for ministry, during World War II the Church more publicly than before called on priests and other religious groups to fully appreciate and understand Mexican American culture. To accept the language and culture of the Spanish speaking was also to accept the people themselves. In a letter to Monsignor Ready in 1943, Father James Tort, C.M.F., of the Claretian order, which possessed a long history of working with Mexicans in the Southwest, underscored the importance of cultural understanding. Tort informed Ready of a recent conversation he had had with Archbishop Mooney about the Church's relationship with Mexicans in that midwestern city. "I told him," the Claretian wrote, "that it is not enough for the Priests in charge of the Mexican people to speak well their language, Spanish, it is also necessary to like them and to understand them, which it is not so frequently found." [60] Ready obtained a copy of a report written by Tort entitled "The Work of the Claretians Among the Mexicans in the United States" in states such as Texas, California, Arizona, and Illinois. "Why and how have the Claretians succeeded so wonderfully in their work among the poor Mexicans, being at the beginning the only laborers in this great field?" Tort rhetorically asked in this document:

> The answer is very simple. Besides the spirit of poverty, self-sacrifice, patience, willingness to undergo privations and other missionary virtues peculiar to the Claretians, the key to their success is mainly the understanding of the character of the Mexicans, resulting from the special education given to Claretian missionaries for work among the poor, the ignorant and the humble and their constant contact with them.[61]

Tort's views were shared by the NCWC as well as by the participants at the San Antonio conference. Cultural respect of the Mexicans was not only important for positive ethnic relations in the Southwest, but for the future of the Church in the region. "A genuine love of these Spanish-speaking people and a sincerely sympathetic attitude towards them on the part of priests and laity," the conference report stressed, "are basic requirements if the Latin-American groups are to be kept close to the Church. In no other ways shall the barriers erected by prejudice be broken down. The Christian law of love must operate." [62]

Cultural coexistence could take various forms. One suggestion was for seminarians and priests to spend some time in Mexico as a way of knowing the people and culture better.[63] More important was the need to participate in Mexican culture in the United States and understand its persistence and evolution. As Father Tort noted, the Claretians had been successful because they accepted Mexican Catholic traditions and customs such as local performances of Los Pastores (The Shepherds' Play) at Christmastime and the "Four Apparitions of Our Lady of Guadalupe" each December plus the reenactment of the Passion and crucifixion of Jesus during Holy Week. Barrio people themselves organized all of these activities. The Claretians likewise adopted traditional sodalities and other Mexican religious associations native to the Southwest or imported by immigrants from Mexico.[64]

Archbishop Cantwell seconded the importance of priests relating to the Mexicans at the cultural grassroots level by taking part in their fiestas and religious processions.[65] Identifying with the religious iconography of Mexican Catholics was another key to cultural awareness for the Church. In the discussion of the work of the Bishops' Committee for the Spanish-Speaking, in particular the construction of parish centers in the barrios, it was suggested that such centers "should be presentable, built, perhaps, in mission style, with a painted representation of Our Lady of Guadalupe and a cross above the entrance."[66] One Church official concluded that all of these efforts to relate to the Mexicans' culture as well as to improve their socioeconomic conditions would be aided by "the protection of Our Lady of Guadalupe, Who is the Mother of these unfortunate people so beloved by Her."[67]

But it wasn't only Anglos in the Church who were in need of cultural knowledge, for some Mexican Americans too, especially in the urban areas, were beginning to lose contact with some of their cultural traditions. To help these people appreciate their rich culture specific strategies were offered, including study clubs conducted in Spanish at which Mexican history could be taught. In addition, certain religious sodalities could be organized that would promote Mexican religious traditions. Such work, it was believed, would help close the gap between Mexican American young people and their Spanish-speaking parents.[68]

Although encouraging the integration of Mexican culture, the Church at the same time was certainly not promoting a form of ethnic cultural nationalism among the Mexicans. Unlike its earlier work with European immigrants such as the Italians and Poles, which focused on "national parishes" structured around the ethnic Catholicism of these groups, as Badillo observes, the Church pursued a more integrationist strategy with Mexicans.[69] As it had done even before World War II in some local areas, the Church instead promoted its version of multicultural unity and a sense that in differences there was strength. Moreover, it consistently condemned the segregation of Mexicans in schools, public facilities, and jobs. It also criticized the segregation of

Mexicans in some Catholic churches and called for integration. To this end, the Church also promoted naturalization and citizenship for Mexican immigrants.[70] One of the committees at the San Antonio conference stated, "The Committee deplores exclusion and segregation of Latin-Americans in mixed parishes as contrary to the spirit of both Christianity and Americanism."[71] Interethnic bonding between Anglos and Mexicans in the Southwest was seen as a way of gaining both national and religious unity. The NCWC especially encouraged such a viewpoint among Anglo-Catholics:

> The Social Action Department [of the NCWC] asks that the English-speaking among the Catholics of the Southwest come to the aid of the Spanish-speaking. They know them better than any other; for they live with them and are of the one Faith. The Spanish-speaking are Americans and their children will be Americans as long as the world lasts. Both to save their souls and to fit them into American life all Catholics should rally together.[72]

Conclusion

The promotion of unity and cultural sensitivity did not mean that some elements within the Church did not continue to display prejudice and discrimination against Mexicans or that even among the pro-Mexican pronouncements there was not some patronization involved. During the war years Mexicans were still referred to as "simple and primitive people" and described as lacking "ambition" or being "indolent" or "charming and lovable" people.[73]

Moreover, many of the efforts at acknowledging the importance of the Spanish speaking to the Church during World War II were largely carried out by Anglo priests and laypeople, with little involvement by the Mexicans themselves. As a result, while it appears that some positive changes resulted (it is not clear how widely the suggested changes were actually implemented), the lack of a larger, more consistent Mexican American/Latino voice and presence behind such efforts limited them. It would take another generation before such a critical mass of Latino priests, sisters, and lay Catholic leaders would surface to expand and to improve on these earlier activities. This later, still-ongoing struggle, along with the profound demographic changes among American Catholics, has clearly led to the Latinization of the Church as a new millennium begins. Already close to half of all American Catholics are of Latino descent. This number will only continue to soar because of high natural birthrates and continued immigration patterns. However, what I have attempted to stress in this chapter is that the roots of such Latinization go deeper into history and are more complicated than some contemporary critics suggest. In 1945, Bruce M. Mohler, the director of the NCWC Bureau of Immigration, observed that a few years before Msgr. John J. Burke, at that time the general secretary of the NCWC, had strongly reacted to a suggestion that Mexican immigrants were not worth any effort on the part of the Church. "His reply," Mohler stated, "was that the Mexican might some day be the salvation of the Church in the United States." Msgr. Burke's prophetic statement would hardly be disputed today.[74]

FIVE

Religion in the Chicano Movement

Católicos Por La Raza

We are demanding that the Catholic Church be Christian.

—CATÓLICOS POR LA RAZA

Do we have to stay out of our own Church? A Church that is not only hypo-critically wealthy, but which does not respect our culture. It is our duty, as Chicanos and Catholics, to return the Catholic Church to us.

—RICHARD CRUZ

Let the poor people in! Let the poor people in!

—CATÓLICOS POR LA RAZA OUTSIDE OF ST. BASIL'S CHURCH,
LOS ANGELES, DECEMBER 24, 1969

WHILE THE CHURCH in the 1940s and 1950s attempted on a larger scale than before to address the needs and interests of its growing Mexican American adherents, especially in the Southwest, by the 1960s events and the new pro-test movements of that politically tumultuous decade outpaced the Church's efforts. Rather than being proactive, the Church now became defensive and subject to increased criticism by Chicano Catholics. If Mexican American Catholics in an earlier period, as exemplified by the work of Cleofas Calleros and Alonso Perales, labored cooperatively with Church reformers, both in-spired by Catholic social doctrine, this new period of unrest in the United States, and indeed worldwide, witnessed the deterioration of this alliance and the emergence of new Chicano oppositional movements against the Church as part of what was perceived as a repressive establishment. This chapter ad-dresses the change in Chicano-Church relations.

The Chicano movement of the late 1960s and early 1970s represented the most significant and widespread protest by Mexican Americans in the his-tory of the United States. Reacting to a legacy of conquest in the Southwest in the nineteenth century, to a history of labor exploitation, and to experiences as second-class citizens characterized by various forms of discrimination and segregation, including lack of access to high-quality education, Mexican Americans by the 1960s challenged the system as never before. The movement was a Chicano uprising.

As part of its agenda, the movement gave birth to Chicano studies, defining it in very strong ethnic, nationalist terms. In turn, Chicano nationalism was largely portrayed as an expression of secular values and goals. The role of religion, especially Catholicism, was not perceived by early students of Chicano studies to have played a major role in the movement. And yet while secularization characterized a good deal of movement politics, religion was not absent. Religion, primarily but not exclusively Catholicism, played a role in the formation of a movement value system focused on social justice. Religion in some cases also proved to be the basis for community organization. Andrew Greeley refers to "cultural Catholics"; however, there were also what I would call "political Catholics."[1]

This chapter is a case study of the role of Catholicism in the Chicano movement in Los Angeles as exemplified by Católicos Por La Raza.[2]

Origins of Católicos Por La Raza

Católicos Por La Raza began as an extension of some of the early movement activities in Los Angeles that had sprung up in reaction to the inspirational struggle of César Chávez and the farmworkers when they struck for union recognition in 1965. Many movement activists in urban locations such as Los Angeles received their political baptism by making a pilgrimage to Delano, the headquarters of the union, to take food to the striking farmworkers and by supporting the initial grape boycott when it was launched in 1967 as a way of pressuring the growers to negotiate with the union. Católicos and the movement in Los Angeles also have to be seen in relation to increased racial tension in Los Angeles, as exemplified by the 1965 Watts riots. That conflict between African Americans and police and state national guard forces led to thirty-four deaths and many casualties.[3]

The school "blowouts" in East Los Angeles during the spring of 1968, when several thousand Mexican American students, inspired by the teacher Sal Castro, walked out of their schools to protest inferior education, likewise helped to ignite the movement in Los Angeles.[4] The walkouts had been preceded by the growing politicization of Chicano youth as a result of the annual Mexican American Youth Leadership Conferences.[5]

Católicos Por La Raza was one of many offshoots of these early protests and interacted with still many others. The movement, at least in Los Angeles, was never fragmented into separate, independent parts. Many activists wore many hats. It was not unusual for a movement activist to be involved as a student leader, as a supporter of the farmworkers, or as an organizer of anti–Vietnam War groups as well as other later manifestations, such as the creation of La Raza Unida Party, an independent Chicano political party.

In retrospect, this interrelationship characterized both the rise and fall of groups such as Católicos Por La Raza. For while much energy could quickly flow into one protest activity, it could just as easily flow out of that effort into another, thus undermining the permanent organization of one form of protest.

Católicos was organized as a result of the coming together of three groups: the Chicano Law Students' Association at Loyola University School of Law (a Jesuit institution), part of a statewide association; *La Raza* newspaper/magazine (a community-based Chicano publication); and United Mexican American Students (umas), a Chicano student group at Los Angeles City College. Richard Martínez, who at the time was the head of umas (later renamed mechma), recalls that he and other Chicano students were inspired by learning about some African Americans in the East who were protesting against mainline Anglo-Protestant churches that they believed were making few if any commitments to the black struggle for self-determination. Martínez began to question the role of the Catholic Church in Los Angeles with respect to Chicanos. "If you have the Church standing with you in making a demand," Martínez remembers thinking, "it's a hell of a lot more powerful than you standing by yourself. If the Bishop is next to me, I'm in good shape."[6] Martínez's statement suggests that he and possibly other organizers of Católicos were influenced by the progressive, activist roles played by the black churches, especially in the southern civil rights struggles of the 1960s led by Dr. Martin Luther King, Jr. They may well have contrasted what they believed to be the lack of such involvement and commitment by the Catholic Church with respect to Chicano civil rights.

Martínez convinced other umas students at his school that they should make the relevance of the Church to the Chicano community one of their top priorities. At Loyola, the Chicano Law Students' Association appears to have started when Richard (Ricardo) Cruz and Miguel García, the only two Chicano law students, along with other progressive students, protested what they claimed was the failure of the school to recruit and support, financially and otherwise, Chicano law students.[7] Cruz referred to himself and García as well as to later Chicano law students at Loyola as "movement babies" because they were politically born as Chicanos in a period of significant Chicano upheaval in Los Angeles. "What a strange feeling it was in those years," Cruz later wrote, "to be studying law in classrooms and simultaneously see[ing] law as it was applied."[8]

Cruz and García were also incensed that there were more Jewish students enrolled at this Catholic institution than Chicanos.[9] This local grievance soon expanded to include the Church's general neglect of the Mexican American community.[10] Of particular concern was the closing of a Catholic parochial school, Our Lady Queen of Angels High School, which had an 87 percent Mexican American enrollment, at the same time that the archdiocese had finished construction of a new three-million-dollar church, St. Basil's, in the trendy Wilshire district.[11] The writer and activist attorney Oscar Zeta Acosta later wrote,

> St. Basil's is [Cardinal James Francis] McIntyre's personal monstrosity.
> He recently bought it for five [sic] million bucks: a harsh structure for
> puritanical worship, a simple solid excess of concrete, white marble and
> black steel. It is a tall building with a golden cross and jagged cuts of
> purple stained glass thirty feet in the air, where bleeding Christ bears
> down on the people of America below. Inside[,] the fantastic organ
> pumps out a spooky religious hymn to this Christ Child of Golden
> Locks and Blue Eyes overlooking the richest drag in town.[12]

At the newspaper *La Raza,* Joe Razo, one of the organizers of the paper, appears to have been involved with various dissident Chicano priests in Los Angeles. In 1969, these priests formed a branch of PADRES, an association of Chicano priests in the Southwest who likewise wanted to make the Church more sensitive to the conditions of Mexican Americans. Razo himself was not a priest.[13]

In late October or early November 1969, Martínez recalls meeting with Cruz, the chair of the Loyola group, to discuss their common concerns. Martínez believes it may have been Razo who arranged the meeting. Cruz, whom Martínez characterized as thoughtful, intelligent, quick-minded, determined, and possessing clear organizational thinking along with a high intensity level, was part of what Martínez referred to as the "Cathedral Mafia"—a group of graduates from Cathedral High School in Los Angeles, a Catholic school run by the Christian Brothers just north of Chinatown and bordering the eastside of the city. Besides Richard and his brother, Ray, members of this "mafia" included Tomás Varela, Percy Duran, Miguel Duran, and Peter Navarro.[14] Raul Ruiz of *La Raza* considers Cruz to have been "a courageous, articulate, and charismatic young man."[15] Members of the mafia went on to college and became activists in the Chicano movement; some were active in Católicos.[16] According to Martínez, the Cathedral Mafia, including Cruz, because they were graduates of parochial schools during the period of the liberal reforms of Vatican Council II championed by Pope John XXIII, knew much more about the politics of the Church than people like Martínez, who had been raised Catholic but who had not gone to Catholic schools.[17]

Richard Cruz, who emerged as the principal leader of Católicos, was a former altar boy and product of the Catholic schools, as were his brothers. He recalled in a 1976 interview that he considered the Christian Brothers to have been great teachers, philosophical and spiritual and yet teaching their students about applying their religious beliefs to the world. "They related to reality more than they [did] to any trimmings and trappings," he observed, "and what I call the dark ages and dark mentality of religion." Cruz further noted that what he and other students took from their Catholic education involved a sense of morality, of good and evil, that they could apply to their social world.[18]

Some years later, Cruz noted that he had been influenced by the life of Jesus—a life he had studied. "More than any of you have," he wrote his parents in 1974, "I at one time loved, sacrificed, understood and, a rare thing indeed, also studied the person, life and times of J. C."[19]

Ray Cruz, Richard's older brother, remembers Richard as a natural-born leader, a great debater in high school, and someone who took his Catholicism seriously. At one point, he even considered a religious vocation. Rosa Martínez, his eventual companion, notes that Richard belonged to a "model Catholic family."[20] In his undergraduate years at Cal State, Los Angeles, where both Richard and Ray participated in the radical Students for a Democratic Society (SDS), Richard majored in philosophy and told Ray, "I am a Hegelian." Although not a Marxist, he appears to have read widely in philosophy, including Karl Marx and Marxist thinkers.[21] "Richard acquired a philosophical and more revolutionary orientation during his undergraduate studies at Cal State, Los Angeles," Ray observes.[22]

Shortly after the meeting between Martínez and Cruz, Católicos Por La Raza was formed to launch an assault by the Chicano movement on the Church in Los Angeles. The actual time line of the organization of Católicos is not certain, although it clearly was formed in 1969. García recalls that the

FIGURE 5.1 Richard Cruz, Católicos Por La Raza Rally at San Fernando State College, 1969. Courtesy Department of Special Collections, Davidson Library, University
of California, Santa Barbara.

group might have been formed earlier than the fall of that year.[23] According
to Raul Ruiz, who became the editor of *La Raza*, Católicos was the brainchild
of Richard Cruz. García concurs. "Richard was the key, the sparkplug," he
stresses. "He kept things moving. Without Richard, Católicos wouldn't have
happened."[24] The Católicos member Bob Gandara agrees. "That son-of-a-
bitch was good," Gandara fondly notes of Cruz; "he was articulate, worked

hard, was open-minded, and believed in what he was doing." As a result, Gandara adds, "we made sure that Richard was the *man*." [25]

Although Cruz was referred to as the cochair of the group, in fact, he was the leader and main spokesperson for Católicos.[26] The name of the group, especially the term *Católicos*, was chosen in order to stress that the members were not anti-Catholic.[27] The term *La Raza* was chosen rather than *Chicano* because Cruz believed it represented a more open and inclusive term, one that integrated the concept of the people and community into the title. The full title expressed the view that the Catholic Church belonged to the people. "Richard was well beyond just being a devout practicing Catholic," his brother Ray stresses. "At the time of Católicos, my brother was focusing on the very meaning of the Church." [28]

Richard Cruz later observed that meeting César Chávez inspired him to think about forming a group such as Católicos. He first met Chávez when he spent time as a law intern with the California Rural Legal Assistance helping farmworkers in Salinas in 1969. What particularly impressed Cruz was that the farm labor leader lamented that while he had received support from a variety of Protestant and Jewish denominations, he had not gotten the public support of the Catholic Church. Upon being introduced to Chávez, Cruz promised he would do what he could do bring the Church to *la causa*. Chávez would later express support for Católicos.[29]

Cruz noted that his pledge to Chávez represented the first reason he founded Católicos. A second factor had to do with Cruz's own Catholic beliefs, what he called a "practice what you preach syndrome." For Cruz, there was no reason the Church should not support Chávez and the farmworkers since Catholic doctrine stressed empathy for the poor. It was hypocritical, he believed, for the Church not to support the struggle. This view came from Cruz's Catholic socialization. "I was a super, super religious person in almost all those years," he recalled. "I was very mystical. . . . So it was my personal religion that made it clear to me that there was just no way on earth that the Church wouldn't of course get behind Chávez once [it] understood what was happening with a little pressure." [30]

A third reason had to do with Cruz's contemplation of the nature of religion. "What the hell is religion? What is its relevance? Is it needed?" These questions Cruz applied to the Church. What was the meaning of the Church if it didn't get involved in social struggles such as that of the farmworkers? [31] Part of Cruz's education was what Raymond Williams refers to as the process of "unlearning," when one begins to question received truths.[32]

Finally, Cruz was inspired to form Católicos out of a belief, given his own Catholic education, that while the Church had done some good in providing Catholic education, it could do much more, especially for Chicanos. He believed, as he put it later, that the Church had to "put its money where its mouth is and start paying for scholarships and all those things."[33]

Influenced by these reasons, Cruz returned to Los Angeles to see what he could do to make the Church more relevant to the Chicano community.

As it prepared to protest against the Church, Católicos moved from being strictly a student effort to an off-campus one as a way of expanding its base. Ruiz stresses that Católicos was a good example of how the Chicano movement was always a mixture of students and community and not composed just of students, as some contend.[34] Still, the three pillars of Católicos were the Loyola law students, *La Raza* newspaper and, later, magazine, and UMAS at Los Angeles City College, which within a short time included UMAS or MEChA students from other schools, such as Long Beach State. Rosa Martínez recalls that representatives of Católicos, including Richard Cruz, went to her campus at Cal State, Northridge, to inform MEChA about Católicos and ask for its support. Martínez notes that the students endorsed the goals of Católicos, but that it was not unanimous because some believed that attacking the Church was going too far. She further remembers Cruz as a "committed, passionate, bright, articulate, and convincing" speaker.[35] Functioning primarily in Los Angeles, Católicos, as Alberto Pulido has noted, inspired the formation of at least one other Católicos group in San Diego.[36]

To announce its formation, Católicos arranged a press conference. Cruz recalled that the only mainstream reporter who showed up was Ruben Salazar of the *Los Angeles Times*.[37] At the press conference, held at the Los Angeles Press Club, Cruz announced the primary objective of Católicos: "We have committed ourselves to one goal—the return of the Catholic Church to the oppressed Chicano community." He added that Católicos wanted the Church "to become as radical as Christ."[38]

Religion and the Chicano Movement

While Católicos was inspired by the individual and group views of the activists who formed it, it was at the same time influenced by other expressions of religiosity in the movement that likewise questioned the Catholic Church's role in the Chicano community. Chávez and the farmworkers' struggle stands as one such influence on Católicos.

In his efforts to organize a largely Mexican American farm labor force in California, Chávez brilliantly combined basic labor union organizing strategies with ethnic and religious ones. As a result, the farmworkers' cause came to represent not just a union, but also a movement for social justice and, as Griswold del Castillo and García stress, a "triumph of spirit."[39]

This strategy likewise involved a direct appeal to Mexican American religious sensibility. A sign in the union hall in Delano, for example, read, "God Is Beside You on the Picketline."[40] Alongside the union's flag, which contained the union's version of the Mexican eagle, Chávez placed the image of the Virgen de Guadalupe, the patron saint of all Mexicans. Chávez himself possessed a special devotion to Guadalupe. In addition, he used the religious symbol of the *peregrinación*, or pilgrimage, to mobilize support for the union's cause. In its famous 1966 Easter march from Delano to Sacramento, the union stressed that the march was more than a political one; that in fact it was a religious pilgrimage and that it would be offered up in penance for the sins of those who participated in it. The marchers were a Mexican American representation of the *penitente* tradition of the Spanish-speaking world. "The penitential tradition is also in the blood of the Mexican-American," Chávez observed, "and the Delano march will therefore be one of penance—public penance for the sins of the strikers, their own personal sins as well as their yielding perhaps to feelings of hatred and revenge in the strike itself. They hope by the march to set themselves at peace with the Lord, so that the justice of their cause will be purified of all lesser motivation."[41]

In 1968 Chávez utilized still another religious symbol in undergoing a twenty-five-day fast ostensibly to suffer for his own sins, but indirectly as a way of shoring up the cause of the farmworkers as the strike entered into its fourth year. Chávez linked his fast and his own personal suffering to Christ's crucifixion to atone for the sins of others. "It is my belief," he stressed, "that only by giving our lives do we find life. I am convinced that the truest act of courage, the strongest act of manliness is to sacrifice ourselves for others in a totally non-violent struggle for justice. To be a man," Chávez concluded, using the nonfeminist terminology of his day, "is to suffer for others. God help us to be men!"[42]

In an essay entitled "The Mexican American and the Church," written or spoken and then transcribed sometime in the late 1960s, Chávez revealed his reservations about the Catholic Church as well as his desire for the Church to become more involved not only in his cause but in that of other Mexican American efforts to achieve social justice. He pointed out how during the early

days of the strike it was not the Church that came to the union's support, especially in the Delano area, but instead a number of socially minded Protestant
ministers through the California Migrant Ministry; this group provided the
religious base of support. "It forced us," Chávez noted, "to raise the question
why our Church was not doing the same."[43]

Chávez, in his version of what in Latin America came to be called liberation theology, called on the Church to acknowledge the needs of its Mexican
American followers—the poor. But this acknowledgment, he insisted, should
not take the form of simple charity. The Church needed to go beyond this and
to provide part of the organized institutional framework for the poor to empower themselves.

Chávez concluded by calling on the Church to reorient its mission and to
once again identify with Christ's mission among the poor: "Finally, in a nut-
shell what do we want the Church to do? We don't ask for more cathedrals.
We don't ask for bigger Churches or fine gifts. We ask for its presence with us,
besides, as Christ among us. We ask the Church to sacrifice with the people for
social change, for justice, and for love of brother. We don't ask for words. We
ask for deeds. We don't ask for paternalism. We ask for servanthood."[44]

Besides the religious manifestations of Chávez and the farmworkers, there
was within the Chicano movement prior to Católicos criticism of the Catholic
Church by other Mexican Americans. In one of the first issues of *Con Safos*, a
creative and iconoclastic Chicano magazine in Los Angeles that featured the
early writings and artwork of some of the major cultural figures of the movement, such as Harry Gamboa, Gronk, Oscar Zeta Acosta, and Raul Salinas,
Eduardo Quevedo, Jr. published an essay entitled "The Catholic Church in
America." In this essay, Quevedo, although never specifically referring to liberation theology, which was at that very moment being conceptualized and
developed in Latin America, provided some evidence of the influence of liberation theology on some Chicanos and the parallel development of an organic
Chicano liberation theology.

Quevedo criticized the Church, as did liberation theologians, for losing its
commitment to the poor and the disempowered and instead pacifying them
by what Quevedo referred to as "the static and death-wish philosophy and
theology of a Thomas Aquinas" through the Church's concentration on salvation in an afterlife in heaven. "Moral betterment and religious goodness, the
child has been told," Quevedo added, "is all that matters." No better example
of this "otherworldly" theology could be found than in Latin America, where,
Quevedo pointed out, the Church build magnificent cathedrals to direct the
countless poor upward while at the same time neglecting their cries of pov-

erty and despair. For Quevedo this did not represent true Catholicism or true Christianity.

By contrast, in observing the growing clamor for social justice by Mexican Americans in the United States and the Church's aloofness toward this movement, Quevedo concluded that in this relationship and process Mexican Americans were emerging as more Christian than the Church itself.[45]

It is not clear whether liberation theology as it emanated from the historic Medellín conference held in Colombia in 1968 had a direct influence on the organization of Católicos.[46] As noted in the Quevedo essay, certain tendencies of liberation theology—particularly the stress on a renewed commitment of the Church to the alleviation of the temporal sufferings of the poor and the Church's further commitment to the empowerment of the poor—are visible. Richard Cruz and other members of the Chicano Law Student Association at Loyola might have encountered liberation theology in some form, although Cruz in a 1976 interview claimed he had never heard of it. Ray Cruz does not recall his brother Richard referring to liberation theology but would not be surprised if Richard was aware of it because of his wide intellectual interests.[47] Ruiz recalls that the idea behind Católicos was in part to propose a "theology of liberation East L.A. style."[48]

Evidence of familiarity with at least some facets of liberation theology do surface in *La Raza* magazine, edited by Ruiz, sometime after Católicos was formed. Ruiz, who was studying Latin American history at Cal State, Los Angeles, under such radical professors as Tim Harding, was quite aware of events in Latin America. At the end of 1968, Ruiz traveled to Cuba as part of a U.S. delegation to help celebrate the tenth anniversary of the Cuban revolution.[49] *La Raza* consistently carried articles on Latin American revolutionary movements, including references to those progressive elements within the Church that supported such movements for social change.[50]

In addition, *La Raza* published articles extolling the exploits of Camilo Torres, the Colombian priest turned revolutionary who was killed by the Colombian military in 1966. In its first magazine edition in early 1970, *La Raza* carried an essay on Torres entitled "The Brotherhood of Priestly Revolutionism" by the Maryknoll priest Blase Bonpane of Los Angeles. Bonpane praised Torres's courage in taking up arms on behalf of the poor and the exploited in Latin America. Bonpane concluded that the worse violence was not armed struggle but in allowing the people of Latin America to continue to suffer. He accused the Church of being an accomplice in this oppression.

Fortunately, Bonpane added, some priests, such as Torres, would no longer tolerate these conditions. "Let it be understood that there is a new breed of religious people in Latin America," Bonpane concluded. "This breed is break-ing with an ugly past. This breed is the catalyst of revolution."[51] Richard Cruz would later name his son Camilo in honor of Torres and Camilo Cienfuegos, one of the leaders of the Cuban revolution.[52]

A Católicos Theology

Influenced directly and indirectly by these various political and theological developments, Católicos put forward its own ideological views and critique of the Church. First and foremost, members of Católicos made it very clear that they identified as Chicano Catholics. In its founding proclamation, Católi-cos stressed that it was precisely the Catholic background of its members that made them conscious of the contradictions of the Church. "We have gone to Catholic schools and understand the Catholic tradition," Católicos pointed out.[53] Although Católicos was not a mass organization, it reminded the Church that Mexican Americans as well as other Latinos were predominantly Catho-lics and made up a large percentage of U.S. Catholics, especially in the South-west.[54] "Mexican-Americans have been most faithful to Catholicism and its traditions," a Católicos press release addressed to Cardinal Francis McIntyre and to the Catholic clergy of the Los Angeles archdiocese stressed. "We have produced saints and martyrs; have given and continue to give truly sacrificial donations to our Catholic Church and for the most part have attempted to live up to Christ's mandate that we love our brother. We believe that you, our spiritual leaders, know these things to be true."[55]

As Catholics, members of Católicos stressed that one of the Catholic tradi-tions they embraced was an identity with the poor. This was an identity that Christ himself had established. "Because of our Catholic training we know," Católicos declared, "that Christ, the founder of Catholicism, was a genuinely poor man. We know that he was born in a manger because His compatriots refused Him better housing. We know that He not only worked and kissed the feet of the poor (Mary Magdalen) but did all in His power to feed and educate the poor."[56]

As Catholics and as Christians, members of Católicos believed that they had no option but to identify with the poor as Christ had done. "We have the duty," Católicos insisted, "to not only love the poor but to be as Christ-like as possible."[57]

Poverty for Chicanos, according to Católicos and other concerned Mexi-can American Catholics, was not a metaphor; it was a living reality. As a

1969 report by Andrés Gallegos and Antonio Tinajero for the Division of the Spanish-Speaking of the U.S. Catholic Conference pointed out, too many Mexican Americans remained poor and marginalized in the country. In the Southwest many Mexican Americans experienced twice the unemployment rate as Anglo-Americans. Eighty percent of Mexican Americans who were employed worked in unskilled or low-skilled jobs. In Texas, 89 percent of Mexican Americans dropped out of school before completing a high school education. Forty percent of Mexican Americans in Texas were functionally illiterate. In California, Mexican Americans composed 14 percent of the public school population but less than ½ of 1 percent of students at the University of California.[58]

It was because poverty existed in the barrios—in the parishes—that Católicos, like liberationists in Latin America, called attention to the contradictions within the Church concerning the poverty of the people and the wealth of the Church. Católicos believed that this contradiction represented hypocrisy on the part of the Church. It preached, on the one hand, that the poor, through their devotion to Christ, would acquire everlasting rewards ("Blessed are the poor"), while at the same time the Church as an institution accumulated wealth beyond the imaginations of the poor.[59]

The contradictions between the poverty of the poor and the wealth of the Church could especially be seen in housing conditions in the barrio and the Church's ownership of property in Los Angeles. While most Chicanos lived in inadequate and deteriorating homes, the Church, despite its vast property holdings, did nothing to reform barrio housing conditions.[60]

Católicos noted that they were raising such questions because of the Church's dominant presence in East Los Angeles, a part of the city that contained among the worst living conditions. Católicos observed that, according to a Los Angeles County survey of housing, 72 percent of dwellings in East Los Angeles violated the building code. What this meant, Católicos pointed out, was congestion, decay, and demoralization for many Chicanos in that part of the city. "And how has the Los Angeles Archdiocese responded to Chicano housing needs?" Católicos asked: "'We're not in the housing business,' a Church spokesman said. And sure enough, the Archdiocese has not built a single unit of low-cost housing. When the chancery claims that their first responsibility is to serve the Mexican American people, it apparently does not include their living conditions."[61]

To further document what Católicos claimed was the Church's hypocrisy with respect to the poor, *La Raza* published a partial listing of Church-owned property acquired from the county assessor's office. According to Católicos, these holdings amounted to a billion dollars. Moreover, this amount covered only Los Angeles County and not the rest of the archdiocese, which included Orange, Ventura, and Santa Barbara counties. *La Raza* further noted that this value might cover only part of the Church's property since it did not include corporations owned by the Church. The properties listed, Católicos believed, did not include just churches, schools, and rectories, but also private homes, apartments, and businesses. According to Ruiz, these holdings included many slum dwellings.[62]

Católicos contrasted certain displays of Church wealth with the conditions of most Chicanos. "We know that the stained glass in Los Angeles' newest Catholic church is worth approximately two hundred and fifty thousand dollars ($250,000)," it pointed out. "We know of this wealth; yet Chicanitos [little children] are praying to La Virgen de Guadalupe as they go to bed hungry and will not be able to afford decent education."[63] Católicos further added, "Compare such wealth to the plight of our people and you begin to wonder, as CPLR [Católicos Por La Raza] has wondered, just who has taken the vow of poverty—the Chicanos or the Catholic Church."[64]

Part of the Church's neglect of the poor, contended Católicos, included a lack of Chicano representation within the Church's structure. Católicos noted that of the twelve million Spanish-speaking people in the United States over 90 percent were Catholics. This made the Spanish speaking the largest single ethnic group within the Church, constituting almost a quarter of all Catholics and 67 percent of those in the southwestern states. In addition, Católicos observed that the total population of La Raza exceeded that of some sixty nations. Latin American countries with smaller populations, including Puerto Rico, possessed their own native church hierarchy and institutions. By contrast, despite their numbers, Spanish-speaking Catholics in the United States had little representation. There was not a single Spanish-speaking bishop. Of the more than 720 priests in the Los Angeles archdiocese only 5 percent were Spanish-speaking.[65] This lack of representation, Católicos observed, in turn discouraged Mexican Americans and other Latinos from entering into vocations. Nevertheless, Chicano Catholics remained loyal Catholics. "What people in the United States have been historically and at present more faithful to the Catholic faith than our people?" Católicos observed.[66]

Chicanos not only needed effective and fair representation in the hierarchy, Richard Cruz contended, but as part of this process the Church had to also understand that, given the growing numbers of Chicano Catholics, the culture of the Church also had to change. "Changing the Church, 'tailoring to our needs,' is one of the aims of Católicos Por La Raza," he told a reporter. "We want to decide who will be the saints of our days. We want Christ to be 'Chuy.'" The reporter noted that "Chuy" was the nickname for the common Mexican name Jesús.[67]

Católicos believed that the Spanish speaking had to be represented at all levels of the Church and that both Chicano clergy as well as laity needed to be part of the decision-making process of the Church in order to give priority to the needs of the poor.[68]

What needed to be done, given the contradictions, hypocrisy, and insensitivity of the Church, was, according to Católicos, to transform the Church from an elite institution to an agency of the people. Católicos stressed that this transformation was justified on the basis of Church doctrines and traditions themselves. "Saint Thomas says that concrete attribution of an authority is made by the people," Católicos noted. "When there is an authority opposed to the people, this authority is illegitimate and tyrannical. As Christians and Catholics, we can and must fight against the mismanagement of OUR Church."[69] Quoting St. Matthew (Matt: 20:28), Católicos reminded the Church of Christ's mission: "I came not to be served, but to serve."[70]

In their own way, Católicos was asserting the profound, new emphasis emerging from Vatican Council II that all Catholics, not just the clergy, represented the Church. According to Father Patrick McNamara, a Jesuit scholar at Loyola University during this period, this new conception of the Church, in his words, "the Church as the people of God," was the most significant pronouncement of the council. It meant, McNamara notes, that the laity, including Católicos, would be agents of change within the Church.[71]

Central to this transformation was the reestablishing of the Church's identity with the poor. "We are demanding that the Catholic Church be *Christian*," Católicos emphasized.[72] Here again Católicos reminded the Church of its origins. Christ was born in poverty, grew up with the poor, had washed their feet, and had died for them. He had loved the poor and now the Church had to once again do the same. "We must return the Church to the poor," Católicos proposed. "Or did Christ die in vain?"[73]

Católicos further believed that by transforming the Church they would assure that the Church came to identify with the Chicano movement. It would transform the clergy into "La Raza Churchmen." "It is long overdue," Católicos observed, "that the Catholic Church in Los Angeles and throughout the Southwest have the moral integrity to identify with *el movimiento*. Católicos Por La Raza will not rest until that day has come."[74]

In their struggle to reconvert the Church, members of Católicos believed they had no better role model than Christ himself. Católicos as well as other Catholic activists in the movement in their version of a Chicano Christology reinterpreted Christ as a revolutionary. "Jesus Christ is being seen as the radical he really is," one New Mexican movement activist proposed. "He is seen as a revolutionist through the eyes of the revolutionaries, for it is from him that we draw strength."[75] As a revolutionary, Jesus, as the Chicano poet Abelardo Delgado wrote, represented the "New Christ" bearing the "New Cross" that would establish the "New Church."[76]

In its call for a "New Church," Católicos made it very clear they were not attacking Catholic beliefs and doctrines, but the current leadership of the Church, which had deviated from these beliefs and doctrines. "I think that we went to great lengths," recalls Ruiz, "to explain every time we spoke or wrote that we were not writing about the ideology or the religion itself, but rather the human aspect of the Church which we felt was very defective."[77]

Richard Cruz later observed that Católicos was simply telling the Catholic clergy "to live like your so-called leader, the one who says . . . 'Be like me' . . . So live with the poor, feed them, get going in other words." Jesus, in Cruz's opinion, lived a "socialistic-communistic life."[78]

Católicos did not see itself as leading a schism from the Church, but as leading it back to its own principles. "It is not the Church or more specifically the religious views that are inadequate to meet the needs of today's poor," Católicos pointed out, "but some of the men who help run the Church." One of these men was Cardinal McIntyre, who, according to Católicos, ran the Los Angeles archdiocese with a tyrannical hand, suppressing both clergy and laity, especially those who identified with the poor. Father McNamara referred to McIntyre's administration as an "authoritarian regime."[79] "Social action, to the Cardinal," Católicos stressed, "is regarded in the same vein as hell."[80]

In its declaration of principles, Católicos concluded that the struggle for the soul of the Church was critical for two basic reasons. One, it was foolish for the movement to neglect the Church as a major institution affecting Chicanos. The Church possessed vast wealth and power, and if that could be converted to aid in the alleviation of poverty and the empowerment of Chicanos, then the movement would have acquired a significant ally. Second, Católicos understood—as did César Chávez—that in any social movement like the Chicano movement, spirituality was essential to maintaining morale and commitment. Católicos believed that a liberated Church would be able to provide this spiritual guidance—a faith-based movement. The movement and the poor needed not an unfriendly Church but a friendly one. This is what Católicos aimed to achieve. "When poor people get involved in a long conflict, such as a strike, or a civil rights drive, and the pressure increases everyday," Católicos observed, "there is a deep need for spiritual advice. Without it families crumble, leadership weakens, and hard workers grow tired. In such a situation the spiritual advice must be given by a friend, not by part of the opposition." [81]

Defining their beliefs and their objectives, members of Católicos, shortly after organizing, likewise drafted a list of demands that it hoped to present to Cardinal McIntyre. These demands reflected Católicos' philosophy, but in a more concrete manner outlined the specific changes it hoped to pressure the Church into accepting. Key to the demands was acquiring a substantive input by the Chicano community into Church decision making. This would be achieved by the creation of a Commission on Mexican American Affairs within the hierarchy of the Church in Los Angeles. The commission would be composed of representatives of Mexican American community organizations as well as of Mexican American priests and nuns. It would concentrate its efforts on reorienting Church policy in the following areas:

1. Education. The commission would be authorized to make periodic accountings, for example, of Church assets in order to determine the available funding for Chicano education programs.
2. Housing. This would involve the Church providing housing loans for the purchase of homes or for repairs. The Church would also build low-cost housing in the barrios.
3. Health. The commission would administer and control all Church hospitals in the Mexican American community as well as provide free or low-cost health insurance for low-income Mexican Americans.
4. Shared Governance. The commission would jointly share with the Church hierarchy policy-making powers on all temporal affairs.
5. Leadership and Orientation. The commission would oversee classes in all barrio parishes concerning leadership and Mexican American culture. The Church would also provide orientation classes on Mexican American history and culture to its seminary students as well as to clergy assigned to barrio parishes.

6. Assignment of Clergy to the Chicano Movement. The Church
   would see to it that concerned priests and nuns would be assigned
   on a full-time basis to work with Chicano community projects and
   organizations.

7. Freedom of speech for all priests and nuns. The Church would guaran-
   tee freedom of speech and would not retaliate against any member of
   the clergy for speaking out on secular issues.

8. Use of Church Facilities. The Church would make available to Chicano
   community groups the use of Church buildings for meetings and other
   events.

9. Public Commitment to the Chicano Movement. The Church would
   publicly support the struggles of the Chicano community in their
   varied manifestations and issues, such as support for the farmworkers,
   for the anti–Vietnam War movement, against racist grand juries in Los
   Angeles, and support for Chicano activists arrested by the police.[82]

By acceding to these demands, the Church, according to Católicos, would
"reflect the social condition of the people it serves."[83] This reconverted
Church, according to Cruz, would no longer practice a patronizing charity
that only involved monetary donations. Instead, it would be a charity based
on a love that would seek to eradicate the root problems facing Chicanos. "I
think charity is love," he concluded, "and if it's not practiced then it's jive."[84]

Católicos stressed that they would persist in their struggle until their demands were met, irrespective of the consequences. "Further understand that
we shall enforce our demands with whatever spiritual and physical powers we
possess even if it means we must be jailed," they told the press.[85]

Confronting the Church

With their demands in hand, Católicos in the fall of 1969 proceeded to devise
a strategy to force the Church in Los Angeles, specifically Cardinal McIntyre,
to agree to them. Meeting at the headquarters of La Raza magazine and later
at the Euclid Community Center on Whittier Boulevard in East Los Angeles,
around twenty hard-core members of Católicos concentrated on devising the
steps they would take. According to García, the members of the Chicano Law
Students' Association of Los Angeles, which comprised students from various Los Angeles schools, were the most active members of Católicos.[86] Rosa

FIGURE 5.2 Católicos Por La Raza, 1969. Courtesy Department of Special Collections, Davidson Library, University of California, Santa Barbara.

Martínez, who volunteered to represent Cal State, Northridge, at Católicos meetings, remembers that between thirty and forty people attended these meetings.[87] It does not appear that the meetings were the occasion for any philosophical discussions. Richard Martínez notes that the issues-oriented and pragmatic aspects of these meetings coincided with what he considered to be Católicos' more populist base, as opposed to a philosophical one.[88]

Despite its relatively small numbers, Católicos organized subcommittees to focus on particular strategies. This included a Lawsuit Committee, composed of the Loyola law students; a Logistics or Action Committee; and a Support Committee to publicize Católicos' concerns to the Chicano community, to recruit Catholic clergy to its side, and to research the Church's position on community needs.[89]

Although some women, such as Rosa Martínez, Alicia Escalante, Lydia López, María Acosta, Gloria Chávez, and Patricia Borjón along with some others, participated in several of these meetings and in later demonstrations, they do not appear to have shared the same authority within Católicos as the men. Martínez recalls that perhaps as many as 50 percent of the activists in some way or another connected with Católicos actions were women; still, they were relegated to less influential positions despite her belief that Richard Cruz attempted to be more inclusive of women. Nevertheless, as she notes, women in the group, as in too many other Chicano movement organizations, "sort of rotated to the kitchen to warm the tortillas and cook the food, type and fold the flyers, etc."[90]

As part of its initial organizing, Católicos contacted the Congress of Mexican-American Unity, an umbrella group representing some sixty Mexican American organizations. It informed the congress of its concerns about the Church and requested that the congress speak directly to Cardinal McIntyre. Considering itself to be a member of the congress, Católicos told the group, "We believe that the Church has sufficient means and power to reform not only those institutions under its control but the whole of society which affects our people." While the congress supported Católicos in its efforts, it is not clear whether it adhered to its request.[91]

Católicos' initial strategy further involved publishing an open letter in *La Raza* to Cardinal McIntyre concerning its demands and attempting to present a copy personally to the cardinal. When Richard Cruz and a few others visited the chancery office to do this on October 15, McIntyre refused to see them, instead leaving his office through a back door and calling the police. No arrests were made. After Católicos persisted in their efforts to see the cardinal, he agreed to meet with them two days later, only to tell them, "Say what you have to say or get out!" Cruz later recalled, "I kiss[ed] [the] Cardinal's ring but he treats us like trash and we split."[92] The Católicos left without presenting their demands since McIntyre refused to treat them with respect. "Do we have to stay out of our own Church?" Cruz remarked. "A Church that is not only hypocritically wealthy, but which does not respect our culture. It is our duty, as Chicanos and Catholics, to return the Catholic Church to us."[93]

Following the cardinal's rebuff, Católicos devised a new, twofold but interrelated strategy. It would call for another meeting with the cardinal and, at the same time, commence picketing of the cardinal's residence at St. Basil's Church in order to force such a meeting. The strategy of confrontation had been part of the debate within Católicos. It appears that some, including Ray Cruz and Bob Gandara, had concerns about a strategy of direct confrontation either because of their lingering loyalty to traditional Church authority or because they doubted it was a sound tactical decision. Such reservations, whether expressed or not, did not win the day. Richard Cruz, Richard Martínez, and Raul Ruiz, as the key inner circle, forcibly and successfully argued for confrontation. They insisted that the only way to get awareness in the community about the failures of the Church was to get publicity, and the only way to get publicity was through confrontation. Not only would they get publicity, they observed, but confrontation, almost as a form of guerilla warfare, would expose the contradictions of the Church. Cruz and the others were convinced that the Church would overreact and even use violence against Católicos. This would prove their point that the Church was a rigid, conservative institution that had no sympathy or support for Chicanos. "You cannot make changes unless you confront the institution," Ray Cruz remembers his brother saying, "and when you do confront them, they're going to react with violence."[94]

According to Ray Cruz, Católicos also seriously discussed the implications of utilizing a confrontational strategy and risking alienating moderate and traditional Mexican American Catholics. They acknowledged the risk but believed that their strategy outweighed it. However, to deal with this potential problem, Católicos likewise recognized that they needed to try to get as much community support as possible. They believed that this was feasible once the people, as a result of Católicos' challenge to the Church, recognized the injustices of the Church.[95]

Católicos specifically targeted Cardinal McIntyre because it understood that he held the power and the purse strings. "We pursued meetings with the Cardinal in our own inimitable way," Martínez stresses, "in your face." García further notes, "We saw that the power was at the archdiocese and that Cardinal McIntyre was much too conservative and much too old and that he really was an obstacle to making the Church more progressive."[96] Picketing included a prayer vigil on Thanksgiving Day in front of St. Basil's.[97] To encourage others to attend, Católicos sent out an appeal and an explanation of the protest a few days before the event. "We are not demanding that the Catholic Church be Christian. For you see, if it is Christian it cannot in conscience retain its fabulous wealth while Chicanos have to . . . beg, plead . . . for better housing, education, legal defense and other Chicano goals which you know so well. . . . And believe us, we don't need your moral support. We need your Chicano bodies and spirit with us—NOW!!!"[98]

The vigil continued the following week on December 7 at the end of the Sunday Masses. About 350 Chicanos and Anglo supporters representing different groups united under the Congress of Mexican-American Unity protested. "We urge Chicanos and all Christians and Catholics to unite with us in our cause," a Católicos press release stated, "and to celebrate with us the day when no members of the Catholic clergy are wealthier than the poorest Mexican-American. The Church will be made relevant. So be it."[99] Gandara remembers that at these protests at St. Basil's, Católicos and its supporters were not allowed to use the bathrooms at the church. By comparison, a nearby

Jewish synagogue did allow them to use their facilities and even provided coffee for the demonstrators.[100]

The protestors attempted to see the cardinal, whose residence was at the rear of the church, but neither he nor any of his staff would meet with Católicos. "We could only wonder what Christ would do if 350 Chicanos would want to see Him," Católicos asserted.[101] In response, McIyntre was reported to have said, "I was here before there were Mexicans. I came to Los Angeles twenty-one years ago."[102]

After receiving no response from the cardinal, Católicos decided to raise the ante. On December 18, 1969, between fifteen and thirty members of Católicos visited the cardinal's offices at the chancery to demand a meeting. They had decided not to take no for an answer.

In 1972 Richard Cruz wrote a paper reflecting on this visit to the cardinal and on the events surrounding the visit to St. Basil's. He noted that he and the others entered the chancery and went up one flight of stairs to where an elderly receptionist greeted them. Cruz and the others requested to meet with McIntyre.

"I'm sorry," the receptionist told them, "His Reverence is not in at the moment and you would simply *have* to have an appointment to see him even if he was."

"Excuse us, ma'am, but he's here. We saw his black limousine parked in back," Cruz replied.

Cruz recalled that two nuns sitting in the waiting room looking like saints began to exchange disturbed, frightened glances with each other and the receptionist.

"What exactly is the nature of your visit?" the receptionist then asked.

"We're Chicanos from various parts of L.A. we told her (todo proud)," Cruz responded, "and we've been trying to see the Cardinal for a long time to talk to him about the poverty of our people and what he and the Church are doing about it!"

When Cruz finished saying this, one of the other Católicos chimed in, "And we're not going to leave until we see him!"

"Now let me see if I have this straight, young men," the receptionist replied with a distraught look, "you're from Chicago and. . . ."

"No," Cruz and the others interrupted, "you've never heard the word Chicano? There's barrios full of Chicanos and all kinds of Raza surrounding this area. You know, Mexican, Mexican-American! Orale—Chicago—chingou!"[103]

Completely taken aback, the receptionist excused herself for a minute or two and upon returning informed the group that one of the cardinal's assistants would see them. Católicos agreed, and three of them, including Richard Cruz and Richard Martínez, were escorted into another room. Unfortunately, this meeting came to naught when the third member of Católicos proceeded to use the occasion to verbally attack the assistant for the Church's neglect of the Chicano community.[104]

After the three representatives of Católicos rejoined the rest of the group, a decision was made to force their way into the cardinal's office. Rosa Martínez, who was part of the contingent, notes that Cruz was not a very patient person and that he finally told the others, "Let's just go in."[105] They forced open the door into the inner corridor in search of the cardinal's office. As startled priests emerged from their offices, they ran down the corridor. Joe Razo led the charge, and when one of the priests tried to stop him, Razo, perhaps an ex–football player, threw a perfect body block, knocking the priest completely off his feet and freeing the other Católicos to move down the hall in search of the cardinal's office. "That's it!" Richard Martínez and the others yelled out. García tried to open the door only to have it shut on him from the inside, pinning his arm between the door and the frame. García recalls acting as if his arm was in serious pain in order to try to get the door open. His ploy worked enough to allow him to force it ajar. As García pushed his way into the office, there, standing no more than three feet away, was a red-faced and very nervous Cardinal McIntyre. "Call the police. Call the police," he said in a faint voice to his staff of two or three priests.[106]

"No, no, we don't need to call the police," Martínez remembers one of the staff responding, "calm down, calm down."[107] Rosa Martínez observes that the cardinal was visibly shaken and that some of his staff seemed to think that she and the other Católicos had come to rob the chancery office.[108] In fact, Martínez herself was somewhat shaken at what was transpiring. "I remember thinking," she says, "that the Holy Ghost was going to come down, as all of my Catholic upbringing came back to me, and I was in terror of being struck down by God."[109]

A livid cardinal agreed to meet with the few Católicos who had managed to enter the office. Other priests who had blocked the entryway to the corridor prevented the other Católicos from doing so.[110] McIntyre listened to their demands, but promised only to look into the issues presented to him. Richard Cruz did all of the talking for Católicos. After several minutes, having forced their meeting with the cardinal, members of Católicos retreated, believing they had at least won a moral victory. "We weren't very sophisticated," Martínez notes, "but that was our strength because with our energy and our enthusiasm we just charged ahead."[111] García recalls that it was a very short encounter with the cardinal because he and the other Católicos believed that the police had been called and would arrive shortly.[112]

A few days passed, and Católicos did not hear back from the cardinal. As a result, the decision was made to organize a large demonstration outside of St. Basil's on Christmas Eve and to disrupt the cardinal's midnight Mass. The service was going to be televised, and Católicos hoped to take advantage to publicize its demands.[113] This more dramatic strategy may have been inspired by the actions of the Católicos group in San Diego, who on November 30 had taken over Camp Oliver, a Catholic youth camp in Descanso just east of San Diego. The San Diego Católicos used the seizure to bring attention to their demands. The takeover ended on December 1.[114]

Richard Martínez recalls that at this point Católicos made increased contact with disaffected priests and nuns such as Father Bonpane. In the meantime, picketing and candlelight vigils outside of St. Basil's resumed. Ruiz notes that large numbers participated in these protests, which included some sleepovers outside of the church.[115]

Richard Cruz further observed that by this time, they had gained support from a wide spectrum of the Chicano movement and from progressive religious clergy. This included Brown Berets, welfare mothers, high school and college students, and community organizers as well as priests and nuns.[116] Rosa Martínez notes that Católicos did not attract just radical activists, but also community people.[117]

Additional preparation for the Christmas Eve demonstration involved recruiting other Chicano student support. This was the task assigned to Martínez and the UMAS group at City College. Martínez remembers that while many students responded positively to the planned demonstration, some raised doubts as to the correctness of attacking the Church. These students believed that the action would offend many Catholics. Moreover, they did not believe that the Church was the real enemy.[118]

In addition to organizing students for the demonstration, Católicos, principally Razo and Richard Cruz, concentrated on gathering community support and participation. They also arranged to have legal representation at the demonstration in case of encounters with the police. Since Católicos were not keeping their demonstration a secret, they assumed the police would be present. Concern about the police had been growing among Católicos. Cruz believed they had tapped his phone. It is possible, according to Cruz's son Camilo that his father and possibly other Católicos carried guns for protection.[119] García corroborates Cruz's suspicions and notes that Chicano members of the Criminal Conspiracy Section of the city police had been "tailing us." He adds, "They knew us and we knew who they were."[120] Gandara, who worked for *La Raza* and was a member of Católicos, recalls some Anglos approaching members of the group trying to sell weapons. The Católicos refused. Gandara believes the sellers may have been undercover police.[121]

Católicos arranged to secure the services of the movement attorney Oscar Zeta Acosta, the "Brown Buffalo." Acosta would later write about the St. Basil's demonstration as well as other movement activities in his book *The Revolt of the Cockroach People* (1972). Additional support for the protest came from a group called the Coalition for Concerned Catholics, which was an organization of Anglo priests, nuns, and laypeople.[122] A flyer apparently produced by this group referred to the upcoming protest as one for peace and justice.[123]

The strategy for the intervention at the cardinal's Mass involved several steps. The assembled crowd would first have an alternative "people's Mass" outside the church at the same time the Mass was being conducted inside of St. Basil's. Both masses would commence at 11 P.M. and conclude around midnight. The alternative Mass would be officiated by some of the priest supporters of Católicos, including Bonpane. It would be timed to end a few minutes before the conclusion of the cardinal's Mass. The group would then line up in a candlelight procession and enter the church. Going through the vestibule, they would enter the sanctuary and proceed down the main aisle. At the foot of the altar railing, they would spread out and face the congregation. Three of them, including Cruz and Martínez, would then take turns reading their demands. This strategy, according to Martínez, "sounded good."[124]

The actual events, however, did not quite turn out that way. It appears that somewhere between 200 and 350 people gathered to participate in the demonstration. Not only activists were encouraged to attend but also families. Ramón Cruz, Richard's father, participated.[125] They assembled at Lafayette Park, about a mile from the church, and then marched to St. Basil's chanting, "Que viva la raza!" "Chicano Power!" and "Catholics for the people."[126] They congregated to the side of the main entrance, next to a large nativity scene. The front entrance to the church is small, so the hundreds of Católicos supporters spilled out into the street.[127] Lydia López, whose husband, Federico López, was a member of Católicos and a onetime Brown Beret, attended the protest. Because she was pregnant and because of the possibility of violence, she was told by her husband, and possibly other Católicos, not to get too close to the church. She stood across the street. A further indication that Católicos expected police violence is that some, including Razo, gave Lydia their wallets and keys to hold for them.[128]

As people arrived for the midnight Mass, some verbal altercations took place between those entering and members of Católicos. Bonpane said the Católicos Mass in Spanish, using a table for the altar. Instead of the regular wafers for communion, he used bits of flour tortilla. Ray Cruz remembers the alternative Mass as "radical but fun." [129] When their Mass ended, the Católicos group formed a procession with lighted candles and prepared to enter the vestibule around 12:15 A.M.[130]

At this point, the sequence of events is not perfectly clear. Zeta Acosta later claimed that Católicos had made prior arrangements, presumably with St. Basil's, to enter the church as long as they left their banners and candles outside.[131] In a letter of December 26 to Cardinal McIntyre, Richard Cruz noted that prior to the commencement of the cardinal's Mass a Sergeant Domínguez of the Los Angeles police had talked to him and other Católicos about their intent with respect to the Mass. "We told him that we had no intention whatsoever of disrupting the service," Cruz wrote. "He advised us that you [McIntyre] had instructed him to inform us that so long as we did not carry our banners and candles within the sanctuary, that we would be welcome to participate in the celebration of the Mass, and that the doors would remain open." [132] On the other hand, Gandara recalls that some priests came out of the church and informed the group that no further room was available.[133]

It appears, however, that upon discovering that the huge, heavy front doors of the church shut electronically, a small contingent of Católicos proceeded to enter the church through a side door. Earlier that evening García had walked to the church parking lot on the west side of the church and had seen a side door leading into the church. Curious, he had entered and discovered that he was in a large basement sanctuary where a second midnight Mass was in progress. He had walked down the side aisle and at the back discovered stairs that led up to the main vestibule or lobby of the church outside of the main sanctuary where the cardinal was saying Mass. When Católicos failed to open the outside door later, García informed some key people of the side entrance. García notes that about twelve to fifteen people followed him into the basement sanctuary, among them Razo and Zeta Acosta. Richard Cruz also joined the group. At least three others, including Rick Sánchez, found still another side entrance that led to the vestibule. Upon ascending the stairs to the main vestibule, García moved to open one of the main doors to allow the others outside to enter the church. "I went directly for the door," he remembers, "and I put my hand on the bar, when this big old undercover cop lifted me up away from the door." [134] In the vestibule, which is quite small, the Católicos had encountered a number of "ushers" who later turned out to be undercover county sheriffs. Monsignor Benjamin Hawkes, the pastor at St. Basil's, later testified that he had requested "extra ushers" from the Anchor Club, an organization of lay Catholics holding public jobs such as county sheriff. He requested them not only because of an anticipated large attendance at the midnight Mass, but because an informant within Católicos had reported the group's strategy for confrontation that evening. [135] Cruz later referred to this encounter as an "ambush." "When one of us merely reached for the door handle to the outside door," Cruz explained, describing García's attempt to open the door, "the usher struck the man in the back of the neck. Immediately, the usher in charge ordered the other ushers to throw us out, and in the twinkle of an eye, they viciously beat upon us and attempted to eject us." [136] However, when García had put his hand on the bar of the door, the automatic doors swung open, allowing some on the outside to come in. [137]

Richard Martínez recalls that as he and other Católicos entered the vestibule, they realized it was not going to be easy to go into the sanctuary, or main part of the church. Blocking the doors to the sanctuary were the ushers. Martínez notes that they were "not small." As Martínez and the others approached the ushers, they started to chant, "Let the poor people in! Let the poor people in!" As they attempted to open the sanctuary doors, Martínez remembers, "All hell broke loose." [138]

As the melee erupted, additional ushers entered from the side of the vestibule. Protestors and ushers in the vestibule and apparently also in the choir loft and basement were throwing punches, wrestling, and shouting at each other. Sánchez notes that he was spared being hit when one of the undercover sheriffs noticed he was wearing a suit and tie; the officer, according to Sánchez, quickly turned and hit someone wearing a guayabera. [139] Ruiz remembers that the congregation inside the church raised their voices in singing "O Come, All Ye Faithful" in an effort to drown out the calls of "Let the poor people in!" Although the Mass was being televised by KTLA, channel 5, viewers never saw the fighting, although the audio did pick up some of the shouting. [140]

In his fictionalized autobiography, Acosta insists that he was one of those inside the vestibule. [141] However, Ruiz, who had entered the church, did not see Acosta inside. "I do recall him being outside the church as the police descended upon us," Ruiz recalls. "Even though Oscar was a lawyer, he also wanted to get arrested. He kept running around yelling, 'Arrest me! Arrest me!' But the police refused to comply knowing he was our lawyer which agitated Oscar to no end."[142] Ruiz's testimony concerning Acosta, however, is contradicted by García, who insists that Acosta's account is accurate. At the same time, García disputes Acosta's claim that he had found the side door to the church. "I take credit for that," García asserts.[143]

Within a few minutes uniformed Los Angeles police in full riot gear who, according to Católicos, had been waiting behind the church in buses reinforced the ushers.[144] Declaring the demonstration to be an "unlawful assembly," the police, or "juras," as Gandara refers to them, moved into the crowd wielding their riot sticks and spraying mace both outside and inside the vestibule. "I felt a strong stream of something cold on my forehead," Pedro Arias, the "old man" of the Católicos, said as he described being maced, "and almost immediately I felt my eyes sting. Because of this, I could hardly see."[145] Ray Cruz still remembers the "angry, ugly faces of the police. You could see the hate in their eyes."[146] Acosta referred to the conflict as a "religious war, a holy riot in full gear."[147]

Inside the church, as the Mass came to an end, an irate Cardinal McIntyre, aware of the disturbance in the vestibule, condemned the action of Católicos. "We are ashamed of the participants," he told the congregation, "and we recognize that their conduct was symbolic of the conduct of the rabble as they stood at the foot of the cross, shouting, 'Crucify Him!'" However, the cardinal asked the congregation to forgive the demonstrators "for they know not what they do." *The Tidings*, the archdiocesan paper, later referred to the action of Católicos as the "new barbarism."[148] One church official called them "militant revolutionaries."[149] In addition, a newscaster, the former Los Angeles chief of police Tom Reddin, accused Católicos of practicing extortion against the Church.[150]

Outnumbered, the demonstrators retreated outside of the church and onto Wilshire Boulevard. In retreating, some of the demonstrators smashed one of the main doors of the church, according to Gandara, by throwing a heavy receptacle for cigarette butts or a pot at it.[151] As the people inside the church began exiting, Martínez recalls seeing one of the churchgoers literally flatten a young student demonstrator, who had to be taken to the hospital. In addition, the police arrested five of the protestors, whom the *Los Angeles Times* the next day referred to as the "club-swinging mob." One of those arrested, Alicia Escalante, was held by two police officers from behind, each holding one of her arms behind her back. Gandara recalls seeing another "jura" approach her as if threatening to hit her with his nightstick. He never got the chance. "I don't know where she got her strength," Gandara says of Escalante, "but she picked up her right foot and kicked the cop right in the *huevos* [testicles]." The officer went down on his knees. Television cameras caught Escalante's action. Those arrested were charged with conspiring to start a riot and assaulting an officer. Two of those arrested were Razo and Ruiz, who spent the rest of Christmas Eve in jail until bailed out the next day. Charges were later dropped, at least for those arrested that night. Zeta Acosta would later call the events of that evening a "police riot."[152] A Católicos news release further protested the actions of the police and of Cardinal McIntyre: "Women, children and innocent bystanders were clubbed without mercy from the police, the Church officials and the Cardinal who allegedly speaks for the Pope and Jesus Christ."[153] Those maced included senior citizens who had attended the Católicos Mass.[154]

Of the demonstration, Richard Cruz told a reporter that it "was a beautiful thing," although he "got it in the gut at the side door with a Billy club."[155] According to Ray Cruz, Richard was not surprised by the police violence. He had expected it, but sensed that the cardinal's use of violence would only reinforce the Católicos' demand for change.[156]

Following the demonstration, Richard Cruz and the other Católicos retreated in the early morning hours to their office at the Euclid Community Center to plot further actions and to secure bail for those arrested. Despite the police intervention, or because of it, Católicos expressed a sense of accomplishment, especially after seeing the wide media coverage the day after the protest. They believed they had gotten their message out, although this was but one step in a larger battle.[157] Gandara notes that he believed the demonstration outside of the church was a success, but he did not relish the "chingazos," or fisticuffs, that followed.[158]

The next day, Christmas Day, between fifty and one hundred protestors returned to St. Basil's and held a vigil across the street from the church in an empty lot on Wilshire. They also picketed in front of the church, some carrying pictures of those who had been injured and arrested the previous evening. They exchanged angry comments with the mostly Anglo parishioners as they entered for Mass. "Go back to Mexico!" some of the churchgoers shouted at the demonstrators. Police in civilian clothes in the meantime snapped photos of the protestors.[159] Outside the church, Richard Cruz told a reporter, "We're not going to stop demonstrating. The Cardinal will have to kill us to get us to stop."[160]

The vigil was marred, however, by the actions of Gloria Chávez, a member of Católicos and a community activist who entered St. Basil's during one of the Christmas Masses with a golf club in hand and proceeded to march down the main aisle before the ushers were aware of what was occurring. Acosta noted that it was a number seven wood.[161] When she reached the altar, she waved the club, scaring off the priest, and then pulled the altar cloth off, spilling the items on it, including the chalice, onto the floor. Police arrested Chávez "on suspicion of disrupting a religious meeting."[162] Lydia López recalls that Chávez's actions were "beyond the pale" and became a polarizing issue. Martínez observes that Chávez's actions were disavowed by most Católicos, who expressed disbelief that Chávez would go so far as to desecrate the altar.[163] García was not particularly surprised that she did such a thing because, according to him, she was "a gutsy woman."[164]

One day later, on December 26, Richard Cruz wrote a letter to Cardinal McIyntre in which he contradicted the cardinal's and the police's views of Católicos as a violent, revolutionary group. Using scriptural references, Cruz stressed that the protests were in keeping with the example of Jesus:

> Father, what we seek is a reformation of our Church even as Our Savior
> sought to regenerate the Pharisees and the Scribes whose concern was
> not with the Kingdom of God. . . . He is our Example, his methods of
> confrontation with the established authority is our strategy, even as
> he drove the money changers out of the Temple of God. . . . And if we
> appear as "rabble rousers crying for His death," we recall that He too,
> was called a glutten [sic] and a winebibber because he lived with and
> championed the cause of the poor and the downtrodden.

And as for those critics who attacked Católicos as being un-American and wanted them "to go back to where you're from" or who redbaited them as Communists, Cruz countered in his letter by observing, "We have no desire to return anywhere because in point of fact, this land is our land. We do not aspire to the communist ideology because we know it to be as reactionary and godless as is the racist reactionary and inhumane government of this country."

Finally, Cruz challenged McIntyre, as the representative of a forgiving Jesus, to act likewise and to forgive Católicos for whatever injury the cardinal believed they had done: "During your sermon on Christmas Eve, you prayed to God that He should forgive us because of our innocence. God cannot forgive us unless you, personally forgive us first. We seek your forgiveness not

FIGURE 5.3 Richard Cruz in front of St. Basil's Church, Los Angeles, December 25, 1969. Courtesy Department of Special Collections, Davidson Library, University of California, Santa Barbara.

only before God, but also before Man. Perhaps we might begin this Christian dialogue by your seeking to have the charges against the demonstrators dismissed." Cruz closed the letter by writing, "En Cristo." [165]

Receiving no response from the cardinal, Católicos continued the vigil at St. Basil's. This included a Mass on December 28 celebrated by Bishop Antulio Parrilla of Puerto Rico and attended by about 350 people. The bishop, in Los Angeles as part of a peace campaign against the war in Vietnam, sympathized with Católicos. "I am a bishop in good standing with the Holy See, in perfect communion with the Holy Father in Rome," he observed in his homily. "I have received permission from him [the Pope] to go preach the gospel to the poor people of our race, and that is what I am doing today. I am totally in support of the Chicano cause." The Mass, held in a vacant lot across from St. Basil's, was concelebrated by Father Mark Day, a Franciscan working with the farmworkers, and Father William Davis, a Jesuit from New York City.[166]

A week later Católicos and its supporters staged a three-day fast outside of St. Basil's.[167] People slept on the grass in front of the church. Of the fast, Richard Cruz stated, "We are Catholics who approach the demonstration of our faith in the spirit of Christ and under the banner of Our Patron Saint, La Virgen de Guadalupe. She is our only power and only source of wisdom, and the staff or La Virgen de Bronze should be our only weapon."[168]

Although Católicos had been in existence for only a couple of months, their demonstration at St. Basil's represented the climax of its short history. St. Basil's symbolized the differences and tensions between Católicos and the Church in Los Angeles. The Christmas Eve protest led to a variety of repercussions. As far as the Church was concerned, it denied the charges that it had been unresponsive to the Mexican American community. It pointed out its numerous educational and charitable services in East Los Angeles. At the same time, Monsignor William Johnson told a reporter that social action was not the main task of the Church. "The Church," he said, "tries to inspire people to live Christian lives, not to dictate particular solutions to social problems."[169] Although rhetorically holding its ground, the Church nevertheless moved to meet Católicos' challenge by instituting certain reforms or at least the appearance of reform.

These moves on the part of the Church were aided by the announced retirement of Cardinal McIntyre in early 1970. Whether the protests initiated against him by Católicos played a role in his retirement is hard to determine. One reporter believed that the cardinal's retirement was welcomed by the Vatican because of his seeming inability to deal with what the reporter called a "theology of resistance" carried out not only by Católicos but also by other discontented factions in the Church.[170]

Richard Cruz called the resignation of McIntyre a firing for his ultraconservative views. "The Pope fired McIntyre," he asserted. "McIntyre was both the symbol and reality of the completely turn-of-the-century mentality—paternalism with respect to the Chicano people. No matter what any historian ever says, no matter what the Church may say, we know that the Pope sent the delegate to can McIntyre's ass—the Pope fired his ass." [171] And in a further sarcastic comment to a reporter, Cruz added about the cardinal's departure, "I miss him. He was an organizer's delight." [172]

One group, the Coordinating Committee on Latin America, with an office in Los Angeles, specifically credited Católicos for the removal of McIntyre. "May I congratulate you upon what must be considered a victory for CPLR [Católicos] as revealed by the news of today," Glenn E. Smiley, the executive director, wrote to García. "I know you realize that the resignation or retiring of the Cardinal is only the first round in the *lucha* [the struggle] por La Raza, and that there is still the job to be done. More power to the people in this case." [173]

Political and Legal Ramifications

With Cardinal McIntyre's departure, the Church was in a better position to address the demands made on it by Católicos. McIntyre's successor, Archbishop Timothy Manning, was more disposed to pursue a conciliatory policy, within certain limits. García found him more "approachable." [174] Shortly after assuming office, Archbishop Manning met with representatives of Católicos and while he never conceded the issue of shared governance, he did proceed to address some of the other concerns of Católicos. For one thing, Manning helped end the grape boycott, which was called off when the growers agreed to recognize the farmworkers' union. Furthermore, Manning authorized additional funds for the Church's social and educational services in East Los Angeles. To deal with the issue of representation, Manning established an interparochial council of clergy and laypeople for the East Los Angeles parishes to serve as an advisory group to the archbishop. Cultural reforms included permission for Spanish-speaking parishes to include Latino music such as mariachis at Mass. Although it is not clear if Manning met again during the next several months with Católicos, he, on his own initiative, visited the home of Richard Cruz later that September and met with some members of Católicos. Ray Cruz recalls that while he, Richard, and the other Católicos present were diplomatic with Manning, his parents, by contrast, were in awe of the archbishop's visit to their home on Avenue 37. [175] Outside of Los Angeles, similar changes took place in other California and southwestern dioceses. [176]

On a broader level, the protests by Católicos as well as a growing restlessness on the part of Chicano clergy made an impression not only on the U.S. hierarchy but in Rome as well. In 1970, for example, the Vatican approved the appointment of the Reverend Patricio Flores of San Antonio as the first bishop of Mexican American decent in the United States. One year later, the Reverend Juan Arzupe, a Latino of Ecuadorian origins, was appointed auxiliary bishop in Los Angeles, a clear concession to Católicos' and other Chicano demands for more Latino representation in the Los Angeles Church. By 1974 three additional Latino priests were appointed bishops in the United States. Moreover, within the U.S. Church, working committees and conferences on the Spanish speaking were organized into the 1970s. This included the Primer Encuentro Hispano de Pastoral (First Hispanic Pastoral Encounter) that met in Washington, D.C., in 1972 under the U.S. Catholic Conference for the Spanish-Speaking and recommended a number of changes to make the Church more relevant to the Latino communities.[177]

For its part, Católicos still believed these concessions by the Church were largely cosmetic. In a February 1970 press release, Católicos declared that a personal meeting with Archbishop Manning had taken place, on January 22, but that Manning's subsequent written response to the group's demands was unsatisfactory, primarily because the archbishop still refused to accept adequate Chicano representation on his advisory committee concerning the Chicano community. Católicos noted that the Congress of Mexican-American Unity supported its position. Católicos also held the Church responsible for the prosecution of those Católicos indicted for their participation in the Christmas Eve protest. They concluded that if Manning did not provide concrete remedies Católicos would go over his head. "Thus, because we have the endorsement of our people, because the Church continues to ignore our just and Christian demands, has perpetrated violence upon us Christmas Eve and is presently treating twenty-one members of CPLR as criminals, because we seek a more relevant Church, we will continue our struggle and will, if necessary in the not-so-distant future, send representatives to the Vatican to plead our cause before the Holy Father, the Pope."[178]

Through 1970 Católicos continued to sponsor periodic vigils and picketing of the Church. On January 24, for example, Católicos mobilized about five hundred members and supporters who marched from downtown Los Angeles to St. Basil's to again call attention to their demands.[179] Later that spring, following Chicano student protests at Roosevelt High School in East Los Angeles, Católicos organized a march of about three hundred Chicano high school

students demanding that the Church do more to improve educational opportunities for Chicanos.[180]

These additional protests were highlighted by a baptismal certificate burning vigil held in front of St. Basil's on September 13, 1970, accompanied by an
outdoor Mass celebrated by Father Luis Jaramilla. This event, called a "Bautismo de Fuego" (Baptism of Fire), was spearheaded by Pedro Arias and his
family, who called on other Chicano Catholics to join them in burning their
baptismal certificates (no doubt influenced by the example of anti–Vietnam
War protestors burning their draft cards) as a way of protesting what Arias
claimed was still a reluctance on the part of the Church to become a Church
of and for the poor.[181] "CPLR [Católicos] will declare invalid their baptism into
the Catholic Church," a flyer announcing the protest read, "and they will baptize themselves into the true spirit of Christianity and Catholicism." [182] In his
homily, Father Jaramilla noted that by burning their baptismal certificates, he
and others "were not leaving the Church . . . we are the Church." [183] Richard
Cruz told a reporter that the ashes from the burned certificates would be sent
to Pope Paul VI as a plea for help in Católicos' struggle.[184]

Although Católicos through its confrontational tactics succeeded, directly
and indirectly, in forcing concessions from the Church, in the process it appears to have also alienated other Mexican American Catholics, especially
those not involved in the Chicano movement. Ruiz believes that, in part, this
was due to the propaganda by the archdiocese against Católicos, but that a
good portion of the blame lay with Católicos, who were not able to convince
other Mexican American Catholics that Católicos was neither anti-Catholic
nor anti-Church. "We miscalculated how deeply faithful Chicano Catholics
were and are towards the Church despite its failures in the community," he
notes. Some in the community told Ruiz, "Raul, tanto que te quiero, pero favor no ataques la iglesia [Raul, as much as we love you, please don't attack the
Church]." [185] One Mexican American, Alejandro Jesús González, wrote a letter
to Richard Cruz expressing his anger over the St. Basil demonstration:

> I had to write to you and state a few comments and reaction of Your
> Own People! I am Mexican! I love this country and I and my family
> work! Do you and your Gang of Hoodlums????
>
> I am thoroughly disgusted and sick at what you all did to St. Basil's
> and our Beloved Cardinal—I watched the Mass on t.v. and we all cried
> to think in this country, with all its goodness, any group would dare do
> such a thing!

If you don't like it here . . . go back to Mexico and live like a dog. . . .
take all your rebels with you too. . . . we don't need you and your
troublemakers![186]

Ruiz's concerns were supported by certain anti-Católicos manifestations
following the Christmas Eve protests. In early January 1970, for example, a
delegation of Mexican American Catholics visited Cardinal McIntyre and issued a prepared statement. They attacked Católicos as not being representative of the Mexican American Catholic community in Los Angeles. "We wish
to make clear our position as conscientious Catholics faithful to the hierarchy," they stressed. "These bearded revolutionary militants are not Mexican
in their totality, nor do they represent the Mexicans of Los Angeles, neither do
they represent Mexican-Catholics." [187] Later that week, this same group, joined
by others, participated in a Mass of Reparations at Our Lady Queen of Angels
Church (La Placita Church) in downtown Los Angeles. At the Mass, they made
their opposition to Católicos clear.[188] In addition, Católicos received hate letters accusing the group of being Communist. One anonymous note read,

> Communists Are Pigs
> Police Are Wonderful
> Support Your Local Police
> Register Commies.[189]

At the same time, Católicos received some letters of support for its actions.
Following the Christmas Eve protest, for example, Lorraine Armendáriz
wrote, "Our Lord said and did many things that upset the hierarchy when he
was here, so don't feel dismayed at the response you get from them." [190]

Although Católicos continued its criticism of the Church, it was significantly hampered by having to defend itself against new legal actions against
it. One month after the St. Basil's demonstration, twenty-one members and
supporters of Católicos were arrested for their participation in the Christmas Eve protest. Zeta Acosta referred to them as the St. Basil Twenty-One.[191]
Officers arrested Richard and Ray Cruz at their parents' home, where they
both lived on and off. They had expected to be arrested because they knew
that a police investigation had commenced after the Christmas Eve action.
Rosa Martínez, who lived with Richard, notes that he believed that the police
tapped his phone and that he was being followed.[192] They spent one night in

jail and then were released on their own recognizance.[193] According to Lydia López, who, although six months pregnant, was arrested along with her husband, Federico, there had been some earlier discussion among Católicos about whether they should go underground if threatened rather than be arrested. They decided to turn themselves in if threatened with arrest.[194] "I didn't want to run," Gandara observes about his arrest.[195] Charges ranged from disturbing the peace to assaulting an officer. Some of the charges were somewhat ludicrous. For example, Ray Cruz was charged with assaulting an officer with his religious candlestick. He was later acquitted.[196] Trying to relieve the pressure of the arrests, Richard Cruz, who in addition to his passion, according to his son Camilo, possessed a great sense of humor, jokingly teased Lydia López, "Lydia, have your baby in court. It'll be good for the movement."[197]

Zeta Acosta was retained as the attorney for the defendants, who were split into two separate trials that together lasted until June 1970. Acosta accused the Catholic Church in Los Angeles of prosecuting not only Católicos, but also all Mexican Americans.[198] The trials were characterized by Zeta Acosta's theatrical antics, as Ian Haney López so well documents concerning other Acosta cases, as does Acosta himself in his semifictional account of the trial in *The Revolt of the Cockroach People*, questioning the legitimacy of the legal process, especially with respect to the exclusion of Chicanos from the jury selection process.[199] He also requested that all Catholics be excluded from the jury since the Church had publicly censured the defendants. According to Acosta, the state was unconstitutionally interfering in a purely religious matter. The court rejected his request.[200] During the trials, the presiding judge found Acosta in contempt of court and sentenced him to three days in jail.[201] García notes that at one point in the trials, Acosta had to be suspended because he had not paid his bar dues.[202] Rosa Martínez, who attended the trials, notes of Acosta, "Zeta was amusing. The jurors loved him. He wore these outrageous ties. He was good. He did the best he could. We had fun. We all had lunch together each day."[203]

In the end, twelve of the defendants were found guilty. Some, like Martínez, Razo, and Richard Cruz, served from two to four months in jail for disrupting a religious service. Others, such as Ruiz and Arias, received minor fines.[204] The presiding judge specifically lectured Cruz upon his sentencing: "You among all the participants should have known better. Government by blow horn and tantrum will not be tolerated."[205] Although García, himself later an attorney, expresses much admiration for Zeta Acosta's commitment, he, in hindsight, now recognizes that Acosta, even though he had some help from at least one other attorney, took too much upon himself by attempting to represent all of the defendants.[206]

To protests the arrests, Católicos in March 1970 staged a rally, march, and prayer service at the Cathedral of St. Vibiana's, the official church of Archbishop Manning in downtown Los Angeles.[207]

Besides the police, the FBI also became involved in investigating Católicos, specifically on the Christmas Eve demonstration. It appears that one or more informants within Católicos reported to the FBI. Copies of the FBI reports were also sent to the Secret Service and, for unexplained reasons, to military officials in southern California.[208]

The distraction of the trials clearly affected the ability of Católicos to maintain its momentum. In addition, Chicano activists, including members of Católicos, because they wore many hats in the movement, were further distracted by the organization of the Chicano anti–Vietnam War movement during 1970. This buildup would itself climax on August 29, when over twenty thousand people, mostly Chicanos, demonstrated against the war in East Los Angeles. Richard Cruz and other Católicos helped organize the demonstration. Like the St. Basil protest but on a much larger scale, this manifestation of growing Chicano discontent and militancy over the war was forcibly attacked and destroyed by the Los Angeles County sheriffs, an act that led to a full-scale riot in East Los Angeles. Three people were killed, including the *Los Angeles Times* reporter Ruben Salazar. Richard Cruz saw this as another example of police overreaction, like that which had occurred at St. Basil's.[209] By that tragic day and certainly into the fall, Católicos for all practical purposes had ceased to exist as still other venues of social protest arose.

The Legacy of Católicos and Richard Cruz

Because of his leadership in Católicos, including his arrest for participating in the St. Basil's demonstration, Richard Cruz, even after graduating from law school in 1971, continued to pay a price for his convictions. He met resistance, along with García, in being certified as a practicing attorney despite passing the bar. The State Bar of California claimed that Cruz had committed "moral turpitude" because of his arrest for disturbing a religious service. Cruz fought this unjust opposition and with the support of the American Civil Liberties Union, along with Chicano community support, gained his right to practice law in 1973. Archbishop Manning, to his credit, testified in support of Cruz.

Like other members of Católicos, Cruz would remain a committed activist and champion of social justice until his death in 1993 at age fifty, the victim of lung cancer.[210] Camilo Cruz observes that his father was considered a "Chicanos' Chicano" because of his leadership.[211] His fellow attorney García, besides admiring Cruz's passion for the underdog, at the same time notes that he had a quick wit and great sense of humor. Cruz also loved to party and could out-party all his friends and colleagues. "In his 50 years," García observes with much fondness, "Richard lived a good 75."[212]

Hernán Sillas, a founding member of the Mexican American Legal Defense and Education Fund (MALDEF), in an obituary of Cruz, recalled as a young attorney meeting Richard and some of the other Chicano law students in the late 1960s. "It was quickly apparent that there were those who would never go back to the barrio and help its residents," he observed. "Richard was different. You knew instantly that he would go back and have an impact." Sillas referred to Cruz as a lawyer always on the right side.[213]

For Richard Cruz, the legacy of Católicos, besides the political issues involved, also had to do with more philosophical and even theological ones. "Personally," he wrote in 1976, "to myself and quite a few others, what it [Católicos] did was allow many of us to really once and for all get down to [the] . . . realities of who are we? Do we need religion?"[214] Cruz would later leave the Church and become an atheist, although still believing in a spiritual force in the world. Richard, Rosa Martínez notes, "was a spiritual person but not religious."[215] Católicos Por La Raza in an existential way proved to be not only a confrontation with the institutional Church, but also a confrontation with the Catholic soul of its participants. Although Cruz moved away from his faith—indeed, he was no longer a practicing Catholic by the time he was active in Católicos—he continued to believe that the Catholic Church had to be always made accountable to the people and had to serve the people. "He never abandoned his principles," Ray Cruz says of his brother.[216]

When Richard Cruz died on July 27, 1993, Camilo paid tribute to his father's commitment and, indirectly, to that of Católicos as a whole. He noted that the struggle had not been in vain and that their story would not be forgotten. "Dear Dad," Camilo eulogized,

Although I can't embrace you physically, I can embrace what you've done for me and our people. I want to especially thank you, my mother, and all the other brave warriors who challenged and fought the many hateful and oppressive institutions of this country. Because of the rebellion of the 1960s young Chicanos of today and the future have a few more chances at making it in this society. We don't have to worry as much as you did about having a voice, an existence, and about calling ourselves 'Chicanos.' In thinking of you, Dad, I think of the tremendous 1960's and the people you were involved with in creating the beautiful Chicano Revolution. Many things are still wrong, of course, but [we] are better now because of what you and others have left for us.[217]

SIX

Padres

Chicano Community Priests and the Public Arena

It is no longer sufficient for Church people to try to straddle a middle course, but it is necessary to advance the concrete application of the principle of justice.

—FATHER JUAN ROMERO

We addressed . . . issues from a justice perspective with the concept that injustice goes contrary to our faith.

—FATHER LUIS QUIHUIS

All of a sudden we had discovered a fascinating new entity—ourselves. . . . [N]ow we could be.

—FATHER VIRGILIO ELIZONDO

CATÓLICOS POR LA Raza marked a new chapter in Chicano/Church relations not only in Los Angeles, but in other areas of the Southwest as well where the majority of Chicano Catholics resided. Certainly movement activists began to demand more support from the Church for its agenda. In addition, some Chicano Catholic priests and sisters, inspired in part by Católicos as well as by Vatican II and liberation theology, represented what the theologian Harvey Cox in 1967 called the "New Breed in American Churches" and began organizing themselves and functioning as a pressure group within the Church to achieve reforms that would reflect Chicano interests.[1] This led to the formation of Padres Asociados para los Derechos Religiosos Educativos y Sociales (PADRES) and Las Hermanas.[2] This chapter concerns not the organization PADRES, but rather presents case studies of three individual Chicano priests, the padres, who, beginning in the movement years and beyond, have functioned as what I refer to as community priests.

In my work in Chicano history, one of the principal themes I have stressed is that of the role of leadership.[3] For the most part, I have addressed political and community leadership. In my recent work in Chicano Catholic history, however, I have been impressed with another form.[4] This is the leadership, both spiritual and temporal, of Chicano Catholic priests. Overlooked in Chicano history as well as in contemporary Chicano studies is the major part that many Chicano priests have played and continue to play in their communities. This gap also reflects the lack of emphasis by scholars on the contributions of Catholic parishes in providing both organization and a sense of community among Chicano Catholics, and here I am using the term *Chicano* in a generic sense, including both Mexican Americans and Mexican nationals. One fine exception is Roberto Treviño's recent study of Mexican American Catholics in Houston.[5]

As leaders, some Chicano priests represent a version of the "worker-priests" that surfaced in post–World War II Western Europe, principally in France. Reacting to the devastation, dislocation, and class unrest unleashed by the war, these priests left the safety of their churches and took the Church directly to the workers. Laboring in factories and industries, worker-priests immersed themselves in working-class life and culture as a way of promoting Catholic social doctrine. At first supported by the French Church hierarchy, many of the worker-priests left their parishes and secured employment in factories as a way of associating with the workers. They no longer lived in their comfortable rectories, but in poor working-class quarters. Some emerged as trade union leaders and merged their faith with socialist beliefs. As the worker-priests became more militant and public, the Church by the 1950s withdrew its support and brought an end to this experiment.[6]

Despite the short life of the worker-priest movement, what strikes me about the leadership they provided in their communities is how in these pre–Vatican II years they were redefining "Church" as "people." By the same token, some Chicano priests in our time, and probably earlier as well, embodied a modified version of worker-priests. By this I mean not that they are to be found working in factories but that, like their French counterparts, they are taking and have taken the Church beyond its institutionalized structure to the people themselves. Through their community leadership they have sought not only to redefine the Church, but also to assist in the empowerment of the Chicano community in the United States. They represent what Richard Martínez, in his study of PADRES, refers to as an "insurgent state of being."[7] As such, they symbolize what I call community priests. To an extent, of course, all Catholic priests are community priests in that they engage with their parish communities. The distinction I would make is that for some Catholic priests community primarily means ministering to the spiritual needs of their members within the institutionalized boundaries of their churches.

By contrast, community priests as I define them are those priests, of whatever ethnic background, who see their spiritual ministry as also involving being part of a community's struggles, or what David Badillo calls "social action," in areas such as civil rights, workers' rights, community empowerment, and community identity and self-respect.[8] Community priest are both inside and outside the institutional Church, but it is a separation that they do not recognize. Reflecting Vatican II influences as well as those of liberation theology, community priests are redefining the meaning of Church and the role of the clergy.

Community priests, however, must be distinguished from worker-priests in that they maintain their foothold in their parishes and rectories rather than apart from them. As a rule, they do not work primarily with labor unions, as did the worker-priests. Instead, community priests engage in a variety of community movements comprised for the most part of working-class Latinos who are not usually members of labor unions. In addition, community priests have not embraced the more radical socialist leanings of the French worker-priests but, instead, have reemphasized Catholic social doctrine as well as civil and human rights principles. Finally, community priests, because of their more moderate politics, have largely had the support of Church leaders in their work.

Still, despite the more moderate or liberal veneer associated with community priests, they share with worker-priests the deep belief that the Church cannot stand aside while its people face exploitation and discrimination. As Chicanos, the community priests identify with their ethnic community and with its suffering. Community priests are distinguished not only by taking the Church to the people, but also by transforming the American Church by bringing the people—Latinos—into the Church and Latinizing it. Latinization is forcing the institution to become even more public in addressing the needs of its growing Chicano and Latino working-class members. In this process, the community priests are examples of the Catholic Church's direct intervention in the public sphere and its relationship to the modern world.

In this chapter I look at examples of Chicano community priests on the basis of the oral histories of three Chicano priests: Father Juan Romero, a diocesan priest in Los Angeles; Father Luis Quihuis, a Jesuit in Santa Barbara;

and Father Virgilio Elizondo, a diocesan priest in San Antonio.[9] These priests embody three models of community priests: (1) the community activist; (2) the community organizer; and (3) the cultural worker. These categories are of significance only for an analysis of the concept of community priest and are not meant to be reductionist. All three priests in one way or another provide leadership in each category. The distinctions are meant only to stress a particular emphasis that characterizes the work of each.

Community Activist

Father Juan Romero has had a long personal involvement in the Chicano community. Born in New Mexico in 1938 during the last years of the Great Depression, Romero has always appreciated his family roots in that state. He is particularly proud of his family connections with Padre José Antonio Martínez, the nineteenth-century *nuevomexicano* priest described by Fray Angélico Chávez, who provided leadership to the Hispano community against the threats posed by the new Anglo-American order following the U.S.-Mexico war. This included challenging the equally new Catholic Church regime led by the French-born archbishop Jean Baptiste Lamy. Father Juan identifies with Father Martínez's struggle for social justice.[10]

Like many other Mexican Americans, Romero's parents migrated to California in order to find work. Romero was a young boy at the time. Settling in East Los Angeles, his father, an accountant, found employment with the newly established aviation industry as World War II broke out.

Raised in a family that was very religious—his father played a leadership role in a variety of Catholic lay groups—and attending Catholic school in East Los Angeles, Romero at a very early age felt he possessed a vocation to the priesthood. He pursued his vocation by entering the local seminary after elementary school. He studied at the minor seminary in Los Angeles and at the newly opened St. John's major seminary in Camarillo. While there, Romero displayed his leadership skills and his interest in and passion for civil rights and social justice. He also knew he wanted to work in the Chicano community and helped organize a Spanish-language radio program, "La Voz Guadalupana," that included religious issues such as the lives of the saints. Situated in a farming community, St. John's was also in close proximity to bracero camps peopled by the Mexican contract workers who had been entering the country under the World War II labor agreement between the United States and Mexico. Romero, along with other seminarians, visited the camps and met with the workers, and he assisted at the Masses at the camps said by the priests from the seminary. "I enjoyed going there and talking with the men," he recalls. "It was a good experience for me." [11]

After his ordination in 1964, Father Juan was first assigned to St. Francis' Church in East Los Angeles, where, because of the impoverished conditions in this parish, he became more politically conscious of social injustice. "It helped radicalize me," he observes.[12] In addition to becoming aware of barrio conditions, Father Juan also witnessed a lack of cultural sensitivity on the part of the Irish American pastor, who, despite the reforms of Vatican II (which allowed priests to say Mass in the vernacular rather than in Latin), refused to allow Father Juan to say Mass in Spanish, despite the fact that about 80 percent of the parishioners were Mexican. The pastor insisted on English-only Masses as his concession to Vatican II. Father Juan thought the pastor had "blinders" on, and this started him questioning the rigidity of the institutional Church.[13]

Two years later, he was sent to Our Lady of Guadalupe Church in Santa Barbara. Here he participated in some of the first *cursillos*, or lay retreats, aimed at promoting religious leadership among Chicano Catholic laypeople.[14] At this time he also developed an interest and association with César Chávez, himself a cursillista. He was invited along with other priests to San Jose to attend a meeting concerning the Church's relationship with Spanish-speaking laity. Chávez addressed the priests and noted that while many Protestant ministers, especially through the Protestant-led Migrant Ministry, were supporting the farmworkers' cause, very few Catholic priests were involved, even though the majority of the workers were Catholic. This impressed Father Juan, who vowed to become one of those committed priests. It was as if Chávez's spiritual power had spoken directly to him. "This was the first time that I had met César," Romero later wrote, "and [I] was greatly impressed with his style, firmness, soft-spoken manner, and the way he very directly challenged church people to be present in the struggle of the farm worker." He was particularly struck by Chávez's wholeness as a person and his spirituality: "[He possessed an] integratedness, a beautiful combination of toughness and gentleness, the best qualities of masculinity and femininity, and his deep spirituality, which some people thought was contrived but it was close enough to see that it really was religious, a conviction of a faithful person." [15]

Father Juan met Chávez again in 1968 in Santa Barbara at the Franciscan seminary where he was recuperating from his twenty-five-day fast. "He had undertaken this fast," Romero noted of Chávez, "as a sacred discipline for himself, to affirm his own commitment to nonviolence, and to be an example to his fellow *campesinos*. It was by no means a show, but a genuinely religious act." [16] Father Juan further noted that Chávez's close connection to the Franciscans and to the teachings of St. Francis, in particular on serving the poor, had given Chávez a "Franciscan spirit." [17] Shortly thereafter, Romero deepened his involvement with the farmworkers' cause when he attended a talk by the Reverend Wayne C. Hartmire, a Protestant minister and one of the leaders of the Migrant Ministry. Hartmire likened the ministers who were working with the union to the famous worker-priests in Europe. Romero had read about the worker-priests in seminary, but now he recognized that he could emulate them by working with the farmworkers. "I thought how ironic it was that priest-workers in the United States," he reflected, "were neither priests in our usual understanding nor were they even Catholics. They were Protestant ministers who took seriously the challenge of the Gospel, and patterned much of their own life and ministry after the noble experiment of the priest-worker movement." [18] Romero joined those ranks and later served as a board member of the interfaith National Farm Worker Ministry (Migrant Ministry). "Advocacy of justice for farm workers through a prayerful strike and boycott," he observed, "is a significant ministry which affirms the human dignity of migrant farm workers." [19]

Beginning in Santa Barbara, Father Juan commenced a three-decade period of involvement with and support of the farmworkers. "Because of the struggle of the United Farm Workers Union (UFW) in the fields of California and the boycott cities of the nation," Romero wrote in 1974, "there is emerging among poor people in general and Mexican farm workers in particular a new consciousness that '¡Sí, se puede!' They can be masters of their own destiny and bring about a change in those socioeconomic and political structures which hold them in bondage." [20] In each of his parishes, he organized support for the strike and for both the grape and lettuce boycotts as well as raised funds for the strikers. In Los Angeles, Romero worked with the Interfaith Committee to Aid Farm Workers. Part of the committee's work involved mediation between agribusiness owners and the UFW. But the committee also advocated justice for farmworkers. "It is no longer sufficient for Church people to try to straddle a middle course," Romero stressed, "but it is necessary to advance the concrete application of the principle of justice." [21] As part of their commitment, Romero and the committee often met with supermarket officials to try to convince them not to sell nonunion grapes.[22] Father Juan further spearheaded a successful effort in 1970 to place an advertisement in *The Tidings*, the archdiocesan paper of Los Angeles, signed by over eighty priests and calling for the right of workers to join a union of their choice and the right to strike

FIGURE 6.1 Father Juan Romero (*right*) with (from *left to right*) Father Luis Olivares, C.M.F., Dolores Huerta, and César Chávez, Los Angeles, circa 1970s. Courtesy Father Juan Romero.

and endorsing the grape boycott.[23] Other efforts by Romero in support of the farmworkers included leafleting in front of supermarkets to promote the grape and lettuce boycotts as well as conducting a survey among farmworkers in the Coachella Valley that revealed strong support among the workers to join the UFW as opposed to rival unions such as the Teamsters.[24]

Along with other priests and sisters, in 1973 he was arrested outside Fresno when a group joined striking workers in opposing restrictions on picketing activities. Romero and the others challenged the morality of the injunction through civil disobedience. They had been inspired to participate in civil disobedience by Chávez. Of this encounter, Romero wrote,

> In his powerful and quiet way, César can truly move a crowd. He was honest, tough and straightforward as he spoke of the importance of unity, union and nonviolence. He underscored the importance of asserting our rights here in Fresno where freedom of assembly and speech is unconstitutionally denied by an unjust injunction. He also asked: "What are you going to say when our children and grandchildren ask you, 'Were you on that strike?' and 'Did you go to jail?'"[25]

A total of sixty clergy and religious leaders were arrested, men and women, Catholic and Protestants, including Dorothy Day, the famed head of the Catholic Workers' Movement. The protestors were held for almost two weeks before being released. Romero later recalled,

> When I joined the picket line on the morning of August 2, the line captains were very careful that we remain on public (state) property . . . and that we not trespass the private property of the grower. The line itself was well ordered and disciplined, although noisy: *Huelga!* [strike] *Vengan compañeros* (join us comrades) *Esquiroles!* (scabs) Chávez sí!, Teamsters no! The point of the pickets and gathering was precisely to challenge the injunction which was calculated to diminish the effectiveness of the strike. Shortly after we arrived, two large Gray Line buses, empty except for the driver, came and waited. A Spanish-surnamed sheriff's officer said he spoke in the name of the people of California, and through his efficient mobile loud speaker system informed us that we were "An unlawful assembly!" . . . By 9 o'clock that morning, most of us were arrested and by 11 o'clock were booked and jailed. Our stay was unexpectedly prolonged for almost two weeks, which became a time of prayer and literal fasting for many of us in order to cast out demons of injustice and oppression which are still the lot of many migrant farm workers in our land.[26]

His longtime support of the farmworkers and migrant workers in general is proof that, in his role as community priest, Father Juan has consistently reminded the Church of its moral obligation to the poor and oppressed. "The Church has traditionally shown its interests and official pastoral concern for people who migrate," he asserts, "but rarely translated that into political action for the benefit of migrants. Policies which favor those economic interests which exploit human beings by treating them as cogs in a machine—pools of temporary cheap labor, only to be discarded when no longer useful, are directly against Gospel values of justice and the dignity of the human person."[27]

Using Chávez as his model of faith and social commitment, Romero in the late 1960s participated in drug rehabilitation programs for *pintos* (Chicanos in prison). Moreover, having been involved in small anti–Vietnam War protests while in Santa Barbara in the mid-1960s, Romero helped organize other Chicano priests and some members of his Orange County congregation to participate in the National Chicano Anti-War Moratorium of August 29, 1970. He had met with Rosalio Muñoz, one of the main organizers of the moratorium, who had requested Chicano priests to join what proved to be a historic protest by about twenty thousand people. Following the police riot that disrupted the proceedings and the killing of Ruben Salazar, a veteran *Los Angeles Times* reporter and the KMEX news director, Romero within a few days arranged for a press conference. Featuring Bishop Patricio Flores of San Antonio, the conference was organized to protest the destructive actions of the Los Angeles County sheriffs and the death of Salazar.

Father Juan's community activism was furthered after the formation of PADRES in 1969. An assembly of Chicano priests from throughout the Southwest that Romero helped to organize, PADRES aimed to foster change within the Catholic Church by increasing the role of Chicanos and empowering the Chicano Catholic community. The formation of PADRES as a Chicano priest advocacy group solidified Romero's political identity as a Chicano. "I felt comfortable calling myself Chicano because it had clear political connotations that I supported."[28] PADRES elicited what Father Juan refers to as the "collective *coraje*," or anger, of its members to combat social injustice.[29]

Although PADRES did not publicly refer to liberation theology, it clearly embraced its key concept of a Church of and for the poor and oppressed. "PADRES promoted a liberation theology and its scriptural hermeneutic," Romero later observed, "which promoted getting involved with the poor and oppressed who have greater need."[30] The emphasis by PADRES on working against social injustice was also in keeping, Romero believed, with Vatican II's call for the Church to be actively involved in the modern world. Of this connection, he commented, "God has inspired individuals and movements to act in new ways and with various styles of leadership in order to try to adequately meet the particular needs and challenges of changing times."[31]

PADRES sought to shift the emphasis, as Romero notes, away from ministry among Hispanics to "Hispanic ministry"—the agency of Chicano priests themselves. Besides calling for the appointment of Chicano bishops (of which there were none in 1969), PADRES endorsed a variety of social issues, such as education of the Mexican American poor through bilingual education, care of the impoverished poor, and support for the UFW grape boycott. It also called for welfare reform, housing and health services for Chicanos, and new youth initiatives to deal with the gang problems.[32]

From 1972 to 1975, Romero served as executive director of the new organization composed of about 130 mostly Chicano priests. One of his central leadership roles was the establishment of what was called the Mobile Team Ministry in connection with the Mexican American Cultural Center in San Antonio and funded by the Campaign for Human Development of the U.S. Catholic bishops. Influenced by the writings and work on literacy and consciousness of Paulo Freire in Brazil and by the developing theology of liberation in Latin America, the Mobile Team Ministry was a traveling contingent of certain PADRES members, along with religious sisters and others, including some Chicano Protestant ministers, who attempted to raise the critical consciousness of poor and disenfranchised Chicanos. The group traveled to parts of the Southwest and also made a few forays into such locations as Chicago, Detroit, New York City, and Miami. The ministry also promoted civic involvement to deal with issues of discrimination and social justice. Voter registration drives formed part of the agenda, and the ministry organized workshops of thirty to fifty people at each location. Romero and his colleagues stressed Freire's concept of *conciencia crítica*, which Father Juan noted was not just consciousness raising but mobilizing people to take action. "*Concientización*," Romero stresses, "was not just a cliché for us; it made sense to us."[33] In applying Freire's concepts, Romero and the ministry aimed to politicize the dignity of the people. This politicization, in turn, would lead to political action by the people to change their conditions. Besides reading Freire's writings, some members of PADRES traveled to Latin America to learn more about his approach. Romero applied to his superiors for permission to travel but was denied.[34]

Besides Freire's influence, the ministry also employed from liberation theology the concept of *comunidades eclesiales de base*, or Christian base communities that involved biblical reflections on particular social problems, but also with the intent to act on these reflections. Here, Father Juan likewise employed St. Thomas Aquinas's call to "observe, judge, and act."[35] "We were beginning to articulate social problems theologically and with a sense of community," Romero recalls.[36]

Although the Mobile Team Ministry was effective up to a point, it was limited with respect to personnel and resources. As a result, Romero and PADRES made arrangements with the Industrial Areas Foundation (IAF) in Chicago, led by Saul Alinsky, to advance and revise the concept of base communities by establishing more extensive and permanent organizations centered around parishes. This represented a logical extension of the ministry concept. The first successful effort was COPS, or Communities Organized for Public Service, in San Antonio, which was formed in the mid-1970s. While not, strictly speaking, a base community (which tend to focus more on small Bible study groups), COPS reflected the *comunidades'* stress on linking reflection with action. It was to serve the poor through base community formation. "It [COPS] tirelessly worked to resolve issues about what people were truly interested and what affected the well-being of the community," Father Juan observed.[37]

Romero was not directly involved in the formation of COPS, but he did help form its Los Angeles counterpart, UNO (United Neighborhoods Organization). After his stint with PADRES, he returned to Los Angeles to his old family church, St. Alphonse, on the east side. There, working with people like Ernie Cortés, who had worked with Alinsky, Romero was one of several priests in East Los Angeles, including Father Luis Olivares (see Chapter Seven), who brought together eighteen parishes to form UNO. Each parish put together councils of priests, religious sisters, and laypeople. They identified issues held in common by all parishes. "Whatever the particular issue that is discussed," Romero commented, "it is always specific, concrete, sometimes controversial, and has a particular name and/or place connected with it. It corresponds to a real and unselfish SELF-INTEREST of the person. It is thus able to move him or her, together with others, into focused action to deal with that situation."[38]

As Romero notes, the trick was to go beyond recognizing problems to focus on issues that help to develop critical thinking. A problem, according to him, is something that nobody can do anything about unless it is first analyzed and dissected. At this point, it moves from being a problem to becoming an issue or issues that "you attach a name to . . . and a place." Issues, Romero contends, are winnable. UNO stressed taking on only issues that were winnable. This created a sense of empowerment in the people. The people were trained to understand the root sources of their problems but then to take practical, accomplishable steps to correct them.[39]

As base communities, UNO and the various parish councils identified specific community issues that would lead to community action and, at the same time, to the development of local organic leadership. Some of the members, including Father Juan, attended leadership-training sessions organized by the

IAF. Romero notes that many of these emerging leaders were Mexican American women, a sizable number of whom were already involved in some form of parish work. Their involvement with UNO was an extension, although a political one, of their church work. "In all parishes that have a Latino population," Romero observes, "the main workers and movers are the women: *abuelitas* and their daughters and their granddaughters. So nothing is going to move without the women."[40]

Through parish meetings, personal interviews, and house meetings, issues were brought forth, and through collective action and pressures on elected officials new leadership surfaced. As Romero said, "Reflecting and acting together on those things [issues] involves a process through which strong relationships of trust and confidence are built, leaders are discovered and formed, and issues for collective action are clarified. In this process, awareness is pricked and awakened. People begin to see that things could be different if they work together to change a bad situation to a much better one. This kind of ongoing survey is much more valuable to pastoral agents of the Southwest."[41]

But UNO, according to Romero, was not a vanguard organization or composed of just an elite group. It represented a mass movement of barrio people to empower themselves. It was this mass that gave them power when by the hundreds they attended public meetings before governmental officials to exert pressure for community reforms. It was clearly a way of refocusing the meaning of *Church*. One of the first successful issues that UNO confronted was the excessive auto insurance rates in East Los Angeles. Through organization and the application of consistent pressure on insurance companies and county supervisors, UNO succeeded in reducing rates up to 38 percent. Parish-based UNO chapters, as Peter Skerry has shown, subsequently pursued other, similar local issues. These included the construction of new street and traffic lights in the barrio.[42]

The success of COPS and UNO helped to raise political consciousness and led to the empowerment of the Chicano communities in both San Antonio and Los Angeles. At the same time, it created a different perception of the Church by laypeople involved. Rather than seeing it as only a religious institution, the laity began to recognize it as a leadership force in the community itself. According to Romero, the laity began to think critically "but not just in an analytical level but at a strategic level that led to political action."[43] And rather than seeing the priests as aloof religious figures, they began to see figures such as Father Juan as key community leaders.

Since 1976 and the formation of UNO, Romero has continued to be active in the community, among other things, by supporting the sanctuary movement for Central American refugees in the 1980s. Today, although retired, Father Juan maintains an active involvement with the issues affecting his parishioners. He remains an example of a Chicano community priest.

Community Organizer

Father Luis Quihuis was the pastor of Our Lady of Sorrows church in downtown Santa Barbara. He was born in 1951 in Phoenix into a large, strongly religious family of Basque ancestry on his father's side with roots in Arizona extending back to the nineteenth century. Quihuis's parents on both sides were from ranching families. His paternal grandfather, like everyone in his family, believed in education. He educated not only his own children, but also the children of his employees. Father Luis's father's name was Francisco Vásquez Quihuis and his mother's was María del Carmen Córdoba. Both were college educated, and his father served in World War II.[44]

Father Luis attended St. Mary's elementary and high school in Phoenix, which was run by the Franciscans and staffed also by the Precious Blood Sisters. But the foundational source of his moral socialization came from his parents and grandparents. His family on both sides was extremely devout and imposed their commitment to their faith on their children.[45]

Furthermore, his family stressed social justice issues and helping those less fortunate. "We were raised traditional Catholics with strong Catholic values," he noted, "but more importantly it kind of forced us to get actively involved in justice related issues, working always on behalf of the downtrodden and poor."[46] In addition to imparting these values to his children, his father, he recalled, was active in local Mexican American Democratic Party politics and was a member of several community organizations, including the Viva Kennedy Clubs in the 1960 presidential election. His mother belonged to several organizations, primarily religious ones such as the Women's Auxiliary of their parish church, and was at one time president of the Women's School Auxiliary at St. Mary's school.[47]

At the dinner table, issues of justice and politics were not uncommon topics of conversation. Father Luis recalled his parents saying, "Discrimination only takes place if you let it overpower you."[48] Religious and political discourse and practice were carried out in an ethnic context so that the Quihuis children grew up with a sense of pride in being Mexican and being bilingual. "We never shunned our identity as mexicanos," he stressed. "We didn't say we were Spaniards. We were not afraid or ashamed to say who we were and I think that's something that my parents always taught us."[49]

Family socialization was buttressed by Quihuis's Catholic education. Attention to the African American civil rights movement led by Dr. Martin Luther King, Jr., and discussions about the Vietnam War were part of his high school classroom learning. "Some would say that we're fighting Communism," he noted of these discussions. "Then the whole question of what is Communism? Do we just accept what the press tells us? Why were we interfering in other peoples' lives and governments and getting rid of governments? We really had no business in telling people how to govern themselves." [50] Father Quihuis believed that the openness at his school to discussing controversial issues was linked to Vatican II and the call for the Church to be more open to the world. "Vatican II opens the door," he observed, "and says that issues are no longer just black and white but that there's a lot of gray and it's good if you look at the gray, too." [51]

Since elementary school, Quihuis believed he had a vocation for the priesthood. He remembered that in the seventh grade he wrote an essay on this topic. "It was probably the first time I began to feel a call." [52] He served as an altar boy through elementary and high school. His parents supported his vocation but left the decision to pursue it up to him: "They gave me total freedom. They said it's your decision, not ours. But if you feel that it's God who's really calling you, then by all means you have our blessing." [53]

At the same time, he wanted to experience more of life before making a final decision. After graduating from high school, he enrolled at Arizona State University (ASU) in Phoenix in 1969 in order to be close to his family, even though he had been accepted at more prestigious schools. He remained in Phoenix also because of his strong reaction to the death of a very close cousin, Michael Barreras, who died tragically in a car accident. His cousin's death made Father Luis appreciate his family even more. At ASU, he majored in business because he loved mathematics and economics; he intended to become a stockbroker, but he was uncertain whether to pursue a secular career or a religious one. As an undergraduate student, Luis displayed the leadership talents that would characterize his later religious and community life. This included being elected in his freshman year to represent the business students in the student government. As a member of the student council, he helped to remove the ROTC requirement for undergraduates. He also participated in Chicano student activities through MEChA and Mexicanos Unidos, especially in organizing cultural events around Cinco De Mayo and El Día de los Muertos. As a strong, practicing Catholic, he joined the Newman Club, the campus Catholic student organization. It was at the Newman Center in the late 1960s that he first learned about liberation theology. "This was just a year after the historic 1968 Medellín conference in Colombia that first set out the key tenets of liberation theology," he noted.

> It was the whole question of poverty and preferential option for the poor that first started to come up. I remember one of the lectures [at the Newman Center] was the whole question of Christ in the face of the poor. It was a Dominican from Mexico City. He asked "who is actually poor?" By this he meant that too many times we fall into the trap of thinking of the poor as simply those who are economically disadvantaged. But the poor is anyone who lacks in being truly a whole person. It could be psychological problems; it could be illness; it could be anything that keeps you away from being a whole and total person. These were all the poor as he described them and how the new theology that was coming out was being called liberation theology. I found this lecture fascinating because it gave me insight into how there are certain barriers that keep people from fully participating as whole human beings.[54]

At the Newman Center, Father Luis also helped to organize the December 12 feast day of Our Lady of Guadalupe: "We would do a procession. There was money available and we would get a mariachi group for the *mañanitas* [early morning songs honoring Guadalupe] at 5 in the morning. But this was not just for Chicanos on campus. We invited everyone. It was a time to share Chicano culture with others."[55]

As an undergraduate, Quihuis was likewise fortunate to take an introduction to anthropology class taught by the eminent scholar Margaret Mead. From her, he learned to further appreciate different cultures and how to avoid the "tendency in the human person to try to paint reality as they want it to be rather than how it really is. That's what I learned from her. In other words, with her it was don't just accept. Question it. Look at it from other perspectives."[56]

It was also at ASU that, like Father Juan, Quihuis had an impressionable encounter with César Chávez. The farm labor leader was in Phoenix in 1972 to promote the lettuce strike and to get people to stop buying lettuce, especially from Safeway stores. To this end, Chávez was engaged in one of his periodic fasts. Along with many other Mexican Americans, Quihuis visited Chávez and expressed his support in prayer sessions during the nine days of his fast in the south Phoenix barrio. Father Luis observed that the nine days were symbolic of a Catholic novena, a period of prayer lasting the same number of days. "César was very much aware of the importance of the Church for the Latino community," Quihuis said. "Everything that César did always involved the Church and Our Lady of Guadalupe."[57] Of this initial encounter with Chávez, Father Luis stressed, "I liked him from the very beginning. My first meeting with him was kind of in awe. Here was a very simple man who had been able to bring a movement together for a just cause."[58] Again like Juan Romero, what impressed Quihuis the most about the farm leader was his deep spirituality and how this seemed to guide and support his politics. "Anybody can have a social movement or a justice movement and may not produce faith," he recalls about his encounter, "but if it is based on faith . . . it will endure forever."[59] The concept of a faith-based movement such as Chávez's would remain a model for Quihuis. "Later as a Jesuit," he stated, "I spoke out against injustice sometimes even within my own order and within the Church."[60]

Following his graduation from ASU in 1973, Quihuis, who had a steady girlfriend in college, still felt that he had a vocation, but he was not ready to pursue it. Instead, he was hired as assistant to the speaker of the Arizona House of Representatives. He was responsible for upgrading and modernizing the legislative process and the reorganization of state agencies so that they could be more effective and efficient in delivering human services. This brought him significant fortune and power at age twenty-three. "They used to say that I was the power behind the throne," he joked.[61] When hired, he was making nearly seventy thousand dollars a year, an amount that, according to him, would today be equivalent to more than double that amount. In his administrative capacity, he focused on social legislation such as health care, which was consistent with his interests and religious and social values. He remained in this position from 1974 to 1982.[62]

Despite his good fortune, and maybe because of it, Quihuis never lost sight of his vocation. He felt a void in his life. Finally, after a thirty-day retreat at the Trappist monastery in Gethsemani, Kentucky, made famous by Thomas Merton, he decided in 1981, at age thirty-one, to enter the Jesuit order. He gave his considerable savings and possessions, including a car and a condominium, to his family and others, keeping only some artwork. As a Jesuit novice, Quihuis was pleased that, besides his studies, he was able to continue to pursue his interests in community and social issues. He worked with the poor in Los Angeles, Orange County, and the Imperial Valley. He returned to work with the sick and dying in Phoenix.

As part of his philosophy studies, he went to Spain for two years, where his interest in liberation theology deepened after he met Gustavo Gutiérrez, the leading liberationist theologian, as well as other Latin American theologians such as Jon Sobrino. Two aspects of liberation theology appealed greatly to him. One was the preferential option for the poor, and the other was the use of economic theory guided in part by Marxist concepts to understand what liberationists call "social sin," that is, the economic injustice prevalent in too many societies.[63] Quihuis's interest in liberation theology later expanded when he traveled to Brazil for additional study. Remaining there for more than three years, he participated in the base communities movement (*comunidades de base*), linking faith to community issues, and met and studied with Dom Helder Camara, Brazil's leading liberationist theologian. From Dom Helder, Quihuis learned that liberation theology should not be linked just to social and economic issues, but also to fostering the popular religiosity of the people. It was their popular religion that kept their faith alive and aided them in their struggle to liberate themselves. In Brazil, Father Luis also immersed himself in the writings and work of Paulo Freire and his concept of *educación popular*, which linked community experience to literacy and education.[64]

Following his return from Spain to the United States and before being ordained, Quihuis was dispatched in the mid-1980s by the Jesuits to be their chief lobbyist in Washington, D.C. as assistant director of social ministries. Here he concentrated on faith and justice issues. He was part of the religious coalition that opposed the Supreme Court nomination of Robert Bork in 1987, a staunchly conservative jurist with little record of being sensitive to civil rights issues.[65] The nomination was defeated. He also helped forge the successful religious organization opposed to reintroducing funding for the Nicaraguan contras, the right-wing military forces supported by the Reagan administration who were fighting to topple the Sandinista revolutionary government.[66]

Skillful in organizing on the basis of his personal talents and his legislative experience, Father Luis, after his ordination in 1992, was assigned to the University of San Francisco (USF), a Jesuit institution. He was specifically asked by the president of the university to organize and launch a new outreach initiative in the Latino community of San Francisco, which was composed of Central Americans, Mexicans, and other Latin American groups. Father Luis eagerly accepted. He was given his own budget and had direct access to the president's office and to all department heads. In the following nine years, Father Luis would become an example of the concept of a community priest and, more directly, of a priest community organizer.[67]

FIGURE 6.2 Father Luis Quihuis, S.J., with Dolores Huerta, San Francisco, 1997.
Courtesy Father Luis Quihuis, S.J.

The Martyrs of El Salvador Project, named after the six Jesuits and two
laypersons killed by the military in El Salvador in 1989 during that country's
civil war, represented USF's effort to take the university to the Latino community. "It was an exercise in the university recapturing part of its motto [as
a university]," Father Luis explained; "so we were moving back into the community."[68] Based on the model of the *comunidades de base* and Freire's concept of *educación popular*, the idea was to develop leaders who were members
of the community rather than having the university do everything. "It was not
the university of the ivory tower coming down with all the answers to tell the
people what their problems and needs were," explained Quihuis.[69] Focusing
on the Mission District, the main Latino area of San Francisco, and center-
ing its activities at St. Peter's, the largest Catholic church in the Mission, the
project first organized community meetings to identify issues. Because of its
location in the barrio, St. Peter's, along with other Latino Catholic churches,
was tuned into what Father Luis called the "pulse of the people."[70] A community board composed of fifteen community leaders, parents, representatives of community groups, and youth, both men and women, was formed; it
met once a month and also attended regular general community meetings at
St. Peter's.[71] "The board would identify its own needs and based on the identi-

fication of these needs, then we would move the resources needed to help solve these issues and problems out in the community."[72] As he further observed, "We were in partnership with the community."[73]

After a series of gatherings, various key issues were identified, the crucial ones being education and health. On education, Father Luis, with the assistance of Sister Ignatius of the Sacred Heart of Mary order, started a tutoring program at the church, USF students serving as the tutors and as teachers' aides. The tutoring program initially focused on St. Peter's parochial school, which, because of its overcrowded conditions, had increased class sizes and thereby diminished the attention that teachers could provide individual students. Over 570 students attended in double sessions. "So you had two kindergartens, two seventh grades, eighth grades, and so forth," Father Luis recalled. "So we began a series of tutoring programs in which we got our students at USF involved in working as either teacher's aides in the classroom or after school and helping to deal with some of the deficiencies one on one with the students." This successful program then expanded to providing tutoring after school to public school children.[74]

In addition, Quihuis got the School of Education at the university to work with the teachers from St. Peter's to assist them in devising new approaches to pedagogy and curriculum. This involved a series of seminars that included child psychology. Other seminars focused on mathematics and science. Cognitive methodology was linked to multicultural approaches. "In a short time," Quihuis proudly recalled, "we began to see tremendous changes in the academic performances of the children."[75]

Moreover, USF started scholarship programs for Latinos as well as recruitment to the university. These scholarships were called Saber es Poder (knowledge is power) and provided five thousand dollars in assistance. To receive one of the scholarships, a student had to agree to work in the community as part of Father Luis's program. Latino enrollment at USF more than doubled during Quihuis's tenure as director of the project, going from less than 5 percent to over 12 percent of the student population.[76]

Community education also involved parenting classes. This centered on socializing Latino parents, impressing upon them the importance of education for their children. In addition, parents were instructed on the negative effects of domestic violence on children's psyche, how that, in turn, affected their performance in school and led students to join gangs to get the support they were not getting at home. Parents were further taught how to deal with their children's drug abuse, including how to search a room without the child feeling that his or her privacy was being violated. Communication between parents and their children was stressed, especially in light of the fact that children were beginning to communicate in English while the parents retained their Spanish. Finally, parents were informed that they had rights with respect to the schools; that even though they spoke only Spanish, they, as parents, could demand to meet with teachers and principals, and that the schools had to provide translators for these meetings. Attendance at these meetings did not pose a problem because financial aid given to St. Peter's students was contingent on parents going to the meetings.[77]

On health issues, the project responded to the lack of school nurses in both the parochial and public schools in the Mission by asking student nurses from the School of Nursing at USF to volunteer at the schools. Health records for the children were updated, including immunization dates, and nutritional classes for both parents and students were started. The student nurses discovered that many of the children arrived at school in quite a hyperactive state, and this made it difficult for them to concentrate on their classes. They referred to this as "concentration defect." By checking the child's blood pressure, the nurses discovered that it was highly elevated in the morning. By noon it had come down, and the student would then suffer a depressive syndrome that made them lethargic and again unable to concentrate on their lessons. Upon inquiring, the nurses discovered that most of these poor children had only sugared coffee and sugared cereal for breakfast. This heavy concentration of sugar, in turn, caused the hyperactivity. To counter this, the student nurses started nutrition classes for the children and parents. "We started a whole campaign that a healthy child is a bright child," Father Luis noted. "And sure enough, it paid off because children began to do a lot better in school."[78]

Eye examinations and hearing tests were likewise administered to the children. "Some needed hearing aids, some needed glasses," Quihuis records, "and we got those for them."[79] Health fairs for the community were organized. Assistance was given to register those qualified for Medi-Cal, especially the young. Medical assistance, referrals, and counseling were made available to Latinos with AIDS. "It's one of the areas that you very seldom talk about in the Latino communities," Father Luis observed, "so we began to hold forums and talk about AIDS, first of all that it was a problem and how to deal with it, and the people who had AIDS, how they should be treated, with dignity and respect."[80]

Finally, with the assistance of some of the city's physicians and the student nurses, a pediatrics clinic was opened at St. Peter's. It was free and open to the public. The establishment of a family practice clinic followed this. Undocumented Latino immigrants especially flocked to both clinics during the tense period generated by Proposition 187 in 1994, when Latinos believed that public clinics and hospitals would now inquire about their legal status. Supported by public health officials and the city of San Francisco, which refused to implement Proposition 187 when it was approved by state voters, Father Luis and his staff allayed the fears of the Latino community and assured people that they would not be asked about their immigrant status.[81]

Because of the immigrant bashing connected to Proposition 187, the project also began free legal services through its legal clinic. For example, law students from USF volunteered to accompany individuals and families to hospitals and clinics to make sure they were not harassed about their status. Moreover, they provided legal counseling on immigrant issues, including the sponsoring of citizenship classes. Such assistance likewise involved what Father Luis referred to as "street law," which informed people of what their rights are if arrested. "Even as an undocumented person, you have rights," he stressed.[82] To help on household budgets and income taxes, business students at USF were organized by Father Luis to provide assistance in completing income tax forms.[83]

Growing gang warfare involving drugs and drive-by shootings in the Mission and centered around key gangs such as the Mexican Mafia, Nuestra Familia, and Mara Salvatrucha was allayed by the project's sponsoring of afternoon tutorial and soccer programs for kids as well as by counseling parents and meeting with gang members. With the cooperation of the various professional sports teams in San Francisco, such as the Giants, the project took kids to sporting events, where they entered free of charge. Father Luis and his assistants in particular concentrated on getting mothers involved in the antigang effort. They became part of a gang task force that met every week. At these meetings—organized around the concept of the *comunidades de base* and liberation theology—mothers did a scriptural reading and then related it to the realities and problems they faced with their children.[84] Mothers walked the streets in the afternoons and evenings to prevent gang violence. "If the mothers are out in the streets," Father Luis stressed, "you're not going to have gang members doing drive-by shootings."[85] According to him, this plan worked. In addition, issues of police abuse, especially against Latino youth, were addressed by organizing community meetings with police officials, including Father Luis's direct appeals on some occasions to Mayor Willie Brown. "It was a matter of just picking up the phone," he noted of his strong relationship with the mayor, "and either calling him personally or calling his staff." In return for Brown's support, Father Luis admitted without qualms that he encouraged Latinos to vote for the mayor.[86]

Cultural and religious traditions were not ignored by the project. It helped organize popular religious activities, especially on the occasions of the feast day of Our Lady of Guadalupe, El Día de los Muertos, and the feast of Santa Cecilia, the patron of musicians. As part of these activities, Father Luis blessed mariachi and other musical groups. Mothers' Day and Cinco de Mayo were additional community celebrations sponsored by the project. Anglo-American cultural traditions like Thanksgiving were also observed. For this holiday, Father Luis organized the USF students in raising funds for food baskets to distribute to the poor in the Mission District and other Latino areas. One year the students raised nineteen thousand dollars and fed nine hundred families.[87]

Finally, community meetings specifically addressed various injustices concerning labor practices, housing, educational services, and the lack of health insurance in the Latino community. These meetings were conducted in Spanish, with English translation provided. "We would speak out on the injustices that were going on in relationship to labor practices," Quihuis recalled. "We would speak out on the injustice concerning housing issues. We would speak out on the injustice of people not having access to health insurance. Employers like the Bank of America would have Latinos only part-time with no benefits. We addressed these issues from a justice perspective with the concept that injustice goes contrary to our faith. We didn't attack individuals. We simply addressed the problems in the community."[88]

The project further encouraged community empowerment by conducting voter registration campaigns as well as promoting naturalization for Latino immigrants.[89] In addition, Father Luis kept in further contact with the community by just walking around the Mission talking to people. "I knew everything that was going on in the community," he recalled; "I was taking time talking to *abuelitos* [grandparents] and . . . the people of the barrio."[90] Father Luis noted that what was crucial to the success of the project was that the people trusted him and the Church. It was the Church's involvement in the community that gained the trust and support of the people. From this experience, he asserted that efforts to successfully organize the Latino community on issues important to them cannot succeed without the role of the Church. "It's where the people are," he concluded.[91]

For nine years Father Luis worked in the Mission District. While his leadership was crucial to the success of the El Salvador project, it was not indis-

pensable and it was not intended to be so. The development of local leadership was to ensure the continuity of the project with or without Father Luis.
"As I look back and reflect over these nine years," he said, "we did a hell of
a lot considering the problems. We not only addressed key issues but we became an active voice in the community."[92] Recognizing this and wanting to
do parish work, he left in 1999 and was assigned to Santa Barbara. At Our
Lady of Sorrows he has successfully duplicated some of the programs of the El
Salvador project. As he looked back on those nine years, Father Luis believed
that the combination of faith and community work, examples he took from
César Chávez, proved to be highly successful. From a theological perspective,
he added, "It was very simple. It was helping to promote faith and justice."[93]
And from a political and sociological angle, Father Luis concluded that his
role as a community organizer and that of the church-based project reveal the
importance of Catholic parishes and priests in the development of organization and a sense of civic community for Latinos. Secular political organizers
need to be cognizant of this and at their risk shun the churches and parishes
as natural organizing centers. Here is where the people are, both citizens and
immigrants. "What it tells us about organizing," Father Luis concluded, "is . . .
that politicians need to listen . . . to . . . the needs of the people by working
more closely with pastors, regardless of what religious denomination because
they [the pastors] have the pulse of the people."[94]

Cultural Worker

Father Virgilio Elizondo is one of the most-recognized theologians of Chicano
religion. At the same time, he is a community priest. In his case, he is what I
call a cultural worker. Like Romero and Quihuis, Elizondo's proclivity to serve
others was part of his early socialization. Born in San Antonio in 1935, part of
what Elizondo refers to as the great frontier between Mexico and the United
States, he grew up in the predominantly Mexican west side. His parents were
immigrants from Mexico—his father, working class from Coahuila, and his
mother from the upper class of Mexico City, but whose family had lost all of
its wealth during the Mexican Revolution of 1910. Thanks to advice from Jewish American acquaintances, Elizondo's father bought property in the barrio
and started a family grocery store, Las Nuevas Colonias. Elizondo recalls that
his interfaith consciousness stems from this help offered to his father. "So that
became part of my sense of humanism later on," he notes, "that it was thanks
to the Jewish people of San Antonio that my dad got going."[95] His mother op-

erated the store while his father sold candy to other *tienditas* (small stores). As he grew up, Elizondo worked in the store and recalls how this socialized him to relating to people of all backgrounds.[96]

Like Romero and Quihuis, Elizondo grew up in a very religious household, although, as he observes, his family was not "churchy." This meant that, because of the family business, his parents did not have time to participate in many organized church groups. "There was a deep sense of God, a deep sense of morals, and a deep sense that God was approximate to us," he notes, "but we weren't a family that always prayed the rosary or went to church together. Religion formed a big part of our life, but I wouldn't say that we were a church family."[97] Nevertheless, he notes the importance of the parish church to his family and to the Mexican American community. "The parish church . . . was our social and religious center of life," he stresses. "We loved and cherished our Mexican-mestizo Catholic tradition with its many colorful ceremonies, processions, pilgrimages, shrines, songs, devotions, and decorations. Church was never dull, for even the snoring old folks provided some good entertainment during the services."[98]

The young Virgilio was sent to Catholic elementary schools but not to a Catholic high school. His memories of these schools are not particularly good ones: he recalls stinking bathrooms, horrible cafeteria food, and the constant discipline of the Ursuline and Divine Providence nuns that involved corporal punishment. Mexican American kids who spoke Spanish at school were punished by having to stand in front of the class and recite "I will never speak Spanish again in my life." This, according to Elizondo, made the children ashamed of their culture.[99] Instead of Catholic high school, he attended the Peacock Military Academy, where a sense of discipline was inculcated. "It was a very rigorous experience, but it was good for me. I also developed self-confidence there."[100]

At home, images of the Sacred Heart and of Our Lady of Guadalupe were permanent icons, especially owing to his grandmother's presence. Religious feast days such as that of Our Lady of Guadalupe, Good Friday, and Ash Wednesday represented particularly impressive events, and some, such as that of Guadalupe, he remembers "were like carnival days."[101] All of these feast days were celebrated in Mexican fashion, a memory and influence that the later Father Virgilio would use to guide him in his ministry. He recalls above all the rituals surrounding Good Friday, or Viernes Santo, and how the Mexican American community celebrated it more than Easter Sunday. They identified with the suffering Jesus. This included a community-wide reenactment of the Passion of the Christ, including the crucifixion. "As I interpret it now," Elizondo observes, "Good Friday was for the people whereas Easter Sunday was a clerical celebration in churches. It also has to do with the Mexican fascination with death that comes from both the Indian and Spanish traditions. Latinos take the incarnation and humanity of Jesus more seriously than Anglo Catholics" [102]

Growing up on the west side also meant that Elizondo was very much aware of his ethnic roots. Mexican culture surrounded him, reinforced by his parents, who spoke Spanish at home. "Everyone knew each other by name," he recalls of his neighborhood, "and had a sincere interest in the needs and goings-on of people in the neighborhood." [103] His father participated in Mexican American community activities, including being a member of several organizations such as the Pan-American Progressive Association (PAPA), the League of United Latin American Citizens (LULAC), and the Mexican Chamber of Commerce. Elizondo recalls that at age ten he helped his parents organize house bingo parties to raise money for the campaign of Henry B. González for the city council (González later became a congressman). Elizondo's father would often remind Virgilio and his sister of their ethnic identity and of how they needed to be proud of it—of "solidarity in nuestro pueblo." [104] Elizondo likewise grew up aware that Mexicans were subordinated and discriminated against in San Antonio.

Elizondo learned from his mother, Doña Anita, the importance of caring for others less fortunate. She assisted and counseled neighborhood youth who were having troubles. Elizondo refers to her as the "neighborhood psychologist." Part of her work with youth included instilling in them a pride of their mexicano background and culture.[105]

Despite the discrimination against Mexicans and blacks in the city, Elizondo grew up in a nurturing environment in which religion and ethnicity complemented one another. This included the staging of *pastorelas* (the Shepherds' Play) and *posadas* (Mary and Joseph seeking shelter) during Christmastime. He remembers that people would purchase Mexican religious calendars from Jewish merchants. They would also get empty cigar boxes from his father's store and put the image of Our Lady of Guadalupe in the *cajita* (box). "They would take the cigar boxes and paint them real pretty con florecitos y todo," Elizondo notes, "and put the *santito* in there and you would have a *nicho*." [106] Moreover, irrespective of some of the nuns' prohibition of Spanish in school, the Spanish language was spoken everywhere, including in the homilies of the masses in the west-side churches. "Once, I remember," Elizondo observes, "they put an English Mass [homily] and people thought *que horror*, it was going to ruin the church with English." [107] Elizondo himself grew up speaking only Spanish until he entered school.

Among the core values stressed by his parents was one that would come to characterize Elizondo's later life, namely, that of service to others. He developed this value very early on when he worked in his father's store and helped the customers, especially the *viejitos* (the elderly), who, according to Elizondo, "were always venerable. Viejitos would come to the store and you always helped them out. I grew up with that sense." [108] Moreover, through elementary and high school Elizondo served as an altar boy. "This is when I learned to appreciate good wine," he jokingly recalls of the Spanish wines used by the predominantly Spanish-born priests in his parish. "As altar boys we used to sip the unconsecrated altar wine." [109]

Education was likewise emphasized. Both the young Virgilio and his older sister were encouraged to attend college, which their parents knew, despite their limited education, was of prime importance. Following his graduation from high school, Virgilio received a scholarship to attend St. Mary's University in San Antonio, where other Mexican Americans of middle-class backgrounds attended. Unlike Romero and Quihuis, Elizondo does not appear to have possessed an early sense of a vocation to the priesthood. This would develop in college. At first, he was more aware and sensitive to racism in San Antonio. He was particularly impressed with the leadership of Archbishop Robert Lucey, who for years had been a champion of Mexican American civil rights.[110] Of Lucey, Elizondo says, "Archbishop Lucey didn't have the vocabulary of later liberation theology, but he was practicing that theology by critiquing the system that kept mexicanos down." [111] Lucey became his role model. Elizondo understood that he was privileged to be attending college, but that this also carried with it social responsibilities. He recalls an English class in which one of the novels he had to read was a Western that had racial references to Mexicans as being dirty and *borracho* (drunk). "The whole class laughed at these stereotypes," he notes, "and the Brother in charge of the class added that these were 'stupid Mexicans.'" Elizondo did not challenge the professor but remembers being very angry inside. "At that time you didn't know how to protest," he adds, "when teachers said something you accepted it. But I remember this as a negative experience." [112]

These changes in his life led Elizondo in his senior year in 1957 to make the decision to become a diocesan priest. He believes that the seeds of this vocation had been placed much earlier, but that they came to fruition in college.

It was a gradual decision, he comments, "it was not a bolt of lightning." [113] He also felt that this was a way of fulfilling social obligations. "I felt that through the priesthood and the Church I could contribute in some way to the betterment of my people," he notes. "I didn't become a priest just to become a social activist. But, on the other hand, I saw that the Church had something to do to help the activists in what was necessary." [114] This sense of social commitment was enhanced in his seminary studies on Catholic social doctrine at Assumption Seminary in San Antonio, studies that, among other things, stressed human rights, the right of workers to unionize, and the right to a just wage. Archbishop Lucey emphasized such training, including Spanish, for all seminarians. [115]

Following his ordination in 1963 and after his initial parish assignments, Elizondo matured in his social consciousness and in his development as a cultural worker within the Church by his close association with Archbishop Lucey. "There was a very good chemistry between us," he notes. [116] The archbishop appointed the young priest to work on religious education and, in time, as director of religious education for the archdiocese. The appointment coincided with the conclusion of Vatican Council II, which, as in the case of Romero and Quihuis, significantly influenced the thinking and praxis of Elizondo. Father Virgilio was particularly affected by the document on the Church in the modern world, especially the idea of the Church returning to its original source as a service to its people. He understood that this involved what he refers to as "collective charity," which is being involved with people and social justice. "That the basic identity of the Church is to be of service to the world," he stresses:

> That the Church doesn't exist for itself alone, but it exists to serve the world. So, therefore, the Church was the best Church when it didn't think as a Church, [but] when it was out organizing the day camps or was helping the peasants to set the water system, or feed[ing] the hungry, [or] give[ing] drink to the thirsty . . . so the Church was not called into existence for itself but to be of service. So the word "service" becomes the key word. [117]

Vatican II likewise impressed Elizondo with the concept of people as Church. This was a concept that had been forgotten by the Church and yet was crucial—"that the Church is fundamentally people, the people of God." [118] Father Virgilio observes that what was remarkable about Vatican II was that it "was so radically new because it was so traditional." By this, he means that what was radical and new was that the Church was stressing returning to its roots as a Church of and for the people, especially the poor and oppressed. This was its roots, and it needed to get back to them if the Church was to be relevant in the modern world.[119]

Father Virgilio's commitment to social justice issues was furthered when he accompanied the archbishop to the conference in 1968 in Medellín, Colombia, where the bishops of Latin American met to discuss implementing the changes of Vatican II and to explore what the council meant for the Catholic Church in Latin America. "The bishops were meeting in Latin America and Archbishop Lucey got invited and he wanted me to go with him," Elizondo points out. "I had no idea what would happen. That's why it was so mind blowing."[120] Here he became acquainted with the beginnings of liberation theology and met some of the early liberationists, such as Gutiérrez. "This was the first time I really met Latin Americans, not just Mexicans," Father Virgilio remembers. "These were brilliant men and women, passionately committed to the Church, but passionately committed to creating a new Church." As he further points out, Medellín aimed to inject "a new soul into the Church."[121] Elizondo was especially struck by the concept of "social sin" and the attention paid to the glaring class and social inequities in Latin America and "turning the Church inside out; instead of the Church siding with the rich, it's the poor that the Church sides with." Of this particular emphasis at Medellín, Elizondo adds,

> That was the thing at Medellín. Sin was always seen as personal, but
> to see that the whole structure could be a sinful structure and that the
> whole structure could be productive of certain circumstances, misery,
> poverty, and all that. I think that's what was radical at Medellín. . . . So
> Medellín stressed that sin was not just personal, but that it's structural,
> and that part of the task of the Church is to denounce such evil and to
> provide new alternatives that people haven't thought about. . . .
> Medellín for me was a great encounter with an aspect of Christian-
> ity that I had never suspected. I knew that the Church was involved in
> social justice concerning just wages, rights for workers, and all of that,
> but that question of what produces injustice was something new.[122]

Accepting liberation theology as practiced in Latin America and including it as part of his religious education, Elizondo, at the same time, expanded it to incorporate issues on culture rather than just of class. Instead of focusing solely on economic and social injustice, he as well as many other U.S. Latino theologians stressed the importance of culture and, in particular, popular religiosity in the liberation struggles of U.S. Latinos. Father Virgilio's orientation toward culture as contested territory in the struggle for social justice first came from his own strong Mexican American cultural background. Vatican II enhanced this with its stress on inculturation and the need for the Church to recognize cultural and ethnic diversity in implementing the changes of the council. This was manifested to Father Virgilio after a one-year stay at the East Asian Pastoral Institute in Manila, where he learned from Asian Catholic theologians an anthropological approach to Christianity. "It was the study of culture and religion in the Catholic faith, but from the perspective of different Asian cultures." [123] It reinforced for him the idea that the Church was culture. As he would stress later in his own writings, Jesus had come into the world not only as a human but specifically as a Galilean and hence of a specific culture. "The basic principle in Christianity is when God became man," Elizondo stresses, "he didn't become any man—he became a Galilean. So, therefore He affirms culture and it's through culture that He celebrates the presence of God." [124] "I was fascinated with this way of approaching this question," he concludes of his Manila experience, "but in some way I felt this was similar to the Chicano struggle in the Southwest where the Church didn't understand our perspective." [125]

The Manila experience impressed upon Elizondo the concept that "culture is the collective soul of the people." "I really came to a profound appreciation of the importance of cultural diversity. Differences did not have to be better or worse, superior or inferior. You have to look at difference as simply a difference. You have to appreciate difference as richness. This became the basis of much of my own future work as a Mexican American Catholic." [126]

Elizondo began to implement these ideas in the early 1970s, after the formation of PADRES, of which he was an early member. PADRES also reflected the influence of the Chicano movement of that period, which, besides its emphasis on political empowerment, stressed a new Chicano identity and cultural awareness. "All of a sudden we had discovered a fascinating new entity—ourselves. . . . [N]ow we could be." [127] As part of the movement, PADRES in 1972 believed it was important to establish a cultural training institute to prepare priests, sisters, and laypeople to work more effectively in the Chicano communities. It started the Mexican American Cultural Center, or MACC, in San Antonio and selected Elizondo as its director. Indeed, Father Virgilio had suggested the idea for the center. For the next eleven years, he headed this effort.

The basic principles of MACC were, one, to further the process of inculturation with respect to Chicanos and the Church and, two, through the legitimization of Chicano culture to empower Chicanos in both sacred and secular terms. By recognizing and validating the Chicano experience, its history and culture, MACC, as part of the Chicano movement, would deal with the identity question among Chicano Catholics and give them a sense of their own self-worth. "We want to be Catholic," Elizondo stresses, "but we don't want to give up all that is precious to us as Chicanos in order to be Catholic." [128] This represents what Gerald Poyo in his study of Cuban American Catholics refers to as "integration without assimilation." [129] Feeling good about themselves and being confident of themselves would empower Chicanos to make changes within the Church and outside of it. "The purpose of MACC," he reflects, "was to provide us as Chicano clergy with a place of our own. Here we could bring in our own leaders and one could develop our own knowledge based on our experience. We acted on the basis that even though we practiced our Catholic faith differently from Anglo Catholics, ours was not inferior. It was not superior, but it was not inferior." [130]

Like other expressions of the Chicano movement, MACC recognized the importance of the cultural wars in the United States and staked out culture as its contribution to liberation theology. As Father Virgilio observes, "That here [in the United States] [it] wasn't just the matter of economic poverty. . . . We were being denied the right to our own existence, to name ourselves. So that was a deeper type of poverty than just economic poverty—the poverty of non-being, the poverty of non-existence. And in that sense I think we were pushing further than in Latin America." [131]

MACC believed that if priests, sisters, and lay leaders, both Chicanos and Anglos, were going to work in Mexican American parishes, they had to prepare themselves as cultural workers by knowing and appreciating the history and culture of the people and being able to communicate in Spanish. By sponsoring cultural leadership, MACC indirectly would also be helping to create organic leadership in the barrios, as its disciples would assist in the empowerment of the communities. [132]

In this effort, MACC, utilizing what Elizondo refers to as "religious imagination," organized institutes and classes on Chicano history and culture, Spanish-language classes, and religious courses in which scriptures would be studied from a Chicano perspective. And by bringing together a variety of scholars, MACC began publishing various texts on Chicano religious culture. [133] As part of its program, the center hosted numerous Chicano artists, musicians, poets, and writers. Through a restudy of the liturgy or ritual of the Church, MACC promoted liturgical inculturation that integrated within barrio churches various Chicano religious traditions, customs, and music. These included renewed attention to feast days such as that of Guadalupe and El Día de los Muertos. "Liturgy needs to involve people," Elizondo stresses,

> and how people enact the sacred. We celebrate the Christian mystery, but we don't do it abstractly, or shouldn't do it abstractly. We celebrate it as it comes in life to us. Each culture has its way of expressing what is sacred.
>
> Jesus had a culture and an ethnic identity. That principle has to continue.[134]

At the same time, MACC worked to stress the importance of Chicano popular religiosity in the form of home altars, popular devotions, *peregrinaciones* (popular pilgrimages), and other expressions of a people's faith. These manifestations were presented not as superstitions, as some in the Church presented them, but as legitimate expressions of the sacred. "This was a very legitimate expression of Christianity," Elizondo observes. "It was different from the U.S. Catholic Church but not inferior."[135] In addition, he invited liberation theologians from Latin America such as Gutiérrez to speak at MACC.[136]

In its leadership program, MACC stressed the importance of Chicano priests serving as community organizers. Working with PADRES and Archbishop Flores, MACC helped to organize COPS in San Antonio as an effective empowering community movement.[137] "Vatican II said that the Church has to be the Church of the people," Father Virgilio notes of his organizing efforts, "and so it cannot be a foreign Church."[138]

As a cultural worker, Father Virgilio further expanded his efforts when in 1983 Archbishop Flores appointed him rector of San Fernando Cathedral in San Antonio. Elizondo became the first rector of Mexican descent since 1840.[139] San Fernando had always been the central church for Mexican Americans in the city, but it had lagged in recent years owing to gentrification, which dislocated many parishioners. Those who remained consisted mainly of viejitos, or the elderly. Because of this, Elizondo's friends cautioned him about taking on the position, but Father Virgilio embraced the challenge. "I was extremely excited," he recalls. "On the other hand, a lot of my friends said 'Don't take it. You're going to waste your time because it's a dying place. Anybody can run the cathedral, but you're doing such great work at MACC.' Well, my inner sense

FIGURE 6.3 Father Virgilio Elizondo, circa late 1990s. Courtesy Father Virgilio Elizondo.

told me to say yes. Especially when Archbishop Flores said 'Here's a chance to put into practice all you've been talking about.' " [140]

At San Fernando, building on his work at MACC and earlier cultural activities at the cathedral by sympathetic Spanish priests, Elizondo—functioning, according to María Del Socorro Castañeda, as an "organic intellectual," or what Foucault called a "specific intellectual" with a specific mission in life— showcased the cathedral as a model of inculturation and cultural empowerment. [141] "We reclaimed our right to express our Catholicism in the way of our ancestors," he asserts. [142] The liturgy was revised to incorporate a whole array of Chicano religious cultural traditions. It focused on Elizondo's concept of church as fiesta. "It was a liturgy with lots of mexicano things," he notes, "a lot of mariachi music and decorations and *danzantes* (dancers). So really a very fiesta Mass." [143] This concept of the Mass as fiesta contrasted with what Elizondo recalled and still notes of predominantly Anglo-American Catholic services. "Mass was recited not celebrated," he observes of this contrast. [144] Such rituals conveyed not only spiritual meanings, but ethnic and community ones as well. "We are poor by society's standards," Father Virgilio writes of the Mexican American community, "and considered inferior by much of the mainline society, but our religion provides us with a sacred space where we can experience a deep sense of dignity, identity, and belonging." [145] One parishioner, Frank Paredes, Jr., reinforced this view by stating, "The public rituals and fiestas at San Fernando strengthen us in our identity by allowing us to pridefully celebrate our culture and faith." [146] These changes or transformations reflect what León refers to as "sacred poetics." "Religious actors can manage the often harsh and potentially overwhelming conditions they confront," he notes, "the battle for survival and more, dignity, love, freedom—by deploying the most powerful weapons in their arsenal: signs, myths, rituals, narratives, and symbols." [147]

Of course, the celebration of the feast day of Our Lady of Guadalupe became a central focus of Elizondo's cultural transformation. The feast day had been celebrated in the past at the cathedral, but Father Virgilio expanded it and attracted many more people. He, more than any other previous pastor, understood the power and attraction of Guadalupe to Mexican Catholics. "There is a power in Guadalupe that is under esteemed by some in the Church," he points out. "I see her attraction to people. It's not a simple piety. I don't think there's a greater force, religious or secular, in the Latino community than Guadalupe." [148]

To increase the range of these changes, he initiated a television Mass each Sunday from the cathedral that was nationally broadcast. This encouraged other Latino churches in the Southwest to follow the cathedral's practices or what Castañeda, borrowing from Pierre Bourdieu, refers to as "symbolic capital." [149] All of these liturgical changes increased church attendance, bringing back many younger Mexican Americans as well as appealing to more recent Mexican immigrants. Of this increased attendance and the enthusiasm that the changes generated, Elizondo jokingly says, "For the first time in the cathedral church, people rushed to get the front pews. Usually, in the church it's the other way around—they rush to get the back pews." [150]

The centerpiece of this liturgical transformation focused on the Passion service during Semana Santa (Holy Week) that Father Virgilio commenced in 1985. Earlier passion plays had been performed in the barrios, but he believed it would have an even greater impact if it moved downtown to use the cathedral as the crucifixion climax. It worked with the aid and leadership of many laypeople, and now each year thousands participate in the procession and ritual. One year, sixteen thousand people attended. Each Good Friday the downtown streets belong to the mexicanos, many of them poor immigrants. Physicality, to borrow from León's astute observations on borderland religion, creates a space of resistance.[151] "This is a living drama," Elizondo notes, "the drama of the pueblo."[152] Such ritual is not only religiously empowering but socially and, indirectly, politically as well. It is a form of mass community demonstration or what the theologian Roberto Goizueta calls "extensions of domestic religious life." "Around San Fernando Cathedral in San Antonio," Father Virgilio observes,

> there is no greater and more beautiful day than Good Friday. This is
> the day when we proclaim Jesus as El Señor del Poder (The God of
> Power). No day of the year brings more people together at one time
> than the reenactment of the trial, crucifixion, and burial of Jesus. . . .
> As a human being and as a pastor, this is truly the most beautiful, most
> moving, and most inspiring day of the year.[153]

Besides the liturgical changes, Father Virgilio used his years as rector to help people in other ways. Medical programs were started, the homeless were given shelter, immigrants were provided legal assistance, and an ecumenical AIDS march that has become an annual event was organized. In addition, Elizondo used his visible position as rector to participate in various civic committees. He accomplished all of these changes without always seeking the archbishop's permission. "I always found that in the Church," he observes, "it's always better to follow an old Spanish principle that it's better to ask for forgiveness than for permission."[154] In a short period of time, he had transformed San Fernando into the center of Chicano Catholic life in San Antonio. "I think San Fernando became effectively the Latino cathedral of the United States," Father Virgilio concludes.[155] In 1995, after twelve years as rector, he stepped down.

Through his work at MACC and San Fernando as well as his writings on Chicano theology, which center on the important role of culture in Chicano religious life, Father Virgilio Elizondo exemplifies the concept of community priest and, in particular, that of cultural worker.

Conclusion

Leadership can be defined in many ways. What I am proposing is that, in studying Chicano history and Chicano studies, we expand that definition beyond the secular to include the religious. The example of Fathers Romero, Quihuis, and Elizondo suggest that some Catholic priests as well as other religious figures provide vital leadership, not just in a spiritual sense but in a temporal one as well. The sacred and the secular are joined in a very powerful way. In this sense, the earlier model of the worker-priests in France is reconfigured in the form of community priests. Through such leadership, churches and parishes become significant organizing centers. Churches are not only where many of the people are, but also where they are motivated by their faith. It is the faith communities, such as the *comunidades de base* in Latin America, that perhaps serve as the model for sustained and permanent community organization in the struggles against injustice. Faith and social consciousness come together, as the example of César Chávez reveals, to propel *la causa* (the struggle). Scholars need to rediscover and understand this tradition.

SEVEN

¡Presente! Father Luis Olivares and the Sanctuary Movement in Los Angeles

A Study of Faith, Ethnic Identity, and Ecumenism

For I was hungry and you gave me food, I was thirsty and you gave me drink, a stranger and you welcomed me, naked and you clothed me, ill and you cared for me, in prison and you visited me.

—MATTHEW 25:35–36

To know God is to do Justice

—JEREMIAH 20:13–16

When aliens reside with you in your land, do not molest them. You shall treat the aliens who reside with you no differently than the natives born among you; have the same love for them as for yourself; for you too were once aliens in the land of Egypt.

—LEVITICUS 19:33–34

A church that doesn't provoke any crisis,
a gospel that doesn't unsettle,
a word of God that doesn't get under anyone's skin, a word of God that doesn't touch the real sin of the society in which it is being proclaimed—
what gospel is that?

—ARCHBISHOP OSCAR ROMERO, 1978

You cannot be witness to human suffering and not be convinced of the existence of social sin. We are all responsible unless we take a stand and speak up.

—LUIS OLIVARES, 1990

ON A WARM September evening in 1990, a rather large congregation of people of different ethnic and religious backgrounds gathered to honor Father Luis

Olivares, the former pastor of Our Lady Queen of Angeles, better known as La Placita Church. Tables were arranged in the public open space by the plaza bandstand adjacent to the Olvera Street marketplace in downtown Los Angeles and directly across from La Placita. Dignitaries such as Mayor Tom Bradley, state representatives who had passed a resolution declaring September 5 Father Olivares Day, city and county officials, who had renamed Olvera Street Father Luis Olivares Street for that day, family members, religious figures from different denominations, movie and entertainment figures such as Martin Sheen and Jackson Browne, as well as friends and colleagues, all came to celebrate the life and accomplishments of this Claretian priest. Also in attendance was the aging icon of the Chicano movement and the farmworkers' struggle, César Chávez.

After greeting one another and mingling in the plaza and enjoying cocktails, the group sat down to a catered Mexican dinner. Father Olivares, looking thinner than usual, but still with a charismatic aura about him, sat next to Chávez, symbolizing their close comradeship over many years. As the affair progressed through dinner, remarks, and songs by Jackson Browne, some began to notice a growing number of what appeared to be homeless Latinos—Central Americans and Mexicans—who began to gather in front of La Placita and outside of the temporary chain-link fence installed to mark off the area designated for the celebration.

But the gathering crowd soon noticed Father Olivares and began to call out to him. "¡Viva Padre Olivares! ¡Que viva el Padre Olivares! ¡Padre Luis Olivares! ¡Presente! ¡Ven con nosotros! ¡Queremos Padre Olivares! ¡Olivares! ¡Olivares! ¡Olivares!" they shouted in unison.

Browne, who was singing one of Olivares's favorite songs, "For Every Man," upon hearing the shouts calling for the esteemed guest, stopped singing and said, "I feel it strangely appropriate that I am being accompanied by the voices of people who spend the night in front of the church. . . . I welcome their accompaniment, just as Father Luis Olivares welcomes them."

The audience broke out in applause and invited the homeless to share the meal. Capturing the drama of the moment, Chávez, in his testimony to Olivares, observed in words that could have just as easily been said of him, "You have been with the people in the bad times and in the good times. Your heart is an open temple for those who seek refuge." [1]

Not quite three years later, Chávez was speaking again of the goodness of his dear friend and confessor. This time, however, the occasion was the funeral of Father Louie, as he was affectionately called. The scene was not La

Placita, which for some would have been more appropriate, but Mission San Gabriel (where Father Luis is buried), managed by the Claretians and located twelve miles northeast of downtown Los Angeles. Within a few weeks Chávez himself would be dead. Father Louie had prophesied Chávez's death, and perhaps that is how it should have been. César Chávez and Luis Olivares in life and in death were joined by their deep Catholic faith and by their commitment to social justice.

Along with Chávez, some two thousand mourners of varying backgrounds and religious faiths came one last time to honor Olivares. They arrived on that morning in March in cars and buses. They wanted to be there early enough to pay their personal respects and say their good-byes to Father Louie as he lay in state in front of the altar. It took quite awhile for the procession of people to make their way to the open casket before the 1 P.M. Mass. "It was like the President of the United States dying," Dámaso Olivares, the eldest of the Olivares siblings, thought to himself.[2] As the men, women, and a few children approached the casket, which was partly covered by a United Farm Worker (UFW) flag, they saw their beloved priest, comrade, and friend looking more gaunt and pale than they remembered him. Still, it was unmistakably Father Louie. As usual, he was dressed as impeccably as a priest can be. Always a sharp dresser with his black silk suits and Gucci shoes, he once again looked elegant and dignified in his collar and suit. As if to remind his people one last time of the importance of social action, Father Louie wore on his lapel a UFW button that read "No Uvas" (No Grapes).

The people touched the coffin as if to feel one last time his radiance and his love for them. Some bent over and tenderly kissed him. Some brought other movement buttons and pinned them on Father Louie. Some read "No War in El Salvador," "Economic Justice," "Women's Rights"; one in particular that caught the attention of Reverend George Regas of the Episcopalian All Saints' Church in Pasadena said, "No Human Need Is Illegal."[3] Even in death, the mourners drew on Father Louie for faith, commitment, and courage. "He was our conscience," Father Matthew DiMaria, a fellow Claretian and longtime friend from their seminary years, told a reporter. "He challenged us. He was a voice for the poor."[4] Dozens of priests concelebrated the Mass of Christian Burial accompanied by the lyrical strains of mariachi violins as well as the stirrings ones from the mariachi brass. Speaking for the family, Henry Olivares said of his younger brother, "Wherever Louie was needed that's where he was. The refugees and immigrants needed him and he rose to the occasion. Wherever there was a need, Louie was willing to do something."[5]

So many had come that even the larger and newer church adjacent to the old Mission could not hold them all, and many had to strain to hear the liturgy as they spilled outside. "Inside and outside the church on the balmy afternoon," Tom Fox of the *National Catholic Reporter* wrote, "people prayed and sang, many holding back tears."[6] And as they had done at the Olvera Street banquet three years earlier, many of the Central American refugees as well as others began to spontaneously call out for Olivares right after the consecration. "¡Viva Luis! ¡Viva Luis Olivares! ¡Presente!" For them, Luis Olivares not only was still present, as the calls symbolized, but the priest who had sheltered them was still doing so.[7] They shed tears along with everyone else as Browne sang at the end of the service "You Are My Hero."[8]

Who was Father Luis Olivares and why did so many people from different walks of life, but particularly Central American refugees and undocumented Mexican immigrants, revere him almost as though he were a saint? And what is Father Olivares's role in history, especially in Chicano/Latino history? Who was this man?

Father Louie was a Catholic priest of the Claretian order who in the 1980s, as pastor of La Placita Church, organized one of the most successful efforts to provide sanctuary for both Central American refugees (primarily Salvadorans) and undocumented Mexican immigrants. The sanctuary movement began around 1982 in other parts of the country and resurrected a centuries-old tradition based on the Old Testament, Roman law, medieval canon law, and English common law in synagogues and churches: that of giving protection or sanctuary to people being persecuted by civil authorities. In the 1980s, what came to be called the sanctuary movement focused on political refugees from El Salvador and Guatemala who were escaping deadly civil wars and repressive authoritarian governments directly or indirectly under military control. In the case of El Salvador, people were fleeing the presence of so-called death squads that terrorized both peasants and city dwellers. This repression, reflecting the dominance in these countries of elite ruling classes, also extended to clergy, especially Catholic priests and sisters, native and foreign, who spoke out against the repression. As a result, some of the clergy were killed and became martyrs of the Central American wars. The most notable victim was Archbishop Oscar Romero of San Salvador, the capital of El Salvador, who was killed while saying Mass in 1980. The U.S. government in turn supported this repression, in particular under the Reagan administration in the 1980s, which supplied military and economic aid to the governments of El Salvador and Guatemala and in addition attempted to overthrow the revolutionary Sandinista government in Nicaragua.[9]

The position of the Reagan administration was that the people fleeing Central America were not political refugees, but rather "illegal aliens" desiring to find jobs in the United States. This contradicted, according to critics of Reagan's policy, the earlier 1980 Refugee Act passed by the U.S. Congress, which paralleled the UN position on refugees, under which Central Americans qualified as legitimate political refugees.[10] While worsening economic conditions did play a role in the refugees' decision to migrate, as the scholars Nora Hamilton and Norma Stoltz point out, the civil wars nevertheless exacerbated these conditions.[11] "Many Central Americans living in Mexico and the United States," Hamilton and Stoltz write, "assert that survival and personal safety are their primary motivation for emigrating."[12] However, the Reagan administration's acceptance of Salvadorans and Guatemalans as political refugees would have been an acknowledgment of the repression and lack of human rights imposed by the governments of those countries. The administration was not about to admit that. No more than 5 percent of Salvadorans, for example, gained legal asylum in the United States.[13]

As a result, many Americans, especially members of churches and synagogues, took it upon themselves to aid, shelter, and protect the Central American refugees—the "feet people."[14] This meant opposing the Reagan administration, especially the Immigration and Naturalization Service (INS), and arguing that there was a higher moral law involved in providing sanctuary for these refugees. Some of these sanctuary workers, including clerics, were arrested, tried, and convicted of breaking the law in harboring what the INS considered illegal aliens. In her study of the origins of the sanctuary movement in Tucson in 1982 Hillary Cunningham observes,

> Broadly speaking, this movement can be defined as a religiopolitical coalition that began as a network of churches and synagogues that decided to offer "safe haven" or "sanctuary" to Central American fugitives denied political asylum by the U.S. Immigration and Naturalization Service (INS). The movement was officially inaugurated during the March 1982 political declaration of Sanctuary by Southside Presbyterian Church and at its height in 1986–1987 it spanned Mexico, the United States, and Canada, included more than four hundred religious congregations, and claimed between sixty and seventy thousand participants.[15]

In Los Angeles, many people, especially liberal Protestants, Jews, and Catholics, including clerics, and some forty churches supported the concept of sanctuary, while opposing U.S. treatment of the refugees as well as American policies in Central America. There is no question, however, that the main leadership of the sanctuary movement in Los Angeles came from Father Olivares and his brave, committed group of colleagues, both Latino and non-Latino, at La Placita. It was Olivares who in 1985 declared La Placita an official sanctuary for Central American refugees, the first Catholic church in Los Angeles to do so. Moreover, La Placita became the site of perhaps the largest sanctuary movement in the country, given the large Central American population that arrived in the 1980s. In addition, Olivares did what no other sanctuary movement did. He extended the concept of sanctuary in 1987 to include undocumented Mexican immigrants. Over a period of some nine years, until his removal as pastor of La Placita in 1990, Father Louie was not only the acknowledged spokesperson of the Central American refugees, but the director of an expansive operation at La Placita to aid refugees and undocumented immigrants. As part of these efforts, his was one of the loudest voices raised against U.S. policies in Central America. In the 1980s, Olivares stood out as one of the most important and influential Chicano and Latino leaders in the United States. There is no question in my mind that Olivares's place in history, certainly in Chicano history, is assured and that he takes his place among the many eminent leaders in that history who symbolize not only opposition to repression, exploitation, and discrimination, but also the active effort of Chicanos/Latinos to make their own history by struggling to bring about social change.[16]

In researching the story of Olivares and the sanctuary movement at La Placita, I was struck by three central themes that characterize this movement. The first concerns the faith-based nature of the struggle. It was Olivares's faith and his particular liberationist tendency that initiated and sustained the movement. The second is what I call the emergence of a pan-Latino identity that brought together Mexican Americans and Central Americans in the effort to provide protection and support to both refugees and undocumented immigrants. The third is the ecumenical (alliances with non-Catholic religious denominations) aspect of the experiment at La Placita, marked by a genuine effort to reach out to people in need. Faith, ethnic identity, and ecumenism came together in a progressive and dynamic historical process at La Placita.

Faith and the Sanctuary Movement

To appreciate the centrality of faith in the sanctuary movement at La Placita one has to understand the evolution of Father Olivares's personal spiritual growth.

Luis was only about six or seven years old and living in his modest west-side home in San Antonio's Mexican barrio when he decided he was going to play at saying Mass. He had keenly studied the priest's rituals at the neighborhood Immaculate Conception Church just a few blocks from the Olivares home. In his mind, he could recreate the priest's movements and give a reasonably accurate rendition of the Latin liturgy. Not content at saying the regular Mass, the young Louie said the more elaborate High Mass. Dressed in vestments especially made for him by his grandmother Inez, he recruited his two older brothers as altar boys and his four sisters as the congregation, all gathered in front of a makeshift altar. On one occasion when a family friend, Father Correa, visited the Olivares home, Louie coaxed him into playing along. The only caveat, however, was that Father Correa, instead of assuming his role as the priest, had to take a back seat to Louie. While the young boy played the priest, Father Correa served as an additional altar boy. At least in the Olivares household, Louie reigned as the high priest. Other religious games involved Louie baptizing his sisters' dolls. There seemed to be no question about what the future held in store for Luis Olivares.[17]

The Olivares family was a very religious, devout Mexican Catholic family. "The church was the center for us," recall some of Olivares's siblings, "Some other families would gather at a picnic. We would be at church or at church activities."[18] Both sides of the family originated in the northern states of Mexico and both fled to the United States during the Mexican Revolution of 1910. They came with their children, among whom were Luis's parents.

Prophecy seems to have always enveloped much of the life of Father Olivares, and it seems to have started with his paternal grandparents. As Catholics, they opposed the strong anticlerical sentiment associated with many of the Mexican revolutionaries, who saw the Church as part of the oligarchy that had ruled Mexico for many years. The most recent manifestation was the dictatorship of Porfirio Díaz, overthrown by the revolution in 1911. Luis's grandparents in response sheltered priests who were being persecuted; this amounted to their version of sanctuary. "I would say that that history was an influence in my brother's life," Henry Olivares says.[19]

After the paternal grandparents left Mexico and went to San Antonio sometime around the late 1910s, they continued to assist and harbor Mexican priests escaping from the continued persecution of the Church in Mexico following the outbreak of anti-Catholic sentiment in the so-called Cristero War of the mid-1920s. This version of an "underground railroad" was practiced by Luis's father. "My dad used to hide priests behind the walls," Olivares remembered, "so he was involved in a kind of sanctuary movement as a young adult!"[20] These priests found refuge in San Antonio and would often visit the Olivares home. They became early role models for the Olivares children as they were growing up. Louie loved to hear these stories from his grandmother Inez. "Tell me again the story of Father so and so," he would plead with her. Little did grandmother Inez, much less Louie, know that years later, Father Luis himself would be sheltering and providing sanctuary for others fleeing persecution.[21] What he also drew on, of course, was that his own family on both sides consisted of immigrants who themselves had fled a civil war. When his sister, Socorro, years later at La Placita good-naturedly teased him about helping people who didn't even pay taxes, Father Louie lectured her: "Socorro, you need to understand that these people are coming just like our grandparents and parents."[22]

Luis's parents were deeply Catholic. His father, Dámaso, a mechanic, and his mother, Victoriana, a pecan sheller in one of San Antonio's many *nuecerías*, or pecan-shelling plants, met at Immaculate Heart Church. Dámaso belonged to the Society of San Luis Gonzaga, and Victoriana was a pious member of the Hijas de María. Married in 1928, they had seven children, including Luis, who was born on February 13, 1934. Tragedy struck the Olivares family when Victoriana died in childbirth in 1938. Luis was only about three and a half years old. He would have few, if any, memories of his mother. Henry, however, a year older, remembers his mother as a very religious and very social person. One of Victoriana's last wishes was that her children be taken care of by her husband's family. That wish was honored, and Dámaso along with his seven children, including the new baby girl, Josefina, moved into a house in the barrio that included grandmother Inez and Dámaso's sister, Concha. Grandmother Inez would play the role of the matriarchal figure, while Tía Concha, affectionately called Tía or Mami by the children, would serve as the mother figure, especially for the younger children, including Luis.[23]

Grandmother Inez, or Abuelita Inecita, as the children called her, looms as a major influence on the Olivares children, especially in their religious and spiritual upbringing. She was the backbone of the family and integrated the family with the Church. To Abuelita the Church was everything, second only to the family. The Church was not only the center of the faith, but also the social center of the community. Luis always remembered his grandmother in relation to his faith. Her memory was constantly with him. During those long, lonely days when he was dying, his memory of her and of the woman who was his virtual mother, Mami, comforted him. "My grandmother raised us," he recalled. "She was very religious—daily Mass, the whole bit. She would take us, my older brother and me, we would go with her at 6:15 in the morning every single day to Immaculate Heart. That's the origin of my vocation. We spent a lot of time in Church."[24] Besides daily and Sunday Mass, the Olivares children had to participate every evening in reciting the rosary at home with Abuelita or going to church for rosary service.[25]

Abuelita's persona was only enhanced for Luis and his siblings by her role as a *curandera*, or healer. She practiced this form of popular religiosity, influenced by Mexican indigenous traditions and practices, in her home and in the barrio. Her good reputation was well known in the Mexican community, and many who were unable to afford a doctor or were suspicious of professional medicine visited the Olivares home to be prayed over and healed by Abuelita. Healing involved both prayers and the use of herbs, thus uniting the spiritual and the physical. On some occasions she would make visits and take the children with her.[26] Healing others, the persecuted, the tortured, the unwanted, would become part of Father Louie's ministry years later.[27]

In addition to being a healer and holy woman, Abuelita further socialized the Olivares children to care for others, especially the poor. Although not a well-to-do woman, she would go out of her way to assist those in need. After daily Mass, she would often bring home hungry people and feed them tortillas and coffee. She would never throw away articles like old clothes and shoes, choosing instead to give them to the poor. This example had a lasting influence on all of the children, including Luis, who came to understand later that in her own way Abuelita, as he would in his own ministry, practiced a "preferential option for the poor." "I think that the seed that Louie got," one of his sisters observes, "was that my grandmother was always helping people. Anybody that would knock at the door would not leave without eating. If they didn't have a place to sleep, they would find a place at the house. Our house was always packed."[28] But it was not just Abuelita who served as a role model in helping the poor; so too did Tía Concha and Dámaso, Luis's father, who for many years belonged to the St. Vincent de Paul Society, which aided the poor and the needy on the west side.

This sacrificing, yet warm and nurturing environment reinforced the importance of the family—*la familia*—to the Olivares children. They were always reminded to stay together and to support each other. "We stuck together," Socorro stresses. "La familia stuck together. Regardless of the differences that we had, we always came out [together]."[29] Socorro, herself later a religious sister, saw this concept of la familia being applied by her brother Louie at La Placita. The refugees and immigrants, in a way, became Father Louie's extended family. "I saw that coming from our home," she says, "to the work that he was doing and all of this was to help these people." [30]

In his youth, Luis exhibited the strong religious upbringing his parents provided. He and his brothers served as altar boys. All of the Olivares children attended Catholic school. Luis went to Immaculate Heart of Mary Parochial School through the eighth grade. Everywhere he turned, Catholicism was present in his life. It was the center of everything, and he fervently accepted it. He believed he had a vocation to the priesthood. He enthusiastically wanted to become a priest. After all, had he not been preparing for this all of his young life? Had he not played the role of priest at home? He wanted not only to be a priest, but a Claretian priest. The Claretians administered their parish church, Immaculate Heart, and for Luis they were a living symbol of the priesthood. He saw himself in them. Of Spanish and Mexican descent, the priests at Immaculate Heart looked like him and came from the same cultural background. They spoke Spanish, as he did at home. They were his role models. And then there was big brother Henry, who blazed the trail and who served as the pioneer. In 1947, one year before Luis, Henry left San Antonio at age thirteen or fourteen to enter the Claretian junior seminary in Compton, California, in the Los Angeles area. One year later, Luis, at age thirteen, followed. He knew he wanted to be a priest, and he never wavered in this desire. His role in history—in Chicano history—would be as a priest. [31]

After thirteen years of seminary training and studies at Claretian institutions in southern California as well as at Catholic University in Washington, D.C., Luis Olivares was ordained a Claretian priest in 1961 in his hometown of San Antonio in the historic San Fernando Cathedral. As a seminarian and student, Olivares displayed qualities that had their roots in his family life: religious commitment, a deep faith, personal leadership, the ability to reach out to others, a charming personality with a good sense of humor, and charisma. Identified by his superiors as a potential leader within the Claretian order, Luis or Louis, as he was now called, very quickly climbed the Claretian ladder, being elected treasurer of the western region of the order after receiving an M.A. degree in financial administration from Notre Dame in 1965. In this position, which he held from 1967 to 1977, he was responsible for investing Claretian funds in various financial institutions both in the United States and Europe. Olivares, in this capacity, lived an exciting, cosmopolitan life, being wined and dined by clients or potential clients. This period in his life has in some circles been criticized for its absence of social action and community involvement. The criticism is not devoid of some truth; however, from Olivares's perspective, he had not abandoned what his parents had instilled in him about helping the poor and less fortunate, for those germs of social justice remained embedded within him and were reinforced by Catholic social doctrine stressed by the Claretians. He seems to have been excited about the reforms of Vatican Council II (1962–1965) and came to believe they were liberating. At the same time, Olivares was a good company man. His loyalty to the Claretian order was unquestioned: he did what he was assigned to do, and he did it well and enjoyed it. He was not in a position to allow his social justice tendencies to flourish. This would change in the mid-1970s.[32]

The changes began within Father Louie. He often spoke of his "conversions," believing that "we go through a series of conversions and . . . are given opportunities along the way to get closer to Christ by the challenges we are presented."[33] By this he didn't mean that, like St. Paul, all of a sudden he was shocked into a new state of mind or conversion. He meant that under different life circumstances, parts of him, latent values and principles that had been dormant, now rose to the surface in the form of a personal resurrection. Conversion did not mean a totally new consciousness, but a rising of a consciousness already planted inside of him and now, being fertilized and watered, was blooming.

By his own admission, Olivares's major conversion came when he encountered César Chávez and the farmworkers' movement. For this, he was indebted to Father Richard Estrada, who at the time was a Claretian seminary student who wanted to do some fieldwork for the UFW in organizing the second grape boycott in East Los Angeles around 1974. To do this, however, he needed a priest-sponsor who would supervise his activity. Father Louie, believing this sponsorship would not take too much of his time, volunteered or perhaps was asked by the order to act as Estrada's supervisor. In this capacity, Olivares met Chávez and was converted. It was as if everything Abuelita Inecita and his parents had taught him about helping the poor rose to the surface. It was as if the new directions, including the changes in the role of the Church in the modern world set off by Vatican II, now became crystallized. In an anonymous interview in 1976 with the sociologist Lawrence Mosqueda, but in which Olivares's identity can be detected, he acknowledged the impact the farmworkers had on him:

I live a double standard as a cleric and I guess, as a Mexican American. One of the greatest things that has happened to me, as to my involvement with the United Farm Workers, is an awareness as to where life really is. The things that are of value to farmworkers give you a totally different perspective. You start seeing the dimensions of the gospel. [It has had] a tremendous influence on me.[34]

With a new sense of purpose Olivares plunged not only into supervising Estrada, but also into joining his student in assisting the farmworkers. Father Louie exhibited the same passion he had displayed in raising money for the order. But now, instead of raising funds, he was working with people. This new role reestablished his affiliation not only with the poor, but also with his Mexican American roots. Along with Estrada, he learned how to be an organizer in the boycott. He picketed, marched, and frequently visited with the farmworkers and with Chávez and the UFW in the Central Valley and elsewhere. He found the experience liberating.[35]

Father Louie also drew closer and closer to Chávez and took on the role of his personal priest. But in a fascinating transformation, Chávez at the same time became Father Louie's spiritual director.[36] Olivares officiated at UFW weddings, baptisms, and funerals. Dolores Huerta, the UFW's dynamic vice president, remembers that Father Louie's homilies were "words like wings." [37] The encounter with Chávez and the farmworkers dramatically changed Olivares's life. "This is the reason I became a social activist," he said. This is where he belonged.[38]

Father Louie and Chávez became spiritual brothers as well as comrades in struggle. Chávez would often visit La Placita after Olivares became pastor.[39] For the rest of their lives, they held to an unbreakable bond. Each in his own way would become a martyr to the cause of social justice. "He tells me about his struggle and I tell him about mine," Father Louie told his brother Henry. "We compare. He's bucking the political authority. I'm bucking the religious authority." [40]

But it was not just Chávez who touched Olivares's life; it was also the farmworkers themselves. He was moved as he visited their homes by their simplicity, sincerity, and hospitality—"Venga, Padre, venga," (come in, Father, come in) they would say, inviting him into their homes. He was also affected by their deep spirituality.[41] He came to understand that those one serves convert one.[42]

Father Louie's conversion expanded when he requested in 1975 to be assigned to Our Lady of Solitude (Soledad) in Boyle Heights. He wanted to be with *la gente* in the barrio. These were his roots. East Los Angeles substituted for the west side of San Antonio. He was back home. He was doing his abuelita's work, caring for the poor and the needy. As pastor at Soledad, Father Louie welcomed the suggestion made to him by fellow Texan and organizer Ernie Cortés to build a grassroots poor people's campaign in East Los Angeles. The idea resonated with Olivares because Cortés had successfully set up just such a campaign in San Antonio called Communities Organized for Public Service (COPS). As an organizer for the Industrial Areas Foundation (IAF), headed by the longtime progressive Saul Alinsky, Cortés stressed community-based leadership focused on specific community issues and the mobilization of mass pressure on local officials to demand reforms. This became the genesis of United Neighborhoods Organization (UNO), started in the early 1970s and officially inaugurated in 1976.[43] UNO focused on issues that, according to it, were "winnable."[44] Through the leadership of Father Louie as well as that of pastors like Juan Romero, UNO utilized the Catholic parishes and the Episcopalian Church of the Epiphany in Lincoln Heights to organize several chapters. Olivares and Cortés knew that it was in the parishes and churches where they could appeal to *la raza* and organize them in what the UNO activist Lydia López, who joined Olivares's staff in the mid-1980s, calls a "new kind of ministry."[45] The connection between reform politics and Catholic and Christian social doctrine characterized UNO and other IAF faith-based movements. As Mark Warren notes, "While Alinksy took a rather utilitarian view of churches as repositories of money and people to be mobilized, the modern IAF developed a close collaboration with people of faith, fusing religious traditions and power politics into a theology of organizing."[46]

The initial issue taken on by UNO, one that became highly publicized, concerned high and discriminatory auto insurance rates in East Los Angeles. Through a series of confrontations, or what UNO referred to as actions, with the insurance companies as well as county officials, UNO succeeded in lowering the rates.[47] UNO could mobilize as many as five thousand people for a public meeting as an expression of participatory democracy. Other issues included evaluating the performance of public school principals, lobbying for tougher anticrime legislation, repairing broken traffic lights, reducing gang violence, and developing better health facilities and programs. Stressing local leadership, UNO trained people how to speak in public and how to organize meetings. In these struggles and campaigns, Father Louie, with his commitment, charisma, and articulate bilingual speaking ability, surfaced as the key spokesperson and spiritual leader of UNO.[48] In his study of UNO Peter Skerry refers to Olivares as "Mr. UNO."[49] It was Father Luis whom the media descended upon for commentary on the issues. It was not leadership and media

FIGURE 7.1 Father Luis Olivares, C.M.F., La Placita Church, Los Angeles, circa late 1980s. Courtesy Department of Special Collections, Charles E. Young Research Library, UCLA.

attention that attracted Olivares, although he didn't shy away from them and even enjoyed them, but rather his involvement with the people themselves. It was they who empowered him. "This is where I saw Louie really loving people," Father Estrada remarks. "This is what made Louie; the people made Louie."[50]

These conversions in the 1970s in a way were laying the groundwork for Father Louie's most important mission: the sanctuary movement at La Placita Church in the 1980s. Olivares astutely recognized that by transferring from Soledad to La Placita would further expand his new ministry to the poor and disenfranchised. La Placita was the historic birthplace of Los Angeles in 1781. Like San Fernando Cathedral in his hometown of San Antonio, La Placita was the heart of Mexican Catholicism in Los Angeles. It drew thousands of Latinos, including growing numbers of newly arriving Central Americans. It was a working-class, working poor, immigrant, and developing refugee population that constituted the parishioners of La Placita. On any given Sunday, some ten thousand people attended the eleven Spanish-language masses. Every weekend two to three hundred baptisms were performed. It was a Claretian parish, and Father Louie wanted to be there. In 1981, he got his chance.[51]

Olivares did not arrive at La Placita with a preconceived plan to organize a sanctuary movement for Central American refugees. His initial goal was to use the church as a center for expanding grassroots organizing through UNO, just as he had been doing at Soledad and throughout East Los Angeles. In this, he was guided by his reawakened identity with the poor. Particular circumstances, however, while not altering his vision, did shift the strategy. What remained fundamental was his commitment, influenced by Chávez and the farmworkers' movement, that only a faith-based movement could sustain the vision of organizing the Latino working poor. He kept in mind Chávez's profound statement: "Today I don't think that I could base my will to struggle on cold economics or on some political doctrine. I don't think these would be enough to sustain me. For me the base must be faith." [52]

While Father Louie's vision on arriving at La Placita remained focused, what changed were the demographics at the parish. Historically Mexican American, La Placita witnessed a growing number of Central American refugees arriving by the early 1980s. The number would reach some three hundred thousand by the end of the decade. [53] Los Angeles became the second largest Salvadoran city next to San Salvador. [54] Many of the refugees were drawn to La Placita not only as a place of worship, but also as a place where, they hoped, they might receive assistance. As the number of refugees increased, Father Luis began to reach out to them and welcome them to La Placita. He not only welcomed them into the parish, but also began to provide support for them. In the Sunday bulletin of La Placita, references began to appear concerning conditions in El Salvador, including spiritual quotes from Archbishop Romero. [55] This assistance and attention, however, became more concrete and integrated into La Placita's mission when Father Michael Kennedy, a Jesuit priest who had spent time in Latin America and who was looking for a parish where he could work with Central American refugees, proposed to Olivares sometime in 1984 or early 1985 the opportunity that La Placita offered to advance such work. The sympathetic pastor with no hesitation immediately seized upon the challenge. With Kennedy's assistance plus his undivided loyalty, Father Louie shifted his attention and energy to assisting the refugees and in declaring sanctuary for them in 1985. [56]

The sanctuary movement at La Placita was faith-based. What motivated it and sustained it despite criticism, opposition, and even death threats was the strongly held belief of Father Louie and his staff—wonderful, dedicated people such as Kennedy, Estrada, and López, to name just a few, as well as many volunteers, including refugees like Arturo López and Mario Rivas—that what they were doing was the work of God. In giving sanctuary, they were representing the real Church and truly living the message of Jesus and the Gospel. Social movements need ideological and, indeed, even spiritual inspiration and motivation, and the sanctuary movement at La Placita is an important example of the marriage of religious belief and social action.

There are several elements to the activities at La Placita as a faith-based movement. One of these is Father Louie's and his staff's belief that their actions constituted a new way of being Church or, one could say, a return to the original roots of the Church. Olivares believed that the Church, by which he meant the hierarchy, had become too complacent, too comfortable with the rich and powerful, too afraid to speak out on social and political issues, and too distant from the poor. Father Louie moved to make La Placita a different kind of Church. His Church would be just the opposite, and the sanctuary movement would reflect this. He understood that the Church was political despite its statements to the contrary, but it was political either in the direction of the power elite or in support of certain public issues such as antiabortion legislation. What he wanted to do was to channel the Church's politics into confronting more directly the issues of poverty and oppression. If the Church did not stand up for the poor and the oppressed, then the Church might as well not exist. He declared, "If it is expected for the Church's survival to align itself with the rich and the powerful, I'd go so far as to say that the Church should not survive." [57] As Susan Bibler Coutin notes, by contrast with other sanctuary movements that represented in their reflections and actions a critical perspective on sectarian U.S. society and middle-class values, Olivares and the sanctuary movement at La Placita added a critique of the U.S. Catholic Church. [58]

He scolded the Church hierarchy, as had Católicos Por La Raza years earlier, for believing that the position of accommodation was the best. If the Church was of the opinion that it could do more for its people by aligning itself with the ruling elite it was sadly mistaken. This would only lead to more oppression of poor working people. Instead, Olivares called for what Father Romero terms a "new evangelization" based on the Gospel and its priority being the poor, the oppressed, and the marginalized. "Through a new method of *concientización*, new ideas of faith will be announced and social injustice denounced," Romero wrote. [59] *La Opinión*, the major Spanish-language newspaper in Los Angeles, referred to this new evangelization practiced at La Placita as "Evangelio en la calle" (evangelization in the streets). [60] Through this evangelization for the poor, not just in words, but also in action, Father Louie wanted to make the sanctuary movement a way not just of assisting the refugees, but of creating a powerful symbol. He very much believed in symbolism and hence thought the movement should stand as a symbol that the Church in the midst of great suffering truly cared.[61]

It was faith in a new kind of Church that inspired and motivated Father Louie and his apostles. It was faith in the teachings of Jesus and in the incarnational (and the Word became flesh) and salvational meaning of the Gospel. In this respect, the sanctuary movement at La Placita was not just a social movement; it was a practice of faith.

Other aspects of this faith-based movement were further articulated and acted upon by Olivares and his supporters. One involved the concept taken from liberation theology of the "preferential option for the poor." Father Louie personally identified with this, what in Christian theology is also referred to as the "holiness of the poor," and he spoke of it as if it disturbed others, including his superiors.[62] He once remarked to his brother Dámaso that God had made the world and its resources not just for some, but for all of God's children. "If there is so much food here," he said, "it should be taken and given to the ones that are less fortunate because it's all God's things."[63] Olivares believed that faithfulness to the Gospel meant identifying with the poor, and not just the economic poor but the refugees, the undocumented, and others of the less fortunate.[64] One of his favorite sayings, one that Henry Olivares calls his brother's mantra, went like this: "When I come to my final judgment the Lord is not going to ask how many times I went to Mass. He won't care if I gave at Sunday collection. I know that I will be asked: When I was homeless, did you give me shelter? When I was hungry, did you feed me? When I was naked, did you clothe me? When I was a foreigner in your midst, did you take me in?"[65]

If Olivares believed that the Church should be overtly political in its option for the poor, then he further accepted the concept that priests needed to be politically and socially involved in their defense and support of the poor and oppressed. Jesus was his role model. He came into the world not only to baptize, but also to practice a new life and not only in philosophical terms, because how then would one explain the crucifixion? Father Louie rejected the idea that priests should stay in their churches and administer the sacraments. "Our ministry," he proclaimed, "has converted us as agents of social transformation. This, in turn, has a political resonance that is inevitable. But we accept this with all of its consequences."[66]

For Olivares, preaching the Gospel went hand in hand with social action. The Church, including priests, could not remain neutral on what liberationists call social sin: oppression, injustice, racism, class exploitation. Olivares said, "You cannot be witness to human suffering and not be convinced of the existence of social sin. We are all responsible unless we take a stand and speak against it."[67] Father Louie recognized that, unfortunately, there was a divide within the Church on the proper role of priests and that this reflected the tension between what he called "iglesia-institución" and "iglesia-pueblo." He identified with the latter and believed that the institutional Church in fact needed those whom he referred to as the "locos" such as himself, Kennedy, Father Greg Boyle (another Jesuit supporter), and others who spoke out against injustice and who were politically involved. "I cannot remain independent of my people's suffering," he said.[68] Those who opposed sanctuary, for example, according to Henry Olivares, used to tell Father Louie, "Go back to your rectory, stay in there. The Church belongs in the church. The priest belongs in the sacristy." But he would respond, "I don't belong there."[69]

Olivares, in redefining the role of the Church and of priests, clearly was influenced not only by the reforms of Vatican II, especially its pronouncement on the "Church in the Modern World," but also by liberation theology. This theology connected Catholic social doctrine with movements for social reform and even revolutionary changes as well as stressing a preferential option for the poor. Olivares knew and read many of the major liberation theologians, as apparently many other Chicano priests at the time did, as the sociologist Gilbert Cadena has documented.[70] Yet, as Kennedy astutely points out, what Father Louie practiced at La Placita was not textbook liberation theology. In fact, Kennedy prefers the term "liberation from the base." By this he means that the people themselves, the refugees and those who aided them, were the real theologians or "spiritual guides" rather than the intellectuals. As one sanctuary Protestant minister in Tucson observed, it was reading the Gospel from the perspective of Central Americans and the refugees.[71] The people did not expound on this theology; they practiced it. But this was nothing new; it was just going back to the Gospel and what Kennedy calls "gospel theology." As he explains it,

> It's like do you serve the poor? Do you visit the people in prison? Do you believe that God's Spirit is working in the whole community? And that it is sinful that a few have so much and the majority don't. Punto. Now does that have consequences in politics? Yes. Does it make [some] people feel uncomfortable? Yes. So don't call it liberation theology. . . . It's theology from the base and that means all of us.[72]

This Gospel theology in Olivares's mind linked the Gospel message with contemporary society and, in particular, with alleviating social sin. He believed that the Church could address both the Gospel and the needs of people through social action. He saw no contradiction and referred to this unity as a "process of education."[73] "He had a genius for bringing together the gospel message with social justice," Father Boyle recalls.[74] In his weekly homilies before hundreds at La Placita, Father Louie preached this message, always connecting the Gospel to the plight of the people, especially the refugees. Sitting inside La Placita one Sunday, Blase Bonpane felt the power of this message: "He took the fourth chapter of Luke when Jesus quotes from Isaiah 'He has sent me to proclaim liberty to captives.' And he linked this to the institutional violence being perpetrated against the people of Central America and of their need for their own liberation."[75]

The people responded to this message with great understanding and enthusiasm. But the message was not solely that of Olivares or of Kennedy: it was also that of the people themselves. Both priests would invite some of the refugees at Mass to go up to the front of the altar, face the congregation, and tell their moving stories. These gripping tales fused, as nothing else could, the Gospel and contemporary social issues. The experience represented what staff member Lisa Martínez calls "living the liturgy."[76] "There was weeping but also laughter" at these Sunday masses, as the Chicana novelist Graciela Limón, a volunteer at La Placita, recalls. "Often there was clapping and speaking out. In all, these were extremely positive moments."[77]

As part of the sanctuary movement as a faith-based process, Olivares stressed the priority of God's law over human law. He believed that if civil society contributes to injustice, then it is the responsibility, if not the duty, of those who believe in the merciful God to first obey his laws even if it means violating Caesar's laws. God is not neutral on injustice, Father Louie believed, and neither should we be. He particularly emphasized this point when he proclaimed, along with Kennedy and Boyle, in 1987 that they, as priests and children of God, would not obey the new Immigration Reform and Control Act passed by the U.S. Congress the previous year because it did not extend amnesty to all undocumented immigrants, mostly from Mexico, and prohibited their employment. They said, "We will not obey this law. We will hire undocumented workers, and we will encourage others to do so. For us the laws of God come before the laws of humans."[78]

Olivares was unquestionably political, but his politics were based on his faith. His belief in God, in a just and merciful Savior, in the Jesus who came to save, in the sanctity of all of God's creatures, and in salvation in this world as well as in the next, all of this oriented Father Louie's politics and that of the sanctuary movement at La Placita. The church symbolized the New Jerusalem and the New Church. It was both reality and symbol. If the reality had its historical moment, the symbol lives on. As Father Boyle said, "Olivares stood as a countersign to the kingdom of power, greed and violence. He pronounced what the kingdom of God should look like, a place in which people share and live in equality." [79]

Pan-Latino Identity and Sanctuary

On a cold but sunny December day in Los Angeles, people from various ethnic backgrounds, among them Central American refugees, anxiously entered the main sanctuary of La Placita Church. The gathering included eighty religious leaders and members of other faiths in an ecumenical show of support for what was soon to transpire. Various film and entertainment celebrities who wished to use their status to call attention to the event joined them. Besides this diverse audience, there was a small army of reporters and television crews covering the unfolding drama. "It was like a national event," Kennedy thought to himself. It also reflected the use of sanctuary as a "public event" or as "public sanctuary" that characterized other well-publicized sanctuary movements as a way of educating the public and the media to the plight of Central American refugees and to the conflicts in Central America. At the appropriate moment, Father Olivares, accompanied by Father Kennedy, entered the sanctuary and stood in front of the main altar. Behind them on the main altar screen, the image of Our Lady of Guadalupe was prominently displayed, flanked by the U.S. flag on one side and the Mexican flag on the other. The priests were dressed in white robes to symbolize a new beginning. Following the service, a news conference was held inside the church. In a strong voice and with a determined look on his face, Olivares announced, "Today, December 12, 1985, on the feast day of Our Lady of Guadalupe, the patroness of the Americas, we here at La Placita Church in unity with our brothers and sisters of other faiths publicly declare the church to be a sanctuary for refugees fleeing persecution and oppression in Central America. These Salvadorans and Guatemaltecos are our brothers and sisters also and we will not turn them away." [80]

With these words, Father Louie not only made La Placita the first Catholic church in Los Angeles to declare itself a sanctuary, but also voiced a new pan-Latino solidarity that had not been widely articulated before in the Chicano community. Indeed, he symbolically reconstructed Guadalupe into a pan-Latino deity by extending her blessing to include Central America and the Central American refugees.[81] "We are all responsible," he had said four days earlier, in order to put the issue in historical perspective, "for what happened in those horrible years of the Holocaust. We were all responsible for what our country did in Vietnam. We must all bear responsibility for what is now going on in Central America."[82]

As an expression of this solidarity, the Mexican American priest introduced a Salvadoran couple and a Guatemalan mother with her three children. They were dressed all in black, and their faces, except for their eyes, were completely covered by black scarves. Their names were not given in order to protect their identities. In plain but moving Spanish, they proceeded to tell their *testimonios*, or stories, to the assembled audience and the media. Their tragic tales were translated for those who did not understand Spanish.[83]

Olivares's acceptance of the Central Americans into what had been historically a Mexican American parish underlined the changing and more complex demographics of Latino Los Angeles and its equally changing ethnic political identity. *Chicano* and *Mexican American* were no longer practical terms of ethnic identity in a parish composed of different Latino ethnic groups. Father Louie understood this and gave expression to a new pan-Latino identity or, to use William Flores's and Rina Benmayor's term, a new form of "cultural citizenship."[84] This marked a clear departure from the strict ethnic and cultural nationalism associated with the earlier Chicano movement. As David Badillo notes, a general Latino-Catholic identity has developed within the Church today; however, what occurred at La Placita represented an organic fusion of identities as opposed to a generic one.[85] It also further dramatized the issue of sanctuary in the city. While the Los Angeles City Council in late November had also declared the city to be a "city of refuge" for Central American refugees, La Placita's embrace of sanctuary would come to possess more of both a symbolic as well as an actual impact on both the refugees and Los Angeles itself.[86]

The issue of sanctuary and the expression of pan-Latino solidarity was not just Olivares's. Father Kennedy had initially proposed it, with Father Louie's enthusiastic endorsement. It was then discussed for at least two months with different parish groups largely composed of Mexican Americans. With little or no opposition, the represented parishioners willingly and proudly accepted the idea of sanctuary. They were endorsing what in fact had already been reality at La Placita. For at least two years, the church had been serving as an

FIGURE 7.2 Father Luis Olivares, C.M.F., with Father Mike Kennedy, S.J., November 23, 1989. Courtesy Department of Special Collections, Charles E. Young Research Library, UCLA.

unofficial sanctuary, offering various services to the refugees. The announcement of sanctuary only made public activities that had already been transpiring, or what Cecilia Menjivar refers to as community networking.[87] These involvements build on an earlier history of La Placita serving as a community-organizing center for Mexican immigrants and Mexican Americans.[88] For Kennedy, going public represented an organic process. "It was a natural consequence of our work," he says. "It wasn't like it dropped down from Heaven."[89]

Declaring sanctuary, according to Kennedy, also upped the ante "by saying we're publicly sheltering people and that's illegal and we're declaring we're doing it and that it's wrong to be selling military aid to El Salvador."[90] In effect, like other sanctuary movements in the country, La Placita became an "alternative political space."[91] In this space, the sanctuary movement at the church and elsewhere further practiced what the Tucson movement referred to as "legal initiative," which suggested that it was not the movement that was breaking the law, but the Reagan administration that refused to uphold national as well as international law concerning refugees.[92] In addition, the public forum provided Olivares and La Placita more of a platform to speak to the issues and to say to the Reagan administration, according to Kennedy, "We feel that what you're doing in El Salvador is evil, it's wrong, it's sinful." [93] "He was very daring," said Lydia López, characterizing Olivares's leadership.[94] Above all, it made La Placita into a symbol of hope for the Central American refugees. Both in Los Angeles and in Central America, the people now knew that there was a church that accepted them and cared for them. This was Olivares's vision. It was his dream.[95] La Placita became more than an "underground church," a term linked to other sanctuary movements. This small Catholic church, by contrast, represented an open and public sanctuary.[96]

This bold move, of course, was not without controversy. The dissension originated not within La Placita, but outside it, among some of the public and some Church officials. Olivares, however, was not intimidated. He didn't care what consequences ensued. He never thought, for example, how this might affect collections or any other pragmatic matters. He knew he was right in pursuing what Coutin calls "the prophetic tradition."[97] He had informed the newly appointed Archbishop Roger Mahony of his intentions. Although the archbishop was initially supportive and had indicated his desire to preside at the Mass and to attend the press conference, he did not appear. Eventually he took what he considered to be a neutral position on sanctuary after the National Conference of Catholic Bishops, while critical of the Reagan administration's position on the refugees, declined to officially endorse the sanctuary movement because it meant breaking the law. On the other hand, Archbishop Mahony did not prohibit or impinge on Olivares's intentions.[98] While Father Louie publicly did not express disappointment at Mahony's absence at the service, privately, according to López and others, he was heartbroken.[99]

The promotion of pan-Latino identity and solidarity at La Placita was not automatic. It was a process. Underlying this, of course, were the demographic changes. In the 1980s thousands of Central Americans entered Los Angeles. In that decade, La Placita was serving one hundred thousand parishioners, including many Central Americans.[100] Olivares recognized what the writer Rubén Martínez calls the "new L.A."[101] "I think that he was at that particular time unique in the sense that he understood that L.A. was no longer just one culture," Kennedy remarks of Olivares. "L.A. will always be predominantly Mexican but there's a church—La Placita—that's different. Louie got it and a lot of people really didn't."[102] But Olivares's reaction was not based just on demographics. It was a human and Christian response to the plight, condition, and needs of the refugees. It was this compassion that led to his embrace of the Central Americans and to his desire to link Mexican Americans with the new arrivals.

The promotion of pan-Latino identity at one level involved La Placita's acceptance of the concept of sanctuary. But, at another level, it included Olivares's work and that of his staff to get rank-and-file Mexican American parishioners not only to welcome the Central Americans, but also to identify with them in becoming Latinos. Kennedy recalls that when he first proposed the idea of sanctuary Olivares astutely recognized that this emphasis would allow him the opportunity to better "fulfill some of his vision of the Gospel in light of the new reality of Central American immigration." [103] At the same time, Father Louie further understood that his Gospel vision had to likewise include bringing other Mexican Americans into this process.[104]

Olivares admitted, however, that at first this new sense of Latino identity was not necessarily easy for some Mexican Americans at La Placita. "Many people even thought I was Salvadoran because of my involvement with Salvadoran refugees," he told Romero.[105] Some accused him of separating from Mexican Americans and going over to the refugees.[106] But these obstacles did not deter Father Louie. He didn't see the Salvadorans in terms of their national backgrounds. He saw them as people in need and thought that those who were better off and more secure, such as some Mexican Americans, should support them.[107] Like other sanctuary movements, the La Placita project, as spearheaded by Olivares, aimed to create a sense of community, although at La Placita it would be focused on a pan-Latino sense of community or Latino Christianity.[108] In theological terms, he was also striving to accomplish the "blessed community." [109] He once told his brother Henry, after returning from a trip to El Salvador during which he feared for his safety but was not afraid to die, "I'm ready to give my life for these people." Henry responded, more out of concern for his brother's safety than for anything else, "But, Louie, they're not even your people, you're Mexican!"

Louie, with no hostility in his voice but as a way of reassuring his big brother, responded, "Oh, no, they're as Latino as I am. We're all people of God. If they were Anglo, I'd do the same thing. I'm ready to give my life for these people." [110]

In further promoting pan-Latino identity, Olivares utilized symbols or what Laurie Sommers calls the "cultural invention of inventing Latinismo." [111] He installed a new side altar in memory of Archbishop Romero. Crosses of Salvadoran design and other Central American iconography were added to the church. In his office, Father Louie had a picture of Emiliano Zapata, the Mexican revolutionary hero, one of Augusto Sandino, the Nicaraguan revolutionary leader, a framed letter from President Daniel Ortega Saavedra, the head of the Sandinista government in Nicaragua, and a picture of La Virgen de Guadalupe. In addition, he invited and hosted various Central American leaders, such as Ortega Saavedra and Archbishop Arturo Rivera y Damas from El Salvador.[112]

In time, Father Louie's example, compassion, and love for the refugees won over most of his Mexican American parishioners. Although some historical and cultural differences existed between Mexican Americans and Central Americans, they quickly discovered that they shared many experiences and characteristics, including the Spanish language, Latino Catholicism, the migration saga, and their working-class and peasant roots. But above all, according to Kennedy, they shared the need to survive in what for many, including Mexican Americans, was still a hostile and discriminatory U.S. environment and hence the need for justice. This recognition made La Placita into what Kennedy calls a "great experiment."[113] Olivares acknowledged this common bonding and shared Latino identity when, six months after publicly declaring sanctuary, he gratefully told his congregation: "It's gratifying to help. But more important is what has happened to our hearts and attitudes on Central America. Before we declared sanctuary, a lot of you thought that La Placita was here for Mexicans alone. But now you have learned that anyone in need is your neighbor."[114]

The construction, or what some would call the invention, of a pan-Latino identity at La Placita, however, involved more than ideology. Indeed, contrary to Benedict Anderson's concept of an "imagined community," in this case involving Latinos, the experiment at La Placita was instead a lived experience.[115] It also was more than what Felix Padilla, in his study of coalition building between Mexican Americans and Puerto Ricans in Chicago, calls "situational Latino ethnic consciousness," in which both groups joined under the umbrella term *Latino* in order to retain needed social services. Rather than an organic fusion, this type of pan-Latino identity was largely based on practicality and a situational context.[116] Undoubtedly, some of this context was at work at La Placita, but Latino identity in this case went much deeper. Mexican Americans and Central Americans at La Placita were not, as they were in Chicago, uniting only to obtain governmental assistance. On the contrary, there was nothing to be obtained. Instead, they became Latino as a result of their faith that they were all children of God. Moreover, they became Latinos by their self-help actions, or what sanctuary workers in other locations called witnessing.[117] Encountering one another through a variety of assistance programs at La Placita made Mexican Americans and Central Americans recognize each other as one people.

Sanctuary as organized at the downtown church under the supervision of Olivares first and foremost consisted of providing shelter. Many of the refugees had no place to live, not knowing anyone in Los Angeles and having little or no money to rent a place for themselves. In the most dramatic and publicized action at La Placita, Olivares and his staff opened up the church to allow as many as two hundred refugees, all men, to sleep on the church grounds. They were allowed to sleep inside the church itself, sleeping either on the pews or underneath them. The church hall in time was also used as a shelter.[118] These facilities served as a version of the "safe houses" provided for the refugees in other U.S. locations.[119] Parishioners provided blankets, sheets, and pillows for the refugees. Others received mats or sleeping bags. "How many churches were doing that?" López asks. "How many priests or ministers were doing that?"[120] During the day, while the refugees looked for work or went to their jobs, a crew of parishioners cleaned up for church services and prepared for the next evening's shelter.[121] "It was a very poignant moment to watch them leaving and watch them coming back," López thought, as she witnessed this ritual every day. "My heart would go out to them."[122]

While many of the refugees were single men—the *solos*—others arrived with families, among them single women and women with children. To shelter them, Olivares's staff attempted to place some of them with Mexican American families. More concretely, they obtained the use of a former convent on the grounds of Blessed Sacrament Church in Hollywood, a predominantly Latino area, and opened up by 1985 Casa Rutilio Grande, named after a martyred Salvadoran Jesuit priest killed in 1977, or Casa Grande, as it was commonly called. Here, up to thirty Central American families and a few single men were housed for a period of time until more permanent housing could be arranged, especially after they acquired jobs.[123]

Shelter was the most immediate need of the refugees, but other ones also had to be met. This was determined by interviewing the refugees as they came to La Placita. Olivares, Kennedy, and the rest of the staff, along with volunteers, talked and listened to the refugees as they told their stories. These narratives were moving and tragic. Many of them had witnessed other family members being killed, raped, or tortured. Some had been tortured themselves. Children exhibited wounds or were maimed as a result of the bombing of their villages. Many were still traumatized.[124] Graciela Limón heard many of these stories.

"We all wept at what we were hearing," she remembers, still affected by the experience. These stories inspired her to visit El Salvador and to write a pan-Latino novel, *In Search of Bernabé* (1993). She adds, "My recollection is that the general condition of the *refugiados* was pretty heartbreaking: raggedy clothing, obvious neglect of person, fright, a feeling of inadequacy, of displacement. However, I also remember a high spirit of hope and a lot of compassion and commiseration one for the other. There was a strong feeling of comradeship and understanding."[125]

To meet the refugees' needs and to coordinate these efforts, Olivares and his staff, including some of the refugees themselves, established the Centro Pastoral Rutilio Grande as early as 1984.[126] Soon directed by Father Kennedy and with offices at La Placita, the centro, staffed by both Mexican American and Salvadoran personnel and volunteers, offered a variety of services to the refugees.[127] Besides providing shelter, it fed the refugees housed at La Placita and at Casa Grande. Hot meals such as beans and rice in the evenings and breakfast were cooked and served by volunteers who were part of the several small base communities organized by the centro. Emulating their liberation theology counterparts in Latin America, these communities focused on three principles: *leer, refleccionar, actuar* (read, reflect, act), with an emphasis on the last.[128]

Finding employment for the refugees was another major service. Through contacts with the wider sanctuary community in Los Angeles and with those working on Central American issues, including mainline Protestant churches as well as Jewish synagogues, the centro was able to secure jobs for some of the refugees. Others looked for jobs on their own while the centro sheltered them. Still others were allowed to sell homemade products such as clothing outside of the church during Sunday Masses.[129] Because employment often necessitated documents concerning immigration status, staff at La Placita at times advised the refugees as well as undocumented immigrants where to go to purchase such documents in the underground immigrant market.[130]

Other forms of assistance included providing money for rent and for bus transportation, donating clothes to the refugees, and making available medical as well as legal assistance.[131] In addition, what Kennedy calls "survival English" was also available. This included learning practical questions such as, "Where do I catch the bus?" Taught mostly by Anglo volunteers, including university students, these classes were offered in the evenings at both La Placita and Casa Grande.[132] A library was made available at Casa Grande.[133] Because many of the refugees had witnessed brutalities in El Salvador or had themselves been tortured, the centro further arranged psychological counseling. Sympathetic psychologists offered their assistance without charge. They treated these patients either at Casa Grande or at the County Hospital. The greatest psychological need involved those suffering from posttraumatic syndrome, including nightmares. "We had people whose whole bodies were covered with scars," Father Kennedy recalls.[134] The sociologists Norma Chinchilla, Nora Hamilton, and James Loucky, in their study of the refugees, noted other psychological and emotional issues. "Those who came in the 1980s in some cases confronted additional difficulties and psychological problems resulting from the experiences of war and violence in their home countries," they write. "Many Central American immigrants left members of the family behind; parents would leave children with grandparents with the hope of earning enough to send money back home for support; parents sent children to live with little-known relatives in the United States; sometimes individuals came alone, leaving both spouse and children in the home country."[135]

Still other forms of help involved supplying money and guidance for refugees going to other parts of the country or seeking sanctuary in Canada. Los Angeles, as the historian María Cristina García notes, in this sense served as a "funnel city."[136] Henry Olivares remembers visiting Father Louie once at La Placita and witnessing this type of assistance.

> "Henry, come with me," Father Louie, who was in a rush, said.
> "I went with him and there was a couple that had come in from El Salvador and they were on their way out of L.A. into the Midwest. [Louie] gave them money and told them what they needed to do because they were fleeing from El Salvador. That's the kind of thing he was doing. He had this desire to help people."
> Henry asked, "Louie, these people are they going to pay you back?"
> "I don't care," his brother compassionately responded. "That's not what I'm interested in. I want to help them because they're fleeing persecution."[137]

In addition to specific social services, Father Louie used the media to promote the case of the refugees. Articulate in both English and Spanish and an excellent extemporaneous speaker, Olivares became the darling of the Los Angeles media, both English-language and Spanish-language, on sanctuary as well as on Central America. The print and electronic media alike were constantly interviewing him. He was often asked to be on television interview shows. He became the official spokesperson for the refugees. "I don't think a day would go by when some national or local news wasn't interviewing him," says Kennedy. What made Olivares especially effective with the media, according to Kennedy, was that he knew and loved the refugees. He could translate their pains and their hopes. "His heart was there," Kennedy adds.[138] Taking advantage of the media was not something that made Olivares uncomfortable. He cultivated reporters and knew how to use the media. "He was a big ham," Father Estrada affectionately says of Olivares's ties to the media.[139] López heard good-natured jokes that there was no television camera that Father Louie didn't like. She admits that the priest had what she calls a "huge ego," but that this wasn't necessarily bad nor did it distance him from others. "I think that you have to have a huge, healthy ego to be involved in public life," López believes, "because you know that you're going to be attacked so you need to know that you're doing the right thing." [140]

Olivares's media exposure, however, appears to have caused some concern with Archbishop Mahony, who probably felt (or perhaps his staff felt) that Olivares was getting more attention than the archbishop. Probably only half-jokingly, Mahony allegedly once asked Olivares, "What's going on here, Louie? Every time you brush your teeth, you're gonna call CBS?" [141]

An additional expression of pan-Latino ethnic identity consisted of Father Louie's frequent trips to El Salvador to make the linkage between La Placita and the war-ridden Central American country. Olivares believed that assisting the people still there was just as important as the work being done in Los Angeles. This was a form of transnational sanctuary. Through his work, he was linking El Salvador to Los Angeles. On these trips, some of them as a participant in ecumenical religious journeys from Los Angeles, Father Louie took cash, which he distributed to Catholic social services in El Salvador that were working with the poor and the dislocated. Some of these funds, collected from groups such as UNO, he took directly to the peasants in the countryside. "Why are you doing this?" Henry Olivares once asked him. "Hey," Louie answered, with passion in his voice, "I'm the only hope that these people have. I'm the only hope that they can safely get out of El Salvador and go to Honduras. If they don't have money, they can't do it. They're totally helpless. People know what they have to do. All I'm providing is just a little help for them." [142]

On some of these trips into the countryside, the people in turn helped Father Louie by occasionally hiding him from the military, which was trying to discover who was dispensing funds. They sheltered the American priest in their homes until the threat abated. As he accepted the peasants' version of sanctuary, Olivares at these moments could not help but remember his own family's sheltering of persecuted priests in Mexico and in San Antonio. "I just trust the people," he said. "They are the best people and they hide me. I feel like Grandma when she was hiding the priests. I feel these people are like my grandmother, hiding me." [143]

Olivares also traveled to Honduras to visit and do what he could for the many Salvadorans living in refugee camps along the border with El Salvador, some of whom were attempting to repatriate themselves back to their homes. Father Louie couldn't help but be moved by their conditions and by their stories, so similar to the ones he heard at La Placita. Olivares likewise met and became friends with progressive Salvadoran priests and religious workers, including Archbishop Rivera y Damas, the successor of the martyred Archbishop Romero, whose burial site Father Louie visited. Although he had never met Romero, Father Louie felt a personal as well as political closeness to him. On some trips, Olivares further met with governmental officials to urge the cessation of the conflict and violence. On one particular trip, he, Kennedy, and an ecumenical delegation delivered some ten thousand letters from concerned people in Los Angeles advocating peace in El Salvador and calling for the Salvadoran government to observe human rights. They personally met with President Napoleón Duarte and hand-delivered the letters to him.[144]

Pan-Latino identity at La Placita went beyond Mexican American–Central American relations. It also came to include recently arrived undocumented immigrants, predominantly from Mexico. They were economic refugees as opposed to the political refugees from Central America. But to Olivares, his staff, and many of his parishioners there was no distinction. They were all people in need, and it was their responsibility to help them. La Placita's response reflected what Badillo refers to as the "new immigrant church."[145] This assistance was already being given to some extent in the early 1980s, but the issue of the undocumented became more serious after the passage of the 1986 Immigration Reform and Control Act. This new immigration law, while extending amnesty to the undocumented who could prove residency up to 1982, at the same time excluded thousands more who either could not prove it or who had entered after that deadline. To make matters worse, the law for the first time imposed criminal penalties on employers who knowingly hired undocumented workers. Many civil libertarians and Latino civil rights groups expressed concern that employers, in order to avoid the possibility of being prosecuted, might discriminate against hiring Latinos, whether citizens or immigrants.

Using the model of the 1985 public proclamation of sanctuary, Olivares and Kennedy, together with Father Boyle, the pastor of Dolores Mission in Boyle Heights, which had also extended sanctuary to the refugees, agreed to publicly declare their resistance to the new law and to extend sanctuary to undocumented Mexican immigrants and any economic refugees. As they had done two years before, the priests made their declaration on the feast day of Our Lady of Guadalupe, December 12, 1987, at 9 A.M.[146] "Louie always used a Guadalupe event as a time to further educate the people about their own liberation story," López notes with admiration. "To him the story was of interest to the poor because Mary didn't appear to the bishop, she appeared to this little Indian and, my goodness, what does that say? That says that God loves us all and he wanted his mother to appear there and to say I love you."[147]

Bishop Gilberto Chávez, the auxiliary bishop of San Diego, joined them on this occasion. Following a Mass at La Placita, they announced their intentions at a press conference inside the church. La Placita was packed with parishioners, undocumented immigrants, refugees, politicians, community leaders, representatives of the religious ecumenical movement, and, of course, the media.[148]

In their proclamation, Olivares, Kennedy, and Boyle stressed that they understood that by declaring sanctuary for the undocumented, by their hiring of them, and by encouraging others to employ the immigrants, they were breaking the law. But, as Olivares had said on other occasions, there was a higher law—God's law—that they were obeying. Calling the immigration law immoral, the three issued a joint statement that said, "When laws trample human rights, they must not be obeyed. When policies subordinate the needs and rights of people to order and convenience, they must be denounced. To the extent that we openly aid, abet and harbor the undocumented, we indeed are breaking the law. The gospel would have us do no other."[149]

They were refusing to obey the law because Jesus would do the same. "This is not guesswork on our part," they told the audience and the media with conviction. "The Gospel is clear and abundantly full of Jesus' concern for the poor, the fearful, the persecuted, those who hunger for peace and justice. It is our strong belief that Jesus would, with ease, find Himself aiding, abetting and harboring our sisters and brothers who have come to our community in hope and instead are hunted because they lack the papers that would allow them to stay."[150]

Boyle later added, "What would Jesus do? Would he ask for papers before he would give someone a job they need to feed their family? Of course not."[151]

Jesus would go even further, they added. He would also publicly condemn these laws as unjust and use such a public pronouncement to change people's hearts about the poor and oppressed. They were only following Jesus' example. For them not to follow Jesus would be to betray not only Him, but biblical tradition as well. Quoting Leviticus 19:33–34, they reminded others of God's message concerning "aliens": "When aliens reside with you in your land, do not molest them. You shall treat the aliens who reside with you no differently than the natives born among you; have the same love for them as for yourselves." [152]

The only crime the undocumented were committing, the priests stressed, was their desire to pursue the fundamental human right to work and to feed their families. Under these circumstances, they could not remain silent. By accepting the undocumented, they were, as with the refugees, endorsing a preferential option for the poor.[153] They called on others to join them. They could do so by signing a pledge of noncooperation with the law and by stating they would assist in the hiring of the undocumented. The assembled crowd at La Placita broke out into thunderous applause.[154] Three hundred people, including forty religious leaders of different faiths, signed the pledge. "This is a real sign of love and concern," Bishop Chávez said as he joyfully voiced his support. "The 300 people who signed are expressing their love for the undocumented who cannot receive amnesty and who are suffering a lot because they have no home and no rights." [155]

This was a historic declaration because by extending the definition of sanctuary to include mostly undocumented Mexican immigrants, La Placita did what no other sanctuary community in the U.S. had done. While others in the movement had restricted their work only to political refugees, the Los Angeles church did away with such distinctions and embraced both political and economic refugees as one people. Indirectly, this was also a way of constructing and promoting a new pan-Latino identity that distinguished neither between national and ethnic identity, nor between residency statuses.

Yet the announcing of sanctuary for undocumented immigrants was not without its negative consequences. Two days after the declaration, the INS director in Los Angeles stated that both La Placita and Dolores Mission would be investigated for possible immigration law violations.[156] The INS also threatened to eliminate the two churches' tax exemptions if they broke the law.[157] An FBI investigation of Olivares, Kennedy, and Boyle may have further ensued after the INS western regional director, Howard Ezell, referred to them as the "three renegade priests." [158] Ezell, in addition, accused Olivares of sponsoring terrorism by undocumented immigrants.[159] This even involved Olivares's standing up to his older brother, Dámaso, a San Antonio policeman, although in a brotherly and friendly fashion. On a visit to Los Angeles at the time of the controversy over La Placita's stance on the undocumented, Dámaso took exception to his younger brother's position.

"Louie, you have to remember I'm a police officer. I'm sworn to uphold the law."

"Well," Father Louie replied, probably with a twinkle in his eye and displaying his wonderful sense of humor, "you enforce the law and I'll break it." [160]

Incensed at Olivares's defiance, Ezell and the INS pressured Archbishop Mahony to try to force the priests to comply with the law. According to Father Boyle, Mahony at one point tried to convince the provincials of both the Claretians and the Jesuits to remove the three priests from their assignments. The provincials refused. [161]

Archbishop Mahony, for his part, felt caught in the middle. He championed immigrant rights and privately also had doubts about the new law, but he did not want to publicly sanction breaking it. He called the three in to meet with him in an attempt to persuade them to obey the law or at least not openly call for violating it. "Will you sign this statement that you will respect the ban on hiring undocumented workers?" he pressured them. [162] They refused. Olivares said that if the law was unjust, it was not to be obeyed. An agitated Mahony countered that if the law was unjust, it should be changed. [163] The two sides were at a standoff. At one point, one of the archbishop's aides angrily said to Olivares: "What right do you have to set policy for the archdiocese?" [164] Knowing he could demand obedience from the priests but not wanting a public confrontation with the popular clerics, Mahony backed off. [165]

Father Boyle notes, however, that Mahony "silenced" them by instructing them not to speak publicly on the issue. The archbishop shortly rescinded his order when media pressure for the three priests to address specific issues concerning undocumented immigrants increased. [166] As members of religious orders rather than diocesan priests, Olivares, Kennedy, and Boyle were not as much under the control of Mahony as the latter and hence more able to act independently. Of this connection between members of religious orders and social action, Cox notes, "Priests who belong to religious orders are more likely to take unpopular stands than are the secular priests who serve parish congregations." [167]

Hence, Olivares and the other two, while respecting their archbishop, continued to publicly address their opposition to the law and the morality of the issue. In a clear and further defiance of both the INS and Mahony, the three

wrote an opinion piece in the *Los Angeles Times* in 1988 reiterating their ratio-
nale for extending sanctuary to the undocumented immigrants.[168] Although,
according to Kennedy, Father Louie never dwelled too much on the tension
with the archbishop, Olivares put these tensions into perspective when he
stated, "And the *migra* [INS] doesn't like it, and the civic authorities don't like
it, and many times our very own ecclesiastical authorities don't like what this
community [La Placita] proclaims: the defense of the poor, the rejected, the
undocumented. But it is precisely because of this that [God's] community de-
serves respect." [169]

The tensions between Archbishop Mahony and Olivares may have also involved other factors as well. The writer Mike Davis proposes that what seemed
to be at stake was a struggle for the leadership of the Latino Catholic community. Davis notes that shortly after becoming archbishop, Mahony moved
to prioritize a new Latino agenda for the Church in Los Angeles to meet some
of the needs of the new majority in the Church and, in part, to confront the
aggressive inroads among Latinos made by Pentecostal groups. This new initiative, however, was to be centrally controlled by Mahony, and hence the
movement by Father Luis out of La Placita was seen as a rival and more radical competition. As Davis puts it, "The civil rights movement of the undocumented poor that Olivares was building raised the specter of 'dual power' in
the archdiocese, a grassroots church of liberation emerging side by side with
the highly centralized chancery." Although publicly correct in their relationship, Mahony and Olivares would continue to have different visions of the role
of the Church in Los Angeles.[170] Ironically, some twenty years later, Cardinal
Mahony would take the same stance as Olivares and call for the Church to
oppose any federal legislation that would criminalize undocumented immigrants and those who supported them.[171]

Besides sheltering, feeding, and providing many of the same services for
the undocumented as for the refugees, La Placita also served as a central organizing center for a pro–immigrant rights coalition that came together during
this period. One such effort involved the Coalition for Humane Immigrant
Rights of Los Angeles (CHIRLA). Serving as a convener and, according to the
CHIRLA member Susan Alva, as the moral leader of the group, Olivares was the
group's first chairperson and most visible spokesperson on the issues. Father
Louie often called upon CHIRLA for legal assistance for the undocumented
who came to him for help. To protest the deportation of the immigrants by
the INS, the group sponsored public protests and civil disobedience that involved some members, including Olivares, chaining themselves to the fence

in the back of INS headquarters to try to prevent the departure of the buses deporting the immigrants. For these actions, Father Louie and the others were arrested. For Olivares, no action was impossible if it furthered the cause of social justice. The undocumented, like the refugees, were his people, and he was their shepherd.[172]

Ecumenism

If a new pan-Latino identity characterized the united front between Mexican Americans and Central Americans in the sanctuary movement at La Placita, still another progressive aspect of this experiment was the ecumenical support system attached to sanctuary. I am using the term *ecumenism* in an interfaith sense rather than only to imply inter-Christian connections. Indeed, even before La Placita began to assist the refugees, other religious groups, including such mainline Protestant ones as Episcopalians, Presbyterians, and Methodists had already been coming together to address the refusal of the Reagan administration to grant asylum to the Central Americans and to oppose U.S. policy in Central America. La Placita's championing of sanctuary only accelerated this ecumenical movement, which brought together Angelinos of different denominations—Christian, Protestant, and Jew—and different ethnic backgrounds. Ecumenism constituted another aspect of Olivares's vision, and that of others, of God's humanity and of the sanctity of all humans. The stress on ecumenism, of course, is in sharp contrast to the acute rivalry that the Catholic Church displayed toward Protestant and Pentecostal denominations in earlier periods, as noted in Chapter Four. Instead of focusing on what the Church had considered the Protestant threat, now, in the post–Vatican II era, it stressed interfaith respect and dialogue. It now considered, for example, all Christians and even non-Christians to be people of God.[173] Father Louie's embrace of ecumenism reflected this change as well as undoubtedly the religious ecumenism espoused by his friend and colleague César Chávez and the UFW through their integration of support from Catholic, Protestant, and Jewish communities in the farmworkers' struggle.

The ecumenical movement in Los Angeles, centered on the refugees and on the Central American wars, predated Olivares's becoming pastor at La Placita in 1981. Bonpane, who had served as a Maryknoll priest in Central America for many years, suggests that the movement's origins in Los Angeles lay in the outraged and stunned reaction to the killing of six Anglo-American religious sisters in El Salvador by the Salvadoran military in 1980. Catholics and members of other faiths attended a special service at La Placita shortly after the news of this massacre broke. Although Father Louie was not yet at La Placita, Bonpane attributes the killing of the sisters to part of Olivares's ongoing conversion.[174] Part of this conversion involved Olivares's embrace of an ecumenical effort to assist the refugees and to protest U.S. policy in Central America. Rabbi Allen Freehling credits the success of this movement to Olivares's influence and stature. "He was a voice of conscience for all of our communities," he says. "He alerted us to the perils that existed in Central America and was a source of hope that if we came together, we could make a difference in these problems." [175]

Through these ecumenical connections, Olivares was further able to provide assistance to the refugees once they arrived at La Placita. Fund raising for the different services depended on this outreach. So too did finding jobs for the refugees. La Placita could not have done what it did for the refugees and later the undocumented immigrants without the support of the ecumenical community, Jewish and Protestant. Part of this success lay in Father Louie's ability to transcend his own religious and ethnic identity and to reach out to others of different faiths and ethnic backgrounds. Kennedy comments that this ecumenism may have been Olivares's major strength. "To be real honest," he says, in good-humor comparing himself with his friend and mentor, "part of Louie's genius was sometimes that he connected better with the Anglos and the ecumenical groups while I connected better with the refugees." Olivares could do this because he possessed what Father Mike calls, "real presidential style." By means of this style and his commitment, Olivares, according to Kennedy, "could engage people and people felt very confident and as a result he could convoke so many people of really high caliber including Congress people, rabbis, ministers, and bishops. He had charisma." [176]

One of the early manifestations of the ecumenical movement that Olivares supported and worked with was the Southern California Ecumenical Council Interfaith Task Force on Central America (SCITCA). Organized apparently in reaction to the killings of the sisters in El Salvador, the task force was brought together by Sister Patricia Krommer and Sister Pat Rief, IHM. Krommer had been working as a boycott organizer for the UFW in Los Angeles. Many of the initial members, including many women, were interfaith pastors of different faiths, some of whom had also been involved in the farmworkers' struggles.[177] The task force concentrated on educating the religious communities in the greater Los Angeles area on the issues involved in the Central American conflicts, the role of the United States in promoting the conflicts, and the plight of the increasing numbers of refugees reaching southern California. Through its sanctuary committee, task force representatives visited churches and synagogues and addressed these issues. Part of these visits—a very crucial aspect of its work—was the inclusion of some of the refugees themselves, who spoke about their experiences. "This was a very good strategy," Krommer stresses.[178] A few churches, such as the First Unitarian Church, declared themselves sanctuaries before La Placita, but these declarations were political statements in support of the concept, according to the Reverend Don Smith, a task force member; the churches did not engage in sheltering refugees.[179]

Seeing the importance of the task force as he accelerated his own work with the refugees, Olivares supported it and became a member of the group. He served on its advisory board and, although not as active as others because of the press of work at La Placita, he did what he could for the task force.[180] His support and encouragement alone meant a great deal to task force members. To Father Louie, the task force and other ecumenical efforts represented not only the ecumenism supported by Vatican II, but, more important, its actual fulfillment. Ecumenism in this context was no longer just a nice-sounding term or occasional interfaith gatherings, but a real movement. Olivares saw himself as part of this. Bonpane, in turn, saw in Father Louie a deep and genuine commitment to an ecumenism that transcended institutional relationships and that instead focused on the humanity of all people irrespective of their religious connections. "He didn't seem to think that his objective was to create a new Catholic necessarily," Bonpane observes. "He was thinking of creating a kingdom of peace and justice. Something broader than anything that could be categorized as sectarian." [181]

Perhaps the pinnacle of the ecumenical movement in Los Angeles vis-à-vis the Central American issues came in 1989 with the formation of the Wednesday Morning Coalition for Peace and Justice in El Salvador and in the United States. Like the task force, the coalition resulted from a tragedy in El Salvador. On November 16, 1989, the Salvadoran military brutally murdered six Jesuits and their female housekeeper and her teenage daughter in San Salvador. The news sent shock waves throughout the world and reemphasized the widespread violence in that country, which had already resulted in the deaths of some seventy-four thousand people. "On hearing the news, most of us," the activist Tom Smolick wrote, "especially those who had met the martyrs or knew of their work, were stunned." [182] The task force, in conjunction with other groups, including representatives from religious denominations such as the Episcopalian, Presbyterian, Methodist, Jewish, and Catholic, and with the support of Olivares at La Placita, quickly responded to this tragedy. In less than a week they organized a mass demonstration to protest the killings and the U.S. role in support of the Salvadoran military. On November 22, the protestors met at La Placita and from there followed what would become a familiar route for several months to the nearby downtown federal building. There, numerous speakers addressed the crowd and volunteers participated in civil disobedience by locking arms and blocking the front entrance to the building. Knowing they would be arrested, they nevertheless symbolically wanted to stress the urgency of changing U.S. policy in Central America. Sixty-five people, including several religious figures such as Olivares, were arrested. From this reaction to the killing of the Jesuits, a new phase of the ecumenical movement was born that came to be known as the Wednesday Morning Coalition.[183] It represented what the initial Tucson sanctuary movement referred to as "covenant ecumenism," a pact between the different faiths to protect the refugees and to protest the U.S. role in the oppression of the people of Central America.[184]

Over the next several months, through June of 1990, the coalition sponsored similar demonstrations involving civil disobedience. Each protest took place on a Wednesday, hence the name of the group. On those Wednesdays when mass protests did not occur, vigils formed in front of the federal building. Besides its religious base, the coalition grew to include a variety of participants, including lay activists, senior citizens, labor unions, health care workers, and educators. In addition, the involvement of prominent actors and entertainers like Sheen, Kris Kristofferson, Ed Asner, Browne, and others aided in bringing media attention to the demonstrations.[185]

The Wednesday protests also came to possess a significant ritualistic character, linking religious symbols and practices with civic ones. The sacred and the profane came together. Faithfully on each scheduled Wednesday, participants met at 7:30 A.M. in the basement hall of La Placita for a short prayer or homily service presided over by different ministers, rabbis, or priests, including Father Louie. From there they marched almost as in pilgrimage to the federal building. Some carried religious signs, such as a Salvadoran cross decorated with religious symbols from that country. "It was a very religious procession by the fact that it was always very ecumenical," Bonpane remembers.[186] These rituals created a sense of community and transformed how people saw their lives.[187]

Each demonstration focused on a theme that linked the oppression of the Salvadoran people with domestic issues in the United States. This transna-

FIGURE 7.3 Father Luis Olivares, C.M.F., arrested in front of Federal Building, Los Angeles, November 22, 1989. Courtesy Department of Special Collections, Charles E. Young Research Library, UCLA.

tional connection featured themes such as labor movement solidarity, educational solidarity, health care professionals' solidarity, lawyers and homeless solidarity, women and children, the tenth anniversary of the death of Archbishop Romero, and the commemoration of the death of Martin Luther King, Jr. The protest on January 31, 1990, stressed the ecumenical nature of the coalition. The speakers included Archbishop Mahony, Bishop J. Roger Anderson of the Lutheran Church, Bishop E. Lynne Brown of the Christian Methodist Episcopal Church, Bishop Jack Tuell of the United Methodist Church, and Rabbi Lennard Thal, executive director of the Union of American Jewish Congregations.[188] Some demonstrations did not have a particular theme, but instead concentrated on civil disobedience.[189] "It was a very powerful process of protesting," Father Chris Ponnet says of all of these actions.[190]

The protests were, of course, highlighted by civil disobedience, such as the blocking of the front entrance of the federal building, but also included pouring human blood on the entrance sign as a symbolic way of calling attention to the culpability of the U.S. government in the killing of Salvadorans.[191] Before each act of civil disobedience, particular individuals, both religious and secular, volunteered to be arrested. Some, Martin Sheen, for one, a close friend of Olivares, were arrested more than once. The high mark of these arrests occurred on January 17, 1990, when 234 persons were arrested.[192] Those arrested were taken to holding cells, one for men and one for women, in the basement of the federal building until arraigned. Most were released on their own recognizance and paid a minor fine.[193]

The time spent together in the holding tanks, usually a few hours, for some proved to be an augmentation of what was already a profound experience. "While waiting to be booked and released," one participant thoughtfully pondered, "we found ourselves sitting on the floor in a basement room and sharing a bit of what had brought us there and what we had felt as we raised our voices to end United States military aid to El Salvador." [194] Sheen, for his part, saw his arrest and that of others as reflecting their willingness to sacrifice in order to save the people of El Salvador. He linked this to the Salvadoran cross he and others carried during the demonstrations to remind themselves of the sacrifices of the Salvadoran people and, of course, of Jesus' own sacrifice to save humanity. "Christ is crucified again in El Salvador through the deaths of our brothers and sisters," Sheen proclaimed. "The very best among us are murdered and we are reminded how much is demanded of us by the Gospel. . . . The cross is the Way and we are constantly reminded by the Scriptures to take up our Cross and follow Christ." [195]

Olivares and his staff actively participated in the coalition. Father Louie had personally known the martyred Jesuits and felt a personal commitment in protesting their deaths.[196] Hence, he played host to the coalition by opening La Placita as the staging area for the demonstrations. But his engagement entailed more than just providing support. Olivares's endorsement gave the coalition a particular moral and spiritual legitimacy. The educator and activist Mary Brent Wehrli credits Father Louie and the Reverend J. M. Lawson, a key African American Methodist leader, with being the "spiritual guides for that amazing period." [197] At the same time, the activism carried a price, as Olivares exposed himself to further controversy over La Placita's criticism of U.S. foreign policy. "Luis was always the heart of this whole thing," Bonpane says of Olivares's relationship to the coalition. "He was the one who was literally sticking his neck out." [198]

Olivares marched and demonstrated at a number of the coalition's protests. He spoke at some of the rallies. At the January 17, 1990, one whose theme was "Send a Message to Congress," Olivares was the featured speaker.[199] According to Kennedy, activists always wanted to have Father Louie speak: "He would always be the number one person. He was inspirational. He could just capture what to say and say it in a way that was eloquent and calling people to action." [200]

Olivares was apparently arrested more than once, or at least that is the impression people have. When he was arrested, he once again reiterated that there are times when unjust laws must be broken.[201] After one of his arrests, his brother Henry, no doubt with tongue in check, said, "Louie, we're not criminals. You're ruining our name." To which, Olivares, again recurring to his keen sense of humor, replied, "I'm ruining your name but not mine." [202]

Olivares's involvement with the coalition continued into 1990 but became limited owing to his illness and his treatment for the AIDS virus. His last speech on Central America, delivered in McArthur Park, came at the celebration of the signing of the peace accords in El Salvador in early 1992. He expressed pleasure and thanks that after so many years and so many sacrifices and deaths the conflict in El Salvador seemed to be at an end. By then, some four hundred thousand Salvadoran exiles lived in southern California, and many became eligible for temporary asylum when provision of the Temporary Protected Status law was finally extended to Central American refugees by the end of 1990.[203] Father Louie was known and loved by many of them. The several thousands, mostly Salvadorans, assembled at McArthur Park saved their loudest ovation for the now clearly sick priest who had sacrificed himself for them. Feeling weak, Olivares seemed to draw strength from the crowd. His voice grew in volume and conviction. For a few moments it was the same Father Louie who had declared sanctuary in 1985 and who two years later extended it to undocumented immigrants. At this time of apparent victory over the oppressive Salvadoran military and the death squads, Olivares, with the compassion and love of humanity that had characterized his ministry, called for forgiveness and reconciliation. In perhaps one of his last public statements, the dying but indomitable cleric, the son of Mexican immigrants, said, "How will we be able to look in the eyes of the men who killed our sons? The Salvadoran people must show the world that it is possible. . . . Let us all make a commitment to continue to work for peace in El Salvador." [204]

Conclusion

Luis Olivares was a complex human being. I cannot do full justice to the meaning of his life, even if that is even possible. But I want to share some thoughts about that meaning offered by others who were close to him. Yes, these are perhaps subjective views, but they are no less real and genuine and no less human for being so. I particularly like some quotes from Father Rosendo Urrabazo, who as a Claretian seminary student studied under Father Louie and later served with him as a fellow priest on the staff at La Placita in the early 1980s. Father Urrabazo calls his mentor a "living hero . . . who taught us a concern for the poor, a willingness to take risks, the courage to say what needs to be said, and his concept of being a public presence in the fight for social justice. . . . He helped me understand that we are called to be prophets on behalf of our people. He showed me that ministry means caring about the day-to-day problems of people and improving the quality of life as well as attending to their spiritual needs."[205] And his friends at the September 1990 banquet on Olvera Street in his honor had this to say of Father Louie's legacy: "Luis' life and ministry are not separate, isolated events, but a vibrant union of word and deed. This is his great gift. For in those of us who know, respect, and love him, the changes he wrought—God willing—will live on."[206] Then there are the words of his beloved family, who knew him as no one else could. They love and revere him as a brother who in their eyes walked this earth as a saint. "My brother can be considered saintly," Henry says, "in the fact that he espoused the Gospel of Jesus and if we mean by that that he pursued that Gospel to the end, then I would say yes. In my eyes, he is a saint. I pray to him to give me guidance. Whenever I need support, I ask him to help me."[207]

I suspect that many of the refugees and immigrants whose lives he touched embrace Father Louie as a prophet, martyr, holy man, good man, and as a saint.

How does one reflect on one's life as death nears? Dying as a result of the AIDS virus, Father Louie, in the last three years of his life until his death on March 18, 1993, from time to time considered his life and in particular his ministry at La Placita. He didn't do so because he felt that he personally was important, but because he believed that what had transpired at La Placita had profound meaning. "You have to laugh at yourself and not take yourself so seriously," he told an interviewer.[208] Nevertheless, he took his work seriously. He understood that those who struggle for change and for a more just and humane world and advocate for the marginalized are themselves marginalized and persecuted. He knew this, experienced this, and accepted it. It was his cross to bear. "Historically," he thought of his own struggles within the Church, "the real changes in the Church have never come out of the institution. They always come out of the periphery."[209] He added, "Even if it meant being ridiculed and rejected, our commitment to the marginalized stands as a sign of contradiction to our society, just as the prophets of Jesus' time."[210] And of his ministry at La Placita, he said, "They look at what we do and ask if we are solving (the parish's) problems. Are we changing (the undocumented, the poor) condition in life? And I admit that . . . we're not. But I lay great stress on the power of symbols to change things. I think our statement is strong enough to change people's attitudes."[211] And in what can be considered perhaps his own personal epitaph, Father Louie observed, "I'm convinced that despite the futility that it might seem, our ministry was justified because it was a transparent sign of a better world . . . an exaggerated sign of God's presence in the midst of the poor."[212]

While Father Louie's role in the sanctuary movement in Los Angeles was crucial, it is also important to reflect on another aspect that is part of his legacy at La Placita. That concerns the significance of faith-based movements in the Chicano/Latino communities. As some of the earlier chapters in this book suggest, faith-based movements such as the civil rights work of Calleros and Perales, Católicos Por La Raza, and the ministry of Fathers Romero, Quihuis, and Elizondo and, of course, the work of César Chávez and the farmworkers bring attention to themselves by stressing the linkage of faith and political action. As noted, this phenomenon has not been adequately treated in Chicano history. Yet faith-based movements such as those surrounding sanctuary at La Placita stress the central importance of religion in organizing the Chicano/ Latino communities. It has been through their faith in many instances that Chicanos and other Latino groups have resisted oppression and found strength and inspiration to mount resistance movements.[213] In making these efforts, they share a connection with other worldwide faith-based liberationist movements. As Cunningham correctly notes, "All of these [faith-based movements] suggest that religion continues, secularization theories notwithstanding, to be a powerful medium through which peoples of *both* the First and the Third Worlds experience social change."[214] The mass demonstrations in 2006 by Latino immigrants to defend themselves against anti-immigrant legislation and nativism possessed a strong faith-based character.

When told by his own order prior to the revelation of his illness that he had to leave La Placita, Olivares felt disappointed, frustrated, and even angry that his work would not go on. He blamed himself for not preparing better for the continuation of the movement. It is possible that during his dying days he still felt some of these emotions. But Father Louie was wrong. His influence, his work with the unwanted and the poor, his acceptance of the stranger in our midst, his sheltering of the homeless, protecting of the persecuted, promoting of peace and justice, his reminding us that AIDS victims are also God's children, and his courageous effort to transform the Church into one of the people and for the people go on. They go on in the lives of the refugees and immigrants whom he helped; they go on in the work of community activists and religious figures who continue to advocate for immigrants and refugees; and they go on even today at La Placita. Father Louie still lives in the memories and in the deeds of all these people. Father Louie, the prophet, still speaks out. He is still present.

¡LUIS OLIVARES! ¡PRESENTE!

EIGHT

Contemporary Catholic Popular Religiosity and U.S. Latinos

Expressions of Faith and Ethnicity

At home a crucifix hung in almost every room, holy water in the cupboard
behind the jam and a box of pretzels. The Bible weighed less than our
medical dictionary, where the dead lay with toes poking through white
sheets. Palm-leaf crosses withered in the kitchen window for our Okie
neighbors to look in awe.

—FROM GARY SOTO, "PINK HANDS," IN GARY SOTO,
NEW AND SELECTED POEMS (1995)

THE RAPIDLY GROWING U.S. Latino population is having a variety of effects on U.S. culture and institutions. This Latinization, for example, is certainly being felt in religious circles. About 40 percent of all U.S. Catholics are Latinos. In turn, this demographic revolution is forcing the Church to react to the strong element of popular religiosity often associated with Latinos. By popular religiosity, *religiosidad popular,* I mean two essential factors: (1) that many aspects of Latino Catholicism are administered and controlled not by clerics or the institutional church, but by the people themselves in what can be considered civil religion or what Ann Taves refers to as "paraliturgical devotions"; and (2) that Latinos engage in a variety of religious expressions and practices—including what Father Virgilio Elizondo calls "foundational faith expressions" and what Roberto Goizueta interprets as "theopoetics"—that in various cases are not officially either recognized by the Church or, in the U.S. context, appreciated. Yet as Latinos in the twenty-first century grow as the result of high birthrates and immigration to become the majority of U.S. Catholics, the Church will more and more have to engage in a dialogue with the changing religious culture of Latinos; accelerate the process of inculturation; and accept an expanded version of Catholicity as suggested by Vatican Council II, or what Elizondo refers to as religious mestizaje.[1]

While we have seen in earlier chapters the themes of resistance and affirmation in Chicano Catholic history in relation to religious civic action, such as in the case, for example, of the sanctuary movement, one critical fundamental form of resistance and affirmation, as noted in Chapter Three, is the role of popular religiosity or "lived religion."[2] While most Chicanos and other Latinos have historically not engaged in the politics of public protest, many, on the other hand, have practiced some form of popular religion as a way of asserting their identity as Chicano or Latino Catholics. Chapter Three stressed the importance of popular religiosity to the Hispanos of northern New Mexico in the 1930s, as documented by the WPA. This chapter, in a sense, comes full circle back to this theme and notes the continuity into a new generation and historical period of the role of popular religion, especially among recent Mexican and Latino immigrants and their children. Other scholars have studied the role of popular religion among Chicanos and Latinos, but my work takes two approaches that set it apart from these earlier studies. One is to stress the persistence of Chicano/Latino popular religion over time and, second, to reveal new sources for the study of this topic. This chapter is a case study of the role that popular religion plays among contemporary Chicanos/Latinos.

I address here not the institutional responses toward inculturation, but some of the various aspects of popular religiosity—what Timothy Matovina refers to as "popular spirituality"—familiar to Latinos, in particular Chicanos, and introduced into the United States by immigration.[3] The basis for this study is oral histories conducted by undergraduate students in Father Elizondo's classes on Latino religion in 1998 and 1999 at the University of California, Santa Barbara. I assisted in the teaching of these classes. This study is based on data gathered from among the more than one hundred oral histories completed. For their projects, students were asked to select a person of Latino descent outside of the classroom and conduct interviews on how religion and spirituality have affected his or her life. Interviews could be conducted with students or nonstudents, young or old, native born or immigrant. Many of the Latino students naturally chose to interview a family member.

These interviews underscore two crucial aspects of the role that popular religiosity plays in the lives of many Latinos. One is obvious and conscious and involves the fact that Latinos express their faith—their sense of the sacred or what Elizondo refers to as the "collective soul"—through their popular religious beliefs and practices. Second, a less obvious and less conscious aspect, is that in the U.S. context, where Latinos, in particular immigrants, feel less secure and more aware of their "otherness," popular religiosity, as Father Elizondo notes, also represents a form of ethnic defensiveness and affirmation. Popular religiosity is a way of attempting to create a shield of security and, at the same time, of affirming one's identity and sense of community. "Others may take everything else away from us, but they cannot destroy our expressions of the divine," Elizondo stresses. "Through these practices [popular religion] we not only affirm ourselves as people, we also resist ultimate assimilation. Thus our religious practices are not only affirmation of faith, but the language of defense and ultimate resistance."[4] Hence, faith and ethnicity channeled through the process of becoming U.S. Latino Catholics are intertwined and inseparable. Latino identity, as a result, cannot be divorced from religious identity.

Role of *Abuelitas* and Females

One of the most fundamental aspects of Latino popular religiosity is its strong female centeredness. Sometimes referred to as "abuelita theology" or "mujerista theology," this expression of Latino female religiosity is extremely powerful and pervasive.[5] Women, in particular *abuelitas* (grandmothers) and mothers, are gatekeepers of much of Latino popular religiosity. Symbolically, they serve, often in a Mexican or Latin American context owing to the absence of priests, as unofficial ministers and as the literal religious and spiritual guardians of Latino youth and of their families. This praxis built around everyday life, or what Ada María Isasi-Díaz refers to as *lo cotidiano*, represents, according to her, a form of liberation theology. At one level, it is a form of resisting oppression and on another a noninstitutional, nonacademic way of humans knowing about God.[6] These women transmit what Jeanette Rodríguez calls "cultural memory."[7] "In my own spirituality," Ana María Díaz-Stevens observes, "I have been often reminded of how women, especially lower-class and peasant women, construct and make use of our world."[8]

In both Mexico and the United States, women, especially abuelitas, serve as the live-in ministers who assume the charge of setting an example of proper religious and spiritual behavior for children and young adults. Hence, its "matriarchal core," as some contend, distinguishes Latino religion. "Within Latino communities it is often women, mothers, and grandmothers who are the leaders of popular religion," observes David Badillo. "The strong Marian spirituality among Latinos results from the dominant role of women in pop-

FIGURE 8.1 Abuelita theology, San Antonio, circa 1990s. Courtesy James L. Shaffer.

ular religion."[9] This includes instructing through oral traditions in popular
religious beliefs and practices or what Juan Carlos Scannone considers to be
the "Catholic wisdom of the common people."[10] Adelina Correa, for example,
who grew up in a small town in Zacatecas in northern Mexico recalls both her
abuelita's and mother's religious role: "Religion was taught to us by word of
mouth. My grandmother and mother would tell us the stories in the vernacular in simple words that would relate to the everyday life."[11]

Adelina notes that in the United States she has continued this religious oral
tradition with her children. "Raised in the old-fashioned way," she stresses,

"verbal explanation takes the place of the written Bible in my house. I am not saying that they do not know about the Bible but they can relate more to my oral tradition than to the text."[12] One interviewee referred to simply as José Angel remembers that in Mexico his grandmother and mother would tell the children about Jesus, the crucifixion, and Our Lady of Guadalupe. Guadalupe, according to him, was "our version of a fairytale."[13] Not all of this instruction was through oral tradition. Miguel Gabriel Contreras notes that his grandmother in Mexico read the Bible to him and his siblings every day.[14]

Besides administering a form of family catechism, abuelitas and mothers also serve as examples of prayerful devotion and of making prayer a central activity within family life, what Taves calls the "household of faith."[15] Paulina Paleo observes that, as she was growing up in southern California, her maternal grandmother was deeply religious. "She often prayed in front of the entire family because she wanted to set an example to the rest of us," Paulina stated. "My grandmother took her faith in God seriously. In fact I remember her telling me, 'God is going to punish you,' in Spanish when I would misbehave."[16] Sometimes prayer sessions included not only one's family, but also others in the barrio. Timothy Badillo recollects an elderly woman in his neighborhood who gathered all of the children together for early afternoon prayer sessions and that this also occurred in other neighborhoods.[17] Mariela Vega, who grew up in East Los Angeles, recalls that as a child she learned a special prayer from her mother, who had learned it from her mother. This was the prayer to the "Santo Angel de mi Guardia" or to her Guardian Angel.[18]

Dichos, or mantras, are another form of abuelita theology. Rocío Valdovinos's grandmother, Epigmenia Larios, says certain dichos throughout the day that convey a spiritual message. These include "Si Dios quiere" (God willing) and, Rocío's favorite, "Dios aprieta, pero no ahorca" (God tightens but never chokes). "That phrase has been a source of inspiration for my grandmother," Rocío notes, "and she uses it to do the same for others. My grandmother feels that through hard times, what might feel like the worst situation in the world is not and will pass with the grace of God."[19] Still another dicho is "No hay mal que por bien no venga" (every bad thing is caused for a good reason). Rocío's grandmother believes that God sometimes allows misfortune in order to bring people closer to him.[20]

One particular abuelita and female devotion that seems to be widespread is the praying of the rosary, a practice that Latina women seem to share with many Catholic women of various ethnic backgrounds. In Mexico, abuelitas and mothers pray the rosary along with other female members and children every evening. Anastacio López remembers seeing his mother sitting by a crucifix at night and praying the rosary.[21] Miguel Gabriel Contreras notes that in his village in Mexico, his grandmother prayed the rosary each evening "para la Virgen María, para que nos protega" (to the Virgin Mary, so she will protect us).[22] Sometimes the rosary would be prayed at home in the morning. One woman, Carmen, born in a village in Jalisco, Mexico, remembers her family praying the rosary in the morning before the adults left for work and the children for school. In the evening, the adults would attend "el rosario" in the village church led by the women.[23]

Teresa Torres's mother in rural Michoacán prayed the rosary three times a day. This included an evening rosary with her four children. "My mother recalls always daydreaming off and sometimes even falling asleep while my grandmother led the *misterios* [mysteries of the rosary]," the student Angelina Torres writes of her mother's experience. "At night my mother would still be praying in her sleep. She would turn to one side and then to the other and in each turn she would say: 'Santa María Madre de Dios. . . .' And 'Dios te salve María, llena eres de gracia. . . .' [God be with you Mary, full of grace]. She would pray all night long."[24]

Praying the rosary at home by abuelitas and other women is not restricted to life south of the border. It also occurs on the U.S. side. Georgia Oropeza observes that her mother in El Paso, Texas, prayed the rosary every day, sometimes several times a day.[25] Praying the rosary at home in some cases among recent immigrants may even substitute for Sunday Mass. Anastacia López, interviewed by her son, Luis, informed him that when her parents crossed the border from Mexico and settled in Simi Valley in southern California in 1971 her parents did not attend church because they did not know where it was. Instead, they prayed "el rosario."[26]

Finally, abuelitas in their roles as family ministers or what Díaz-Stevens refers to as the "matriarchal core" of Latino Catholicism, also are responsible, along with parents, for the blessing of children.[27] One Chicano student at UC Santa Barbara, José Angel, recalls being blessed by his abuelita with these words: "Ay Dios mío. ¿Cómo has estado, mi corazoncito? Que Dios nos de licencia. Y que Dios te bendiga" (Dear God. How have you been, my loved one? God willing. And may God bless you).[28]

Parental Blessings

In addition to the abuelita blessing, parental blessings are part of family popular religiosity. Serving almost as surrogate ministers, mothers and fathers extend their blessings to their children throughout the life cycle, even into adulthood. Miguel Gabriel notes that every evening before bed or when he and his siblings would go out, they would kneel, pray, and be blessed by both parents.[29] Gildardo Manuel Rivas, who grew up in Stockton, California, was always blessed by his mother when he left for school with these words—words familiar to many other Latinos on both sides of the border: "Que Dios te bendiga, hijo" (May God bless you, my child).[30]

These parental blessings continue, and the practice is passed from one generation to another. Moreover, blessings, as one parent interviewed by her daughter astutely pointed out, represent a religious discourse no less valid than the blessings administered by the priest to the people at the end of each Mass. This parent, Olga Caballero Melgoza, told her daughter, Laura,

> Besides all the icons and religious practice that existed within our home and that continue in my traditions today, religion was and still is present in my everyday language. Without realizing it, we spoke in a religious way all of the time. My mother would always bless me before I left my home to go anywhere. She would make the sign of the cross with her fingers and bless me. This practice still goes on today, for I do it with you and your brothers because I know that without ever realizing it, when you *mija* [daughter] leave the house and when you get into your car, you make the sign of the cross and bless yourself. What you don't see, is that I make the sign of the cross right behind you![31]

Parental blessings are not just physical signs but can be conveyed through letters, by telephone, and today even by e-mail. One student pointed out that she becomes distraught if, after talking to her mother on the phone, her mother forgets to give her "la bendición" or blessing. "I've learned that it is a blessing when others pray for you," she observes, "I believe that the Lord listens to those mothers who pray for their children. It is hard to believe everything is okay without her blessing."[32]

Home Altars

Latino popular religiosity centered in the family is also best expressed through the widespread use of home altars, or *altarcitos*, which extends the metaphor of family members, especially abuelitas and mothers, as surrogate ministers or what León refers to as "religious specialists."[33] Home altars, as William Beez-

FIGURE 8.2 Ida Martínez's personal shrine, Arroyo Hondo, New Mexico, circa late 1990s. Courtesy Siegfried Halus.

ley observes, have a long history in Europe, Africa, and indigenous America.[34] "Women believed the altarcitos brought the divine into the home," Treviño notes of his study of Mexican American Catholicism in Houston, "and that the religious images of the altar represented a home's 'spiritual family.'"[35] Home altars are a way of bringing the Church into the home and emphasizing the expanded definition of Church. "The [home] altar was our personal church while in the home," María Hinojosa notes about her home in Mexico. "We prayed over it, we put items upon it in the intention to worship Jesus and his teachings, and we had our own little religious ceremonies with it."[36] Latinos pray and express their faith in multiple ways, including praying at the local church as well as in their family churches or altarcitos. For recent immigrants, home altars, like praying the rosary, can be temporary substitutes for Sunday Mass because of work schedules or unfamiliarity with the local church scene. This was the case with Raquel Balderas de Quiroga when she and her husband first arrived in California. Because her husband worked on weekends, Raquel had to stay with her young children and could not attend Sunday Mass. Instead, she prayed before her home altar.[37]

Home altars, rather than representing a simple or "primitive" faith, in fact reveal complicated and multiple expressions of faith or what Orlando Espín refers to as "faithful intuition" or the *sensus fidelium*.[38] The often ornate and varied icons displayed on these altars witness this complexity. José Angel describes his mother's altarcito:

> There are so many pictures and figures crowded together. There is La Virgen de Guadalupe's image in a *veladora* [candle], a big crucified Jesus made out of *yeso* [plaster] and a few saints, half of whom I don't even recognize. In the center of the altar sits a wooden chapel-shaped box. In the front side you can see a porcelain doll dressed in a purple dress and holding a golden cane. I swear that sometimes it moves its eyes and stares even when I try to hide. My mom tells me that it is el Santo Niño de Atocha (the Christ child). Mami always says that the saint brings her good luck.[39]

Altarcitos, however, are not restricted just to saintly figures. Sometimes along with the saints, Latinos place the photos of loved ones, both living and dead. This is especially the case with sons serving in the military. Latinos do not pray to them per se, although sometimes they do to the deceased, but they are put there as a sign of reverence as well as to petition the saints on the altar to protect and care for those in the photos. Veronica González's father recalled that on his parent's altarcito in Calexico, California, they placed a photo of his grandparents, who had died in Mexico.[40] Seventy-six-year-old María Serrano in Santa Barbara does the same thing. Besides the images of Jesus and the Virgin of Guadalupe surrounded by candles and flowers, she has pictures of family members.[41]

Particular devotions at home altars are often linked to special causes related to personal and family problems. Alfredo Figueroa recalls that his grandmother in California made an offering to the Santo Niño de Atocha, a Christ child figure originally from Spain, on her home altar after she lost a son, Rudy, because the Santo Niño "is the saint of lost children." She also had an image of San Martín de Porres, and Alfredo believes that this had to do with San Martín being the patron saint of interracial justice and of the sick, which makes him a popular saint among the poor.[42] Moreover, *mandas* or *promesas*, which involve a person requesting a special favor from Jesus, Our Lady of Guadalupe, or a particular saint, are often made at one's altarcito. If the favor is granted, the person returns the favor with an offering or by making a pilgrimage to a sacred site.

On special feast days, such as that of Our Lady of Guadalupe on December 12, some home altars are transformed into singular devotions. Adelina Luna Correa remembers that in her town in Zacatecas on the feast day of Guadalupe, a national symbol in Mexico, her entire family was responsible for decorating the home altar in honor of *La Virgen*. This activity included men and women as well as children. Flowers and candles were placed around the image of Guadalupe, and next to the Virgen were placed pictures of loved ones who had passed away.[43]

In some cases, home altars can be expanded to represent neighborhood or barrio altarcitos. Timothy Badillo placed a four-foot statue of Guadalupe in front of his home in the eastside barrio of Santa Barbara. He surrounded the statue with rosebushes and at night illuminated the site. He believes the Virgen has made his garden grow nicer. Neighbors come to pray before the statue throughout the year, but especially on December 12, when many leave flowers.[44]

Altarcitos span generations, linking immigrants with U.S.-born and more acculturated Latinos. José Angel, who used to be scared of the many images on his mother's home altar, now has his own at the university "where I keep the saints that I love and look to for spiritual healing."[45] Alfredo Figueroa notes that some generational changes are affecting Latinos when he comments, "My nana [grandmother] burnt candles as offerings, now we burn them because they smell good and are soothing." Still, he also observes that religious traditions such as home altars are very much alive and well among U.S.-born Latinos. "Many such traditions," he told his son Andrés, "are finding their way back because they give us a sense of safety, comfort, and strength *porque es parte de nuestra cultura*" (because it is part of our culture).[46]

Home Icons

If home altars symbolize the family as church, many Latino homes as a whole represent church. Not only are home altars present, but also the entire house is made a sanctuary of faith through the numerous religious icons distributed throughout each room. These are meant to add to the devotions made by the families. Icons represent a visual text of Latino religious beliefs. As Elizondo notes, "Mexican Americans are not satisfied with *reading* the truth; they want to *see* the truth."[47] They also indicate the need of poor Latinos from both sides of the border to appeal for divine protection and favors since they have very little else to rely on.

Like many other traditions in Latino popular religiosity, home icons originate for the most part in Mexico and in other Latin American countries. Olga Caballero Melgoza recalls that in her family in Michoacán the two most dominant icons were the Virgen de Guadalupe and the bleeding Jesus on the cross. "The image," she says of Jesus, "was a symbol of protection for my family." In addition, beautiful rosaries adorned each bedroom.[48] As immigrants cross the border, this tradition persists. Georgia Oropeza, who was born in El Paso in 1931, remembers that her mother hung religious pictures throughout the house as well as crosses made out of palms received at Palm Sunday, which hung above each door. A container of holy water was positioned, as in a church, at the entrance to the house. Outside, religious statues adorned the front yard. She notes that her grandmother's house in El Paso was identical in appearance.[49]

This diverse Latino religious iconography is apparent in other regions of the United States. Gildardo Manuel Rivas observes that at his parent's home in Stockton, California, there are portraits of saints such as San Miguel and El Angel de la Guarda everywhere. There is also a statue of Guadalupe that his mother had brought from Mexico and crucifixes that she nailed above each bedroom. His mother has a special devotion to El Sagrado Corazón de Jesús (the Sacred Heart of Jesus) and had built a special little altar, or *cajita*, to hold a wooden portrait of this image. When his father was away, his mother would sleep with the cajita clinched to her chest and with lighted candles for protection until her husband returned.[50] Paula Paleo recalls that her home in Fresno, California, was very similar in appearance. The one difference was that her mother always bought candles that had a saint and a prayer on the outside of the candle. One of her mother's favorite saints was St. Anthony of Padua, and she would say a prayer to him before she lit the candle and another one after the candle burned out.[51]

Like Paleo's mother, other Latinos favor particular saints, Jesus figures, or the Virgin Mary. In Paula Bautista's family, her father had a special devotion to the Virgen de Tonaya in Jalisco. Each year, he would make a *peregrinación* (pilgrimage) there and return with an image of the Virgen. Family and friends would be invited to Paula's house to venerate the image. A collection would be taken up and the funds sent to the church in Jalisco dedicated to the Virgen. Paula's mother, on the other hand, who is from Guatemala, has a special devotion to El Señor de Esquipulas, or the Black Christ. Every time the family visits Guatemala a peregrinación is made to the town of Esquipulas to honor the Black Christ. In their Fresno home, Paula's mother has a statue of El Señor and prays to him every day and especially when a problem arises. "I know that whenever there are worries at my house," Paula notes, "the first thing you hear from my mom is 'ayúdanos Cristo Negro' or 'Ay Señor de Esquipulas'" (help us Black Christ).[52]

Paula, a student at UC Santa Barbara, carries this tradition with her to the campus. Her special devotion is to San Martín de Porres because her parents gave her a statue of him when she was young. "I can say he is my patron savior," she stresses, "I was young, but I felt attached and therefore would call him 'mi negrito.' I even remember once when moving into another house I dropped [him] and he broke. I remember my first reaction was 'I killed him,' so my dad explained that no, I did not kill him and he could be fixed with a little bit of Krazy Glue. I still have him."[53]

Popular Saints

The tradition of venerating particular saints or holy figures—the communion of saints—is strong among Latino Catholics. Some of these saints are not formally recognized by the Church—Goizueta refers to them as "hidden saints"—such as the figure of Juan Soldado, the helper of undocumented immigrants in Tijuana and Don Pedrito Jaramillo, the healer of south Texas, or even the pop icon Selena after her death.[54] Another good example is the Santo Niño de Atocha, who, among other things, is the patron of travelers. "In our devotion to the saints," whom Elizondo likens to an extended family for Latinos and about whom he also observes, "the doctrines of our Church are personalized and become human stories."[55] The mother of Jennifer Enríquez is one such devotee of the Santo Niño. She told her daughter about a serious car accident she suffered in 1989 in Santa Barbara. Prior to the accident, Mrs. Enríquez had bought a little figure of the Santo Niño and, after having it blessed by a priest, put it on the dashboard of her car. As she explained it,

> The day of the car accident the figure fell on my lap at the moment of impact. I truly believe that El Santo Niño de Atocha saved my life. The truck had hit my door with full force, smashing the door completely. Nothing happened to me, not even a scratch while my best friend on the passenger side, right next to me, died instantly. No one could explain how nothing happened to me; they said it must have been a miracle, but

I know it was a miracle of that saint. Since that day I know that God was watching over me. For that I will always be in debt with God.[56]

For her part, María Serrano prayed to the Santo Niño when she could not get pregnant after five years of marriage. Her mother-in-law encouraged María to pray to the Santo Niño, who protected children. "I began to pray to him every night in order for him to grant me my pregnancy," María says, "After one year of desperately waiting, I became pregnant and gave birth to a baby boy named Manuel like his father."[57] When she later had complications on her fifth pregnancy, María again appealed to the Santo Niño and made a *promesa*, or promise, that if the Santo Niño helped her have a safe delivery she would name the child after the Santo Niño. She gave birth to a health baby boy and named him Atocha.[58]

Consuelo Munguia's special devotion, besides that to Our Lady of Guadalupe, is to St. Jude, who is the saint of desperate situations. "I've been in a lot of these," she says, "but after I pray to him, everything seems to turn out fine in the end."[59] Rocío Valdovinos observes that one of her grandmother's favorite saints when she still lived in Mexico was San Antonio de Padua, the saint of those who travel. She would pray to San Antonio to protect her children and grandchildren who traveled back and forth from the United States to Mexico.[60]

The veneration of santos is also linked to saint's names given to children when they are born. Teresa Torres, for example, was named after Santa Teresa and recalls how her family celebrated in her honor the feast day of Santa Teresita every year. "The actual day a person was born did not have as much significance as the day of one's santo," her daughter, Angelina, notes. "The saints play a major role in the Latino community. Many children are named after saints because it is believed that they are the ones who bring about peace and harmony to the world. They are the ones 'que interceden ante Dios Nuestro Señor' (who intercede for us with God)."[61]

Our Lady of Guadalupe

Of all the popular saints, however, there is no question, at least among mexicano immigrants and Chicanos, that the most loved and worshiped is the Virgen de Guadalupe. Of course, the same is true on the Mexican side of the border. Lelia Esparza Quiroga, who was born in the state of Durango, makes

FIGURE 8.3 Guadalupanas, East Los Angeles, circa 1970s. Courtesy Department of Special Collections, Davidson Library, University of California, Santa Barbara.

an interesting but telling observation: "In Mexico, 90 percent of the people are Catholic, but 100 percent are guadalupanos [devotees of Guadalupe]." [62] Revered as "la morenita" (the dark virgin) and as a symbol of mestizo Christianity (the syncretism between indigenous religious beliefs and Spanish Catholicism), Guadalupe over the years has captured the religious imagination of millions throughout Latin America and in the United States, and even in

FIGURE 8.4 Our Lady of Guadalupe mural, Chicano Park, San Diego. Courtesy Mario T. García.

other parts of the world. Almost every person interviewed in Father Elizondo's classes confirmed this exceptional devotion to Guadalupe.

For some Latinos, Guadalupe is seen as more than the mother of Jesus or as the Immaculate Conception. She is recognized as equal with God or, as one interviewee asserted, as a representative of God in Mexican culture.[63] "It is weird," Paula Bautista stated in her interview, "but I hold La Virgen de Guadalupe and God on the same level. Sometimes I pray to her so she can help me get what I need, maybe because I can relate to her more. If the favor I asked for does not happen, I then pray to God."[64] Matovina, in his study of the veneration of Guadalupe in San Antonio over the years, affirms this intense devotion. "If doubts ever creep into the hearts and minds of Guadalupe's devotees," he notes, "they are loath to mention them. Their trust and confidence in her maternal care are so absolute that the mere notion that she failed to listen, respond, or bring about some greater good from tragedy seems a conceptual impossibility."[65]

Besides paying homage to Guadalupe daily in their homes and at church, many Latinos on both sides of the border participate and help organize impressive celebrations on December 12, the feast day of Guadalupe. These may include a reenactment of the apparition of Guadalupe to Juan Diego. Some, of course, including Mexicans from the United States, also make a peregrinación to her shrine in Mexico City on her feast day. Some women, in addition, belong to Las Guadalupanas, a voluntary association of Latinas in the United States who pay particular veneration to Guadalupe and who organize parish activities for Latinos.[66] The role of women in organizing Guadalupe celebrations is noted by Matovina, who sees this as an opportunity for Mexican American women to assert leadership in a sometimes constricted patriarchic culture. "In this context," he writes of San Antonio, "women's roles in planning Guadalupe celebrations, directing recitations of the rosary and other prayers, and accompanying their patroness as attendants provided them with rare opportunities to exercise public community leadership."[67] Gildardo Manuel Rivas remembers that his mother in Stockton was a Guadalupana. She would attend weekly meetings to plan fundraisers as well as visit the sick and hold rosaries for the deceased. Once a year members would host a *Jamaica* or *Quermés* (bazaars), and each Sunday the Guadalupanas would sell *menudo* (tripe soup) after each Mass to raise money to hire mariachis to play the *mañanitas* (morning song) on December 12 in honor of Guadalupe.[68]

Above all, Guadalupe symbolizes hope and protection to people of Mexican and Latin American descent. She is the loving mother who cares for her children, especially the poor and those who seek her protection in their migrations to the United States in the hope of a better life. Lucío Ibarra expressed such sentiments to his son, Leopoldo:

> The whole story of La Virgen de Guadalupe was . . . the single most
> inspirational idea or image to me and the family, but especially to me.

As the story goes, La Virgen appeared to the poor Juan Diego, and that gave me and my family knowledge and hope that La Virgen is also looking over us because we also were very poor and we needed help in life, and that is where our faith came into play. For me personally, La Virgen helped me to get across the border and into the United States with the strength and the courage to get a good job and to eventually bring my wife to the States so that we could start a family here with a chance at success. I always prayed to God and to La Virgen for strength when I thought that I was not going to make it, so I give all of the credit to my religion for my success.[69]

This turning to Guadalupe for support and assistance is echoed by Consuelo Munguía, who recalled that when she was unemployed on the U.S. side of the border for a long time or could find only low-paying cleaning jobs, she prayed to Guadalupe for a *milagro*, or miracle. "I prayed to her everyday," she told her daughter, "and I told her in my prayers that if she helped me find a good job, that I would make an altar for her in my house." About a week later, Consuelo says, she got a job at a Target store. She attributes this to Guadalupe and, true to her word, Consuelo prepared an altar for Guadalupe in her home.[70]

Church as Fiesta

Celebrations of Our Lady of Guadalupe are also manifestations of what Father Elizondo has referred to as "Church as fiesta." That is, much of Latino religion is centered on celebrations, festivities, pageantry, and rituals that, according to Elizondo, "express the core identity of the Mexican American population."[71] In contrast to U.S. Anglo-Catholicism, which tends to be more literate, solemn, and even Protestant in its liturgy and religious culture, Latino Catholicism is more physical, body-oriented, and festive, although no less devotional. "Just as important as the written texts of tradition (or, in fact, more important)," Espín stresses, "is the living witness and faith of the Christian people."[72] This "popular wisdom," as Goizueta further observes, "is expressed primarily, though not exclusively, through symbol and ritual."[73] Rooted in villages and towns in Mexico, many of these religious ceremonies—a version of the Puerto Rican "oxcart Catholicism"—express the need by the poor to find occasion to celebrate life and to express their agency in organizing, sometimes without any Church support, their own particular religious fiestas based on their own liturgical calendar.[74] José Angel recalls his parents telling him of the feast day celebration in Rentería, a small rancho in the northern state of Durango. Other feast days would include that of San Juan de los Lagos, Santo Niño de Atocha, and various other patron saints. The festivities would be in the community since there was no church in the area.[75]

Gildardo Manuel Rivas recalls growing up in Sahuaya, a small village in Michoacán, where one of the principal feast days featured the town's patron saint, Santo Santiago. People from neighboring pueblos would participate in a peregrinación to José Angel's town. He remembers the pilgrimage as being massive.[76] And Adelina Luna Correa notes that her mother, born in Tepechitlán, Zacatecas, often would tell her that in her village every Catholic day of obligation or saint's day would be an opportunity for people to get together and have a fiesta.[77]

The feast day of Our Lady of Guadalupe on December 12, of course, is widely celebrated throughout Mexico, as it is by Latinos in the United States. Olga Caballero Melgoza remembers the events surrounding Guadalupe in her village of Punebero, Michoacán. She observes that the festivities began on the evening of December 11, when many people stayed up all night praying and contemplating the image of La Virgen. The next morning at 5 A.M. the entire pueblo would march to the local church, where they sang the mañanitas, proclaiming a new life, to Guadalupe and laid flowers before her image. During the rest of the day a community fiesta was held in the town plaza.[78]

Carmen, interviewed by Eva Huizar, notes that in her hometown in Jalisco, the Guadalupe celebration would include *el novenario*, or novena, from December 4 to December 12 in honor of La Virgen. The singing of las mañanitas and the praying of the rosary on the morning of the twelfth would be the highlight. "Singing and praying were done with such devotion," she stresses, "there was a pleasing feeling that she was there present listening to us." Later that day a parade would be held with floats depicting scenes of the apparition of La Virgen. After Mass at midday, *danzantes* (dancers) dressed in native costumes would perform, after which food was served and children's games like piñatas were organized. A big community dance concluded the festivities. In other villages and towns in Mexico, as well as in large cities, similar Guadalupe celebrations take place.[79]

Christmastime among Mexican immigrants, naturally, as in other Christian cultures, is a period of much festivity. Immigrants recall special traditions at this time, such as *pastorelas* (the shepherd's play) and *posadas* (Mary and Joseph seeking shelter). Axel Hernández remembers the posada celebrations before Christmas Day. For several days his whole neighborhood in Mexico would march around the town, following townspeople portraying Joseph and Mary on a donkey. After being rejected at the first eleven houses, the Holy Family would be invited into the twelfth, where a fiesta would take place. This community drama was repeated every night for twelve nights until Christmas Eve. "As a kid," Axel notes, "I loved the ritual for the delicious tostadas, tacos, and burritos, as well as the piñata full of candies that were absolute parts of the fiesta. It was a party for everybody, and everyone was in a good mood."[80]

Olga Caballero Melgoza observes that in her town in Michoacán the posadas lasted nine days before Christmas. In her barrio, instead of Mary and Joseph seeking shelter, *El Niño Dios* (the baby Jesus) was carried around by the people. Each home would reject El Niño until the last one offered him shelter. Everyone would be invited in, and the celebration would begin. Olga recalls such foods as tamales, *atole* (a drink made from cornmeal), and *buñuelos* (Mexican doughnuts) being served. A band played, and people danced into the night. Although for the rest of the year her father would not allow Olga and her sisters to attend dances, he would relent during the posadas and a few other religious holidays. "I was able to dance and be out with my friends on religious fiesta days," she fondly remembers. "That to me was one more reason to celebrate!"[81] Consuelo Munguía notes the importance of the posadas to her children growing up in California: "I encouraged my children to participate every year because it was the best way for them to learn about the birth of Jesus Christ."[82] Others recall at Christmastime the singing of *alabados* (religious hymns), the piñatas for the children, and the praying of the rosary as the people with lighted candles followed Mary and Joseph during the posada.[83]

Christmas festivities in the Mexican tradition on both sides of the border include El Día de Los Reyes Magos (the feast of the Three Wise Men), celebrated on January 6, the Feast of the Epiphany. Children wake up early in the morning and find gifts left for them by Los Reyes Magos. They and the adults are then served a special crowned-shaped sweet bread called a *rosca* decorated with fruit and symbolizing the crown of the baby Jesus. Inside the bread is a tiny figure of a baby Jesus hidden in the dough before baking. Whoever finds the baby in their serving has to host a party on or before February 2, when all Christmas festivities conclude.[84]

The church as fiesta is also manifested in Mexico and in the United States following Sunday Mass, when food booths and music appear outside the church. Baptisms and weddings are still other occasions for fiesta. José Angel recalls that the *bautizo*, or baptism, of his sister was followed by "la birría [barbecued goat], arroz [rice] y frijoles [beans]" as well as a piñata and dancing at his family's home. "Bautizos serve as family reunions," he notes, "and when a new baby is born everybody gets ready for *el bailazo* [dance] or the *pachanga* [party]." [85]

While not all of these customs are fully reenacted in the United States, many of them are. Although for immigrants it is never quite the same as in their hometowns in Mexico, still the religious fiestas remind them of what they left behind and of the importance of memory and tradition in their adjustment to life "en el otro lado," on the other side. As Olga Caballero Melgoza stresses about the Guadalupe celebration, "Personally, I feel that the religious festivals are the very best. Now that I live here in the United States, this celebration still continues within the Mexican Catholic population. We try hard to make us feel as if we are back home, but it still feels a bit different." [86]

Other Rituals and Popular Religiosity

Less festive but just as rich in ritual are the community-based observations of *Semana Santa*, or Holy Week. The crucifixion, as Goizueta notes, is one of the central themes of Latino religiosity owing to the identification of many poor and marginalized Latinos with Christ's suffering. "The Hispanic devotion to the crucified Jesus," he stresses, "is born of the courageous refusal to be denied our human right to weep, without which there can be no liberation." [87] In many villages and towns in Mexico most, if not all, of this ritual is in the hands of the people themselves. Gildardo de Manuel Rivas remembers that in his hometown in Michoacán the townspeople would organize the *Vía Crucis*, the reenactment of Christ's passion and death first practiced in Europe during the Middle Ages. [88] The people would portray the soldiers, the Roman officials, Jesus' followers, and Jesus Himself. The Vía Crucis would involve several miles of peregrinación. "The journey is an exhausting one," he says, "and consists of miles of walking, praying and acting out scenes throughout the entire town." The acted-out crucifixion would take place at sunset followed by Mass. Rivas stresses that all of this was very realistic. [89] In her village, also in Michoacán, Teresa Torres as a young girl played the role of Mary Magdalene. [90] Raquel Balderas de Quiroz observes that in her village in Mexico, Good Friday would begin with the *ayuno*, or breakfast, usually consisting of atole. The people would then go up into the hills and pray. Afterward, they would participate in the Vía Crucis, which would involve the Stations of the Cross scattered throughout the village. [91] Adelina Luna Correa recalls that in her home in Tepechitlán, Zacatecas, each person would get a particular penance on Good Friday that

FIGURE 8.5 Vía Crucis, Good Friday, San Antonio, circa late 1990s. Courtesy
Mario T. García.

would involve a surprise. Each person's penance would be determined by a
town lottery. "The person in charge," she explains, "would write on pieces of
paper a number of *penitencias*, or penances, and put them in a basket for the
lottery. Each of us would get to pick a piece of paper out of the basket, and that
was the penitencia we would do for that Semana Santa."[92]

In the United States, Latino immigrants and their families continue observing some of these Holy Week traditions, although in many cases these
celebrations become more organized by culturally sensitive Latino priests in
parishes with sizable Latino congregations. A good example of this is the impressive Semana Santa rituals at San Fernando Cathedral in San Antonio, as
noted in Chapter Six, highlighted by the Vía Crucis on Good Friday. However,
one additional way in which some Latinos continue to participate in familiar
Semana Santa activities is by returning to their home communities in Mexico
during Holy Week. One interviewee noted that after arriving in California
from Jalisco, she and her U.S.-born children have returned periodically to her
hometown for Semana Santa and in particular to participate in the Passion
play. This involves walking for eight hours beginning at 3 A.M., but she feels it
is an experience she wants her children to appreciate, if not now then later. "I

took them with us," she says of her children, "so that they could get a feel for sacrifice."[93]

Peregrinaciónes characterized by physical suffering are linked to devotions to a host of saints or virgins and holy sites. Mexican immigrants sometimes return to their home areas in Mexico to participate in these, especially after making *mandas*, or promises, that have been answered by the saints. María Serrano did just that and recalls what she witnessed: "I joined several pilgrimages, and I remember seeing people barefooted, some crawling and others walking on their knees all the way to the altar of the church. During the pilgrimages, people would sing and others would bring *prendas*, special objects to give as gifts to the saints. Some would bring baby shoes, flowers, candles, and many other meaningful items as gifts. Some even took food for the saints because people believe that the saints take a human form."[94]

One other ritualistic and festive religious occasion in the Mexican and Central American tradition is, of course, El Día de los Muertos, or Day of the Dead. This is celebrated on All Soul's Day, November 2. Not to be confused with Halloween, when people express fear of the dead, El Día de los Muertos celebrates and honors the dead. It is, according to Elizondo, in fact the "day of the living—the day of those who have defied death and are more alive than ever."[95] Rooted in pre-Columbian religions, this day emphasizes the importance of keeping alive the memories—*recordando*—of those who have passed away. In this way, the deceased continue to live. As Elizondo further stresses to his students, "Nothing is worse than when there is no one left to remember you. Then you are really dead."[96]

Michelle Romero recalls that in Mexico, El Día de los Muertos started out with people from miles around gathering at the local church in her town. The congregation then marched in procession to the cemetery, where they cleaned the area around the graves and laid flowers. Music and food accompanied this ritual.[97] In Guatemala, similar practices are observed. Zoila Vásquez notes that on El Día de los Muertos, she and her family would take flowers to the cemetery to honor family members who had died. This was more than a religious occasion; it was a national holiday, as no one worked that day. Special foods and candy would be prepared and eaten at the cemetery as a way of sharing with the deceased. Indians would take foods as well as beer to the cemetery and leave them at the gravesites. The Indians believe that the dead come out at night and eat the food and drink the beer.[98]

Some Mexican immigrants return to Mexico to celebrate El Día de los Muertos. Consuelo Munguía, for example, returns each year to her family home in Culiacán, Sinaloa, where her mother is buried. "My mother has been dead for almost eleven years now," she told her daughter. "Every year, when me and my brothers go to visit her grave on the Day of the Dead, I feel that on that day she is with me again, even if it is just for one day. It's a feeling that I carry with me for the whole year, and I thank God for that." With her brothers and her father, Consuelo places at her mother's grave her favorite food, her favorite book, her favorite clothes as well as beautiful flowers. At midnight, the family hires a *banda* to play her mother's favorite songs. All throughout the day and into the evening, the family recalls all the good memories of Consuelo's mother. This is done to ensure that her memory will never be forgotten.[99]

In the United States, El Día de los Muertos is not as widely celebrated because, among other things, many recent Latino immigrants do not have dead relatives buried in this country. Nevertheless, some Latinos still observe this day at both special church services, organized in many cases by Latino priests, or at community-sponsored events. It is also an observance that has made a generational as well as a status crossover in that more acculturated Chicano university students, for example, today organize Día de los Muertos activities on campuses. Some, such as Paula Bautista, a student at UC Santa Barbara, celebrate El Día de los Muertos simply by going to Mass and praying for their deceased family members.[100]

Additional Expressions of Latino Popular Religiosity

Latino Catholic popular religiosity is further expressed in sundry other ways. These include making personal novenas, in which people pray or visit church for several days or in some cases weeks, often to a specific saint in order to ask for a special favor or *promesa*. Velorios, or wakes, are often still observed in a Latino fashion. These sometimes involve people going to pray the rosary at the home of the person dying. *Quinceañeras*, or the celebration of a girl's fifteenth birthday, is still another Latino popular religious tradition. These coming-of-age events can in fact become quite elaborate and expensive. Quinceañeras celebrated in the United States, while predominantly Catholic, in some cases involve Latino Protestants. Yet another expression of popular religiosity and agency is that in which Mexican immigrants, as part of the funds they send to family and to home communities in Mexico, contribute to the local churches in their villages and towns. Mireya Chávez, who grew up in Oxnard, California, observes that Mexican immigrants from her village in Mexico, El Maguey in Guanajuato, collect money to send to help pay for the construction of a new church there.[101] Finally, at least two interviewees noted that their families at times visit *santeros* or *curanderos*, who drive away evil spirits through *brujería*, or evil omens, even though the Church does not approve of this practice. Martha Hernández observes that even though she considers herself a strong Catholic she sometimes goes to a santero if she believes someone is trying to do her harm by casting an evil spirit on her. "The church can only do so much for its people," she concludes, "so sometimes one just has to look elsewhere for salvation and answers, even though I do look to God first for guidance and solutions."[102]

Conclusion

At one level, the interviews cited above suggest that popular religiosity continues to be a strong influence among Latinos in the United States. Having much of its base south of the border, popular religiosity is transferred to this side by immigrants who themselves often remain closely connected to that base as a result of family ties, cyclical migration patterns, and the constant infusion of new immigrants. Hence Latino popular religiosity becomes transnational. As León concludes, "Religion in Chicano communities is a continuation and radical modification of religion in Mexico, and religion in Mexico is inevitably affected by religious developments north of the border: the transnational movements of people back and forth across the border necessarily result in the two mutually influencing one another."[103]

Second, although popular religiosity is modified as a result of the immigrant experience and the immigrants' inculturation with U.S.-based Catholicism, the persistence, albeit sometimes in modified forms, of what Matovina calls "immigrant Catholicism" suggests that popular religiosity is a strong and growing factor, one that must be taken into account in understanding not only Latino Catholicism but also, as Latinos become the majority Catholic group, Catholicism as a whole in the United States.[104]

Third, the extension and persistence of popular religiosity among Latinos, even in many cases among acculturated U.S.-born Latinos, suggest that the study of Latino ethnic identity cannot be divorced from religious identity. Religion, both in its popular religious manifestation as well as in its more institutionalized form, remains a very powerful influence among many Latinos in the United States. Its influence on values, practices, and consciousness is profound. As a consequence, one cannot, as unfortunately is too often done in Chicano/Latino studies, separate ethnic identity from religious identity. As

Elizondo stresses, "Because of the historical process that has been taking place over the past four hundred years and continues today, the cultural elements in the Mexican-American identity cannot be fully separated from religious elements." [105] And, finally, the manifestation of Latino popular religiosity among the growing Latino Catholic population underlines an issue of critical importance: the U.S. Catholic Church must accelerate the processes of understanding and not fearing the implications of these influences on U.S. Catholicism. If the Church can recognize the opportunities offered to it by embracing these powerful religious feelings as a way of refreshing the Catholic faith in this country, the Church stands to lead rather than follow this significant transformation that will affect U.S. Catholicism in the twenty-first century and beyond.

Reflections

From Catholic communities as well as Catholic metaphors there is often no escape.

—ANDREW GREELEY

AS I NOTED in the introduction, I grew up as a Chicano Catholic. It was and still is part of my identity. It isn't all of who I am, but it's an important part. This book on Chicano Catholic history reflects this aspect of my identity. I don't have a problem with this. Religion is not something I am ashamed of. Am I a practicing Catholic? I attend Mass. I pray. There is no question that I'm guided by my Catholic socialization and, to borrow from Father Andrew Greeley, my Catholic imagination.[1] Catholicism has influenced my values and my politics.

But my Catholicism isn't a generic one. It's a Chicano Catholicism. For years, as I've researched various topics in Chicano history, I've been in search of the Chicano side. I've found myself in Chicano history. But what was missing was my Catholic side. This book is about my search for the Catholic side of Chicano history. I believe that in *Católicos*, I've finally bridged these two critical parts of my identity.

In doing so, I hope I've also done the same in a general way. The absence of Catholic and religious history in Chicano history and Chicano studies has represented, as noted earlier, a huge gap. As in my own case, this partly reveals the ambivalence about religion that other Chicano historians have experienced in their own personal stories. Yet this ambivalence has regrettably shut out a significant part of the Chicano historical narrative. Religion and especially Catholicism permeates the Chicano and other Latino communities, but as historians and scholars we could not or did not want to see this. But this says more about us than about the role of religion in Chicano life. We need now, first, to acknowledge this omission and, second, move to correct it. Chicano history is incomplete without Chicano religious history.

But the divide is not just in Chicano history. My mentor, Ramón Ruiz, not a religious man, once told an audience composed mostly of Chicanos that they couldn't afford to just look at their navels. Ruiz wasn't averse to being direct and blunt. Yet I agree with him. My work in Chicano history has always attempted to link the Chicano experience with the general contours of U.S. history. I've done my part in integrating Chicano history into U.S. history. If U.S. historians of other ethnic backgrounds have not reciprocated that's been their problem and biases. The same holds for my new explorations in Chicano Catholic history. If there is a wide gulf in Chicano history concerning religion, there is an equally wide one in U.S. Catholic history concerning Chicano/Latino Catholicism. This book hopefully will also begin to reverse this neglect.

Just as Chicano history is incomplete without the inclusion of Catholic history, so U.S. Catholic history and Catholic studies are incomplete without the inclusion of Chicano/Latino Catholic history. This does not mean creating a new kind of melting pot in the expectation of producing some generic American Catholic. But it does mean, as Father Virgilio Elizondo has always stressed in his work, the creation of a new mestizaje or synthesis that recognizes and respects differences, but that also produces a new unity strengthened by this diversity.[2] I respect, for example, Irish American Catholicism while at the same time being inspired by particular Chicano religious traditions, such as the devotion to Our Lady of Guadalupe. Both are equal and valid Catholic expressions. One is not better than the other, although they are different. In respecting and accepting these differences, I can become a better Catholic. The key here is respect. The work we do in history lays the foundation for this respect.

In reflecting on the meaning of my book, I believe it provides various insights that can lead to a new analysis of both Chicano history and U.S. Catholic history. There may be other meanings I cannot see because of my closeness to the text, but as best I can interpret my work, let me share the following *pen-samientos*, or thoughts.

Influenced by the Chicano movement and its stress on a rediscovery and renaissance of Chicano culture—cultural nationalism—Chicano studies, including Chicano history, has emphasized the role of ethnic/cultural identity in the evolution of Chicano history. Affected by a history of Yankee conquest and discrimination based on their "Mexicanness," Chicanos as people of Mexican descent have reacted in part by resisting and affirming their Chicano being. This is what some scholars refer to as "cultural citizenship."[3] "Cultural citizenship," assert William V. Flores and Rina Benmayor, "names a range of social practices which, taken together, claim and establish a distinct social space for Latinos in this country."[4] That is, one part of being a citizen and a political subject is recognition of the cultural context surrounding the public persona. All U.S. citizens are cultural citizens in that they reflect a particular ethnic/cultural story. At times, this has meant a very direct cultural expression, such as a pronounced Irish or Italian one. However, owing to acculturation and assimilation, for some Americans this has meant at later periods a more generic U.S. cultural expression that reveals a "white" cultural citizenship. At the same time, for those ethnic and racialized groups, such as Chicanos and African Americans and other so-called people of color, because of segregation, discrimination, and greater degrees of marginalization, their cultural citizenship is not only still much more "ethnic," but more assertive in order to claim their rights and identity as cultural citizens. Indeed, cultural citizenship is not in all cases synonymous with legal citizenship. It includes all people within a society who, through their work and community endeavors, contribute to the general good of society. This cultural citizenship among Chicanos, for example, has been well documented by historians. Chicanos have struggled to become part of the United States by organizing as a specific ethnic group with particular issues.

However, what *Católicos* suggests is that cultural citizenship is not just secular. It also possesses a religious dimension. This is what has been missing in the discourse concerning the concept of citizenship in Chicano history.[5] Chicanos have not resisted and affirmed their cultural citizenship just in secular terms. Father Elizondo tells his students that for years after the U.S. takeover of the Southwest the only public place where Mexican Americans could feel secure in who they were and affirm who they were was largely in their churches and sacred spaces. But this affirmation (that is also resistance to ethnic/cultural discrimination) is practiced as Chicano Catholics and not just as Chicanos. This form of cultural citizenship, or what Flores and Benmayor also refer to as "new citizenship," can be observed in the various manifestations of popular religiosity noted in *Católicos*. But one can also see it in public life: the influence of Catholic social doctrine in Chicano civil rights efforts; the role of religion in the Chicano movement; the work of activist Chicano priests; and the embrace of the concept of sanctuary, as noted. All of these factors address a more public role of cultural citizenship. What this implies is that the discussion of cultural citizenship has to be much more inclusive in what is meant by culture. Religion is a central component of Chicano culture, and it needs to be integrated into this consideration.[6]

At the same time, it is important not to essentialize the Chicano Catholic experience. It is no more homogeneous than secular Chicano history. The Chicano Catholic experience has evolved and changed over the years. As stressed throughout the work of Fray Angélico Chávez, native Mexican Americans like the Hispanos of New Mexico retained much of their pre–U.S. Catholic traditions rooted in popular culture as a way of both defending and asserting their ethnic status at a time of transition. Early immigrants in the first quarter of the twentieth century introduced a mexicano religious culture still closely tied to the popular religiosity of their villages and towns, but even here there was much diversity. Acculturation to U.S. society both by immigrants and their children began to reflect religious as well as cultural changes. Immigrants in some cases, for example, began to become more open to Protestant proselytizing. U.S.-born Mexican American Catholics, as noted in Chapter Two, as part of their "Americanization," pursued bilingual and bicultural approaches, including being influenced more directly by the U.S. Catholic Church, as in the case of the application of Catholic social doctrine.

While the Church in the United States struggled to make itself relevant to Chicano Catholics, much bias and even racism continued into the second half of the century. The ethnic revival movements of the 1960s, such as the Chicano movement introduced a new chapter of Chicano-Church relations. Emboldened by the mass protest movements of that era, including civil rights struggles, a new generation of Chicano Catholics, as witnessed by Católicos Por La Raza, despaired of the ability of the Church on its own to integrate Chicanos. Earlier Mexican American Catholic leaders such as Perales and Calleros had believed such an integration to be possible, but the new generation instead chose direct confrontation with the Church. This generation of

Chicano Catholics proved to be more questioning, as were their peers among post–Vatican II Catholics in general. Influenced by this confrontational politics, Chicano Catholic clerics likewise developed a new ethnic consciousness to complement their religious one and organized as Chicano Catholic clerics in groups such as PADRES and Las Hermanas to reform the Church from within. As part of this change in consciousness, faith-based movements among Chicanos further expanded to include a pan-Latino identity, as Catholicism was transformed in cities such as Los Angeles with the influx of Central American refugees. In addition, Chicano faith-based movements such as the sanctuary movement in Los Angeles led by Father Olivares abandoned the more ethnic and cultural nationalism of earlier groups like Católicos and PADRES and embraced an interethnic ecumenism.

The arrival in the last third of the twentieth century of new waves of Mexican and Latino immigrants into the United States has, at one level, reinforced earlier manifestations of popular religiosity but, at another, has revealed greater secular influences in their countries of origin as well as among their U.S.-born children. The juncture of the secular and the profane is much more visible among this generation of Latino immigrants. At the same time, this new Latino generation, unlike earlier immigrants, is much more inclined to participate in faith-based oppositional movements, as indicated by the mass demonstrations throughout the country in 2006 by Latino immigrants against legislation proposed by nativist and anti-immigrant interests. Many of these pro-immigrant manifestations were faith-based. The fact is that the Chicano Catholic experience has never been monolithic and static. It has evolved and changed while retaining a core identity. A central focus of this identity has been the recognition, both consciously and unconsciously, that religion, in this case Catholicism, has been and still is a way for Chicanos and other Latinos to defend their integrity and honor as a people and as a way to affirm their very being. Resistance and affirmation are fundamental characteristics of historical Chicano Catholicism.

Chicano studies has also made much of the concept of mestizaje, or the interaction and synthesis of cultures to produce a hybrid Chicano culture. Through the work of Gloria Anzaldúa, Chicano mestizaje has expanded to include diverse sexual expressions such as lesbianism.[7] The concepts of border cultures and border crossing metaphorically complement mestizaje. Chicano culture is seen as a dynamic intersection of cultural influences, including not only transborder ones, as in the case of Mexico and the United States, but internal border transactions within U.S.-based Chicano culture (Spanish-speaking versus English-speaking; immigrants versus native born; urban versus rural; working class versus middle class, etc.).

Such concepts as mestizaje and border culture make for new and diverse ways of thinking about the Chicano experience. Yet, here again the role of religion has largely been obfuscated. Religion is seen in static terms and as representing only traditional church institutions. Yet, for many Chicanos the expression of mestizaje has also included the world of religion. Living in the United States and being influenced by Anglo forms of Catholicism, for example, Chicano Catholics, as in my own case, reflect a form of Catholic mestizaje or Catholic border culture. Mexican Catholic traditions interact, both positively and, sometimes, negatively with Anglo-Catholic ones. Chicano identity based on ethnic/cultural conditions has included strong religious dimensions. Hence, my book, with its various suggestions of where and how Chicano Catholic influences have encountered Anglo-Catholic ones, both in popular religiosity and public life, hopefully helps to lay the basis for a rethinking of mestizaje that includes the role of religion.

In the case of U.S. Catholic history, mestizaje, which conveys cultural diversity and cultural mixing, will also influence a revision of what we mean by U.S. Catholic culture. There is no question in my mind that most U.S. Catholic scholars, when they speak or write about American Catholics, are not including Chicanos/Latinos. This has to change. Historically and in the present, Catholic culture, centered in the Southwest but increasingly found nationwide, has meant and continues to mean the interaction of Chicano Catholic practices and traditions with those of other ethnic Catholics. This mestizaje needs to be incorporated into future discussions of U.S. Catholic history and Catholic studies.

The concept of mestizaje further suggests that Chicano Catholicism will never, as observed in historical terms, remain static and essentialist. Mestizaje means constant change and evolution as cultures intersect with one another and borrow and reject from each other. This has been true historically and it is true today and will be in the future. Chicano and Latino Catholicism today in many ways is different from what it was a hundred years ago and it will be different a hundred years from now (perhaps vastly different, given the increasing impact of globalization). Change does not wipe away all vestiges of the traditional, but it does mean that what we define as traditional changes. Continued immigration will repeatedly refresh what is traditional, but generational acculturation and even assimilation as a result of increased education, class mobility, intermarriage, and biethnic children will also, as is visible already, transform the meaning of Chicano and Latino Catholicism. The possibility of being a Chicano and Latino Catholic will not be eliminated, but being such will bring even greater complexity and hybridity.

In my previous work, I attempted to stress what I call the historical agency of Chicanos. That is, Chicanos have not just been victims of history, but they have made history. My studies of the Mexican American Generation of the 1930s through the 1950s are examples of what I mean by historical agency. Despite the fact that most critics continue to believe that I define the Mexican American Generation only as the expression of middle-class leadership, the fact is that if they read carefully and go beyond their biases against the middle class, they will have to acknowledge that my work includes working-class leaders and radicals. Whether focused on the middle class, the working class, or radicals, my studies concentrate on leadership and hence on historical agency. Through my collective biographies, individual biographies, and *testimonios*, or oral histories, I have attempted to show how Chicanos, despite the various obstacles and opposition they meet, have taken their lives into their own hands and struggled to achieve social justice, dignity, respect, and first-class citizenship.

Despite my emphasis on historical agency, I have neglected, until now, to consider historical agency related to religion, especially Chicano Catholicism. I failed, as have other historians, to understand that at certain points in Chicano history, leadership has emanated from faith-based groups and movements. For example, Chicano or Hispano priests in the post–U.S.-Mexico War period in New Mexico, priests such as Father Antonio Martínez and Father José Manuel Gallegos, about whom Fray Angélico Chávez wrote, exercised considerable community leadership in their resistance to both Anglo secular and religious colonization. Fray Angélico himself, as an intellectual but also in his ministry, is an example of religious-based historical agency. In the twentieth century, there are other cases of Chicano priests, especially in public life, representing oppositional leadership on behalf of Chicanos. In *Católicos*, I discuss leadership by such priests as Juan Romero, Luis Quihuis, Virgilio Elizondo, and Luis Olivares.

But faith-based historical agency, of course, has not been the realm just of Chicano priests. Lay Chicano Catholics have likewise expressed such leadership. Guided and inspired by their Catholic faith, they have involved themselves in public life to counter racism and discrimination. Lay Catholics like

Alonso Perales and Cleofas Calleros are representatives of such leadership. Others, such as Richard Cruz and Católicos Por La Raza, have used their historical agency to reform the Church itself to make it more sensitive and relevant to the Chicano community.

It is this Chicano Catholic historical agency that has been marginalized in Chicano history. Indeed, my book only begins to suggest the possibilities for extending the study of leadership and community struggles centered on Catholic parishes and Catholic lay leadership. This leadership had not always expressed itself as publicly as my examples reveal. Some leadership can be more internal to the faith, such as in the Chicano Catholic lay sodalities that provide a spiritual and supportive environment for both men and women centered on particular devotions like that to Our Lady of Guadalupe. In the late 1950s and into the 1960s, many Mexican Americans, men and women, also participated in the Cursillo movement, which aimed to develop lay Catholic leadership through spiritual retreats. César Chávez was a cursillista. More needs to be known about such leadership.[8]

The study and incorporation of Chicano Catholic historical agency will fill in large gaps not only in Chicano history, but also in U.S. Catholic history. Studies of U.S. Catholic religious and lay leadership need to also acknowledge and integrate the role and contribution of Chicano Catholics. The relationship of faith to historical agency needs considerable further attention.

A new emphasis on Chicano Catholic and religious history may also open up new opportunities to study the role of women in Chicano history. Although I am guilty of not doing enough in this area, I do note that women, at least in my book, were involved in making Chicano Catholic history at two levels. The first involves the importance of popular religiosity to Chicano cultural life. As noted in Chapters Three and Eight, which focus on popular religious traditions and practices, women have been at the center of these expressions of faith, expressions controlled by the people themselves and operated without clerical influence. The role of grandmothers and mothers in keeping the faith alive through various forms of popular religion in the home and in the community is a further indicator of lay leadership and historical agency. What some theologians refer to as "abuelita theology" is reflective of this role. Hence, the study of the relationship of women to popular religion provides a new way of exploring and adding to our knowledge of women in Chicano history.

Moreover, women—Chicanas—have also been involved in Chicano Catholic public life. They have been part of Catholic-inspired social movements.

The role women played in Católicos Por La Raza and in the Los Angeles sanctuary movement is evidence of such involvement. This does not mean, of course, that women did not meet with male resistance in their efforts to participate. However, despite such obstacles, women did engage and furthered the struggle of such groups and movements. We need to learn more about such Chicana Catholic lay activism in public life.

Finally, although my study does not include this topic, the role of Chicana Catholic sisters or nuns in the Chicano community must be explored. The recent work by Lara Medina on Las Hermanas, the organization of Chicana sisters organized in the early 1970s as part of the Chicano movement, is an excellent example of research in this area. Other research concerning Chicana sisters in a variety of religious orders and community work is needed.

Historians have lamented the lack of studies on women in Chicano history. While the role of women has not been as neglected as some suggest (and women's history is expanding, as in the work of Gina Marie Pitti on the role of Mexican and Latina women in the organization of Sociedades Guadalupanas), much more needs to be done.[9] What I am proposing is that new attention to Catholic and religious history may open novel, exciting opportunities in this pursuit.

Needless to say, the excavation of the role of Chicana and Latina Catholics is instructive not only for Chicano history, but for U.S. Catholic history as well. The history of women in the Church cannot be reserved for those of European descent. It has to be inclusive of other women, such as Chicanas, who, in many ways, have been and continue to be the backbone of Chicano Catholicism in the United States. With the continued increase among Latino Catholics, the role of women will only expand.

Religion, of course, is also ideology. But unlike much of the Chicano movement that considered religion, including Catholicism, a one-way ideology whose sole or main intent was to dominate and disempower Chicanos, religion, in fact, is more complicated. It is dialectic. It can be an ideology of control and suppression, an ideology used to justify people's resignation. On the other hand, religion, including Catholicism, can also be empowering. With its stress on God's special embrace of the poor, on justice, on right and wrong, on human dignity, as well as other Christian values, Catholic theology can and has inspired progressive movements that have been oppositional against oppression. My chapters on Catholic social doctrine and Mexican American political thought, on the role of Chicano community priests, as well as Católicos

Por La Raza underscore this side of Catholic ideology grounded in social justice issues. This, in turn, suggests that the study of Chicano political thought should examine not only secular political influences, but also religious and Catholic ones. Chicano intellectual history needs to consider this religious dimension. The same holds true for a new study of Catholic political theory in the United States. The inclusion of Chicano Catholic political theories such as liberation theology, for example, likewise expands the parameters of Catholic thought.

What further strikes me about the issues and themes explored in *Católicos* is how religious influences such as Catholic social doctrine, liberation theology, and expressions of popular religiosity have empowered many in the Chicano community. This empowerment has been realized in both the public and the private arenas. Chicano Catholicism, with its particular traditions and celebrations, has helped to make Chicanos feel good about themselves and their culture. As Father Luis Quihuis often said, "Chicano/Latino Catholic practices validate the self-worth of the people." [10] Everything else around them, such as the schools and the media may negate being Chicano, but within the culture and especially in religious circles, the people—*la gente*—can validate their experiences; this is an area in which, paraphrasing the words of Elizondo, "Chicanos can be Chicanos." Religion, along with other cultural traditions, lays the foundation for both self and community empowerment. Communities cannot struggle for liberation unless the people believe in themselves. Religion, including Chicano Catholicism, can be part of this process.

The political implications of recognizing the relationship between Chicano Catholicism and self, but especially community empowerment, are profound. Chicano/Latino political leaders need to understand (and some do), that faith-based movements (César Chávez and the farmworkers' movement is an excellent example) can be of great significance. Faith-based movements represent deep commitment on the part of the people and can thus be of substantial duration. Moreover, in these movements is where the people are. You may not see many Chicanos at secular gatherings, but they are in the churches and at specific Chicano religious events, such as the feast day of Our Lady of Guadalupe. This, then, is where political leaders need to be if they expect to organize the people. If you want to register Chicanos to vote, for example, do not try to do it during a weekday but go to the Chicano parishes on Sundays after the Masses and you'll find hundreds there. The same is true for holding meetings on political and community issues. Chicanos may not go on a weeknight because of work pressures, but they will on a Sunday afternoon after Mass.

These same political implications apply to the U.S. Catholic Church as a whole. The future of the Church very much involves Chicanos/Latinos. The recognition and inclusion of Chicano/Latino religious traditions in the liturgy and practices of the Church can only empower the Church itself. In turn, an empowered Chicano/Latino Catholic community can strengthen the Church at a time of much crisis. The Church, in many ways, already understands this, but much more needs to be done, especially about educating Anglo-Catholics about the inculturation of Chicano/Latino Catholicism. The future of the Church, as Virgilio Elizondo predicts, is mestizo (Chicano/Latino). Or, as Héctor Avalos contends about Latino and Third World Christianity, "Whereas in earlier times Europeans came to 'Christianize' the Third World, we may now have a case where the 'Third World' will see itself as re-Christianizing America and the rest of the 'First World.'" [11]

Whenever I face a crisis in my life, and there have been some, I instinctively pray. This is almost natural to me. I suspect the same has been true of many other Chicanos in the past and in the present. It is this religious and especially Catholic impulse and imagination that I've sought to capture in this book and that has been of significant importance in Chicano history. It is what has been missing in the still-growing field of Chicano history. My book is an effort to recapture that impulse and imagination and to integrate it into Chicano and U.S. Catholic historiography. I hope others will do likewise.

Notes

Introduction

1. See Ania Loomba, *Colonialism/Postcolonialism* (London: Routledge, 1998), 173.
2. Andrew Greeley, *The Catholic Imagination* (Berkeley and Los Angeles: University of California Press, 2000).
3. Michael P. Carroll, *The Penitente Brotherhood: Patriarchy and Hispano-Catholicism in New Mexico* (Baltimore: Johns Hopkins University Press, 2002), 211.
4. Timothy Matovina, *Guadalupe and Her Faithful: Latino Catholics in San Antonio, from Colonial Origins to the Present* (Baltimore: Johns Hopkins University Press, 2005), 21.
5. Liberation theology was the response by the Latin American Church to the reforms of Vatican II and its call for the Church to become more relevant to the modern world. Its leading theologian was Gustavo Gutiérrez. See, for example, Gustavo Gutiérrez, *A Theology of Liberation: History, Politics, and Salvation* (Maryknoll, N.Y.: Orbis Books, 1973); Gustavo Gutiérrez, *The Power of the Poor in History* (Maryknoll, N.Y.: Orbis Books, 1983); Philip Berryman, *Liberation Theology* (New York: Pantheon Books, 1987); Michael

Löwy, *The War of Gods: Religion and Politics in Latin America* (London: Verso, 1996); and Daniel H. Levine, ed., *Religion and Political Conflict in Latin America* (Chapel Hill: University of North Carolina Press, 1986).

6. Mario T. García, *Desert Immigrants: The Mexicans of El Paso, 1880–1920* (New Haven: Yale University Press, 1981).

7. Carlos Fuentes, *This I Believe: An A to Z of a Life* (New York: Random House, 2005), 172.

8. Examples of Chicano historiography that exhibit this social justice sensibility include Alberto Camarillo, *Chicanos in a Changing Society: From Mexican Pueblos to American Barrios in Santa Barbara and Southern California, 1848–1930* (Cambridge: Harvard University Press, 1979); Arnoldo De Leon, *The Tejano Community, 1836–1900* (Albuquerque: University of New Mexico Press, 1982); Richard Griswold del Castillo, *The Los Angeles Barrio, 1850–1890: A Social History* (Berkeley and Los Angeles: University of California Press, 1979); Robert J. Rosenbaum, *Mexicano Resistance in the Southwest: The Sacred Right of Self-Preservation* (Austin: University of Texas Press, 1981); Ricardo Romo, *East Los Angeles: History of a Barrio* (Austin: University of Texas Press, 1983); Francisco E. Balderrama, *In Defense of La Raza: The Los Angeles Mexican Consulate and the Mexican Community, 1929 to 1936* (Tucson: University of Arizona Press, 1982); Rodolfo Acuña, *Occupied America: A History of Chicanos*, 3d ed. (New York: Harper and Row, 1988); Neil Foley, *The White Scourge: Mexicans, Blacks, and Poor Whites in Texas Cotton Culture* (Berkeley and Los Angeles: University of California Press, 1997); Ignacio M. García, *United We Win: The Rise and Fall of the Raza Unida Party* (Tucson: Mexican American Studies and Resource Center, University of Arizona, 1989); Juan R. García, *Mexicans in the Midwest, 1900–1932* (Tucson: University of Arizona Press, 1996); Richard A. García, *Rise of the Mexican American Middle Class: San Antonio, 1929–1941* (College Station: Texas A&M Press, 1991); Juan Gómez-Quiñones, *Chicano Politics: Reality and Promise, 1940–1990* (Albuquerque: University of New Mexico Press, 1990); David G. Gutiérrez, *Walls and Mirrors: Mexican Americans, Mexican Immigrants, and the Politics of Ethnicity* (Berkeley and Los Angeles: University of California Press, 1995); Benjamin Márquez, LULAC: *The Evolution of a Mexican American Political Organization* (Austin: University of Texas Press, 1993); Armando Navarro, *Mexican American Youth Organization: Avant-Garde of the Chicano Movement in Texas* (Austin: University of Texas Press, 1995); Emma Pérez, *The Decolonial Imaginary: Writing Chicanas into History* (Bloomington: University of Indiana Press, 1999); Vicki L. Ruiz, *Cannery Women/Cannery Lives: Mexican Women, Unionization, and the California Food Processing Industry, 1930–1950* (Albuquerque: University of New Mexico Press, 1987); George J. Sánchez, *Becoming Mexican American: Ethnicity, Culture, and Identity in*

Chicano Los Angeles, 1900–1945 (New York: Oxford University Press, 1993);
Zaragoza Vargas, *Proletarians of the North: A History of Mexican Industrial Workers in Detroit and the Midwest, 1917–1933* (Berkeley and Los Angeles: University of California Press, 1993); Emilio Zamora, *The World of the Mexican Worker in Texas* (College Station: Texas A&M Press, 1993); Douglas Monroy, *Rebirth: Mexican Los Angeles from the Great Migration to the Great Depression* (Berkeley and Los Angeles: University of California Press, 1999); Craig A. Kaplowitz, LULAC: *Mexican Americans and National Policy* (College Station: Texas A&M University Press, 2005); Tomás Almaguer, *Racial Fault Lines: The Historical Origins of White Supremacy in California* (Berkeley and Los Angeles: University of California Press, 1994); Clete Daniel, *Chicano Workers and the Politics of Fairness: The FEPC in the Southwest, 1941–1945* (Austin: University of Texas Press, 1991); Dennis Nadín Valdés, *Al Norte: Agricultural Workers in the Great Lakes Region, 1917–1970* (Austin: University of Texas Press, 1991); Dennis Nadín Valdés, *Barrio Norteño: St. Paul and Midwestern Mexican Communities in the Twentieth Century* (Austin: University of Texas Press, 2000); Devra Weber, *Dark Sweat, White Gold: California Farm Workers, Cotton, and the New Deal* (Berkeley and Los Angeles: University of California Press, 1994); Gilbert G. González, *Labor and Community: Mexican Citrus Worker Villages in a Southern California County, 1900–1950* (Urbana: University of Illinois Press, 1994); Julie Leininger Pycior, LBJ *and Mexican Americans: The Paradox of Power* (Austin: University of Texas Press, 1997); Erasmo Gamboa, *Mexican Labor and World War II: Braceros in the Pacific Northwest, 1942–1947* (Austin: University of Texas Press, 1990); Zaragoza Vargas, *Labor Rights Are Civil Rights: Mexican American Workers in Twentieth-Century America* (Princeton: Princeton University Press, 2005); Matt García, *A World of Its Own: Race, Labor, and Citrus in the Making of Greater Los Angeles, 1900–1970* (Chapel Hill: University of North Carolina Press, 2001).

9. Mario T. García, *Mexican Americans: Leadership, Ideology and Identity, 1930–1960* (New Haven: Yale University Press, 1989).

10. García, *Memories of Chicano History: The Life and Narrative of Bert Corona* (Berkeley and Los Angeles: University of California Press, 1994); García, ed., *Ruben Salazar, Border Correspondent: Selected Writings, 1955–1970* (Berkeley and Los Angeles: University of California Press, 1995); Frances Esquibel Tywoniak and Mario T. García, *Migrant Daughter: Coming of Age as a Mexican American Woman* (Berkeley and Los Angeles: University of California Press, 2000).

11. See, for example, citations in note 8 as well as more recent publications such as Armando C. Alonzo, *Tejano Legacy: Rancheros and Settlers in South Texas, 1734–1900* (Albuquerque: University of New Mexico Press, 1998); Patrick J. Carroll. *Felix Longoria's Wake: Bereavement, Racism, and*

the Rise of Mexican American Activism (Austin: University of Texas Press, 2003); Eduardo Obregón Pagán, *Murder at the Sleepy Lagoon: Zoot Suits, Race, and Riot in Wartime L.A.* (Chapel Hill: University of North Carolina Press, 2003); Stephen J. Pitti, *The Devil in Silicon Valley: Northern California, Race, and Mexican Americans* (Princeton: Princeton University Press, 2003); John M. Nieto-Phillips, *The Language of Blood: The Making of Spanish-American Identity in New Mexico, 1850–1940* (Albuquerque: University of New Mexico Press, 2004); Lorena Oropeza, *¡Raza Sí! ¡Guerra No!: Chicano Protest and Patriotism during the Vietnam War Era* (Berkeley and Los Angeles: University of California Press, 2005); Miroslava Chávez-García, *Negotiating Conquest: Gender and Power in California, 1770s to 1880s* (Tucson: University of Arizona Press, 2004).

12. Roberto R. Treviño, *The Church in the Barrio: Mexican American Ethno-Catholicism in Houston* (Chapel Hill: University of North Carolina Press, 2006), 14.

13. Ana María Díaz and Anthony M. Stevens-Arroyo, *Recognizing the Latino Resurgence in U.S. Religion: The Emmaus Paradigm* (Boulder: Westview Press, 1998), 2.

14. David Badillo, *Latinos and the New Immigrant Church* (Baltimore: Johns Hopkins University Press, 2006), 1.

15. Luis D. León, *La Llorona's Children: Religion, Life, and Death in the U.S.-Mexican Borderlands* (Berkeley and Los Angeles: University of California Press, 2004), ix.

16. As quoted in Moises Sandoval, ed., *Fronteras: A History of the Latin American Church in the USA Since 1513* (San Antonio: Mexican American Cultural Center, 1983), viii.

17. On Chicanismo, see Ignacio M. García, *Chicanismo: The Forging of a Militant Ethos* (Tucson: University of Arizona Press, 1997). For an excellent discussion and analysis of Chicano cultural nationalism, see George Mariscal, *Brown-Eyed Children of the Sun: Lessons from the Chicano Movement, 1965–1975* (Albuquerque: University of New Mexico Press, 2005).

18. On the concept of Aztlán, see Rudolfo A. Anaya and Francisco A. Lomeli, eds., *Aztlán: Essays on the Chicano Homeland* (Albuquerque: University of New Mexico, 1991); Luis Leal, "In Search of Aztlán," *Denver Quarterly* 16, no. 3 (Fall 1981).

19. For literature on what I call the "conquered generation" in Chicano history, see, for example, Camarillo, *Chicanos in a Changing Society*; Griswold del Castillo, *Los Angeles Barrio*; Douglas Monroy, *Thrown Among Strangers: The Making of Mexican Culture in Frontier California* (Berkeley and Los Angeles: University of California Press, 1990); William Deverell, *Whitewashed Adobe: The Rise of Los Angeles and the Remaking of Its Mexican Past* (Berkeley and Los Angeles: University of California Press, 2004); Pitti, *The Devil in Silicon Valley.*

20. I borrow the term "collective personality" from the African writer L. S. Senghor, as quoted in Loomba, *Colonialism/Postcolonialism*, 211.

21. León, *La Llorona's Children*, 5.

22. Gaston Espinosa, Virgilio Elizondo, Jesse Miranda, eds., *Latino Religions and Civic Activism in the United States* (New York: Oxford University Press, 2005), 3.

23. See Gary Gutting, *Foucault: A Very Short Introduction* (Oxford: Oxford University Press, 2005), 32–33.

24. Timothy Matovina and Gerald E. Poyo, eds., *¡Presente! U.S. Latino Catholics from Colonial Origins to the Present* (Maryknoll, N.Y.: Orbis Press, 2000), xvii.

25. Andrés G. Guerrero, *A Chicano Theology* (Maryknoll, N.Y.: Orbis Books, 1987), 2.

26. See Díaz-Stevens and Stevens-Arroyo, *The Latino Resurgence*.

27. As quoted in Eduardo C. Fernández, *La Cosecha: Harvesting Contemporary United States Hispanic Theology (1972–1998)* (Collegeville, Minn.: Liturgical Press, 2000), 73. Also see Justo L. González, *Santa Biblia: The Bible Through Hispanic Eyes* (Nashville: Abingdon Press, 1996), and Justo L. González, *Mañana: Christian Theology from a Hispanic Perspective* (Nashville: Abingdon Press, 1990).

28. For an excellent overview of Latino theological development, see Fernández, *La Cosecha*. Also see Arturo J. Bañuelas, ed., *Mestizo Christianity: Theology from the Latino Perspective* (Maryknoll, N.Y.: Orbis Press, 1995); Ada María Isasi-Díaz and Fernando F. Segovia, eds., *Hispanic/Latino Theology: Challenge and Promise* (Minneapolis: Fortress Press, 1996); Ada María Isasi-Díaz, *Mujerista Theology* (Maryknoll: N.Y.: Orbis Press, 1996). On the work and influence of Father Virgilio Elizondo, see Timothy Matovina, ed., *Beyond Borders: Writings of Virgilio Elizondo and Friends* (Maryknoll, N.Y.: Orbis Press, 2000).

29. See, for example, Alberto L. Pulido, *The Sacred World of the Penitentes* (Washington, D.C.: Smithsonian Institution Press, 2000); León, *La Llorona's Children*. Also see Timothy Matovina and Gary Riebe-Estrella, eds., *Horizons of the Sacred: Mexican Traditions in U.S. Catholicism* (Ithaca: Cornell University Press, 2002).

30. Moises Sandoval, *On the Move: A History of the Hispanic Church in the United States* (1990; reprint Maryknoll, N.Y.: Orbis Press, 2006).

31. Jay P. Dolan and Gilberto M. Hinojosa, eds., *Mexican Americans and the Catholic Church, 1900–1965* (Notre Dame: University of Notre Dame Press, 1994).

32. Timothy M. Matovina, *Tejano Religion and Ethnicity: San Antonio, 1821–1860* (Austin: University of Texas Press, 1995). Also see Matovina, *Guadalupe and Her Faithful: Latino Catholics in San Antonio from Colonial Origins to the Present* (Baltimore: Johns Hopkins University Press, 2005).

33. Lara Medina, *Las Hermanas: Chicana/Latina Religious-Political Activism in the U.S. Catholic Church* (Philadelphia: Temple University Press, 2004).

34. Richard Edward Martínez, PADRES: *The National Chicano Priest Movement* (Austin: University of Texas Press, 2005).

35. Félix D. Almaráz, Jr., *Knight Without Armor: Carlos Eduardo Castañeda, 1896–1958* (College Station: Texas A&M Press, 1999).

36. For this additional literature, see Treviño, *The Church in the Barrio*; David A. Badillo, *Latinos and the New Immigrant Church* (Baltimore: Johns Hopkins University Press, 2006); and Anthony Quiroz, *Claiming Citizenship: Mexican Americans in Victoria, Texas* (College Station: Texas A&M University Press, 2005). Some additional sources include José Roberto Juárez, "La Iglesia Católica y el Chicano en Sud Texas, 1836–1911," *Aztlán* (Fall 1974): 217–255; Antonio R. Soto, "The Chicano and the Church in Northern California, 1848–1978: A Study of an Ethnic Minority Within the Roman Catholic Church" (Ph.D. diss., University of California, Berkeley, 1978); Thomas G. Kelliher, Jr., "Hispanic Catholics and the Archdiocese of Chicago, 1923–1970" (Ph.D. diss., University of Notre Dame, 1996). Also, Ricardo Ramírez, "The Hispanic Peoples of the United States and the Church from 1965 to 1985," *U.S. Catholic Historian* 9 (Spring 1990): 165–177; Linda Gordon, *The Great Arizona Orphan Abduction* (Cambridge: Harvard University Press, 1999); Gina Marie Pitti, "The Sociedades Guadalupanas in the San Francisco Archdiocese, 1942–1962," *U.S. Catholic Historian* 21 (Winter 2003): 83–98. A developing history of Chicano Protestantism is likewise beginning to develop; see, for example, Paul Barton, *Hispanic Methodists, Presbyterians, and Baptists in Texas* (Austin: University of Texas Press, 2006), and Rudy V. Busto, *King Tiger: The Religious Vision of Reies López Tijerina* (Albuquerque: University of New Mexico Press, 2005). Also see R. Douglas Brackenridge and Francisco O. García-Treto, *Iglesia Presbiteriana: A History of Presbyterians and Mexican Americans in the Southwest*, 2d ed. (San Antonio: Trinity University Press, 1987); Gaston Espinosa, "Borderland Religion: Los Angeles and the Origins of the Latino Pentecostal Movement in the U.S., Mexico, and Puerto Rico, 1900–1945" (Ph.D. diss., University of California, Santa Barbara, 1999); Arlene M. Sánchez Walsh, *Latino Pentecostal Identity: Evangelical Faith, Self, and Society* (New York: Columbia University Press, 2003). An excellent personal account of growing up as a Mexican American Protestant is David Maldonado, Jr., *Crossing Guadalupe Street: Growing up Hispanic and Protestant* (Albuquerque: University of New Mexico Press, 2001). Also see Daniel Ramírez, "Borderland Praxis: The Immigrant Experience in Latino Pentecostal Churches," *Journal of the American Academy of Religion* 67 (September 1999): 573–596; Daisy L. Machado, *Of Borders and Margins: Hispanic Disciples in Texas, 1888–1945* (New York: Oxford University Press, 2003).

37. Matovina and Poyo, eds., *¡Presente!*, xv.

38. As quoted in Dolan and Hinojosa, eds., *Mexican Americans*, 131.

39. Lawrence J. Mosqueda, *Chicanos, Catholicism and Political Ideology* (Lanham, Md.: University Press of America, 1986).

40. Matovina and Riebe-Estrella, eds., *Horizons of the Sacred*, 7.

41. Sandoval, *On the Move*, xiii. Two recent texts on U.S. Catholicism briefly mention Hispanic Catholics, but no effort is made to integrate this history with that of other Catholics, especially those of European descent. See Charles R. Morris, *American Catholic: The Saints and Sinners Who Built America's Most Powerful Church* (New York: Vintage Books, 1997); and Chester Gillis, *Roman Catholicism in America* (New York: Columbia University Press, 1999). On a better effort to address the role of Latinos in U.S. Catholic history, see Jay P. Dolan, *In Search of an American Catholicism: A History of Religion and Culture in Tension* (New York: Oxford University Press, 2002).

42. Richard Griswold del Castillo, Teresa McKenna, Yvonne Yarbro-Bejarano, eds., *Chicano Art: Resistance and Affirmation, 1965–1985* (Los Angeles: Wright Art Gallery, UCLA, 1991).

43. Ibid., 27.

44. This book is similar to my *Mexican Americans*, which is also an anthology in which I have written all the chapters.

45. Díaz-Stevens and Stevens-Arroyo, *The Latino Resurgence*, 96, 103. Also Guerrero, *Chicano Theology*, 25.

46. Matovina and Riebe-Estrella, eds., *Horizons of the Sacred*, 9.

47. Treviño, *Church in the Barrio*, and Pitti, "Sociedades Guadalupanas," 83.

48. Dolan and Hinojosa, eds., *Mexican Americans*, 1.

49. As quoted in note 32 in ibid., 46.

50. Treviño, *The Church in the Barrio*, 24.

51. Matovina, *Guadalupe and Her Faithful*, 19.

52. Allan Figueroa Deck, S.J., *The Second Wave: Hispanic Ministry and the Evangelization of Cultures* (New York: Paulist Press, 1989), 14.

53. Hinojosa, "Mexican-American Faith Communities in Texas and the Southwest," part I in Dolan and Hinojosa, eds., *Mexican Americans*, 82.

54. León, *La Llorona's Children*, 20.

55. Ricardo Ramírez, "Foreword," in Sandoval, *On the Move*, viii.

56. Expression often made by Fr. Elizondo in his Latino religions classes at the University of California, Santa Barbara, in the late 1990s.

57. Treviño, *The Church in the Barrio*, 18.

58. Sandoval, *On the Move*, xiii.

59. Figueroa Deck, *The Second Wave*, 109.

60. See, for example, recent texts that focus on evolution of ethnic identity among Hispanos in New Mexico in the post–Mexico War period,

such as A. Gabriel Meléndez, *So All Is Not Lost: The Poetics of Print in Nuevomexicano Communities, 1834–1958* (Albuquerque: University of New Mexico Press, 1997); Doris Meyer, *Speaking for Themselves: Neomexicano Cultural Identity and the Spanish-Language Press, 1880–1920* (Albuquerque: University of New Mexico Press, 1996); and John M. Nieto-Philips, *The Language of Blood: The Making of Spanish-American Identity in New Mexico, 1880s–1930s* (Albuquerque: University of New Mexico Press, 2004).

61. Hinojosa, "Mexican-American Faith Communities," in Dolan and Hinojosa, eds., *Mexican Americans*, 109. Also see David Gutiérrez, "Migration, Emergent Ethnicity, and the 'Third Space': The Shifting Politics of Nationalism in Greater Mexico," *Journal of American History* (September 1999): 481–517, and Pitti, "Sociedades Guadalupanas," 89–92.

62. See Figueroa Deck, *The Second Wave*, 124, 116.

63. Sandoval, *On the Move*, 37, and Sandoval, "Mexican Migration to the Midwest and East," in Sandoval, ed., *Fronteras*, 261.

64. Sandoval, *On the Move*, 42.

65. Jeffrey M. Burns, "The Mexican Catholic Community in California," part II in Dolan and Hinojosa, eds., *Mexican Americans*, 192.

66. Sandoval, "Effects of World War II on the Hispanic People," in Sandoval, ed., *Fronteras*, 343.

67. Díaz-Stevens and Stevens-Arroyo, *The Latino Insurgence*, 43.

68. See Isasi-Díaz, *Mujerista Theology*.

69. See Richard Rodríguez, *Hunger of Memory: The Education of Richard Rodríguez* (Boston: David R. Godine, 1981); *Days of Obligation: An Argument with My Mexican Father* (New York: Viking Press, 1992); and *Brown: The Last Discovery of America* (New York: Viking, 2002). And Rubén Martínez, *The Other Side: Notes from the New L.A., Mexico City, and Beyond* (London: Verso Press, 1992).

70. Figueroa Deck, *The Second Wave*, 113, 156.

71. Elizondo, "Foreword," in Philip E. Lampe, ed., *Hispanics in the Church: Up From the Cellar* (San Francisco: Catholic Scholars Press, 1994), viii.

Chapter One

1. Rodolfo Acuña, *Occupied America: The Chicano Struggle Toward Liberation* (San Francisco: Canfield Press, 1972). For examples of the New Western history, see Patricia Nelson Limerick, *The Legacy of Conquest: The Unbroken Past of the American West* (New York: W. W. Norton, 1987), and Richard White, *It's Your Misfortune and None of My Own: A New History of the American West* (Norman: University of Oklahoma Press, 1991). Also see William Cronon, George Miles, and Jay Gitlin, eds., *Under An Open Sky: Rethinking America's Western Past* (New York: W. W. Norton, 1992).

2. For a discussion of the shifts in Chicano historiography, see Alex M. Saragoza, "Recent Chicano Historiography: An Interpretive Essay," *Aztlán* 19 (Spring 1988–1990): 1–77.

3. See Genaro Padilla, *My History, Not Yours: The Formation of Mexican American Autobiography* (Madison: University of Wisconsin Press, 1993), 153–195; Rosaura Sánchez, *Telling Identities: The Californio Testimonios* (Minneapolis: University of Minnesota Press, 1995).

4. See García, *Mexican Americans*, 231–290; also see Almaráz, *Knight Without Armor*.

5. On Jovita González, see introduction by José Limon to González, *Caballero: A Historical Novel*, ed. Limon and María Cotera (College Station: Texas A&M Press, 1996). Josefina Niggli wrote several novels, such as *Mexican Village* (Chapel Hill: University of North Carolina Press, 1945). Ernesto Galarza wrote a great deal on Mexican farm labor in California; see his classic *Merchants of Labor: The Mexican Bracero Story* (Charlotte, N.C.: McNally and Loftis, 1964); also see his autobiography *Barrio Boy* (Notre Dame: University of Notre Dame Press, 1971). On Américo Paredes, who wrote on Mexican American folklore as well as fiction, see Paredes, *With His Pistol in His Hands: A Border Ballad and Its Hero* (Austin: University of Texas Press, 1958), as well as Ramón Saldivar, *The Borderlands of Culture: Américo Paredes and the Transnational Imagination* (Durham: Duke University Press, 2006). Luis Leal, the dean of Mexican American intellectuals, has published countless books, articles, and reviews on Mexican and Chicano literature; for an introduction to his life and career, see Mario T. García, *Luis Leal: An Auto/Biography* (Austin: University of Texas Press, 2000). On José Villareal, see his classic novel *Pocho* (Garden City, N.Y.: Doubleday, 1959).

6. For an excellent bibliography on Fray Angélico, see Phyllis S. Morales, *Fray Angélico Chávez: A Bibliography* (Santa Fe: Lightning Tree, 1980).

7. On the colonial history of New Mexico, see Ramón A. Gutiérrez, *When Jesus Came, the Corn Mothers Went Away: Marriage, Sexuality, and Power in New Mexico, 1500–1846* (Stanford: Stanford University Press, 1991); James F. Brooks, *Captives and Cousins: Slavery, Kinship, and Community in the Southwest Borderlands* (Chapel Hill: University of North Carolina Press, 2002); Ross Frank, *From Settler to Citizen: New Mexico Economic Development and the Creation of Vecino Society, 1750–1820* (Berkeley and Los Angeles: University of California Press, 2000); David J. Weber, *The Spanish Frontier in North America* (New Haven: Yale University Press, 1992). Also see Thomas E. Chávez, *New Mexico: Past and Future* (Albuquerque: University of New Mexico Press, 2006).

8. Nieto-Philips, *The Language of Blood*, 4.

9. See Richard Griswold del Castillo, *The Treaty of Guadalupe Hidalgo: A Legacy of Conflict* (Norman: University of Oklahoma Press, 1990).

10. See David J. Weber, *Foreigners in Their Native Land: Historical Roots of the Mexican Americans* (Albuquerque: University of New Mexico Press, 1973).

11. See Joseph P. Sánchez, *The Spanish Black Legend: Origins of Anti-Hispanic Stereotypes* (Albuquerque: Spanish Colonial Research Center, 1990).

12. See Nieto-Philips, *The Language of Blood*; Robert E. Fleming, *Charles Lummis* (Boise: Boise State University Press, 1981); Deena J. González, *Refusing the Favor: The Spanish-American Women of Santa Fe, 1820–1880* (New York: Oxford University Press, 1999); Ramón A. Gutiérrez, "Charles Fletcher Lummis and the Orientalization of New Mexico," in *Nuevomexicano Cultural Legacy: Forms, Agencies, and Discourse* (Albuquerque: University of New Mexico Press, 2002); Howard Lamar, *The Far Southwest, 1846–1912: A Territorial History* (New York: W. W. Norton, 1970); Charles Fletcher Lummis, *The Land of Poco Tiempo* (New York: Scribner's, 1893); Doris Meyer, *Speaking for Themselves: Neomexicano Identity and the Spanish-Language Press, 1880–1920* (Albuquerque: University of New Mexico Press, 1996); A. Gabriel Meléndez, *So All Is Not Lost: The Poetics of Print in Nuevomexicano Communities, 1834–1958* (Albuquerque: University of New Mexico Press, 1997); María Montoya, *Translating Property: The Maxwell Land Grant and the Conflict over Land in the American West, 1840–1900* (Berkeley and Los Angeles: University of California Press, 2002); Robert J. Rosenbaum, *Mexicano Resistance in the Southwest: "The Sacred Right of Self Preservation"* (Austin: University of Texas Press, 1984); Marc Simmons, *Coronado's Land: Daily Life in Colonial New Mexico* (Albuquerque: University of New Mexico Press, 1991).

13. As quoted in Robert Huber, "Fray Angélico Chávez: 20th-Century Renaissance Man," *New Mexico Magazine* 48 (March-April, 1970), 19.

14. Fray Angélico Chávez, "Southwestern Bookshelf," *New Mexico Magazine* (September-October 1970), 47.

15. See Steele's foreword to the 1993 edition of Fray Angélico Chávez, *My Penitente Land* (Santa Fe: Museum of New Mexico Press, 1993), v.

16. Ibid., 5. For different facets of Fray Angélico, see Ellen M. McCracken, ed., *Fray Angélico Chávez: Poet, Priest, and Artist* (Albuquerque: University of New Mexico Press, 2000).

17. Fray Angélico Chávez, "New Mexico Place-names from Spanish Proper Names," *El Palacio* (December 1949), 371.

18. Chávez, *Origins of New Mexico Families: A Genealogy of the Spanish Colonial Period* (Santa Fe: William Gannon, 1975), xix; Carey McWilliams, *North from Mexico: The Spanish-Speaking People of the United States* (1948; reprint New York: Greenwood Press, 1969), 35–47.

19. See Chávez, "The Authentic Spanish New Mexican—A Question of Identity," in *Environment, People, and Culture: The Inaugural Papers*, vol. 1, part 2 (Las Cruces: New Mexico State University Press, 1971).

20. Ibid., xix.

21. Chávez, *But Time and Chance: The Story of Padre Martínez of Taos, 1793–1867* (Santa Fe: Sunstone Press, 1981). Also see E. A. Mares, ed., *Padre Martínez: New Perspectives from Taos* (Taos: Millicent Rogers Museum, 1988); Juan Romero, "Begetting the Mexican American: Padre Martínez and the 1847 Rebellion" in Thomas J. Steele, S.J., Paul Rhetts, and Barbe Awalt, eds., *Seeds of Struggle/Harvest of Faith: The Papers of the Archdiocese of Santa Fe Catholic Cuarto Centennial Conference on the History of the Catholic Church in New Mexico* (Albuquerque: LPD Press, 1998), 345–372.

22. Chávez, *Penitente Land*, 227

23. See, for example, ibid., xii.

24. Chávez, *Coronado's Friars* (Washington, D.C.: Academy of American Franciscan History, 1968), 87. On Bolton, see Herbert Eugene Bolton, *The Spanish Borderlands: A Chronicle of Old Florida and the Southwest* (New Haven: Yale University Press, 1921). Also see David J. Weber, "Turner, the Boltonians, and the Borderlands," *American Historical Review* 91, no. 1 (February 1986): 66–87.

25. Chávez, "Ruts of the Santa Fe Trail," *New Mexico Magazine* (July–August 1972), 21.

26. For a discussion of both Sánchez and Castañeda as revisionist historians, see García, *Mexican Americans*, 231–272.

27. Chávez, *Penitente Land*, 28.

28. Carroll, *The Penitente Brotherhood*.

29. Chávez, "New Mexico Religious Place Names Other Than Those Of Saints," *El Palacio* (January 1950), 24–25.

30. Chávez, *Archives of the Archdiocese of Santa Fe, 1678–1900* (Washington, D.C.: Academy of American Franciscan History, 1957), 5.

31. See Daniel Bell, *The End of Ideology: On the Exhaustion of Political Ideas in the Fifties* (Glencoe, Ill.: Free Press, 1960).

32. Chávez and Eleanor B. Adams, eds., *Missions of New Mexico, 1776: A Description by Fray Francisco Atanasio Domínguez With Other Contemporary Documents* (Albuquerque: University of New Mexico Press, 1956), xviii.

33. Chávez, "Santa Fe Trial," 22.

34. See, for example, W. W. H. Davis, *El Gringo, or New Mexico and Her People* (1857; reprint New York: Arno Press, 1973); Josiah Gregg, *Commerce of the Prairies: The Journal of a Santa Fe Trader* (New York: Henry G. Langley, 1844).

35. Willa Cather, *Death Comes for the Archbishop* (New York: Modern Library, 1926). Also see Paul Horgan, *Lamy of Santa Fe, the Life and Times* (New York: Farrar, Straus and Giroux, 1975).

36. Chávez, *Padre Martínez*, 158; also see Chávez, *Tres Macho—He Said: Padre Gallegos of Albuquerque, New Mexico's First Congressman* (Santa Fe: William Gannon, 1985), 37.

37. Chávez, *Gallegos*, 37

38. Chávez, "Dona Tules: Her Fame and Her Funeral," *El Palacio* (August 1950), 227, 230–231.

39. Chávez, *Gallegos*, 45.

40. Chávez, "Dona Tules," 230–231.

41. Ibid.

42. Carroll, *The Penitente Brotherhood*, 137–154.

43. Chávez, *Padre Martínez*, 24, 32–33, 47, 50.

44. Ibid., 51.

45. Ibid., 56.

46. Ibid., 81.

47. Chávez, *Gallegos*, 2.

48. Ibid. 6. On the origins of post–Mexican War Hispano identity, see Nieto-Phillips, *The Language of Blood*.

49. Chávez, *Padre Martínez*, 160.

50. Chávez, *Penitente Land*, 254.

51. Ibid., 258.

52. Ibid., xi.

53. Ibid., 267.

54. Ibid., xiv.

55. Ibid., 269.

56. Ibid., 232.

57. Ibid., 267.

58. Chávez, "New Mexico's Bonnie Prince Chile," *New Mexico Magazine* (May–June, 1974), 31.

59. Chávez, *Penitente Land*, 186.

60. Ibid., 255.

61. Chávez, "Southwestern Bookshelf," *New Mexico Magazine* (September–October 1970), 47.

62. Ibid., (March–April 1973), 46.

63. Ibid., (May 1976), 307.

64. Chávez, "La Conquistadora Is a Paisana," *El Palacio* (October 1950), 307. On La Conquistadora, see Chávez, *La Conquistadora, the Autobiography of an Ancient Statue* (Paterson, N.J.: St. Anthony's Guild Press, 1954), and Luis Leal, "La Conquistadora as History," in McCracken, *Fray Angélico Chávez*, 37–44.

Chapter Two

1. David Montejano, *Anglos and Mexicans in the Making of Texas, 1836–1986* (Austin: University of Texas Press, 1987); Foley, *White Scourge*.

2. Zamora, *World of the Mexican Worker*.

3. Montejano, *Anglos and Mexicans*; Foley, *White Scourge*.

4. Ibid.

5. Matovina, *Guadalupe and Her Faithful*.

6. See Virgilio Elizondo and Timothy Matovina, *San Fernando Cathedral: Soul of the City* (Maryknoll, N.Y.: Orbis Books, 1998); García, *Desert Immigrants*, 212–223; and Treviño, *Church in the Barrio*, 1–175.

7. See Orlando O. Espín, "Popular Catholicism Among Latinos," in Dolan and Figueroa Deck, eds., *Hispanic Catholic Culture in the U.S.*, 308–359; Fernando Garza Quiroz, *El Niño Fidencio: Un Personaje Desconocido* (Monterrey, Mexico: Editorial Alfonso Reyes, 1970); Octavio Romano, "Don Pedrito Jaramillo: The Emergence of a Mexican-American Folk Saint" (Ph.D. diss., UC Berkeley, 1964); Kay F. Turner, "Mexican American Women's Home Altars: The Art of Relationship" (Ph.D. diss., University of Texas at Austin, 1990); García, *Desert Immigrants*, 222–223; James S. Griffith, *Folk Saints of the Borderlands: Victims, Bandits and Healers* (Tucson: Rio Nuevo, 2003); Vanderwood, *Juan Soldado*.

8. See García, *Mexican Americans*. For an overview of Latino politics and religion, see Edwina Barvosa-Carter, "Politics and the U.S. Latina and Latino Religious Experience," in Héctor Avalos, ed., *Introduction to the U.S. Latina and Latino Religious Experience* (Boston/Leiden: Brill Academic, 2004), 261–279.

9. See García, *Desert Immigrants*; *Mexican Americans*; and *Memories of Chicano History*.

10. See García, *Mexican Americans*.

11. Ibid.

12. See Charles E. Curran, *Catholic Social Teaching 1981–Present: A Historical, Theological, and Ethical Analysis* (Washington, D.C.: Georgetown University Press, 2002), 45.

13. Franz H. Mueller, *The Church and the Social Question* (Washington, D.C.: American Enterprise Institute, 1984), 93.

14. See, for example, Nieto-Phillips, *The Language of Blood*; Meléndez, *So All Is Not Lost*; Meyer, *Speaking for Themselves*.

15. See basic facts on Perales's life in Alonso Perales, *En Defensa de Mi Raza* (San Antonio: Artes Gráficos, 1937).

16. See, for example, García, *Desert Immigrants*, and George Sánchez, *Becoming Mexican American*.

17. See clippings in the Cleofas Calleros Collection, Southwest Collection, El Paso Public Library. For more on Calleros, see Mario T. García, "Mexican Americans and the Politics of Citizenship: The Case of El Paso, 1936," *New Mexico Historical Quarterly* 59 (April 1984): 187–204.

18. Curran, *Catholic Social Teaching*, 131.

19. See Archbishop Robert E. Lucey's notes to his talk to a Teachers Institute, Central Catholic High School, San Antonio, November 15, 1943, 3, in Arch-

bishop Robert E. Lucey Collection in Catholic Archives in San Antonio, Archdiocese of San Antonio, Chancery Office; hereafter cited as Lucey Collection.

20. Leo XIII, *Rerum Novarum* (Boston: Pauline Book and Media, 1942), 19.

21. Ibid., 21–22.

22. See Lucey's notes to his talk "The Future of Our Spanish-Speaking South-west" at Sixth Regional Conference, Catholic Council for the Spanish Speaking, Albuquerque, July 15, 1953, in Lucey Collection.

23. See quote in Perales, *En Defensa*, iv.

24. Kenneth Duane Yielding, "The Apostle of the Border: Cleofas Calleros," seminar paper, Department of History, Texas Western College, May 1960, Southwest Collection, El Paso Public Library.

25. See Program of Alba Club of the University of Texas at Austin Sixth Annual Banquet honoring Perales, May 3, 1952, in Alonso S. Perales folder in Carlos E. Castañeda Collection in Benson Latin America Library, University of Texas at Austin; hereafter cited as Castañeda Collection.

26. See "Excerpts from Address by his Excellency Most Rev. Robert E. Lucey, S.T.D., Archbishop of San Antonio, October 9, 1949, at Conference of Austin Diocesan Council of Catholic Women" in Lucey Collection.

27. Lucey to Reverend and Dear Father, San Antonio, April 5, 1954, in Lucey Collection. Lucey used this general salutation in correspondence to all of his parish pastors.

28. Curran, *Catholic Social Teaching*, 31.

29. David J. O'Brien, *American Catholics and Social Reform: The New Deal Years* (New York: Oxford University Press, 1981), 183.

30. Perales, *En Defensa*, ii.

31. Ibid., 29–30.

32. As quoted in *La Prensa*, October 26, 1947, 3.

33. *La Prensa*, November 18, 1945, 6.

34. Ibid., December 28, 1947, 3.

35. See "National Catholic Welfare Conference," 31, Calleros Collection, Southwest Collection, El Paso Public Library.

36. Ibid., 26.

37. Ibid., 27.

38. See Calleros to Bruce Mohler, El Paso, July 28, 1933; and Mohler to Calleros, Washington, D.C., August 2, 1933, Cleofas Calleros Collection, ACC 933, box 31, fld. 3, Special Collections, University of Texas at El Paso (UTEP).

39. In 1949, for example, Lucey appointed Perales as vice chairman for the Spanish-speaking on a newly created Archdiocesan Credit Union Committee; see Lucey to Rev. and Dear Father, San Antonio, August 2, 1949, in Lucey Collection.

40. See typescript copy of Archbishop Lucey's address to the Conference on Spanish-Speaking People of the Southwest, San Antonio, July 20, 1943, as well as additional correspondence on the conference in Calleros Collection, Southwest Collection, El Paso Public Library.
41. See clipping, *Los Angeles Times*, March 31, 1930, Calleros Scrapbook, Calleros Collection, Southwest Collection, El Paso Public Library.
42. As quoted in *La Prensa*, November 16, 1947, 3.
43. Mueller, *Church and Social Question*, 124.
44. See clipping, *El Paso Times*, June 9, 1931, Calleros Scrapbook.
45. See Calleros, "Social and Welfare Problems with Mexicans in Texas," typescript, Calleros Collection, ACC 933, box 31, fld. 3 in Special Collections, UTEP.
46. Perales, *En Defensa*, 67.
47. As quoted in Perales's column, *La Prensa*, November 16, 1947, 3.
48. Calleros, "Social and Welfare Problems."
49. *La Prensa*, November 2, 1947, 3.
50. As quoted in clipping, July 20, 1943, Calleros Collection, Southwest Collection, El Paso Public Library.
51. *La Prensa*, December 3, 1939, 3, 6.
52. See clipping, *Los Angeles Times*, April 30, 1930, Calleros Scrapbook.
53. Mueller, *Church and Social Question*, 123.
54. O'Brien, *American Catholics*, 135.
55. Curran, *Catholic Social Teaching*, 137, 144.
56. O'Brien, *American Catholics*, 135.
57. Ibid., 51.
58. Ibid., 70.
59. *La Prensa*, August 1, 1937, 7.
60. See clipping, *Los Angeles Times*, April 30, 1930, Calleros Scrapbook.
61. As quoted in Archbishop Robert E. Lucey, "Migrant Labor, a Moral Problem," speech to Catholic Council on Working Life, Chicago, November 21, 1959, in Lucey Collection.
62. See Calleros to Mohler, El Paso, August 29, 1962, Calleros Collection, Southwest Collection, El Paso Public Library.
63. Calleros, "Social and Welfare Problems."
64. See clipping, *Southern Messenger*, October 16, 1930, Calleros Scrapbook.
65. *La Prensa*, December 29, 1940, 2.
66. Castañeda to Perales, Austin, August 22, 1935; also see Castañeda to Perales, Austin, August 30, 1935, in Perales folder in Castañeda Collection. On Castañeda, see Almaráz, *Knight Without Armor*.
67. Perales to Castañeda, San Antonio, September 2, 1935, in Castañeda Collection.
68. Castañeda to Perales, Austin, August 22, 1935, and Castañeda to Perales, August 30, 1935, in ibid. On Johnson involvement with the NYA, see Robert

Dallek, *Lone Star Rising: Lyndon Johnson and His Times, 1908–1960* (New York: Oxford University Press, 1991). Dallek does not mention this incident involving Perales and Castañeda with LBJ.

69. See Gutiérrez, *Walls and Mirrors*; Márquez, LULAC; and García, *Mexican Americans*. In his study of Mexican American civil rights struggles in Texas during World War II Guglielmo concurs that Mexican Americans included Mexican nationals in their struggles against discrimination and segregation; see Thomas A. Guglielmo, "The Struggle for Caucasian Rights: Mexicans, Mexican Americans, and the Transnational Struggle for Civil Rights in World War II Texas," *Journal of American History* 92, no. 4 (March 2006): 1232.

70. Pitti, "Sociedades Guadalupanas."

71. See "Se Abre La Escuela Gratis," in Perales folder in Castañeda Collection.

72. See Abraham Hoffman, *Unwanted Mexican-Americans in the Great Depression: Repatriation Pressures, 1929–1939* (Tucson: University of Arizona Press, 1974), and Francisco E. Balderrama and Raymond Rodríguez, *Decade of Betrayal: Mexican Repatriation in the 1930s* (Albuquerque: University of New Mexico Press, 1995).

73. See untitled clipping, January 18, 1932, Calleros Scrapbook.

74. See Calleros, "New Mexican Immigrants Into the United States," typescript, undated, Calleros Archives, vol. 16, Carbon Copy Letters, 1958–1960, Southwest Collection, El Paso Public Library.

75. Interview with Calleros by Oscar Martínez, September 14, 1972, Institute of Oral History, UTEP, transcript no. 157.

76. Balderrama and Rodríguez document the same tragedy of U.S.-born Mexican American children being sent back to Mexico, where they had never been before; Balderrama and Rodríguez, *Decade of Betrayal.*

77. For excerpts from Calleros's 1934 report, see Mohler to Alice W. O'Connor, Washington, D.C., August 11, 1936, Calleros Collection, ACC 933, box 2, fld. 2, Special Collections, UTEP.

78. See, for example, Calleros to Mohler, El Paso, October 12, 1933, Calleros Collection, ACC 933, box 31, fld. 3, Special Collections, UTEP.

79. Rev. John J. Burke to Frank Gross, Washington, D.C., September 21, 1929, Calleros Collection, ACC 933, box 31, fld. 3, Special Collections, UTEP.

80. Curran, *Catholic Social Teaching*, 67.

81. Perales, *En Defensa*, 10.

82. See Gutiérrez, *Walls and Mirrors*, and Márquez, LULAC. Also see Guglielmo, "Fighting for Caucasian Rights," 1212–1237, and García, "Mexican Americans and the Politics of Citizenship."

83. Perales, *En Defensa*, 82, 85.

84. See Perales's speech, June 13, 1940, in Perales folder, Castañeda Collection.

85. Michael Omi and Howard Winant, *Racial Formation in the United States: From the 1960s to the 1980s* (New York: Routledge, 1986); Foley, *White Scourge*; Tomás Almaguer, *Racial Faultlines: The Historical Origins of White Supremacy* (Berkeley and Los Angeles: University of California Press, 1994); David R. Roediger, *The Wages of Whiteness: Race and the Making of the American Working Class* (New York: Verso, 1991).

86. Perales, *En Defensa*, 3, 11, 23, 51, 69, 100.

87. Ibid., 27.

88. On Mexican Americans and World War II, see Maggie Rivas-Rodríguez, ed., *Mexican Americans and World War II* (Austin: University of Texas Press, 2005).

89. *La Prensa*, June 4, 1944, 1–2; April 22, 1945, 6.

90. Gilbert G. González, *Chicano Education in the Era of Segregation* (Philadelphia: Balch Institute Press, 1990); Guadalupe San Miguel, *"Let All of Them Take Heed": Mexican Americans and the Campaign for Educational Equality in Texas, 1910–1981* (Austin: University of Texas Press, 1987); García, *Mexican Americans*; John D. McCafferty, *Aliso School "For the Mexican Children"* (Santa Barbara: McSeas Book, 2003).

91. Perales to Castañeda, San Antonio, May 30, 1940, in Perales folder, Castañeda Collection.

92. *La Opinión*, August 25, 1928, 3.

93. Perales, *En Defensa*, 14.

94. See clipping in *La Prensa*, in Perales folder, Castañeda Collection.

95. See clipping, untitled, no date, Calleros Scrapbook, vol. 2, Southwest Collection, El Paso Public Library. For other biased views on intelligence and Mexican American students in this period, see González, *Chicano Education*, and García, *Mexican Americans*.

96. See clipping, *El Paso Times*, May 10, 1940, Calleros Scrapbook, El Paso Public Library.

97. Ibid.

98. Perales to Carlos E. Castañeda, San Antonio, June 26, 1939, in Perales folder, Castañeda Collection.

99. See Guglielmo, "The Struggle for Caucasian Rights."

100. *La Prensa*, December 21, 1942, 3. Also see Guglielmo, "The Struggle for Caucasian Rights."

101. Perales, *En Defensa*, 73.

102. *La Prensa*, June 4, 1944, 1–2.

103. Calleros, "LULAC and Its Origin," typescript, Calleros Archives, vol. 16, Carbon Copy Letters, 1958–1960, Southwest Collection, El Paso Public Library.

104. See Rivas-Rodríguez, *Mexican Americans*.

105. *La Prensa*, October 12, 1941.

106. Ibid., March 18, 1945, 2; February 27, 1944, 3, 6. Also see Daniel, *Politics of Fairness*.

107. Perales to Castañeda, San Antonio, April 26, 1952, in Perales folder, Castañeda Collection.

Chapter Three

1. See examples from introduction; also see Anita De Luna, *Faith Formation and Popular Religion: Lessons from the Tejano Experience* (Lanham, Md.: Rowman and Littlefield, 2002).

2. "Religion emerges in memory," León observes; see León, *La Llorona's Children*, 17.

3. See Treviño, *The Church in the Barrio*, 42–80, and León, *La Llorona's Children*.

4. As quoted in Jerre Mangione, *The Dream and the Deal: The Federal Writers' Project, 1935–1943* (Boston: Little, Brown, 1972), 42. Also see Monty Noam Penkower, *The Federal Writer's Project: A Story in Government Patronage of the Arts* (Urbana: University of Illinois Press, 1977). For Hispano WPA artists in New Mexico, see Tey Marianna Nunn, *Sin Nombre: Hispana and Hispano Artists of the New Deal Era* (Albuquerque: University of New Mexico Press, 2001).

5. See *The WPA Guide to 1930s New Mexico* (1940; reprint, Tucson: University of Arizona Press, 1989).

6. Mangione, *The Dream*, 8. Also see Writers' Project of the Work Projects Administration in the State of New Mexico, *New Mexico: A Guide to the Colorful State* (New York: Hastings House, 1940).

7. Suzanne Forrest, *The Preservation of the Village: New Mexico's Hispanics and the New Deal* (1989; reprint, Albuquerque: University of New Mexico Press, 1998), 15.

8. Ibid., 119.

9. See Dennis Peter Trujillo, "Commodification of Hispano Culture in New Mexico: Tourism, Mary Austin, and the Spanish Colonial Arts Society" (Ph.D. diss., University of New Mexico, 2003).

10. On Brown, see Lorin W. Brown with Charles L. Briggs and Marta Weigle, *Hispano Folklife of New Mexico: The Lorin W. Brown Federal Writers' Project Manuscripts* (Albuquerque: University of New Mexico Press, 1978). On Lucero-White, see "Aurora Lucero-White Lea," *The Santa Fe Scene* (January 9, 1960), 4–7. Also see Aurora Lucero-White, *Literary Folklore of the Hispanic Southwest* (San Antonio: Naylor, 1953). For a more recent compilation of WPA oral histories of Hispano women, although not focused specifically on religion, see Tey Diana Rebolledo and María Teresa Márquez, *Women's Tales from the New Mexico WPA: La Diabla a Pie* (Houston: Arte Public Press, 2000).

11. Badillo, *Latinos*, 190.

12. León, *La Llorona's Children*, ix.

13. Badillo, *Latinos*, xiii. Also see León, *La Llorona's Children*, 42.

14. Treviño, *The Church in the Barrio*, 23.

15. Sarah Deutsch, *No Separate Refuge: Culture, Class, and Gender on an Anglo-Hispanic Frontier in the American Southwest, 1880–1940* (New York: Oxford University Press, 1987).

16. As quoted in Brown, *Hispano Folklife*, 192.

17. Ibid., ix. Also see Gilberto Benito Córdova, ed., *Bibliography of Unpublished Materials Pertaining to Hispanic Culture in the New Mexico WPA Writers' Files* (Santa Fe: New Mexico State Department of Education, 1972).

18. See WPA *Guide*.

19. Reyes N. Martínez, "Meager Contributions," n.d, WPA 5-5-2 #48, 1, in Fray Angélico Chávez History Library of the Museum of New Mexico, Santa Fe; hereafter cited as WPA Files. All further WPA citations come from the Chávez History Library.

20. No author, "Three Saints," n.d., WPA Files 5-5-58 #24, 1.

21. No author, "Fiesta in New Mexico: San Antonio's Day," n.d., WPA 5-5-56 #11, 1.

22. Ibid., 1.

23. For an excellent study of the *matachines* in New Mexico, see Sylvia Rodríguez, *The Matachines Dance: Ritual Symbolism and Interethnic Relations in the Upper Rio Grande Valley* (Albuquerque: University of New Mexico Press, 1996).

24. Ibid., 2–4.

25. Reyes N. Martínez, "Spanish Customs," n.d., WPA 5-5-2 #36, 1–3.

26. Ibid., 3.

27. No author, "Fiestas in New Mexico: San Ysidro's Day in Cordova," n.d., WPA 5-5-56 #1, 1.

28. Ibid., 1.

29. Lorin W. Brown, "San Ysidro Labrador," September 1, 1938, WPA 5-5-20 #32, 1.

30. "Fiestas in New Mexico: San Ysidro's Day," 2.

31. Brown, "San Ysidro," 2.

32. "Fiestas in New Mexico: San Ysidro's Day," 3–4.

33. Lorin W. Brown, "Nuestra Señora de Dolores," January 23, 1939, WPA 5-5-2 #26, 1–2.   Also Edward P. Dozier, "Spanish Catholic Influences on Rio Grande Pueblo Religion," *American Anthropologist* 60 (1958): 441–448.

34. "Fiestas in New Mexico: San Ysidro's Day," 4. On Hispano folklore in New Mexico, see Arthur L. Campa, *Spanish Folk-Poetry in New Mexico* (Albuquerque: University of New Mexico Press, 1946); Aurelio M. Espinosa, *The Folkore of Spain in the American Southwest: Traditional Spanish Folk Literature in Northern New Mexico and Southern Colorado*, ed.

J. Manuel Espiñosa (Norman: University of Oklahoma Press, 1985); Aurora Lucero-White, *Los Hispanos: Five Essays on the Folkways of the Hispanos as Seen through the Eyes of One of Them* (Denver: Sage Books, 1947); Marta Weigle and Peter White, *The Lore of New Mexico* (Albuquerque: University of New Mexico Press, 1988); Nasario García, *Recuerdos de los viejitos: Tales of the Rio Puerco* (Albuquerque: University of New Mexico, 1987).

35. A. Lucero-White, "El Velorio," August 1936, WPA 5-5-21 #1, 1.

36. Reyes N. Martínez, "Communal Spirit Preserved by Some Religious and Social Customs," January 18, 1939, WPA 5-5-4 #1, 1.

37. Lucero-White, "El Velorio," 1.

38. Annette H. Thorp, "Velorio," February 11, 193? (date obscure), WPA 5-5-53 #2, 2.

39. Martínez, "Communal Spirit," 1.

40. Thorp, "Velorio," 4.

41. Ibid., 3–5.

42. Brown, "The Wake," April 9, 1937, WPA 5-5-60 #12, 2.

43. Lucero-White, "El Velorio," 2.

44. Martínez, "Communal Spirit," 2.

45. Brown, "The Wake," 1.

46. Ibid., 2.

47. Ibid., 1.

48. Thorp, "Velorio," 8.

49. Lucero-White, "El Velorio," 5.

50. Ibid., 5–6. On the santos of New Mexico and the santero tradition of local artists who constructed the imgages, see Thomas J. Steele, S.J., *Santos and Saints: The Religious Folk Art of Hispanic New Mexico* (Santa Fe: Ancient City Press, 1982); William Wroth, *Images of Penance, Images of Mercy: Southwestern Santos in the Late Nineteenth Century* (Norman: University of Oklahoma Press, 1991); Barbe Awalt and Paul Rhetts, *Our Saints Among Us: 400 Years of New Mexican Devotional Art* (Albuquerque: University of New Mexico Press, 1998); Charles L. Briggs, *The Wood Carvers of Córdova, New Mexico: Social Dimensions of an Artistic "Revival"* (Albuquerque: University of New Mexico Press, 1989); Marie Romero Cash, *Santos: Enduring Images of Northern New Mexican Village Churches* (Niwot: University Press of Colorado, 1999); E. Boyd, *Saints and Saint Makers of New Mexico* (Santa Fe: New Mexico Laboratory of Anthropology, 1946).

51. Ibid., 6.

52. Brown, "Descansos," October 29, 1938, WPA 5-5-2 #30, 1.

53. Ibid., 2.

54. Ibid.

55. Kenneth Fordyce, "Spanish American Prayer Crosses," n.d., WPA 5-5-21 #2, 1.

56. Lucero-White, "El Velorio," 4.

57. Nina Otero-Warren and John P. Flores, "Christmas in New Mexico," n.d., WPA 5-5-33 #1, 1. On Otero-Warren, see Charlotte Whaley, *Nina Otero-Warren of Santa Fe* (Albuquerque: University of New Mexico, 1994); also see Lucero-White, *Literary Folklore*.

58. Ibid.

59. Ibid., 2.

60. Ibid., 5.

61. Ibid.

62. Ibid., 5–6.

63. Ibid., 6–7.

64. Ibid., 7.

65. Brown, "Los Pastores and Other Plays Brought to New Mexico By the Spanish and Presented at Different Seasons," n.d., WPA 5-5-46, #4, 3.

66. Otero-Warren and Flores, "Christmas in New Mexico," 7.

67. Ibid., 8–12. Also see Manuel Berg, "Adoración de los Reyes," August 25, 1937, WPA 5-5-42 #3; and "Shepherds on the Road (Camino de la Pastorela)," September 3, 1937, WPA 5-5-52 #22.

68. Brown, "Los Pastores and Other Plays," 1.

69. Ibid., 2.

70. Lucero-White, "Los Moros (Danza y Pieza)," n.d., WPA 5-5-37 #1, 1–8.

71. Brown, "Los Pastores and Other Plays," WPA 5-5-46 #4, 1. Also see Rodríguez, *The Matachines Dance*.

72. Manuel Berg, "An Allegorical Drama," WPA 5-5-13 #1, 3.

73. Martínez, "Meager Contributions," 1–3.

74. Dr. Lester Raines, "A Vision," Aug. 2, 1936, WPA 5-5-9 #17, 1 3.

75. Bright Lynn, "La Promesa (The Promise)," February 1, 1939, WPA 5-5-7#10, 1–3. Also see Reyes N. Martínez, "The Cross that Ascended Toward Heaven," January 4, 1940, WPA 5-5-47 #7.

76. L. W. Brown, "Tia Lupe: Santa Barbara's Protection," n.d., WPA 5-5-26, 1.

77. On curanderas and curanderos, see Art Kiev, *Curanderismo: Mexican-American Folk Psychiatry* (New York: Free Press, 1968); Eliseo Torres, *The Folk Healer: The Mexican-American Tradition of Curanderismo* (Kingsville, Tex.: Nieves Press, 1985); Robert T. Trotter and Juan Antonio Chavira, *Curanderismo* (Athens: University of Georgia Press, 1981); and Eliso 'Cheo' Torres with Timothy L. Sawyer, Jr., *Curandero: A Life in Mexican Folk Healing* (Albuquerque: University of New Mexico Press, 2005); Bobette Perrone, H. Henrietta Stockel, and Victoria Krueger, *Medicine Women, Curanderas, and Women Doctors* (Norman: University of Oklahoma Press, 1989); Luis León, "'Soy una Curandera y Soy una Católica': The Poetics of a Mexican Healing Tradition," in Matovina and Riebe-Estrella, eds., *Horizons of the Sacred*, 95–118. Also see León, *La Llorona's Children*, 129–162.

78. Thorp, "The Curandera," n.d., WPA 5-5-2 #70, 1–3.

79. Ibid., 4.

80. Mrs. Lou Sage Batchen, "An Old Native Custom: La Curandera," n.d., WPA 5-5-49 #45, 1.

81. Ibid., 2–3.

82. Ibid., 3.

83. Ibid., 4–10.

84. See Chávez, *My Penitente Land.*

85. See Marta Weigle, *Brothers of Light, Brothers of Blood: The Penitentes of the Southwest* (Santa Fe: Ancient City Press, 1976); Alice Corbin Henderson, *Brothers of Light: The Penitentes of the Southwest* (New York: Harcourt, Brace, 1937); Richard E. Ahlborn, *The Penitente Moradas of Abiquiú* (Washington, D.C.: Smithsonian Institution Press, 1968); Alberto López Pulido, *The Sacred World of the Penitentes* (Washington, D.C.: Smithsonian Institution Press, 2000); Thomas J. Steele, S.J., and Rowena Rivera, *Penitente Self-Government: Brotherhoods and Councils, 1797–1947* (Santa Fe: Ancient City Press, 1985); and Carroll, *The Penitente Brotherhood.*

86. See Weigle, *Brothers of Light.* Weigle herself only sparingly used the WPA records.

87. Lucero-White, "The Penitentes of New Mexico, 1936," August 1936, WPA 5-5-32 #13, 8.

88. Ibid., 9.

89. See Pulido, *The Sacred World.* Also see Weigle, *Brothers of Light*; Steele, S.J., and Rivera, *Penitente Self-Government*; and Ruben E. Archuleta, *Land of the Penitentes, Land of Tradition* (Pueblo West, Colo.: El Jefe, 2003).

90. Forrest, *Preservation of the Village,* 27.

91. WPA *Guide,* 123.

92. Lucero-White, "The Penitentes," August 2, 1936, WPA 5-5-32#7, 2–3.

93. Ibid., 9–10.

94. Ibid., 3–4.

95. Ibid., 6.

96. Reyes N. Martínez, "Unmasked," March 26, 1937, WPA 5-5-9 #4, 1–2.

97. See John D. Robb, *Hispanic Folk Music of New Mexico and the Southwest: A Self-Portrait of a People* (Norman: University of Oklahoma Press, 1980); John B. Rael, *The New Mexican "Alabado"* (Stanford: Stanford University Press, 1951); Thomas J. Steele, S.J., ed., *The Alabados of New Mexico* (Albuquerque: University of New Mexico, 2005).

98. WPA *Guide,* 144.

99. Martínez, "Alabados: Cristo Nuestro Redentor/Christ Our Redeemer," n.d., WPA 5-5-5 #96, 1–2.

100. Martínez, "A Jesús Quiero Acudir/ I wish to Have Recourse to Jesus," n.d., WPA 5-5-5 #53. 1.

101. Martínez, "A La Madre del Rosario/To the Mother of the Rosary," n.d., WPA 5-5-5 #11, 1.
102. No author listed, "A La Virgen de Guadalupe/To the Virgin of Guadalupe," n.d., WPA 5-5-5 #108, 1–2.
103. Lorin W. Brown, "La Ave María de los Borrachos/The Hail Mary of the Drunkards," n.d., WPA 5-5-20 #9, 1.

Chapter Four

1. On PADRES, see Martínez, PADRES; on Las Hermanas, see Medina, *Las Hermanas*.
2. See Juan Hurtado, "An Attitudinal Study of Social Distance Between the Mexican American and the Church" (Ph.D. diss., U.S. International University, 1976). Also see Sandoval, *On the Move*; Jeffrey M. Burns, "Establishing the Mexican Catholic Community in California: A Story of Neglect?" in Dolan and Hinojosa, eds., *Mexicans and the Catholic Church*, 129–147; Philip E. Lampe, ed., *Hispanics in the Church: Up from the Cellar* (San Francisco: Catholic Scholars Press, 1994); and Albert López Pulido, "Race Relations within the American Catholic Church: An Historical and Sociological Analysis of Mexican American Catholics" (Ph.D. diss., University of Notre Dame, 1989).
3. Treviño, *Church in the Barrio*, and Badillo, *Latinos*.
4. Gilberto M. Hinojosa, "Mexican-American Faith Communities in Texas and the Southwest," in Dolan and Hinojosa, eds., *Mexican Americans and the Catholic Church*, 11–125; Burns, "Mexican Catholic Community," 159. Also see Treviño, *Church in the Barrio*; Badillo, *Latinos*; and Alberto López Pulido, "Nuestra Señora de Guadalupe: The Mexican Catholic Experience in San Diego," *Journal of San Diego History* 37 (Fall 1991): 236–254.
5. See García, "Catholic Social Doctrine and Mexican American Political Thought," 292–311.
6. See "Spanish-Americans in the Southwest and the War Effort," Confidential Report No. 24 of Special Services, Bureau of Intelligence, Office of War Information in Catholic Social Action File 1942–1943, in Files of the National Catholic Welfare Conference (NCWC) in Department of Archives and Manuscripts of The Catholic University of America, Washington, D.C.; hereafter—Catholic Social Action File.
7. On Mexican Americans and the Good Neighbor Policy, see García, *Mexican Americans*, 231–272; Alonso Perales, *Are We Good Neighbors?* (San Antonio: Artes Gráficas, 1948). Also see Marquard Dozier, *Are We Good Neighbors? Three Decades of Inter-American Relations, 1930–1960* (Gainsville: University Press of Florida, 1959); J. Lloyd Mecham, *A Survey of United States–Latin American Relations* (New York: Houghton Mifflin,

1965); Fredrick B. Pike, FDR's *Good Neighbor Policy: Sixty Years of Gentle Chaos* (Austin: University of Texas Press, 1995).

8. "Spanish-Americans in the Southwest and the War Effort," 13.

9. Ibid.

10. Ready to Eugene J. Butler, Washington, D.C., October 12, 1942, in Catholic Social Action File, 1942–1943. Also see R. Keith Lane, Chief, Bureau of Intelligence, Office of War Information to Butler, Washington, D.C., October 23, 1942, in ibid; and memo of Butler to Ready, Washington, D.C., November 2, 1942, in ibid.

11. Memo of Montovan to Ready, Washington, D.C., November 18, 1942, in Catholic Social Action File, 1942–1943.

12. Ibid.

13. On the Bracero program, see Galarza's classic study, *Merchants of Labor*; Erasmo Gamboa, *Mexican Labor and World War II: Braceros in the Pacific Northwest, 1942–1947* (Austin: University of Texas Press, 1990); Barbara A. Driscoll, *The Tracks North: The Railroad Bracero Program of World War II* (Austin: Center for Mexican American Studies, 1999); Kitty Clavita, *Inside the State: The Bracero Program, Immigration, and the I.N.S.* (New York: Routledge, 1992).

14. See Walter Prendergast to Joseph T. McGucken, Auxiliary Bishop of Los Angeles, Washington, D.C., March 24, 1943; Prendergast to Ready, March 25, 1943; memo of Rev. R. A. McGowan to Ready, Washington, D.C., April 19, 1943; "Proposal of a Conference on Spanish-Americans in the Southwest," April 28, 1943; and Percy L. Douglas to Ready, Washington, D.C., June 21, 1943, all in Catholic Social Action File, 1942–1943.

15. See Lucey's opening address entitled "Are We Good Neighbors?" and document on opening of conference, no title, July 20, 1943, in Catholic Social Action, 1942–1943 file. On Lucey, see Saul E. Bronder, *Social Justice and Church Authority: The Public Life of Archbishop Robert E. Lucey* (Philadelphia: Temple University Press, 1982); Stephen A. Privett, *The U.S. Catholic Church and Its Hispanic Members: The Pastoral Vision of Archbishop Robert E. Lucey* (San Antonio: Trinity University Press, 1988).

16. See Percy L. Douglas, Acting Coordinator of Inter-American Affairs to Monsignor Reedy, June 21, 1943, in Catholic Social Action, 1942–1943.

17. See documents pertaining to the Denver conference and to the Bishops' Committee in the files of the NCWC. Also see Brother Albeus Walsh, "The Work of the Catholic Bishops' Committee for the Spanish Speaking in the United States" (M.A. thesis, University of Texas at Austin, 1952).

18. Badillo, *Latinos*, 26.

19. Matovina, *Guadalupe and Her Faithful*, 99.

20. Treviño, *The Church in the Barrio*, 33.

21. See García, *Desert Immigrants*, 219–222; and Sánchez, *Becoming Mexican Americans*, 151–170. Also see Emory S. Bogardus, *The Mexican in the United*

States (Los Angeles: University of Southern California Press, 1934); Rev. Vernon M. McCombs, *From Over the Border: A Study of the Mexicans in the United States* (New York: Council of Women for Home Missions, 1925).

22. Badillo, *Latinos*, 187.

23. See Karl Rahner, *The Church After the Council* (New York: Herder and Herder, 1966); Karl Rahner, *The Christian of the Future* (New York: Herder and Herder, 1967).

24. Rev. Amleto Giovanni Cicognani, D.D., to Ready, Washington, June 22, 1944, in Catholic Social Action File, 1944.

25. "Work Among the Mexicans in the United States," in Catholic Social Action File, 1944, 1.

26. Ibid., 1.

27. Ibid., 2.

28. Ibid., 14.

29. See García, *Mexican Americans*, and García, *Memories of Chicano History*.

30. Lucey, "Are We Good Neighbors?" 11–12.

31. See Acuña, *Occupied America*.

32. "The Spanish Speaking of the Southwest and West," report of the San Antonio conference on "The Spanish Speaking of the Southwest and West," published in 1944 by the NCWC in Catholic Social Action File, 1944.

33. See report of the Committee on Migratory Workers, San Antonio conference, in Catholic Social Action File, 1944, 39.

34. See "Bishops' Committee for the Spanish Speaking," in Catholic Social Action, 1945–1947 File, 16.

35. See report of Committee on Scattered Communities, San Antonio Conference, in Catholic Social Action File, 1944, 32.

36. "Work Among the Mexicans," 6.

37. Ibid., 14, 8.

38. Ready to J. F. McGork, Washington, D.C., August 23, 1943, in Catholic Social Action File, 1942–1943.

39. See report of Committee on Large Populations in Cities and Towns, San Antonio conference in Catholic Social Action File, 1944, 21.

40. Committee on Migratory Workers, in Catholic Social Action File, 1944, 36.

41. Ibid.

42. Committee on Small Scattered Communities, 32.

43. Committee on Large Selected Groups, 27–28.

44. See Denver conference document, "Recommendation of the Seminar on Spanish-Speaking People, 1945," in Catholic Social Action File, 1945, 2.

45. Committee on Migratory Workers, 37.

46. "Work Among the Mexicans," 6.

47. Ibid., 15.

48. See copy in Catholic Social Action File, 1944.

49. Ready to Rev. Lawrence Schott, Washington, D.C., April 13, 1944, in Catholic Social Action File, 1944.
50. Report of San Antonio conference, 32.
51. Ready to Schott, Washington, D.C., April 13, 1944, in Catholic Social Action File, 1944.
52. Father Collins to Ready, Washington, D.C., April 13, 1944, in ibid.
53. "Work Among the Mexicans," 5.
54. Rev. Solomon Rahaim, S.J., "The Problem of the Spanish-American in the United States," in Catholic Social Action File, 1944, 6.
55. Committee on Small or Scattered Communities, 31.
56. "Work Among the Mexicans," 6.
57. Ibid., 10.
58. Report of the San Antonio conference, 20.
59. Committee on Small or Scattered Communities, 30–31.
60. Tort to Ready, Fresno, May 21, 1943, Catholic Social Action File, 1942–1943.
61. "The Work of the Claretians Among the Mexicans in the United States," in Catholic Social Action File, 1942–1943.
62. Committee on Migratory Workers, 36.
63. Committee on Large Population in Cities and Towns, 22, and "Work Among the Mexicans," 10.
64. "Work of the Claretians."
65. "Work Among the Mexicans," 10.
66. Minutes of 26th Annual Meeting of the Bishops of the United States, November 15, 1944, in Catholic Social Action File, 1945–1947.
67. "Problem of the Spanish-American," 8.
68. "Work Among the Mexicans," 15, and "Problem of the Spanish-American," 6.
69. For a fuller discussion of this difference, see Badillo, *Latinos*.
70. Committee on Small and Scattered Communities, 33.
71. Committee on Large Settled Rural Groups, 27.
72. Report of San Antonio conference, 15.
73. "Work Among the Mexicans," 13; "Problems of the Spanish-American," 2–3; Lucey, "Are We Good Neighbors?" 3.
74. Mohler to Rev. John J. Birch, Washington,D.C., October 2, 1945, in Catholic Social Action File, 1945–1947.

Chapter Five

1. See Greeley, *The Catholic Imagination*.
2. For a study of the Chicano movement and the Church in Houston, see Treviño, *The Church in the Barrio*, 176–205.
3. On the Watts riots, see Gerald Horne, *Fire This Time: The Watts Uprising and the 1960s* (New York: Da Capo Press, 1997).

4. On the movement in Los Angeles, see Ernesto Chávez, *¡Mi Raza Primero!*
*Nationalism, Identity, and Insurgency in the Chicano Movement in Los
Angeles, 1966–1978* (Berkeley and Los Angeles: University of California
Press, 2002). On the movement in general or other aspects of the move-
ment, see Carlos Muñoz, Jr., *Youth, Identity, and Power: The Chicano
Movement* (London: Verso Press, 1989); Alma M. García, *Chicana Feminist
Thought: The Basic Historical Writings* (New York: Routledge, 1997); García,
United We Win; José Angel Gutiérrez, *The Making of a Chicano Militant:
Lessons from Cristal* (Madison: University of Wisconsin Press, 1998);
Richard Santillan, *La Raza Unida* (Los Angeles: Tlaquilo Publications,
1973); Jesús Salvador Trevino, *Eyewitness: A Filmmaker's Memoir of the
Chicano Movement* (Houston: Arte Publico Press, 2001); Ernesto Vigil, *The
Crusade for Justice: Chicano Militancy and the Government's War on Dissent*
(Madison: University of Wisconsin Press, 1999); Oropeza, *¡Raza Sí! ¡Guerra
No!*; Mariscal, *Brown-Eyed Children of the Sun*; Navarro, *Mexican Ameri-
can Youth Organization*; Navarro, *The Cristal Experiment*; Juan Gómez-
Quinones, *Chicano Politics: Reality and Promise, 1940–1990* (Albuquerque:
University of New Mexico Press, 1990); Martínez, PADRES; Medina, *Las
Hermanas*.

5. On the blow-outs, see Muñoz, *Youth, Identity, Power*, 64–72; Dolores
Delgado Bernal, "Chicana School Resistance and Grassroots Leader-
ship: Providing an Alternative History of the 1968 Blowouts" (Ph.D. diss.,
UCLA, 1997); Mario T. García, "Research Note—Blow-Out: The Sal Castro
Story," in UCLA program on "Sal Castro and the Chicano Youth Leader-
ship Conference: The Development of Chicano Leadership Since 1963,"
UCLA, May 26, 2006; and Mario T. García, "Pedagogy of Chicano Power:
Sal Castro, Paulo Freire, and the Mexican American Youth Leadership
Conferences, 1963–1968," unpublished paper presented at UCLA confer-
ence on Sal Castro and the Chicano Youth Leadership Conference, May 26,
2006.

6. Interview with Richard Martínez, Los Angeles, January 21, 1996. Mosqueda
in his study makes the following statement concerning the founding of
CPLR that in my estimation is incorrect: "It appears that CPLR was not
founded by radicals, but by persons who were very religious (including members of the clergy), somewhat religious, and those who were not
religious but who recognized the Church as an institution which needed to
be challenged in the Chicano community." See Mosqueda, *Chicanos*, 103. I
disagree that CPLR founders were not radicals.

7. Interview with Ray Cruz, April 25, 2003. Richard Cruz attended Loyola
University School of Law from 1967 to 1971; see document, August 30, 1972,
in Ricardo Cruz/Católicos Por La Raza Collection, California Ethnic and
Multicultural Archives (CEMA 28) in Special Collections, University of
Calif., Santa Barbara. Hereafter cited as Cruz/Católicos Col.

8. See document, n.d., in box 1, fld. 2, in Cruz/Católicos Col.

9. Note from Ray Cruz to Mario T. García, April 24, 2003.

10. Interview with Raul Ruiz, March 1, 1993.

11. *Los Angeles Times*, April, 5, 1968, part II, 6.

12. Oscar Zeta Acosta, *The Revolt of the Cockroach People* (1973; reprint, New York: Vintage Books, 1989), 11–12.

13. Martínez interview. Also see, Martínez, PADRES.

14. Ray Cruz note.

15. Ruiz interview and part of my unpublished manuscript entitled "Chicano Power: Testimonios of the Chicano Movement in Los Angeles," 107.

16. Ray Cruz interview.

17. Ibid. Also "Católicos Por La Raza," undated document in possession of Pedro Arias.

18. Richard Cruz interview, December 18, 1976, contained in private collection of his son, Camilo Cruz; hereafter cited as Camilo Cruz Collection. Also see Camilo Cruz, "Tribute to a Barrio Lawyer: Ricardo V. Cruz," in *La Neta del "border" y la frontera* (April 1994), 17–19, in Camilo Cruz Collection.

19. Cruz to Mom & Dad, n.d., 1974 in box 1, fld. 5 in Cruz/Católicos Col.

20. Rosa Martínez interview, June 14, 2005.

21. Ray Cruz interview and interview with Paloma Cruz Martínez, April 25, 2003. Ray Cruz notes that SDS became a model for Chicano movement organizations, including Católicos.

22. Ray Cruz note.

23. Interview with Miguel García, July 11, 2005.

24. García interview.

25. Interview with Bob Gandara, September 4, 2005.

26. Ray Cruz interview and Ruiz interview.

27. Ruiz interview

28. Ray Cruz interview.

29. Ibid. and Richard Cruz interview.

30. Richard Cruz interview.

31. Ibid.

32. As quoted in Loomba, *Colonialism/Postcolonialism*, 66.

33. Ibid.

34. Ibid. Also Muñoz, Jr., *Youth, Identity, Power.*

35. Interview with Rosa Martínez, June 14, 2005. Martínez became Ricardo Cruz's companion and would later bear his two children, Paloma and Camilo Cruz.

36. See Alberto L. Pulido, "Are You An Emissary of Jesus Christ?: Justice, the Catholic Church, and the Chicano Movement," *Explorations in Ethnic Studies* 14, no. 1 (January 1991): 17–34.

37. Richard Cruz interview. Ruben Salazar was the leading Latino journalist of his time. He was the only Chicano writing for a mainstream English-language newspaper in the 1960s. On August 29, 1970, Salazar was tragically killed while covering the large National Chicano Anti-War Moratorium in East Los Angeles. On Salazar, see Mario T. García, ed., *Ruben Salazar, Border Correspondent: Selected Writings, 1955–1970* (Berkeley: University of California Press, 1995).

38. Undated press clipping in Cruz/Católicos Col.

39. Ibid.

40. Luis Valdez and Stan Steiner, eds., *Aztlán: An Anthology of Mexican American Literature* (New York: Vintage Books, 1972), 384.

41. César Chávez, "Peregrinación, Penitencia, Revolución," undated, reproduced in ibid., 386.

42. Ibid., 387.

43. See Jacques Levy, *César Chávez: Autobiography of La Causa* (New York: W. W. Norton, 1975).

44. César Chávez, "The Chicano y la Iglesia," in *La Verdad* (San Diego), December 1969, 3. For the best analysis of Chávez's spirituality, see Frederick John Dalton, *The Moral Vision of César Chávez* (Maryknoll, N.Y.: Orbis Books, 2003). For an excellent survey of Chávez's life that has some discussion of his spirituality, see Richard Griswold del Castillo and Richard A. García, *César Chávez: A Triumph of Spirit* (Norman: University of Oklahoma Press, 1995).

45. *Con Safos* (Fall 1968), 11.

46. On the Medellín conference and the emergence of liberation theology, see Penny Lernoux, *Cry of the People* (New York: Penguin, 1982).

47. Richard Cruz interview; Ray Cruz interview.

48. Ruiz interview.

49. Ibid.

50. *La Raza* (1970), vol. 1, 34.

51. Ibid. Also see "The Revolutionary Church is the Only Church of the People—The Church of the People is the Revolution," *La Raza*, vol. 1, no. 6, 71, and "Camilo Torres: Profeta de Nuestro Tiempo," ibid., 63.

52. Rosa Martínez states that it was her idea that her and Richard's son be named Camilo in honor of the two revolutionaries; Rosa Martínez interview. On Camilo Torres, see John Gerassi, ed., *Camilo Torres, Revolutionary Priest: His Complete Writings and Messages* (Middlesex, England: Penguin Press, 1973).

53. "Católicos Por La Raza," *La Raza* (February 1970), reprinted in Valdez and Steiner, *Aztlán*, 391.

54. "Conference of Catholic Bishops," *La Raza*, 29.

55. Católicos press release, December 4, 1969, in Camilo Cruz Collection.

56. Valdez and Steiner, *Aztlán*, 391.

57. Ibid., 392.

58. "Conference of Catholic Bishops," *La Raza* (1970), vol. 1, 39.

59. Poem in compilation of *La Raza* articles on Católicos in Camilo Cruz Collection.

60. "Católicos Por La Raza and Mexican Americans," *La Raza* (January 1970), 2.

61. Ibid. 2.

62. "Blessed Are the Poor," *La Raza*, vol. 1, no. 2, 55–65; Ruiz interview.

63. Católicos press release, December 4, 1969, in Camilo Cruz Collection.

64. Católicos Public Letter, November 29, 1969, in Camilo Cruz Collection.

65. "The Catholic Church and La Raza," *La Raza* (January 1970).

66. Católicos Public Letter in Camilo Cruz Collection.

67. News clipping, no citation or date in Cruz/Católicos Collection.

68. "Católicos" in Valdez and Steiner, *Aztlán*, 392.

69. "The Church: The Model of Hypocrisy," 9.

70. *L.A. Free Press*, January 16, 1970, 4.

71. Interview with Father Patrick McNamara, April 13, 1996.

72. Católicos press release, December 26, 1969, in Camilo Cruz Collection.

73. "The Church: The Model of Hypocrisy," 9; "Church Hypocrisy," 53–54; and "Católicos," in Valdez and Steiner, eds., *Aztlán*, 392.

74. Ibid.

75. Dolores del Grito, "Jesus Christ as a Revolutionist," in ibid., 393–394.

76. Abelardo Delgado, "The New Christ," "The Organizer," and "A New Cross," poems in ibid., 394–397.

77. Ruiz interview.

78. Richard Cruz interview.

79. McNamara interview. Rodolfo Acuña notes that McIntyre "single-handedly attempted to hold back the reforms of Pope John XXIII and Vatican II," Acuña, *Occupied America: A History of Chicanos*, 3d ed. (New York: Harper Collins, 1988), 344–345.

80. "The Catholic Church and La Raza," 8.

81. Ibid., 4.

82. See demands in *La Raza*, vol. 1, no. 1 (1970), 25; also Letter to Congress of Mexican-American Unity, no date, in Camilo Cruz Collection.

83. See demands in *La Raza*, vol. 1, no. 1 (1970), 25.

84. Richard Cruz interview.

85. Católicos press release, December 4, 1969, in Camilo Cruz Collection.

86. García interview.

87. Rosa Martínez interview.

88. Martínez interview. Some meetings were also held at the Church of the Epiphany; interview with Lydia López, October 24, 1996.

89. "Catholic Church and the Chicano Community," undated document in Camilo Cruz Collection.

90. E-mail note from Rosa Martínez to Mario T. García, June 15, 2005.

91. Letter from Católicos to Congress of Mexican-American Unity, no date, in Camilo Cruz Collection. In a later resume, Richard Cruz noted that he and Joe Aragón met with Cardinal McIntyre on October 11. However, this is very likely a mistake since the letter from Católicos to the Congress written at the time notes October 17 as the date of the meeting with the cardinal; see Richard Cruz resume, box 1, fld. 11, in Cruz/Católicos Col.

92. See Cruz resume in box 1, fld. 11, in Cruz/Católicos Col.

93. Ibid.

94. Ray Cruz interview; Gandara interview.

95. Ibid.

96. García interview.

97. Richard Martínez interview.

98. Católicos Por La Raza to Hermanos y Hermanas, November 29, 1969 in box 5, fld. 1, in Cruz/Católicos Col.

99. Católicos press release, December 4, 1969, in Camilo Cruz Collection.

100. Gandara at one of these demonstrations carried a sign that read "McIntyre is a puto [asshole]"; Gandara interview.

101. Católicos press release, December 15, 1969, in Camilo Cruz Collection.

102. Undated La Raza clipping but apparently around the time of the vigil protests in Camilo Cruz Collection.

103. Richard Cruz, "Católicos Por La Raza Revisited—Three Years Later," handwritten document in Camilo Cruz Collection.

104. Martínez interview; La Raza, vol. 1, no. 1 (1970), 24; The Tidings, January 2, 1979, 3.

105. Rosa Martínez interview.

106. García interview.

107. Martínez interview.

108. Rosa Martínez interview.

109. Ibid.

110. García inteview.

111. Martínez interview.

112. García interview; also see Richard Cruz resume.

113. Rosa Martínez interview.

114. Martínez interview and Pulido, ""An Emissary of Jesus Christ," 25–27.

115. Martínez interview; Ruiz interview.

116. Richard Cruz interview.

117. Rosa Martínez interview.

118. Martínez interview.

119. Untitled class paper written by Camilo Cruz for a class at Oberlin College in Camilo Cruz Collection. Included among Camilo Cruz's collection is a shotgun that belonged to his father; see Xerox copy of shotgun in box 1, fld. 10, Cruz/Católicos Col.

120. García interview.

121. Gandara interview.

122. Martínez interview; Ruiz interview; *L.A. Free Press*, January 16, 1970, 4.

123. Flyer in Pedro Arias Collection.

124. "Open Letter to Cardinal McIntyre," *La Raza*, vol. 1, no. 2, 49; Martínez interview.

125. Ray Cruz interview.

126. Camilo Cruz class paper.

127. Rosa Martínez interview.

128. Lydia López interview.

129. Ray Cruz interview.

130. Martínez interview.

131. *Los Angeles Times* clipping, no date, in Camilo Cruz Collection.

132. Cruz to Rev. James Francis McIntyre, December 26, 1969, in Camilo Cruz Collection.

133. Gandara interview.

134. García interview; interview with Rick Sánchez, May 30, 2006.

135. See clipping, *Los Angeles Herald-Examiner*, March 3, 1970, in box 5, fld. 4, in Cruz/Católicos Col.

136. Richard Cruz interview.

137. García interview; Martinez interview; *The People's World*, January 3, 1970, 1, 12; *Los Angeles Times*, December 25, 1969, and December 26, 1969, 3; *L.A. Free Press*, January 9, 1970, 2, and January 16, 1970, 4; *The Militant*, January 23, 1970, 1; *La Raza*, vol. 1, no. 1, 31.

138. Martinez interview.

139. Sánchez interviw.

140. Ibid.; Ruiz interview; *Los Angeles Times*, December 26, 1969, 3. Also see clipping, no title, February 6, 1970, in box 5, fld. 5, Cruz/Católicos Col. and Gandara interview.

141. See Acosta, *Cockroach People*, 11–21.

142. Ruiz interview.

143. García interview.

144. Ray Cruz interview.

145. *L.A. Free Press*, January 16, 1970, 4; undated Arias statement. Also Gandara interview.

146. Ray Cruz interview.

147. Acosta, *Cockroach People*, 17.

148. *Los Angeles Times*, December 26, 1969, 32; *L.A. Free Press*, January 16, 1970, 4; *The Tidings*, no date, 1.

149. In *Los Angeles Times* clipping, December 29, 1969, in Camilo Cruz Collection.

150. See clipping "Militants Mar Mass" from a compilation of articles by *The Tidings*, no date, in Pedro Arias Collection.

151. Gandara interview.

152. Martinez interview; Ruiz interview; *Los Angeles Times*, December 25, 1969, 1, and January 1, 1970, 3; *La Raza*, vol. 1, no. 1 (1970), 31, 69; *The People's World*, January 3, 1970, 12; *L.A. Free Press*, January 16, 1970, 2; Gandara interview.

153. "No Room at St. Basil's for Chicanos," undated document in Camilo Cruz Collection.

154. Gandara interview.

155. Clipping from *The People's World*, January 3, 1970, in Camilo Cruz Collection.

156. Ray Cruz interview.

157. Ibid.

158. Gandara interview.

159. Clipping in Cruz/Católicos Collection; Lydia López interview; Gandara interview.

160. *Los Angeles Times*, December 26, 1969, 32.

161. Acosta, *Cockroach People*, 21.

162. Clipping from *Los Angeles Times*, December 26, 1969, in Pedro Arias Collection.

163. Ibid.; *The People's World*, January 3, 1970, 12; Lydia López interview; Richard Martínez interview.

164. García interview. García further notes that Gloria Chávez would crack up meetings at Católicos by coming in and saying to the men, "Manos pa arriba, calzones pa bajo" [hands up, underpants down].

165. Cruz to McIntyre, December 26, 1969 in Camilo Cruz Collection.

166. Clipping from *Los Angeles Times*, December 29, 1969, 3, 20, in Camilo Cruz Collection. Also see Richard Cruz resume.

167. *Los Angeles Times*, December 26, 1969, 32; *The People's World*, January 3, 1970, 12; Martinez interview.

168. Richard Cruz, "The Fast of Católicos Por La Raza . . . St. Basil's, January 2, 3, & 4," document in Camilo Cruz Collection and Richard Cruz resume.

169. Clipping from *Herald-Examiner*, January 4, 1970, in Camilo Cruz Collection.

170. *L.A. Free Press*, January 23, 1970, 4.

171. Richard Cruz interview.

172. Undated and untitled clipping in Cruz/Católicos Collection.

173. Smiley to García, January 21, 1970, in Camilo Cruz Collection.

174. García interview.

175. *The Tidings*, January 29, 1971; *Los Angeles Times*, September 14, 1970, 18; Martínez interview; Ray Cruz interview.

176. *The Tidings*, January 29, 1971, 1; *Los Angeles Times*, September 14, 1970, 18; Martínez interview.

177. *Los Angeles Times*, July 28, 1974, part II, 1; *La Voz Católica* (Oakland), July 1973. Also see Badillo, *Latinos*.

178. Católicos press release, February 24, 1970, in Camilo Cruz Collection.

179. Newspaper clipping, no citation, no date, in Camilo Cruz Collection.

180. Clipping from *La Raza*, no date, in Cruz/Católicos Collection.

181. "Católicos Por La Raza Bautismo de Fuego," flier in Pedro Arias Collection; *Herald-Examiner*, September 14, 1970, A-3. Into 1970, it appears that Católicos also organized and operated what they called a Freedom School for high school students at the Euclid Community Center in East Los Angeles. See newspaper clipping from *Herald-Examiner*, March 14, 1970, in Camilo Cruz Collection.

182. "Bautismo de Fuego."

183. Clipping from *Los Angeles Times*, September 14, 1970, 18, in Pedro Arias Collection.

184. Clipping from *Herald-Examiner*, September 14, 1970, in Pedro Arias Collection.

185. Ruiz interviews.

186. González to Cruz, n.d., box 5, fld. 2 in Cruz/Católicos Col.

187. Clipping from *L.A. Free Press*, February 6, 1970, in Cruz/Católicos Collection.

188. Ibid.

189. Note to Católicos, n.d. in box 5, fld. 2, Cruz/Católicos Col.

190. Armendáriz to Richard Cruz, January 8, 1970, in box 5, fld. 2, Cruz/Católicos Col.

191. See Acosta, *Cockroach People*, 137.

192. Rosa Martínez interview.

193. Ray Cruz interview.

194. Lydia López interview. López was acquitted of all charges.

195. Gandara interview.

196. Ray Cruz interview.

197. Lydia López interview.

198. Clipping from *El Popo*, n.d., box 5, fld. 4, in Cruz/Católicos Col.

199. See Ian F. Haney López, *Racism on Trial: The Chicano Fight for Justice* (Cambridge: Harvard University Press, 2003). Although Haney López does not discuss the CPLR cases, he mistakenly notes that Acosta "secured the acquittal of a group of activists, Católicos Por La Raza," 39. While it is true that some were acquitted, others were not.

200. Clipping from *El Popo*, March 10, 1970, in Cruz/Católicos Collection.

201. Clipping from *Herald-Examiner*, May 22, 1970, in Pedro Arias Collection.

202. García interview.

203. Rosa Martínez interview.

204. *Herald-Examiner*, June 6, 1970, A-3.

205. *Los Angeles Times* clipping, n.d., box 5, fld. 4, in Cruz/Católicos Col.

206. García interview; clipping from *Los Angeles Times*, May 10, 1972, in box 5, fld. 4, Cruz/Católicos Col.; Gandara interview.

207. Clipping from *Herald-Examiner*, March 14, 1970, in Camilo Cruz Collection.

208. FBI, Freedom of Information, "Católicos Por La Raza," File # 157-6-26-1726. The FBI report is rather short and focused on the Christmas Eve protest.

209. Ray Cruz interview. For the best study of the Chicano antiwar movement, see Oropeza, *¡Raza Sí! ¡Guerra No!*

210. Ibid.; see obituary on Richard Cruz, "Richard Cruz: Chicano Rights Lawyer," in *Los Angeles Times*, July 24, 1993, in Camilo Cruz Collection. Miguel García, who, like Cruz, graduated from law school in 1971, received his certificate to practice law apparently a year before Cruz; see "The Fight for Miguel García and Richard Cruz," box 1, fld. 1 in Cruz/Católicos Col. A signature drive gathered five thousand signatures in support of Cruz and García to practice law; see clipping from *Justicia . . . O?*, vol. 1, no. 11, 6, in box 1, fld. 8, in Cruz/Católicos Col.

211. Interview with Camilo Cruz, April 25, 1997.

212. García interview.

213. See Sillas obituary in *Hispanic Link Weekly*, August 16, 1993, 3 in box 1, fld. 9, Cruz/Católicos Col. At its 1993 awards banquet, MALDEF awarded its Legal Service Award posthumously to Cruz. See program for Nineteenth Award, Los Angeles Award Dinner, MALDEF, November 4, 1993, in box 1, fld. 9, Cruz/Católicos Col.

214. Richard Cruz interview.

215. Rosa Martínez interview.

216. Ray Cruz interview.

217. Camilo Cruz euology in Camilo Cruz Collection. Richard Cruz is buried at Forest Lawn Memorial Park in Los Angeles; see Certificate of Death, July 27, 1993, in box 1, fld. 9, Cruz/Católicos Col.

Chapter Six

1. Harvey Cox, "The 'New Breed' in American Churches: Sources of Social Activism in American Religion," *Daedalus* (Winter, 1967): 135–150. Also see David J. O'Brien, "The American Priest and Social Action," in John Tracy Ellis, ed., *The Catholic Priest in the United States: Historical Investigations* (Collegeville, Minn.: Saint John's University Press, 1971), 423–469.

2. See Martínez, PADRES and Medina, *Las Hermanas*. Also see Timothy M. Matovina, "Representation and the Reconstruction of Power: The Rise of PADRES and Las Hermanas," in Mary Jo Weaver, ed., *What's Left: Liberal American Catholics* (Bloomington: Indiana University Press, 1999), 220–237; Badillo, *Latinos*, 158–160.

3. See, for example, García, *Mexican Americans*; García, *Memories of Chicano History*; García, *Making of a Mexican American Mayor*; García and Francis Esquibel Tywoniak, *Migrant Daughter*; and García, *Luis Leal: An Auto/Biography* (Austin: University of Texas Press, 2000).

4. See, for example, García, "Catholic Social Doctrine and Mexican American Political Thought," 292–311; and García, "Fray Angélico Chávez, Religiosity, and New Mexican Oppositional Historical Narrative," in McCracken, ed., *Fray Angélico Chávez*, 25–36.

5. Treviño, *The Church in the Barrio*, 176–205.

6. See, for example, Oscar L. Arnal, *Priests in Working-Class Blue: The History of the Worker-Priest, 1943–1954* (New York: Paulist Press, 1986).

7. Martínez, PADRES, 3.

8. Badillo, *Latinos*, 168.

9. Oral histories with Juan Romero, Luis Quihuis, and Virgilio Elizondo.

10. See Rev. Juan Romero, *Reluctant Dawn: A History of Padre Antonio José Martínez, Cura de Taos*, 2d ed. (Palm Springs: Taos Connection, 2006).

11. Romero interview, June 18, 1998.

12. Ibid.

13. Ibid.

14. On cursillos and Latino Catholics, see Badillo, *Latinos*.

15. See Juan Romero, "Ministry to Farm Workers: Experience in Advocacy," *Notre Dame Journal of Education* (Summer 1974): 186–187.

16. Ibid., 187.

17. Romero interview, June 18, 1998.

18. Ibid

19. Romero, "Ministry to Farm Workers," 190.

20. Ibid., 184.

21. Ibid., 188.

22. Ibid.

23. Ibid.

24. Ibid., 189.

25. Ibid., 190.

26. Ibid.

27. Ibid., 191.

28. Romero interview, June 18, 1998.

29. Father Juan Romero, "Charism and Power: An Essay on the History of PADRES," *U.S. Catholic Historian*, nos. 1, 2 (Winter/Spring 1990): 161.

30. Ibid., 160.
31. Ibid., 147.
32. Ibid. 161, 151.
33. Romero interview, July 1, 1998.
34. Juan Romero, "Religiosidad Popular as Locus for Theological Reflection and Springboard for Pastoral Action," unpublished paper in possession of author.
35. Interview with Romero, July 1, 1998.
36. Ibid.
37. Romero, "Charism and Power," 158.
38. Romero, "Usefulness of Hispanic Survey to Ministers of the Southwest," 6, unpublished paper in possession of Father Romero.
39. Ibid.
40. Romero interview, July 1, 1998.
41. Romero, "Hispanic Survey," 11.
42. See Peter Skerry, *Mexican Americans: The Ambivalent Minority* (New York: Free Press, 1993); also Mosqueda, *Chicanos*, 158.
43. Romero interview, July 1, 1998.
44. Interview with Father Luis Quihuis, September 9, 1999.
45. Ibid., September 15, 1999.
46. Interview with Quihuis, September 15, 1999.
47. Ibid.
48. Ibid.
49. Ibid.
50. Quihuis interview, September 30, 1999.
51. Ibid.
52. Quihuis interview, September 15, 1999.
53. Ibid., September 30, 1999.
54. Ibid., October 5, 1999.
55. Ibid.
56. Ibid.
57. Ibid.
58. Ibid.
59. Ibid.
60. Ibid.
61. Ibid.
62. Ibid.
63. Ibid., October 26, 1999.
64. Ibid., November 30, 1999, and December 7, 1999.
65. Ibid., October 26, 1999.
66. Ibid.
67. Ibid., March 28, 2000.

68. Ibid.

69. Ibid., February 1, 2000.

70. Ibid.

71. Ibid.

72. Ibid., November 30, 1999; December 7, 1999.

73. Ibid., March 28, 2000.

74. Ibid., February 1, 2000.

75. Ibid.

76. Ibid., March 28, 2000.

77. Ibid., November 30, 1999; December 7, 1999; March 28, 2000.

78. Ibid., February 1, 2000; November 30, 1999; December 7, 1999.

79. Ibid., March 28, 2000.

80. Ibid.

81. Ibid.

82. Ibid., November 30, 1999; December 7, 1999.

83. Ibid., February 1, 2000.

84. Ibid.

85. Ibid.

86. Ibid., March 28, 2000.

87. Ibid.

88. Ibid.

89. Ibid.

90. Ibid.

91. Ibid., February 1, 2000.

92. Ibid., March 28, 2000.

93. Ibid.

94. Ibid.

95. Interview with Father Virgilio Elizondo, February 10, 1997, 1–2. For an introduction to Elizondo's work, see Matovina, ed., *Beyond Borders*.

96. Interviw with Elizondo, February 10, 1997.

97. Ibid.

98. Virgilio Elizondo, *A God of Incredible Surprises, Jesus of Galilee* (Lanham, Md.: Rowman and Littlefield, 2003), 143.

99. Elizondo interview, Febraury 10, 1997.

100. Ibid.

101. Interview with Elizondo, February 10, 1997. On the celebration of Our Lady of Guadalupe in San Antonio, see Matovina, *Guadalupe*.

102. Ibid.

103. As quoted in Elizondo, *The Future Is Mestizo: Life Where Cultures Meet* (Boulder: University Press of Colorado, 2000), 5.

104. Elizondo interview, February 10, 1997.

105. Elizondo, *Future Is Mestizo*, 9.

106. Elizondo interview, February 10, 1007.

107. Ibid.

108. Ibid.

109. Ibid.

110. Ibid.

111. Ibid., February 13, 1997.

112. Ibid.

113. Ibid.

114. Ibid.

115. Ibid.

116. Ibid., February 20, 1997.

117. Ibid.

118. Ibid.

119. Ibid.

120. Ibid.

121. Ibid., April 21, 1998.

122. Ibid.

123. Ibid.

124. Ibid., May 11, 1998, 15–17. Also see Elizondo, *Galilean Journey: The Mexican-American Experience*, 2nd ed. (Maryknoll, N.Y.: Orbis Books, 2000).

125. Interview with Elizondo, April 21, 1998.

126. Ibid.

127. Elizondo, *Future Is Mestizo*, 39.

128. Elizondo interview, April 21, 1998. On MACC, see Badillo, *Latinos*, 160–162. Also see María del Socorro Castañeda, "Mexican American Spirituality and Conscientization: The Symbolic Capital of the Mexican American Cultural Center" (M.A. thesis, University of California, Santa Barbara, 2001).

129. Gerald E. Poyo, "'Integration Without Assimilation': Cuban Catholics in Miami, 1960–1980," *U.S. Catholic Historian* 20 (Fall 2002): 91–109.

130. Elizondo interview, May 11, 1998.

131. Ibid.

132. Ibid.

133. Ibid.

134. Ibid.

135. Ibid.

136. Ibid.

137. On COPS, see Skerry, *Mexican Americans*; also see Dennis Shirley, *Valley Interfaith and School Reform: Organizing for Power in South Texas* (Austin: University of Texas Press, 2002).

138. Ibid.

139. Matovina, *Guadalupe and Her Faithful*, 144.

140. Elizondo interview, May 27, 1998.
141. Castañeda, "Mexican American Spirituality," 33; Gutting, *Foucault,* 23.
142. Elizondo interview, May 11, 1998.
143. Ibid., May 27, 1998.
144. Elizondo, *Future Is Mestizo,* 16.
145. Elizondo, *A God of Incredible Surprises,* 143.
146. As quoted in Timothy Matovina, "Latino Catholics and Public Life," in Andrew Walsh, ed., *Can Charitable Choice Work? Covering Religion's Impact of Urban Affairs and Social Services* (Hartford, Conn.: Leonard E. Greenberg Center for the Study of Religion in Public Life, 2001), 66.
147. León, *La Llorona's Children,* 5.
148. Elizondo interview, May 27, 1998. Also Matovina, *Guadalupe and Her Faithful.*
149. Castañeda, "Mexican American Spirituality," 37. Of the concept of "symbolic capital," Castañeda writes, "As Pierre Bourdieu rightly argues, symbols accrue value the more they are borrowed freely by others. In the context of the U.S. Catholic Church, the more the Catholic Church borrows Latina/o religious practices, the more value such practices gain. Similarly, the more the Church as a whole uses or borrows Latina/o practices (such as hymns or rituals), the more value is given to these hymns, rituals, or other practices, by both the Latina/o community and the rest of the Church."
150. Ibid.
151. León, *La Llorona's Children,* 18, 27.
152. Elizondo interview, May 27, 1998.
153. Elizondo, *A God of Incredible Surprises,* 103. See Goizueta quote in Badillo, *Latinos,* 181.
154. Elizondo interview, May 27, 1998.
155. Ibid.

Chapter Seven

1. See *The Tidings,* no date, Olivares Family Collection; *Los Angeles Times,* December 16, 1990, 2; interview with Henry Olivares, May 18, 2002; Rubén Martínez, *The Other Side: Notes from the New L.A., Mexico City and Beyond* (New York: Vintage Books, 1992), 141–142.
2. Interview with Olivares Family, March 30, 2002.
3. See Father Luis Olivares, C.M.F., X Anniversary Program, April 7, 2003.
4. *National Catholic Reporter.* Hereafter cited as NCR, April 2, 1993, 2.
5. Henry Olivares interview.
6. Ibid.
7. Olivares Family interview; also see, *Los Angeles Times,* March 20, 1993, B-1.
8. Blase Bonpane interview, January 13, 2003.

9. On the sanctuary movement, see, for example, Hilary Cunningham, *God and Caesar at the Rio Grande: Sanctuary and the Politics of Religion* (Minneapolis: University of Minnesota Press, 1995); Renny Golden, *Sanctuary: The New Underground Railroad* (Maryknoll, N.Y.: Orbis Press, 1986); Susan Bibler Coutin, *The Culture of Protest: Religious Activism and the U.S. Sanctuary Movement* (Boulder: Westview Press, 1993); Ann Crittenden, *Sanctuary, a Story of American Conscience and the Law in Collision* (New York: Weidenfeld and Nicolson, 1988); Miriam Davidson, *Convictions of the Heart: Jim Corbett and the Sanctuary Movement* (Tucson: University of Arizona Press, 1988); Robert Tomsho, *The American Sanctuary Movement* (Austin: Texas Monthly Press, 1987); Ignatius Bau, *The Ground Is Holy: Church Sanctuary and Central American Refugees* (Mahwah, N.J.: Paulist Press, 1985); Gary MacEoin, "A Brief History of the Sanctuary Movement," in *Sanctuary: A Resource Guide for Understanding and Participating in the Central American Refugee Struggle* (San Francisco: Harper and Row, 1985). For an excellent and powerful novel of the sanctuary movement, see Demetria Martínez, *Mother Tongue* (New York: Balantine Books, 1994). For an international perspective on sanctuary comparing refugee policies in Mexico, the United States, and Canada, see María Cristina García, *Seeking Refuge: Central American Migration to Mexico, the United States, and Canada* (Berkeley and Los Angeles: University of California Press, 2006). Also see Sergio Aguayo and Patricia Weiss Fagen, *Central Americans in Mexico and the United States: Unilateral, Bilateral, and Regional Perspectives* (Washington, D.C.: Hemisphere Migration Project, Center for Immigration Policy and Refugee Assistance, 1988); Elizabeth G. Ferris, *The Central American Refugees* (New York: Praeger, 1987). On Romero, see Archbishop Oscar Romero, *Voice of the Voiceless* (Maryknoll, N.Y.: Orbis Press, 1990); Placido Erdozaín, *Archbishop Romero: Martyr of Salvador* (Maryknoll, N.Y.: Orbis Press, 1981); James R. Brockman, S.J., ed., *Oscar Romero, The Violence of Love* (Maryknoll, N.Y.: Orbis Press, 2004); and Jon Sobrino, *Archbishop Romero: Memories and Reflections* (Maryknoll, N.Y.: Orbis Press, 1990). The literature on the Central American wars of the 1980s is extensive. Some examples include Robert Armstrong and Janet Schenck, *El Salvador: The Face of Repression* (Boston: South End Press, 1981); John H. Coatsworth, *Central America and the United States: The Clients and the Colossus* (New York: Twayne, 1994); John E. Findling, *Close Neighbors, Distant Friends: United States–Central American Relations* (Westport, Conn.: Greenwood Press, 1987); Walter LaFeber, *Inevitable Revolutions: The United States in Central America*, 2d ed. (New York: W. W. Norton, 1993); William M. LeoGrande, *Our Own Backyard: The United States in Central America, 1977–1992* (Chapel Hill: University of North Carolina Press, 1998).

10. See Cunningham, *God and Caesar at the Rio Grande*, xv. According to the 1980 Refugee Act, a refugee was any person "unable or unwilling to avail himself or herself of the protection of [his or her own country] because of persecution or a well-founded fear of persecution on account of race, religion, nationality, membership in a particular social group or political opinion." As quoted in David Quammen, "Seeking Refuge in a Desert: The Sanctuary Movement: Exodus redux," *Harper's*, 273 (December 1986), 59.

11. Nora Hamilton and Norma Stoltz, "Central American Migration: A Framework for Analysis," *Latin American Research Review* 26, no. 1 (1991): 75. Hamilton and Stoltz correctly note that a variety of factors influenced Central American migration, including economic and political ones.

12. Cunningham, *God and Caesar at the Rio Grande*, 101.

13. Cecilia Menjívar, "Salvadoran Migration to the United States in the 1980s: What Can We Learn about It and from It?" *International Migration* 32 (1994): 377.

14. Cunningham, *God and Caesar at the Rio Grande*, 19.

15. Ibid., xiii, 32. In addition to All Saints Church in Tucson, a number of other churches, mostly Protestant, also declared sanctuary on March 24, 1982; see Coutin, *Culture of Protest*, 30.

16. Although Quakers and Protestants pioneered the sanctuary movement in the early 1980s, Catholic churches in time also played a leading role; see Cunningham, *God and Caesar at the Rio Grande*, 65; also Badillo, *Latinos*, 198.

17. Olivares Family interview; Henry Olivares interview; *L.A. Weekly*, September 6–12, 1991, 23.

18. Olivares Family interview.

19. Henry Olivares interview.

20. Denis Lynn Daly Heyck, "Father Luis Olivares Interview," in Denis Lynn Daly Heyck, ed., *Barrios and Borderlands: Cultures of Latinos and Latinas in the United States* (New York: Routledge Press, 1994), 216.

21. Henry Olivares interview; Olivares Family interview.

22. Olivares Family interview. For a description of San Antonio's immigrant community in the early twentieth century, see Badillo, *Latinos*, 23–44, and Matovina, *Guadalupe and Her Faithful*, 82–91.

23. Olivares Family interview; Heyck, "Olivares," 215–216; Henry Olivares interview.

24. Heyck, "Olivares," 215–216.

25. Ibid.; Olivares Family interview; Henry Olivares interview.

26. Henry Olivares interview.

27. Ibid.; Heyck, "Olivares," 216.

28. Olivares Family interview.

29. Ibid.

30. Ibid.

31. Olivares Family interview; *L.A. Weekly*, September 6–12, 1991, 23.

32. Henry Olivares interview.

33. Heyck, "Olivares," 220.

34. See Mosqueda, *Chicanos*, 143–144.

35. *L.A. Weekly*, September 6–12, 1991, 24.

36. Henry Olivares interview.

37. Marita Hernández, "The Last Fight of Father Olivares," *Los Angeles Times Magazine*, December 16, 1990, 4.

38. Program for Olivares Dinner, September 5, 1990; Heyck, "Olivares," 221, 223.

39. Lydia López interview, December 14, 2002.

40. Henry Olivares interview.

41. Interview with Father Richard Estrada, August 24, 2002.

42. *Los Angeles Times Magazine*, December 16, 1990, 4.

43. Lydia López interview. On the Industrial Areas Foundation, see Mary Beth Rogers, *Cold Anger: A Story of Faith and Power Politics* (Denton: University of North Texas Press, 1990), and Mark Warren, *Dry Bones Rattling: Community Building to Revitalize American Democracy* (Princeton: Princeton University Press, 2001).

44. Ibid.

45. Ibid.

46. As quoted in Timothy Matovina, "Latino Catholics and American Public Life," in Andrew Walsh, ed., *Can Charitable Choice Work? Covering Religion's Impact on Urban Affairs and Social Services* (Hartford, Conn.: Leonard E. Greenberg Center for the Study of Religion in Public Life, 2001), 61.

47. Ibid.

48. Ibid. Also Matovina, "Latino Catholics," 63.

49. See Skerry, *Mexican Americans*, 198.

50. Estrada interview; *Los Angeles Times Magazine*, December 16, 1990, 4; *Los Angeles Times*, July 9, 1986, clipping in Olivares Family Collection; Heyck, "Olivares," 223–224; Henry Olivares interview; *L.A. Weekly*, September 6–12, 1991, 24.

51. Heyck, "Olivares," 225; *L.A. Weekly*, September 6–12, 1991, 22, 26.

52. As quoted in John C. Hammerback and Richard J. Jensen, *The Rhetorical Career of César Chávez* (College Station: Texas A&M Press, 1998), 30.

53. See Nora Hamilton and Norma Stoltz Chinchilla, *Seeking Community in a Global City: Guatemalans and Salvadorans in Los Angeles* (Philadelphia: Temple University Press, 2001). Also, Norma Stoltz Chinchilla and Nora Hamilton, "Seeking Refuge in the City of Angels: The Central American Community," in Gerry Riposa and Carolyn Deusch, eds., *City of Angels* (Dubuque: Kendall/Hunt, 1992), 84–100; and Norma Chinchilla, Nora

Hamilton, and James Loucky, "Central Americans in Los Angeles: An Immigrant Community in Transition," in Joan Moore and Raquel Pinder-hughes, eds., *In the Barrios: Latinos and the Underclass Debate* (New York: Russell Sage Foundation, 1993), 51–78.

54. Xavier Gorostiaga and Peter Marchetti, "The Central American Economy: Conflict and Crisis," in Nora Hamilton et al., eds., *Crisis in Central America: Regional Dynamics and U.S. Policy in the 1980s* (Boulder: Westview Press, 1988) 133.

55. See Sunday bulletins of La Placita Church at Our Lady Queen of the Angels Church in Los Angeles. For a study of Salvadoran refugees in San Francisco, see Cecilia Menjívar, *Fragmented Ties: Salvadoran Immigrant Networks in America* (Berkeley and Los Angeles: University of California Press, 2000).

56. Interview with Father Michael Kennedy, August 24, 2002.

57. *L.A. Weekly,* June 29-July 5, 1990, 12.

58. Coutin, *Culture of Protest,* 154.

59. Father Juan Romero, "Tension Between Cross and Sword: A Profile of Father Luis Olivares," unpublished paper, courtesy of Father Romero, 17.

60. *La Opinión,* August 6, 1990, 7.

61. Heyck, "Olivares," 227.

62. Clipping from NCR, December 22, 1989, in Olivares Family Collection. Also see Cox, "New Breed," 142.

63. Olivares family interview.

64. Ibid; *La Opinión,* August 6, 1990, 7.

65. Program for Commemorative Mass for Father Luis Olivares, March 17, 1995; Henry Olivares interview.

66. *La Opinión,* no date, clipping in Olivares Family Collection.

67. As quoted in *Los Angeles Times Magazine,* December 19, 1990, 5.

68. *La Opinión,* no date, clipping in Olivares Family Collection; Ibid., August 6, 1990, 7, clipping in Olivares Family Collection. On Father Greg Boyle, see Celeste Fremon, *G-Dog and the Homeboys: Father Greg Boyle and the Gangs of East Los Angeles* (Albuquerque: University of New Mexico Press, 2004).

69. Henry Olivares interview.

70. Gilbert R. Cadena, "Chicano Clergy and the Emergence of Liberation Theology," *Hispanic Journal of Behavioral Sciences* 11, no. 2 (May 1989): 107–121.

71. Coutin, *Culture of Protest,* 77.

72. Kennedy interview. On the concept of "spiritual guides," see Cunningham, *God and Caesar at the Rio Grande,* 139.

73. *La Opinión,* August 13, 1989.

74. *L.A. Weekly,* September 6–12, 1991, 26.

75. Bonpane interview.

76. Lisa Martínez interview, August 29, 2002.

77. E-mail note from Graciela Limón to Mario T. García, June 11, 2002; also, Henry Olivares interview.

78. Program for Commemorative Mass for Olivares.

79. As quoted in *L.A. Weekly*, June 29–July 5, 1990, 12.

80. See *Los Angeles Times*, December 13, 1985, part 2, 1–2.

81. Here I extend León's concept of Guadalupe as a transborder blessed virgin connecting Mexico City to Los Angeles; León, *La Llorona's Children*, 94.

82. Olivares letter to editor, *Los Angeles Times*, December 8, 1985, 4. Also Cunningham, *God and Caesar at the Rio Grande*, 39, and Quammen, "Seeking Refuge," 61.

83. Henry Olivares interview.

84. See William V. Flores and Rina Benmayor, *Latino Cultural Citizenship: Claiming Identity, Space, and Rights* (Boston: Beacon Press, 1997).

85. See Badillo, *Latinos*, 175–181.

86. *L.A. Weekly*, September 6–12, 1991, 24; *Los Angeles Times*, November 23, 1985, sec. II, 1; ibid., December 6, 1985, sec. II, 1.

87. Menjívar, "Salvadoran Migration," 385.

88. León, *La Llorona's Children*, 6.

89. Kennedy interview; Estrada interview; Henry Olivares interview.

90. Kennedy interview.

91. Cunningham, *God and Caesar at the Rio Grande*, 97.

92. Coutin, *Culture of Protest*, 108–109.

93. Ibid.

94. López interview.

95. Ibid.

96. On the concept of the "underground church," see Cunningham, *God and Caesar at the Rio Grande*, 157–201.

97. Ibid. Also see Coutin, *Culture of Protest*, 192–193.

98. Heyck, "Olivares," 225–226; *L.A. Weekly*, September 6–12, 1991, 25; Kennedy interview; *Los Angeles Times*, December 6, 1985, sec. II, 1, 4.

99. López interview.

100. *L.A. Weekly*, June 29-July 5, 1990, 12. Also see García, *Seeking Refuge*.

101. Martínez, *The Other Side*.

102. Kennedy interview.

103. Ibid.

104. As quoted in Romero, "Cross and Sword," 10.

105. Ibid., 11.

106. Henry Olivares interview.

107. Ibid.

108. Cunningham, *God and Caesar at the Rio Grande*, 130, 136.

109. Cox, "New Breed," 143.

110. Cunningham, *God and Caesar at the Rio Grande*, 130, 136.

111. Laurie Kay Sommers, "Inventing Latinismo: The Creation of 'Hispanic' Panethnicity in the United States," *Journal of American Folklore* 104 (1991): 50.

112. *La Opinión*, August 15, 1989, clipping, Olivares Family Collection

113. Kennedy interview.

114. *Los Angeles Times*, July 7, 1986, clipping in Olivares Family Collection.

115. Benedict Anderson, *Imagined Communities* (London: Verso Editions, 1983).

116. See Félix Padilla, *Latino Ethnic Consciousness: The Case of Mexican Americans and Puerto Ricans in Chicago* (Notre Dame: University of Notre Dame Press, 1985).

117. Coutin, *Culture of Protest*, 193.

118. Romero, "Cross and Sword," 11; *L.A. Weekly*, September 6–12, 1991, 25.

119. Cunningham, *God and Caesar at the Rio Grande*, 25.

120. López interview.

121. Kennedy interview; Henry Olivares interview.

122. López interview.

123. *Los Angeles Times Magazine*, December 16, 1990, 6.

124. Kennedy interview.

125. Limón to García, June 11, 2002.

126. Martínez interview.

127. Kennedy interview.

128. Ibid; Henry Olivares interview.

129. Kennedy interview; Henry Olivares interview.

130. Confidential source, July 9, 2005.

131. *La Opinión*, August 13, 1989, clipping in Olivares Family Collection.

132. Kennedy interview.

133. Ibid.

134. Ibid.

135. Chinchilla, Hamilton, and Loucky, "Central Americans in Los Angeles" in Moore and Pinderhughes, eds., *In the Barrios*, 51–78.

136. García, *Seeking Refuge*, 100.

137. Henry Olivares interview; *Los Angeles Times*, July 9, 1986, clipping Olivares Family Collection.

138. Kennedy interview.

139. Estrada interview.

140. López interview.

141. Henry Olivares interview.

142. Ibid.

143. Ibid.

144. Kennedy interview.

145. Badillo, *Latinos*.

146. *L.A. Weekly,* September 6–12, 1991, 26.

147. López interview.

148. *Los Angeles Times,* December 13, 1987, part II, 13.

149. Ibid., September 21, 1988.

150. Ibid.

151. NCR, November 11, 1988.

152. *Los Angeles Times,* September 21, 1988.

153. Ibid.

154. *L.A. Weekly,* September 6–12, 1991, 26.

155. *Los Angeles Times,* December 13, 1987, part II, 13.

156. Kieran Prother, "Father Luis Olivares," in *Peace Sharings* (Summer, 1993), 3, in Father Juan Romero Collection.

157. *La Opinión,* August 13, 1989, 3.

158. *L.A. Weekly,* June 29-July 5, 1990, 12.

159. Romero, "Cross and Sword," 13.

160. Olivares Family interview.

161. Interview with Father Greg Boyle, November 22, 2005.

162. *Los Angeles Times Magazine,* December 16, 1990, 5.

163. Romero, "Cross and Sword," 13.

164. *Los Angeles Times Magazine,* December 16, 1990, 5.

165. Romero, "Cross and Sword," 13.

166. Boyle interview.

167. Cox, "New Breed," 142.

168. See *Los Angeles Times,* September 21, 1988, and *L.A. Weekly,* September 6–12, 1991, 26.

169. ACLU Program honoring Father Luis Olivares, December 6, 1991, in Olivares Family Collection.

170. Mike Davis, *City of Quartz: Excavating the Future in Los Angeles* (New York: Vintage Books, 1992), 356.

171. See media coverage of Mahony's position in early 2006 against a House of Representatives bill that, among other things, would criminalize undocumented immigrants and groups, such as the Church, that supported them.

172. Susan Alva interview, November 26, 2002.

173. See Badillo, *Latinos,* 183.

174. Bonpane interview.

175. *L.A. Weekly,* September 6–12, 1991, 26.

176. Kennedy interview.

177. Interview with Patricia Krommer, February 3, 2003, and e-mail from Krommer to Mario T. García, April 22, 2003.

178. Krommer interview.

179. Interview with Rev. Donald Smith, December 6, 2002.

180. Ibid.

181. Bonpane interview; Smith interview.
182. "The Wednesday Morning Coalition: A Call to Conscience," courtesy of Rev. Donald Smith.
183. NCR, December 8, 1989, 7; "Wednesday Morning Coalition"; interview with Father Chris Ponnet and Patricia Krommer, February 2, 2003.
184. Cunningham, *God and Caesar at the Rio Grande*, 100.
185. "Wednesday Morning Coalition"; Bonpane interview.
186. Bonpane interview.
187. "Wednesday Morning Coalition."
188. Ibid.
189. Ibid.
190. Ponnet/Krommer interview.
191. "Wednesday Morning Coalition."
192. Ibid.
193. Bonpane interview.
194. "Wednesday Morning Coalition."
195. *The Tidings* clipping in Olivares Family Collection.
196. Kennedy interview.
197. E-mail from Mary Brent Wehrli to Mario T. García, April 24, 2003.
198. Bonpane interview.
199. "Wednesday Morning Coalition."
200. Kennedy interview.
201. *L.A. Weekly*, December 16, 1990, 5.
202. Henry Olivares interview.
203. Chinchilla, Hamilton, and Loucky, "Central Americans in Los Angeles," 71–72; *Los Angeles Times*, December 20, 1990. It is estimated that about 20 percent of El Salvador's five million people arrived in the United States during the 1980s; see Menjívar, "Salvadoran Migration to the United States in the 1980s," 374.
204. *Los Angeles Times*, January 19, 1992, clipping in Olivares Family Collection. On the peace process, see Jack Child, *The Central American Peace Process, 1983–1991* (Boulder: Lynne Riener, 1992).
205. *Los Angeles Times Magazine*, December 6, 1990, 6; column by Father Rosendo Urrabazo, San Antonio paper, no title, no date in Olivares Family Collection.
206. Program for Olivares dinner, September 5, 1990, 1.
207. Henry Olivares interview.
208. *L.A. Weekly*, September 6–12, 1991, 27.
209. *Los Angeles Times Magazine*, December 16, 1990, 5.
210. *The Tidings*, September 14, 1990, Olivares Family Collection.
211. ACLU Program, December 6, 1991.
212. *Los Angeles Times Magazine*, December 16, 1990, 2.

213. See, for example, Matovina, *Guadalupe*; Badillo, *Latinos*; and Treviño, *Church in the Barrio.*

214. Cunningham, *God and Caesar at the Rio Grande*, 2.

Chapter Eight

1. See Virgilio Elizondo, *The Future Is Mestizo*; Virgilio Elizondo and Timothy M. Matovina, *Mestizo Worship: A Pastoral Approach to Liturgical Ministry* (Collegeville, Minn.: Liturgical Press, 1988), 3; Roberto S. Goizueta, "U.S. Hispanic Popular Catholicism as Theopoetics," in Ada María Isasi-Díaz and Fernando F. Segovia, eds., *Hispanic/Latino Theology: Challenge and Promise* (Minneapolis: Fortress Press, 1996), 261–288; also see Meredith McGuire, "Linking Theory and Methodology for the Study of Latino Religiosity in the United States Context," in Anthony M. Stevens-Arroyo and Ana María Díaz-Stevens, eds., *An Enduring Flame: Studies on Latino Popular Religiosity* (New York: Bildner Center for Western Hemisphere Studies), 196. Also see Ann Taves, *The Household of Faith: Roman Catholic Devotions in Mid-Nineteenth-Century America* (Notre Dame: University of Notre Dame Press, 1986), 22–23.

2. Matovina, *Guadalupe and Her Faithful*, 14.

3. Timothy M. Matovina, "Liturgy, Popular Rites, and Popular Spirituality," in Elizondo and Matovina, *Mestizo Worship*, 82.

4. Virgilio Elizondo, "Popular Religion as the Core of Cultural Identity in the Mexican American Experience," in Stevens-Arroyo and Díaz-Stevens, eds., *An Enduring Flame*, 116–117; also see Virgilio Elizondo, *Christianity and Culture* (1975; reprint, San Antonio: Mexican American Culture Center, 1983), 174.

5. See Ada María Isasi-Díaz, *En la Lucha: Elaborating a Mujerista Theology* (Minneapolis: Fortress Press, 1993).

6. Ada María Isasi-Díaz, *Mujerista Theology* (Maryknoll, N.Y.: Orbis Books, 1996), 59–82.

7. Jeanette Rodríguez, "Contemporary Encounters with Guadalupe," *Journal of Hispanic/Latino Theology* 5, no. 1 (August 1997): 48–60. Rodríguez defines "cultural memory" in this way: "Cultural memory is evoked around image, symbol, or event precisely because it keeps alive and transforms those events of the past, creating an effective response that continues to give meaning to the present. If a cultural memory becomes static, no longer reinterpreted and impacted by the present, then it no longer serves the function of communal identity, resistance, and/or survival," 53.

8. Ana María Díaz-Stevens, "Analyzing Popular Religiosity for Socio-Religious Meaning," in Stevens-Arroyo and Diaz-Stevens, eds., *An Enduring Flame*, 25–26.

9. Badillo, *Latinos*, xv. Also see Carroll, *The Penitente Brotherhood*, 213.

10. As quoted in Figueroa Deck, *The Second Wave*, 116.

11. Adelina Luna Correa interviewed by Elizabeth Luna Correa, Spring, 1999, 4. The student papers did not provide interview dates; however, all were conducted in the spring quarters of either 1998 or 1999.

12. Ibid., 7.

13. Angel interviewed by Javier Angullo, Spring 1999, 4.

14. Miguel Gabriel Contreras interviewed by Marcela Plascencia, Spring 1998.

15. Taves, *Household of Faith*.

16. Paulina Paleo interviewed by Anthony R. Soria, Spring 1999.

17. Timothy Badillo interviewed by Cecilio Valdivia, Spring 1998.

18. Mariela Vega interviewed by Veronica Saldana, Spring 1999, 7.

19. Epigmenia Larios interviwed by Rocío Valdovinos, Spring 1999, 5.

20. Ibid., 8.

21. Anastacia López interviewed by Luis E. López, Spring 1998, 4.

22. Contreras interview, 4

23. Carmen interviewed by Eva Huizar, Spring 1999.

24. Teresa Torres interviewed by Angelina Torres, Spring 1999, 4–5.

25. Gregoria Oropeza interviewed by Michelle Oropeza, Spring 1998.

26. López interview.

27. Badillo, *Latinos*, 189; Matovina, *Guadalupe and Her Faithful*, 18; Lara Medina, "Women: The U.S. Latina Religious Experience," in Avalos, ed., *Introduction*, 284.

28. José Angel by Javier Angullo, Spring 1999, 1.

29. Contreras interview, 2.

30. Gildardo Manuel Rivas interviewed by Monica Valdez, Spring 1998.

31. Olga Caballero Melgoza interviewed by Laura Melgoza, Spring 1999.

32. Raquel Balderas de Quiroga interviewed by Raquel Quiroga, Spring 1998.

33. León, *La Llorona's Children*, 95.

34. William H. Beezley, "Home Altars: Private Reflection of Public Life," in Ramón A. Gutiérrez, ed., *Home Altars of Mexico* (Albuquerque: University of New Mexico Press, 1997), 91–107.

35. Treviño, *The Church in the Barrio*, 55.

36. María Hinojosa interviewed by Suzanne Carey, Spring 1999, 7.

37. Ibid.

38. Orlando O. Espin, "Tradition and Popular Religion: An Understanding of the Sensus Fidelium," in Arturo J. Bañuelas, ed., *Mestizo Christianity: Theology from the Latino Perspective* (Maryknoll, N.Y.: Orbis Books, 1995), 150.

39. José Angel interview.

40. Rafael González interviewed by Veronica González, Spring 1999, 5.

41. María Serrano interviewed by Edith Nava, Spring 1999, 1.

42. Alfredo Figueroa interviewed by Andrés Figueroa, Spring 1998, 3–4

43. Correa interview, 7–8.

44. Timothy Badillo interviewed by Cecilio Valdivia, Spring 1998.

45. José Angel interview.

46. Figueroa interview, 4.

47. Elizondo, "Living Faith: Resistance and Survival," in Elizondo and Matovina, *Mestizo Worship*, 14.

48. Caballero Melgoza interview.

49. Oropeza interview.

50. Manuel Rivas interview.

51. Paleo interview, 4.

52. Paula Bautista interviewed by Ana Lilia Gonzáles, Spring 1999.

53. Ibid.

54. Goizueta, "Popular Catholicism," 267; Taves, *Household of Faith*, 48. On Juan Soldado, see Paul J. Vanderwood, *Juan Soldado: Rapist, Murder, Martyr, Saint* (Durham: Duke University Press, 2004).

55. Elizondo, "The Treasure of Hispanic Faith," in Elizondo and Matovina, *Mestizo Worship*, 72.

56. Mrs. Enriquez interviewed by Jeniffer Enriquez, Spring 1999, 7.

57. María Serrano interview, 7.

58. Ibid., p. 8.

59. Consuelo Munguia interview, 7.

60. Epigmenia interview, 7.

61. Teresa Torres interview, 8.

62. Lelia Esparza Quiroga interviwed by Alejandro Esparza, Spring 1998, 5. The literature on Guadalupe is extensive, but see, for example, Matovina, *Guadalupe*; D. A. Brading, *Mexican Phoenix: Our Lady of Guadalupe, Image and Tradition Across the Centuries* (Cambridge: Cambridge University Press, 2001); Jeanette Rodríguez, *Our Lady of Guadalupe: Faith and Empowerment among Mexican American Women* (Austin: University of Texas Press, 1994); Virgilio Elizondo, *La Morenita: Evangelizer of the Americas* (San Antonio: Mexican American Cultural Center, 1980); Jody Brant Smith, *The Image of Guadalupe*, 2d ed. (Macon, Ga.: Mercer University Press, 1994); Ana Castillo, ed., *Goddess of the Americas/La Diosa de las Américas: Writings on the Virgin of Guadalupe* (New York: Riverhead Books, 1996); Stafford Poole, *Our Lady of Guadalupe: The Origins and Sources of a Mexican National Symbol, 1531–1797* (Tucson: University of Arizona Press, 1996); Mary E. Odem, "Our Lady of Guadalupe in the New South: Latino Immigrants and the Politics of Integration in the Catholic Church," *Journal of American Ethnic History* 24 (Fall 2004): 26–57; William B. Taylor, "The Virgin of Guadalupe in New Spain: An Inquiry into the Social History of Marian Devotion," *American Ethnologist* 14, no. 1

(February 1987): 9–33; Jeanette Favrot Peterson, "The Virgin of Guadalupe: Symbol of Conquest or Liberation?" *Art Journal* 51, no. 4 (Winter 1992): 39–47; Eric R. Wolf, "The Virgin of Guadalupe: A Mexican National Symbol," *Journal of American Folklore* 71 (January–March 1958): 34–39; Kristy Nabhan-Warren, *The Virgin of El Barrio: Marian Apparitions, Catholic Evangelizing, and Mexican-American Activism* (New York: New York University Press, 2005). Also see León's insightful discussion of Guadalupe on both sides of the border in *La Llorona's Children*, 59–126.

63. Ibid., 6.

64. Bautista interview.

65. Matovina, *Guadalupe and Her Faithful*, 16.

66. Figueroa interview.

67. Matovina, *Guadalupe and Her Faithful*, 81.

68. Manuel Rivas interview.

69. Lucio Ibarra interviewed by Leopoldo Ibarra, Spring 1999.

70. Consuelo Munguia interview, 6–7.

71. Elizondo, "Popular Religion," in Stevens-Arroyo and Díaz-Stevens, eds., *An Enduring Flame*, 127.

72. Espin, "Tradition and Popular Tradition," in Bañuelas, ed., *Mestizo Christianity*, 150.

73. Goizueta, "Popular Catholicism," 269.

74. See Ana Maria Diaz-Stevens, *Oxcart Catholicism on Fifth Avenue: The Impact of the Puerto Rican Migration Upon the Archdiocese of New York* (Notre Dame: University of Notre Dame Press, 1993).

75. José Angel interview.

76. Manuel Rivas interview.

77. Correa interview.

78. Caballero Melgoza interview.

79. Carmen interview; some "noveñarios" start eight days before December 12; see Correa interview; also see Anastacio López interviewed by Luis E López, Spring 1998.

80. Axel Hernández interviewed by Nazanin Firouztaleh, Spring 1998.

81. Caballero Melgoza interview.

82. Consuelo Munguia interviewed by Mabel Munguia, Spring 1999, 3.

83. Contreras interview, 6, and Carmen interview.

84. Consuelo Munguia interview, 4.

85. José Angel interview.

86. Caballer Melgoza interview.

87. Goizueta, "Popular Catholicism," 278.

88. Taves, *Household of Faith*, 33.

89. Rivas interview.

90. Teresa Torres interview, 9.

91. Balderas de Quiroga interview.

92. Luna Correa interview, 4.

93. Carmen interview.

94. María Serrano interview, 7. On the concept of pilgrimage, see Elizondo and Freyne, eds., *Pilgrimage.*

95. Elizondo, "Popular Religion," 128.

96. Father Virgil Elizondo's lectures at uc Santa Barbara, Spring 1998 and Spring 1999.

97. Michelle Romero interviewed by Mark Yalen, Spring 1998, 4.

98. Zoila Vásquez interviewed by Ana Pérez, Spring 1998, 5.

99. Consuelo Munguía interview, 4–5.

100. Bautista interview.

101. Mireya Chávez interviwed by Gení Greene, Spring 1998, 5.

102. Martha Hernández interviewed by Héctor Baltazar, Spring 1999; José Angel interview; Contreras interview; Virginia Gaona interviewed by Pablo E. Landeros, Spring 1998.

103. León, *La Llorona's Children,* 244.

104. Matovina, "Liturgy, Popular Rites," 88.

105. Elizondo, "Living Faith," 18.

Reflections

1. Greeley, *The Catholic Imagination.*

2. See Elizondo, *The Future Is Mestizo.*

3. See Flores and Benmayor, eds., *Latino Cultural Citizenship.*

4. Ibid., 1.

5. Ibid.

6. Ibid. The role of religion and specifically Catholicism in the formation of cultural citizenship is hinted at in this influential volume on the concept of cultural citizenship, but not heavily developed. The one exception is Richard R. Flores's essay on Chicano Catholic performances of "Los Pastores" in San Antonio, 124–151.

7. Gloria Anzaldúa, *Borderlands/La Frontera* (San Francisco: Aunt Lute Books, 1987).

8. For an excellent discussion of the cursillo movement in California, see Burns, "The Mexican Catholic Community in California," part II in Dolan and Hinojosa, eds., *Mexican Americans.*

9. Pitti, "Sociedades Guadalupanas."

10. As witnessed in classes taught by Father Luis Quihuis at uc Santa Barbara.

11. Héctor Avalos, "Conclusion," in Avalos, ed., *Introduction,* 305.

Bibliography

Oral History Interviews

Alva, Susan. Interviewed by Mario T. García, November 26, 2002.
Angel, José. Interviewed by Javier Angullo, Spring 1999.

Badillo, Timothy. Interviewed by Cecilio Valdivia, Spring 1998.
Balderas de Quiroga, Raquel. Interviewed by Raquel Quiroga, Spring 1998.
Bautista, Paula. Interviewed by Ana Lilia Gonzáles, Spring 1999.
Bonpane, Blase. Interviewed by Mario T. García, January 13, 2003.
Boyle, Father Greg. Interviewed by Mario T. García, November 22, 2005.

Calleros, Cleofas. Interviewed by Oscar Martínez, September 14, 1972.
Chávez, Mireya. Interviewed by Geni Greene, Spring 1998.
Contreras, Miguel Gabriel. Interviewed by Marcela Plascencia, Spring 1998.
Correa, Adelina Luna. Interviewed by Elizabeth Luna Correa, Spring 1999.
Cruz, Camilo. Interviewed by Mario T. García, April 25, 1997.
Cruz, Ray. Interviewed by Mario T. García, April 25, 2003.

Elizondo, Father Virgilio. Interviewed by Mario T. García, Spring 1997; Spring 1998.
Estrada, Father Richard. Interviewed by Mario T. García, August 24, 2002.

Figueroa, Alfredo. Interviewed by Andrés Figueroa, Spring 1998.

Gandara, Bob. Interviewed by Mario T. García, September 4, 2005.
Gaona, Virginia. Interviewed by Pablo E. Landeros, Spring 1998.
García, Miguel. Interviewed by Mario T. García, July 11, 2005.
González, Rafael. Interviewed by Veronica González, Spring 1999.

Hernández, Alex. Interviewed by Nazanin Firouztaleh, Spring 1998.
Hernández, Martha. Interviewed by Héctor Baltazar, Spring 1999
Hinojosa, María. Interviewed by Suzanne Carey, Spring 1999.

Ibarra, Lucio. Interviewed by Leopoldo Ibarra, Spring 1999.
Iglesia, Ada. Interviewed by Oralia de Oca, Spring 1999.

Kennedy, Father Michael. Interviewed by Mario T. García, August 24, 2002.
Krommer, Patricia. Interviewed by Mario T. García, February 3, 2003.

Larios, Epigmenia. Interviewed by Rocío Valdovinos, Spring 1998.
López, Anastacia. Interviewed by Luis E. López, Spring 1998.
López, Lydia. Interviewed by Mario T. García, October 24, 1996; December 14,
    2002.

Martínez, Lisa. Interviewed by Mario T. García, August 29, 2002.
Martínez, Paloma Cruz. Interviewed by Mario T. García, April 25, 2005.
Martínez, Richard. Interviewed by Mario T. García, Los Angeles, January 21,
    1996.
Martínez, Rosa. Interviewed by Mario T. García, June 14, 2005.
McNamara, Father Patrick. Interviewed by Mario T. García, April 13, 1996.
Melgoza, Olga Caballero. Interviewed by Laura Melgoza, Spring 1999.
Munguía, Consuelo. Interviewed by Mabel Munguía, Spring 1999.

Olivares family. Interviewed by Mario T. García, March 30, 2002.
Olivares, Henry. Interviewed by Mario T. García, May 18, 2002.
Oropeza, Gregoria. Interviewed by Michelle Oropeza, Spring 1998.

Paleo, Paulina. Interviewed by Anthony R. Soria, Spring 1999.

Quihuis, Father Luis. Interviewed by Mario T. García, Fall 1999; Spring 2000; Fall
    2000.

Rivas, Gildardo Manuel. Interviewed by Monica Valdez, Spring 1998.
Romero, Father Juan. Interviewed by Mario T. García, Summer 1998.

Romero, Michelle. Interviewed by Mark Yalen, Spring 1998.
Ruiz, Raul. Interviewed by Mario T. García, March 1, 1993.

Sánchez, Rick. Interviewed by Mario T. García, May 30, 2006.
Serrano, María. Interviewed by Edith Nava, Spring 1999.
Smith, Reverend Donald. Interviewed by Mario T. García, December 6, 2002.

Vásquez, Zoila. Interviewed by Ana Pérez, Spring 1998.
Vega, Mariela. Interviewed by Veronica Saldana, Spring 1999.

Archival Sources

Archbishop Robert E. Lucey Collection in Catholic Archives at San Antonio, Texas, Archdiocese of San Antonio, Chancery Office.

Camilo Cruz Private Collection.
Carlos E. Castañeda Collection in Benson Latin America Library, University of Texas at Austin.
Católicos Por La Raza FBI Files, Freedom of Information, FBI.
Cleofas Calleros Collection, Southwest Collection, El Paso Public Library.
Cleofas Calleros Collection, Special Collections, University of Texas at El Paso.

Father Juan Romero Private Collection.

Los Angeles Times Photo Archives, Special Collections, UCLA Charles E. Young Research Library.

National Catholic Welfare Conference (NCWC) Files in Department of Archives and Manuscripts of The Catholic University of America, Washington, D.C.
New Mexico Commission of Public Records, State Records Center and Archives, Santa Fe, New Mexico.

Olivares Family Private Collection.
Our Lady Queen of Angeles Sunday Bulletin Collection, Our Lady Queen of Angeles Rectory, Los Angeles.

Pedro Arias Private Collection on Católicos Por La Raza.

Photo Archives, Museum of New Mexico, Palace of the Governors, Santa Fe, New Mexico.

Reverend Donald Smith Private Collection.

Ricardo Cruz/Católicos Por La Raza Collection, California Ethnic and Multicultural Archives (CEMA) in Special Collections, University of California, Santa Barbara.

UCSB Student Oral History Projects in Father Virgilio Elizondo Classes, in possession of Mario T. García.

WPA (Works Progress Administration) Files in Fray Angélico Chávez History Library of the Museum of New Mexico, Santa Fe.

Newspapers and Newsletters

Con Safos (Los Angeles)

El Paso Times
El Popo (Cal State, Northridge)

Hispanic Link Weekly

L.A. Free Press (Los Angeles)
L.A. Weekly
La Prensa (San Antonio)
La Opinión (Los Angeles)
La Raza (Los Angeles)
La Verdad (San Diego)
La Voz Católica (Oakland)
La Voz del Pueblo (Berkeley)
Los Angeles Herald Examiner
Los Angeles Times
Los Angeles Times Magazine

National Catholic Reporter

The People's World
The Militant
The Tidings (Los Angeles)

Selected Secondary Sources

Acosta, Oscar Zeta. *The Revolt of the Cockroach People.* 1973; reprint, New York: Vintage Books, 1989.
Aguayo, Sergio, and Patricia Weiss Fagen. *Central Americans in Mexico and the United States: Unilateral, Bilateral, and Regional Perspectives.* Washington, D.C.:

Hemisphere Migration Project, Center for Immigration Policy and Refugee Assistance, 1988.

Ahlborn, Richard E. *The Penitente Moradas of Abiquiu.* Washington, D.C.: Smithsonian Institution Press, 1968.

Almaráz, Jr., Félix D. *Knight Without Armor: Carlos Eduardo Castañeda, 1896–1958.* College Station: Texas A&M Press, 1999.

Archuleta, Ruben E. *Land of the Penitentes, Land of Tradition.* Pueblo West, Colo.: El Jefe, 2003.

Arnal, Oscar L. *Priests in Working Class Blue: The History of the Worker-Priest, 1943–1954.* New York: Paulist Press, 1986.

Avalos, Hector, ed. *Introduction to the U.S. Latina and Latino Religious Experience.* Boston/Leiden: Brill Academic Publishers, 2004.

Awalt, Barbe, and Paul Rhetts. *Our Saints Among Us: 400 Years of New Mexican Devotional Art.* Albuquerque: University of New Mexico Press, 1998.

Badillo, David. *Latinos and the New Immigrant Church.* Baltimore: Johns Hopkins University Press, 2006.

Bañuelas, Arturo J., ed. *Mestizo Christianity: Theology from the Latino Perspective.* Maryknoll, N.Y.: Orbis Press, 1995.

Barton, Paul. *Hispanic Methodists, Presbyterians, and Baptists in Texas.* Austin: University of Texas Press, 2006.

Barvosa-Carter, Edwina. "Politics and the U.S. Latina and Latino Religious Experience," in Héctor Avalos, ed., *Introduction to the U.S. Latina and Latino Religious Experience.* Boston/Leiden: Brill Academic Publishers, 2004.

Bau, Ignatius. *The Ground Is Holy: Church Sanctuary and Central American Refugees.* Mahwah, N.J.: Paulist Press, 1985.

Beezley, William H. "Home Altars: Private Reflection of Public Life," in Ramón A. Gutiérrez, ed., *Home Altars of Mexico.* Albuquerque: University of New Mexico Press, 1997.

Berryman, Philip. *Liberation Theology.* New York: Pantheon Books, 1987.

Boyd, E. *Saints and Saint Makers of New Mexico.* Santa Fe: New Mexico Laboratory of Anthropology, 1946.

Brackenridge, R. Douglas, and Francisco O. García-Treto. *Iglesia Presbiteriana: A History of Presbyterians and Mexican Americans in the Southwest.* 2d ed. San Antonio: Trinity University Press, 1987.

Brading, D. A. *Mexican Phoenix: Our Lady of Guadalupe, Image and Tradition Across the Centuries.* Cambridge: Cambridge University Press, 2001.

Briggs, Charles L. *The Wood Carvers of Córdova, New Mexico: Social Dimensions of an Artistic "Revival."* Albuquerque: University of New Mexico Press, 1989.

Brockman, S.J., James R., ed., *Oscar Romero: The Violence of Love.* Maryknoll: Orbis Press, 2004.

Bronder, Saul E. *Social Justice and Church Authority: The Public Life of Archbishop Robert E. Lucey.* Philadelphia: Temple University Press, 1982.

Brown, Lorin W., Charles L. Briggs, and Marta Weigle. *Hispano Folklife of New Mexico: The Lorin W. Brown Federal Writers' Project Manuscripts.* Albuquerque: University of New Mexico Press, 1978.

Burns, Jeffrey M. "The Mexican Catholic Community in California," Part II in Jay Dolan and Gilberto Hinojosa, eds., *Mexican Americans and the Catholic Church, 1900–1965.* Notre Dame: University of Notre Dame Press, 1994.

Busto, Rudy V. *King Tiger: The Religious Vision of Reies López Tijerina.* Albuquerque: University of New Mexico Press, 2005.

Cadena, Gilbert R. "Chicano Clergy and the Emergence of Liberation Theology." *Hispanic Journal of Behavioral Sciences* 11, no. 2 (May 1989): 107–121.

Campa, Arthur. *Spanish Folk-Poetry in New Mexico.* Albuquerque: University of New Mexico Press, 1946.

Carroll, Michael P. *The Penitente Brotherhood: Patriarchy and Hispano Catholicism in New Mexico.* Baltimore: Johns Hopkins University Press, 2002.

Casarella, Peter, and Raul Gómez, eds. *El Cuerpo de Cristo: The Hispanic Presence in the U.S. Catholic Church.* New York: Crossroad, 1998.

Cash, Marie Romero. *Santos: Enduring Images of Northern New Mexican Village Churches.* Niwot, Colo.: University Press of Colorado, 1999.

Castañeda, María Del Socorro. "Mexican American Spirituality and Conscientization: The Symbolic Capital of the Mexican American Cultural Center." M.A. thesis, University of California, Santa Barbara, 2001.

Castillo, Ana, ed. *Goddess of the Americas/La Diosa de las Americas: Writings on the Virgin of Guadalupe.* New York: Riverhead Books, 1996.

Chávez, César. "The Chicano y La Iglesia." *La Verdad.* San Diego (December 1969).

———. "Peregrinación, Penitencia, Revolución." Reprinted in Luis Valdez and Stan Steiner, eds., *Aztlán: An Anthology of Mexican American Literature.* New York: Vintage Books, 1972.

Chávez, Ernesto. *¡Mi Raza Primero! Nationalism, Identity and Insurgency in the Chicano Movement in Los Angeles, 1966–1978.* Berkeley: University of California Press, 2002.

Chávez, Fray Angélico. "Southwestern Bookshelf." *New Mexico Magazine* (September–October, 1970), 7.

———. *My Penitente Land.* Santa Fe: Museum of New Mexico Press, 1993

———. "New Mexico Place-names from Spanish Proper Names." *El Palacio* (December 1949), 367–382.

———. *Origins of New Mexico Families: A Genealogy of the Spanish Colonial Period.* 1954. A facsimile of the first edition. Santa Fe: William Gannon, 1975.

———. *But Time and Chance: The Story of Padre Martínez of Taos, 1793–1867.* Santa Fe: Sunstone Press, 1981.

———. *Coronado's Friars.* Washington, D.C.: Academy of American Franciscan History, 1968.

———. "Ruts of the Santa Fe Trail." *New Mexico Magazine* (July–August, 1972), 18–29.

———. "New Mexico Religious Place Names other Than Those of Saints." *El Palacio* (January 1950), 24–25.

———. *Archives of the Archdiocese of Santa Fe, 1678–1900.* Washington, D.C.: Academy of American Franciscan History, 1957.

———, and Eleanor B. Adams, eds. *Missions of New Mexico: 1776, A Description by Fray Francisco Atanasio Domínguez with Other Contemporary Documents.* Albuquerque: University of New Mexico Press, 1956.

———. *Tres Macho—He Said: Padre Gallegos of Albuquerque: New Mexico's First Congressman.* Santa Fe: William Gannon, 1985.

———. "New Mexico's Bonnie Prince Chile." *New Mexico Magazine* (May–June 1974), 31.

———. "La Conquistadora is a Paisana." *El Palacio* (October 1950), 299–307.

———. *La Conquistadora, the Autobiography of an Ancient Statue.* Paterson: St. Anthony's Guild Press, 1954.

———. "The Authentic Spanish New Mexican—A Question of Identity." *Environment, People, and Culture: The Inaugural Papers,* Vol. 1, Part 2. Las Cruces: New Mexico State University Press, 1971.

Chávez, Thomas E. *New Mexico: Past and Future.* Albuquerque: University of New Mexico Press, 2006.

Child, Jack. *The Central American Peace Process, 1983–1991.* Boulder: Lynne Rienner, 1992.

Coatsworth, John H. *Central America and the United States: The Clients and the Colossus.* New York: Twayne, 1994.

Córdova, Gilberto Benito, ed. *Bibliography of Unpublished Materials Pertaining to Hispanic Culture in the New Mexico WPA Writers' Files.* Santa Fe: New Mexico State Department of Education, 1972.

Coutin, Susan Bibler. *The Culture of Protest: Religious Activism and the U.S. Sanctuary Movement.* Boulder: Westview Press, 1993.

Cox, Harvey. "The 'New Breed' in American Churches: Sources of Social Activism in American Religion." *Daedalus* (Winter 1967): 135–150.

Crittenden, Ann. *Sanctuary, A Story of American Conscience and the Law in Collision.* New York: Weidenfeld and Nicolson, 1988.

Cruz, Camilo. "Tribute to a Barrio Lawyer: Ricardo V. Cruz." *La Neta del "border" y la frontera* (April 1994).

Cunningham, Hilary. *God and Caesar at the Rio Grande: Sanctuary and the Politics of Religion.* Minneapolis: University of Minnesota Press, 1995.

Curran, Charles, ed. *Catholic Social Teaching 1891–Present: A Historical, Theological, and Ethical Analysis.* Washington, D.C.: Georgetown University Press, 2002.

Dalton, Frederick John. *The Moral Vision of César Chávez*. Maryknoll, N.Y.: Orbis Books, 2003.

Davidson, Miriam. *Convictions of the Heart: Jim Corbett and the Sanctuary Movement*. Tucson: University of Arizona Press, 1988.

Davis, Mike. *City of Quartz: Excavating the Future in Los Angeles*. New York: Vintage Books, 1992.

Deck, Allan Figueroa, S.J. *The Second Wave: Hispanic Ministry and the Evangelization of Cultures*. New York: Paulist Press, 1989.

———, and Jay P. Dolan, eds. *Hispanic Catholic Culture in the U.S.* Notre Dame: University of Notre Dame Press, 1994.

Delgado, Abelardo. "The New Christ," "The Organizer," and "A New Cross." Poems in Valdez and Steiner, eds., *Aztlán*.

Del Grito, Dolores. "Jesus Christ as a Revolutionist." In Valdez and Steiner, eds., *Aztlán*.

De Luna, Anita. *Faith Formation and Popular Religion: Lessons from the Tejano Experience*. Lanham, Md.: Rowman and Littlefield, 2002.

Díaz, Ana María, and Anthony M. Stevens-Arroyo. *Recognizing the Latino Resurgence in U.S. Religion: The Emmaus Paradigm*. Boulder: Westview Press, 1998.

———. *Oxcart Catholicism on Fifth Avenue: The Impact of the Puerto Rican Migration Upon the Archdiocese of New York*. Notre Dame: University of Notre Dame Press, 1993.

Dolan, Jay P. *In Search of an American Catholicism: A History of Religion and Culture in Tension*. New York: Oxford University Press, 2002.

———, and Gilberto M. Hinojosa, eds. *Mexican Americans and the Catholic Church, 1900–1965*. Notre Dame: University of Notre Dame Press, 1994.

Elizondo, Virgilio. *Christianity and Culture*. San Antonio: Mexican American Cultural Center, 1975.

———. *The Future Is Mestizo: Life Where Cultures Meet*. Boulder: University Press of Colorado, 2000.

———. *Galilean Journey: The Mexican-American Experience*. Maryknoll: Orbis Books, 2000.

———, and Timothy M. Matovina. *Mestizo Worship: A Pastoral Approach to Liturgical Ministry*. Collegeville, Minn.: Liturgical Press, 1988.

———. *A God of Incredible Surprises, Jesus of Galilee*. Lanham, Md.: Rowman and Littlefield, 2003.

———. *La Morenita: Evangelizer of the Americas*. San Antonio: Mexican American Cultural Center, 1980.

———, and Sean Freyne, eds. *Pilgrimage*. London: Concilium, 1996.

Erdozain, Placido. *Archbishop Romero: Martyr of Salvador*. Maryknoll, N.Y.: Orbis Press, 1990.

Espín, Orlando O. "Popular Catholicism Among Latinos." In Jay P. Dolan and Allan Figueroa Deck, eds., *Hispanic Catholic Culture in the U.S.* Notre Dame: University of Notre Dame Press, 1994.

———. "Tradition and Popular Religion: An Understanding of the Sensus Fidelium." In Arturo J. Bañuelas, ed., *Mestizo Christianity: Theology from the Latino Perspective.* Maryknoll: Orbis Books, 1995.

Espiñosa, Aurelio M. *The Folklore of Spain in the American Southwest: Traditional Spanish Folk Literature in Northern New Mexico and Southern Colorado.* Ed. J. Manuel Espiñosa. Norman: University of Oklahoma Press, 1985.

Espinosa, Gaston. "Borderland Religion: Los Angeles and the Origins of the Latino Pentecostal Movement in the U.S., Mexico, and Puerto Rico, 1900–1945." Ph.D. diss., University of California, Santa Barbara, 1999.

———, Virgilio Elizondo, and Jesse Miranda, eds. *Latino Religions and Civic Activism in the United States.* New York: Oxford University Press, 2005.

Fernández, Edward C. *La Cosecha: Harvesting Contemporary United States Hispanic Theology (1972–1998).* Collegeville, Minn.: Liturgical Press, 2000.

Ferris, Elizabeth G. *The Central American Refugees.* New York: Praeger, 1987.

Flores, William V., and Rina Benmayor. *Latino Cultural Citizenship: Claiming Identity, Space, and Rights.* Boston: Beacon Press, 1997.

Forrest, Suzanne. *The Preservation of the Village: New Mexico's Hispanics and the New Deal.* Albuquerque: University of New Mexico Press, 1998.

Freire, Paulo. *Pedagogy of the Oppressed.* 1970; reprint, New York: Continuum, 2005.

García, Alma M. *Chicana Feminist Thought: The Basic Historical Writings.* New York: Routledge, 1997.

García, María Christina. *Seeking Refuge: Central American Migration to Mexico, the United States, and Canada.* Berkeley and Los Angeles: University of California Press, 2006.

García, Mario T. *Desert Immigrants: The Mexicans of El Paso, 1880–1920.* New Haven: Yale University Press, 1981.

———. *Mexican Americans: Leadership, Ideology, and Identity, 1930–1960.* New Haven: Yale University Press, 1989.

———. *Memories of Chicano History: The Life and Narrative of Bert Corona.* Berkeley and Los Angeles: University of California Press, 1994.

———, ed. *Ruben Salazar, Border Correspondent: Selected Writings 1955–1970.* Berkeley: University of California Press, 1995.

———. *The Making of a Mexican American Mayor: Raymond L. Telles of El Paso.* El Paso: Texas Western Press, 1998.

———. *Luis Leal: An Auto/Biography.* Austin: University of Texas Press, 2000.

———, and Frances Esquibel Tywoniak. *Migrant Daughter: Coming of Age as a Mexican American Woman.* Berkeley: University of California Press, 2000.

———. "Mexican Americans and the Politics of Citizenship: The Case of El Paso, 1936." *New Mexico Historical Quarterly* 59 (April 1984): 187–204.

———. "Catholic Social Doctrine and Mexican American Political Thought." In *El Cuerpo de Cristo: The Hispanic Presence in the U.S. Catholic Church*, ed. Peter Casarella and Raul Gómez. New York: Crossroad, 1998.

García, Nasario. *Recuerdos de los viejitos: Tales of the Rio Puerco*. Albuquerque: University of New Mexico Press, 1987.

García, Richard A. *Rise of the Mexican American Middle Class: San Antonio, 1929–1941*. College Station: Texas A&M Press, 1991.

Gerassi, John, ed. *Camilo Torres, Revolutionary Priest: His Complete Writings and Messages*. 1971; reprint, Middlesex, England: Penguin Press, 1973.

Gillis, Chester. *Roman Catholicism in America*. New York: Columbia University Press, 1999.

Goizueta, Roberto S. "U.S. Hispanic Popular Catholicism as Theopoetics." In Ada María Isasi-Díaz and Fernando F. Segovia, eds., *Hispanic/Latino Theology: Challenge and Promise*. Minneapolis: Fortress Press, 1996.

Golden, Renny. *Sanctuary: The New Underground Railroad*. Maryknoll: Orbis Press, 1986.

González, Gilbert G. *Labor and Community: Mexican Citrus Worker Villages in a Southern California County, 1900–1950*. Urbana: University of Illinois Press, 1994.

———. *Chicano Education in the Era of Segregation*. Philadelphia: Balch Institute Press, 1990.

González, Justo L. *Santa Biblia: The Bible Through Hispanic Eyes*. Nashville: Abingdon Press, 1996.

———. *Mañana: Christian Theology from a Hispanic Persepctive*. Nashville: Abingdon Press, 1990.

Gorostiaga, Xavier, and Peter Marchetti. "The Central American Economy: Conflict and Crisis." In Nora Hamilton et al., eds., *Crisis in Central America: Regional Dynamics and U.S. Policy in the 1980s*. Boulder: Westview Press, 1988.

Greeley, Andrew. *The Catholic Imagination*. Berkeley and Los Angeles: University of California Press, 2000.

Griffith, James S. *Folk Saints of the Borderlands: Victims, Bandits and Healers*. Tucson: Rio Nuevo, 2003.

Griswold del Castillo, Richard. *The Los Angeles Barrio, 1850–1890: A Social History*. Berkeley and Los Angeles: University of California Press, 1979.

———. *The Treaty of Guadalupe Hidalgo: A Legacy of Conflict*. Norman: University of Oklahoma Press, 1990.

———, and Richard A. García. *César Chávez: A Triumph of Spirit*. Norman: University of Oklahoma Press, 1995.

———, Teresa McKenna, and Yvonne Yarbro-Bejarano. *Chicano Art: Resistance and Affirmation, 1965–1985*. Los Angeles: Wright Art Gallery, UCLA, 1991.

Guerrero, Andrés G. *A Chicano Theology*. Maryknoll, N.Y.: Orbis Books, 1987.

Guglielmo, Thomas A. "The Struggle for Caucasian Rights: Mexicans, Mexican Americans, and the Transnational Struggle for Civil Rights in World War II Texas." *Journal of American History* 92, no. 4 (March 2006): 1212–1237.

Gutiérrez, David G. *Walls and Mirrors: Mexican Americans, Mexican Immigrants, and the Politics of Ethnicity.* Berkeley and Los Angeles: University of California Press, 1995.

———. "Migration, Emergent Ethnicity, and the 'Third Space': The Shifting Politics of Nationalism in Greater Mexico." *Journal of American History* 86, no. 2 (September 1999): 481–517.

Gutiérrez, Gustavo. *A Theology of Liberation: History, Politics, and Salvation.* Maryknoll, N.Y.: Orbis Books, 1973.

———. *The Power of the Poor in History.* Maryknoll, N.Y.: Orbis Books, 1983.

Gutiérrez, Ramón A. *When Jesus Came, the Corn Mothers Went Away: Marriage, Sexuality, and Power in New Mexico, 1500–1846.* Stanford: Stanford University Press, 1991.

———, ed. *Nuevomexicano Cultural Legacy: Forms, Agencies, and Discourse.* Albuquerque: University of New Mexico Press, 2002.

Hamilton, Nora, and Norma Stoltz. "Central American Migration: A Framework for Analysis." *Latin American Research Review* 26, no. 1 (1991): 75–110.

———, and Norma Stoltz Chinchilla. *Seeking Community in a Global City: Guatemalans and Salvadorans in Los Angeles.* Philadelphia: Temple University Press, 2001.

———, Norma Chinchilla, and James Loucky. "Central Americans in Los Angeles: An Immigrant Community in Transition." In Joan Moore and Raquel Pinderhughes, eds., *In the Barrios: Latinos and the Underclass Debate.* New York: Russell Sage Foundation, 1993.

Hammerback, John C., and Richard J. Jensen. *The Rhetorical Career of César Chávez.* College Station: Texas A&M Press, 1998.

Henderson, Alice Corbin. *Brothers of Light: The Penitentes of the Southwest.* New York: Harcourt, Brace, 1937.

Hernández, María. "The Last Fight of Father Olivares." *Los Angeles Times Magazine* (December 16, 1990).

Heyck, Deni Lynn Daly. "Father Luis Olivares Interview." In Deni Lynn Daly Heyck, ed., *Barrios and Borderlands: Cultures of Latinos and Latinas in the United States.* New York: Routledge Press, 1994.

Horgan, Paul. *Lamy of Santa Fe, the Life and Times.* New York: Farrar, Straus and Giroux, 1975.

Huber, Robert. "Fray Angélico Chávez: 20th Century Renaissance Man." *New Mexico Magazine* 48 (March–April 1970), 19.

Hurtado, Juan. "An Attitudinal Study of Social Distance Between the Mexican American and the Church." Ph.D. diss., U.S. International University, 1976.

Isasi-Díaz, Ada María. *En la Lucha: Elaborating a Mujerista Theology.* Minneapolis: Fortress Press, 1993.
————. *Mujerista Theology.* Maryknoll: Orbis Press, 1996.

Juárez, José Roberto. "La Iglesia Católica y el Chicano en Sud Texas, 1836–1911." *Aztlán* (Fall 1974): 217–255.

Kelliher, Thomas G., Jr. "Hispanic Catholics and the Archdiocese of Chicago, 1923–1970." Ph.D. diss., University of Notre Dame, 1996.
Kiev, Art. *Curanderismo: Mexican-American Folk Psychiatry.* New York: Free Press, 1968.

Lampe, Philip E., ed. *Hispanics in the Church: Up from the Cellar.* San Francisco: Catholic Scholars Press, 1994.
Leal, Luis. "In Search of Aztlán." *Denver Quarterly* 16, no. 3 (Fall 1981): 16–22.
Leo XIII. *Rerum Novarum.* Boston: Pauline Book and Media, 1942.
León, Luis D. *La Llorona's Children: Religion, Life, and Death in the U.S.-Mexican Borderlands.* Berkeley: University of California Press, 2004.
————. " 'Soy una Curandera y Soy una Católica': The Poetics of a Mexican Healing Tradition." In Matovina and Riebe-Estrella, eds., *Horizons of the Sacred.*
Lernoux, Penny. *Cry of the People.* New York: Penguin, 1982.
Levine, Daniel H., ed. *Religion and Political Conflict in Latin America.* Chapel Hill: University of North Carolina Press, 1986.
Levy, Jacques. *César Chávez: Autobiography of La Causa.* New York: W. W. Norton, 1975.
López, Ian F. Haney. *Racism on Trial: The Chicano Fight for Justice.* Cambridge: Harvard University Press, 2003.
Löwy, Michael. *The War of Gods: Religion and Politics in Latin America.* London: Verso, 1996.
Lucero-White, Aurora. *Los Hispanos: Five Essays on the Folkways of the Hispanos as Seen Through the Eyes of One of Them.* Denver: Sage Books, 1947.
————. *Literary Folklore of the Hispanic Southwest.* San Antonio: Naylor, 1953.

MacEoin, Gary. "A Brief History of the Sanctuary Movement." In *Sanctuary: A Resource Guide for Understanding and Participating in the Central American Refugee Struggle.* San Francisco: Harper and Row, 1985.
Machado, Daisy L. *Of Borders and Margins: Hispanic Disciples in Texas, 1888–1945.* New York: Oxford University Press, 2003.
Maldonado, David, Jr. *Crossing Guadalupe Street: Growing up Hispanic and Protestant.* Albuquerque: University of New Mexico Press, 2001.
Mangione, Jerre. *The Dream and the Deal: The Federal Writers' Project, 1935–1943.* Boston: Little, Brown, 1972.

Mares, E. A., ed. *Padre Martínez: New Perspective from Taos*. Taos: Millicent Rogers Museum, 1988.

Mariscal, George. *Brown-Eyed Children of the Sun: Lessons from the Chicano Movement, 1965–1975*. Albuquerque: University of New Mexico Press, 2005.

Martínez, Demetria. *Mother Tongue*. New York: Balantine Books, 1994.

Martínez, Richard Edward. PADRES: *The National Chicano Priest Movement*. Austin: University of Texas Press, 2005.

Martínez, Rubén. *The Other Side: Notes from the New L.A., Mexico City and Beyond*. New York: Vintage Books, 1992.

Matovina, Timothy, and Gary Riebe-Estrella, eds. *Horizons of the Sacred: Mexican Traditions in U.S. Catholicism*. Ithaca: Cornell University Press, 2002.

———. *Tejano Religion and Ethnicity: San Antonio, 1821–1860*. Austin: University of Texas Press, 1995.

———. *Guadalupe and Her Faithful: Latino Catholics in San Antonio from Colonial Origins to the Present*. Baltimore: Johns Hopkins University Press, 2005.

———, and Gerald E. Poyo, eds. *¡Presente! U.S. Catholics from Colonial Origins to the Present*. Maryknoll: Orbis Press, 2000.

———, ed. *Beyond Borders: Writings of Virgilio Elizondo and Friends*. Maryknoll: Orbis Press, 2000.

———. "Representation and the Reconstruction of Power: The Rise of PADRES and Las Hermanas." In Mary Jo Weaver, ed., *What's Left: Liberal American Catholics*. Bloomington: Indiana University Press, 1999.

———. "Latino Catholics and American Public Life." In Andrew Walsh, ed., *Can Charitable Choice Work? Covering Religion's Impact on Urban Affairs and Social Services*. Hartford, Conn.: Leonard E. Greenberg Center for the Study of Religion in Public Life, 2001.

McCracken, Ellen M., ed. *Fray Angélico Chávez: Poet, Priest, and Artist*. Albuquerque: University of New Mexico Press, 2000.

McGuire, Meredith. "Linking Theory and Methodology for the Study of Latino Religiosity in the United States Context." In Anthony M. Stevens-Arroyo and Ana María Díaz-Stevens, eds., *An Enduring Flame: Studies on Latino Popular Religiosity*. New York: Bidner Center for Western Hemispheric Studies, 1994.

Medina, Lara. *Las Hermanas: Chicana/Latina Religious-Political Activism in the U.S. Catholic Church*. Philadelphia: Temple University Press, 2004.

Meléndez, A. Gabriel. *So All Is Not Lost: The Poetics of Print in Nuevomexicano Communities, 1834–1958*. Albuquerque: University of New Mexico Press, 1997.

Menjívar, Cecilia. "Salvadoran Migration to the United States in the 1980s: What Can We Learn About It and From It?" *International Migration* 32 (1994): 371–401.

———. *Fragmented Ties: Salvadoran Immigrant Networks in America*. Berkeley and Los Angeles: University of California Press, 2000.

Meyer, Doris. *Speaking for Themselves: Neomexicano Cultural Identity and the Spanish-Language Press, 1880–1920.* Albuquerque: University of New Mexico Press, 1996.

Morales, Phyllis S. *Fray Angélico Chávez: A Bibliography.* Santa Fe: Lightning Tree, 1980.

Morris, Charles R. *American Catholic: The Saints and Sinners Who Built America's Most Powerful Church.* New York: Vintage Books, 1997.

Mosqueda, Lawrence J. *Chicanos, Catholicism and Political Ideology.* Lanham, Md.: University Press of America, 1986.

Mueller, Franz H. *The Church and the Social Question.* Washington: American Enterprise Institute, 1984.

Muñoz, Carlos, Jr., *Youth, Identity, and Power: The Chicano Movement.* London: Verso Press, 1989.

Nabhan-Warren, Kristy. *The Virgin of El Barrio: Marian Apparitions, Catholic Evangelizing, and Mexican-American Activism.* New York: New York University Press, 2005.

Navarro, Armando. *The Cristal Experiment: A Chicano Struggle for Community Control.* Madison: University of Wisconsin Press, 1998.

———. *Mexican American Youth Organization: Avant-Garde of the Chicano Movement in Texas.* Austin: University of Texas Press, 1995.

Nieto-Phillips, John M. *The Language of Blood: The Making of Spanish-American Identity in New Mexico, 1850s-1940.* Albuquerque: University of New Mexico Press, 2004.

Nunn, Tey Marianna. *Sin Nombre: Hispana and Hispano Artists of the New Deal Era.* Albuquerque: University of New Mexico Press, 2001.

O'Brien, David J. *American Catholics and Social Reform: The New Deal Years.* New York: Oxford University Press, 1968.

———. "The American Priest and Social Action." In John Tracy Ellis, ed., *The Catholic Priest in the United States: Historical Investigations.* Collegeville, Minn.: Saint John's University Press, 1971.

Odem, Mary E. "Our Lady of Guadalupe in the New South: Latino Immigrants and the Politics of Integration in the Catholic Church." *Journal of American Ethnic History* 24 (Fall 2004): 26–57.

Oropeza, Lorena. *¡Raza Sí! ¡Guerra No!: Chicano Protest and Patriotism During the Vietnam War Era.* Berkeley: University of California Press, 2005.

Padilla, Genaro. *My History, Not Yours: The Formation of Mexican American Autobiography.* Madison: University of Wisconsin Press, 1993.

Penkower, Monty Noam. *The Federal Writers' Project: A Story in Government Patronage of the Arts.* Urbana: University of Illinois Press, 1977.

Perales, Alonso. *Are We Good Neighbors?* San Antonio: Artes Gráficas, 1948.
———. *En Defensa de Mi Raza.* San Antonio: Artes Gráficas, 1973.
Perrone, Bobette, H., Henrietta Stockel, and Victoria Krueger. *Medicine Women, Curanderas, and Women Doctors.* Norman: University of Oklahoma Press, 1989.
Peterson, Jeanette Favrot. "The Virgin of Guadalupe: Symbol of Conquest or Liberation?" *Art Journal* 51, no. 4 (Winter 1992): 39–47.
Pitti, Gina Marie. "The Sociedades Guadalupanas in the San Francisco Archdiocese, 1942–1962." *U.S. Catholic Historian* 21 (Winter 2003): 83–98.
Pitti, Stephen J. *The Devil in Silicon Valley: Northern California, Race, and the Mexican Americans.* Princeton: Princeton University Press, 2003.
Poole, Stafford. *Our Lady of Guadalupe: The Origins and Sources of a Mexican National Symbol, 1531–1797.* Tucson: University of Arizona Press, 1996.
Poyo, Gerald E. " 'Integration Without Assimilation': Cuban Catholics in Miami, 1960–1980." *U.S. Catholic Historian* 20 (Fall 2002): 91–109.
Privett, Stephen A. *The U.S. Catholic Church and Its Hispanic Members: The Pastoral Vision of Archbishop Robert E. Lucey.* San Antonio: Trinity University Press, 1988.
Prother, Kieran. "Father Luis Olivares." *Peace Sharings* (Summer 1993): 3.
Pulido, Alberto L. "Are You an Emissary of Jesus Christ?: Justice, the Catholic Church, and the Chicano Movement." *Explorations in Ethnic Studies* 14, no. 1 (January 1991): 17–34.
———. "Nuestra Señora de Guadalupe: The Mexican Catholic Experience in San Diego." *Journal of San Diego History* 37 (Fall 1991).
———. "Race Relations within the American Catholic Church: An Historical and Sociological Analysis of Mexican American Catholics." Ph.D. diss., University of Notre Dame, 1989.
———. *The Sacred World of the Penitentes.* Washington, D.C.: Smithsonian Institution Press, 2000.

Quammen, David. "Seeking Refuge in a Desert: The Sanctuary Movement: Exodus Redux." *Harper's* 273 (December 1986).
Quiroz, Anthony. *Claiming Citizenship: Mexican Americans in Victoria, Texas.* College Station: Texas A&M University Press, 2005.
Quiroz, Fernando Garza. *El Niño Fidencio: Un Personaje Desconocido.* Monterrey, Mexico: Alfonso Reyes, 1970.

Rael, John B. *The New Mexican 'Alabado'.* Stanford: Stanford University Press, 1951.
Ramírez, Daniel. "Borderland Praxis: The Immigrant Experience in Latino Pentecostal Churches." *Journal of the American Academy of Religion* 67 (September 1999): 573–596.
Ramírez, Ricardo. "The Hispanic Peoples of the United States and the Church from 1965 to 1985." *U.S. Catholic Historian* 9 (Spring 1990): 165–177.

Rebolledo, Tey Diana, and María Teresa Márquez. *Women's Tales from the New Mexico WPA: La Diabla a Pie*. Houston: Arte Public Press, 2000.

Rivas-Rodríguez, Maggie, ed. *Mexican Americans and World War II*. Austin: University of Texas Press, 2005.

Robb, John D. *Hispanic Folk Music of New Mexico and the Southwest: A Self-Portrait of a People*. Norman: University of Oklahoma Press, 1980.

Rodríguez, Jeanette. "Contemporary Encounters with Guadalupe." *Journal of Hispanic/Latino Theology* 5, no. 1 (August 1997).

———. *Our Lady of Guadalupe: Faith and Empowerment among Mexican American Women*. Austin: University of Texas Press, 1994.

Rodríguez, Sylvia. *The Matachines Dance: Ritual Symbolism and Interethnic Relations in the Upper Rio Grande Valley*. Albuquerque: University of New Mexico Press, 1996.

Romano, Octavio. "Don Pedrito Jaramillo: The Emergence of a Mexican-American Folk Saint." Ph.D. diss., University of California, Berkeley, 1964.

Romero, Archbishop Oscar. *Voice of the Voiceless*. Maryknoll: Orbis Press, 1990.

Romero, Father Juan. "Tension between Cross and Sword: A Profile of Father Luis Olivares." Unpublished paper, courtesy of Father Romero.

———. "Ministry to Farm Workers: Experience in Advocacy." *Notre Dame Journal of Education* (Summer 1974).

———. "Charism and Power: An Essay on the History of PADRES." *U.S. Catholic Historian* (Winter/Spring 1990): 147–163.

———. "Religiosidad Popular as Locus for Theological Reflection and Springboard for Pastoral Action." Unpublished paper in possession of author.

———. "Usefulness of Hispanic Survey to Ministers of the Southwest." Unpublished paper in possession of author.

———. "Begetting the Mexican American: Padre Martínez and the 1847 Rebellion." In Thomas J. Steele, S.J., Paul Rhetts, and Barbe Awalt, eds. *Seeds of Struggle/Harvest of Faith: The Papers of the Archdiocese of Santa Fe Catholic Cuarto Centennial Conference on the History of the Catholic Church in New Mexico*. Albuquerque: LPD Press, 1998.

Ruiz, Vicki L. *Cannery Women/Cannery Lives: Mexican Women, Unionization, and the California Food Processing Industry, 1930–1950*. Albuquerque: University of New Mexico Press, 1987.

Saldívar, Ramón. *The Borderlands of Culture: Américo Paredes and the Transnational Imagination*. Durham: Duke University Press, 2006.

Sánchez, George J. *Becoming Mexican American: Ethnicity, Culture, and Identity in Chicano Los Angeles, 1900–1945*. New York: Oxford University Press, 1993.

Sánchez, Joseph P. *The Spanish Black Legend: Origins of Anti-Hispanic Stereotypes*. Albuquerque: Spanish Colonial Research Center, 1990.

Sánchez, Rosaura. *Telling Identities: The Californio Testimonios.* Minneapolis: University of Minnesota Press, 1995.

Sandoval, Moises, ed. *Fronteras: A History of the Latin American Church in the USA Since 1513.* San Antonio: Mexican American Cultural Center, 1983.

———. *On the Move: A History of the Hispanic Church in the United States.* 2d ed. Maryknoll, N.Y.: Orbis Press, 2006.

Saragoza, Alex M. "Recent Chicano Historiography: An Interpretive Essay." *Aztlán* 19 (Spring 1988–1990).

Shirley, Dennis. *Valley Interfaith and School Reform: Organizing for Power in South Texas.* Austin: University of Texas Press, 2002.

Simmons, Marc. *Coronado's Land: Daily Life in Colonial New Mexico.* Albuquerque: University of New Mexico Press, 1991.

Skerry, Peter. *Mexican Americans: The Ambivalent Minority.* New York: Free Press, 1993.

Smith, Jody Brant. *The Image of Guadalupe.* 2d ed. Macon, GA: Mercer University Press, 1994.

Smith, Rev. Donald. "The Wednesday Morning Coalition: A Call to Conscience." Ca. 1990.

Sobrino, Jon. *Archbishop Romero: Memories and Reflections.* Maryknoll: Orbis Press, 1990.

Sommers, Laurie Kay. "Inventing Latinismo: The Creation of 'Hispanic' Panethnicity in the United State." *Journal of American Folklore* 104 (1991): 32–53.

Soto, Antonio R. "The Chicano and the Church in Northern California, 1848–1978: A Study of an Ethnic Minority within the Roman Catholic Church." Ph.D. diss., University of California, Berkeley, 1978.

Steele, Thomas J., S.J. *The Alabados of New Mexico.* Albuquerque: University of New Mexico Press, 2005.

———. *Santos and Saints: The Religious Folk Art of Hispanic New Mexico.* Santa Fe: Ancient City Press, 1982.

———, and Rowena A. Rivera. *Penitente Self-Government: Brotherhoods and Councils, 1797–1947.* Santa Fe: Ancient City Press, 1985.

Taves, Ann. *The Household of Faith: Roman Catholic Devotions in Mid-Nineteenth-Century America.* Notre Dame: Notre Dame University Press, 1986.

Taylor, William B. "The Virgin of Guadalupe in New Spain: An Inquiry into the Social History of Marian Devotion." *American Ethnologist* 14, no. 1 (February 1987): 9–33.

Tomsho, Robert. *The American Sanctuary Movement.* Austin: Texas Monthly Press, 1987.

Torres, Eliseo. *The Folk Healer: The Mexican-American Tradition of Curanderismo.* Kingsville, Tex.: Nieves Press, 1985.

————, and Timothy L. Sawyer, Jr. *Curandero: A Life in Mexican Folk Healing.* Albuquerque: University of New Mexico Press, 2005.

Treviño, Roberto R. *The Church in the Barrio: Mexican American Ethno-Catholicism in Houston.* Chapel Hill: University of North Carolina Press, 2006.

Trotter, Robert T., and Juan Antonio Chavira. *Curanderismo.* Athens: University of Georgia Press, 1991.

Trujillo, Dennis Peter. "Commodification of Hispano Culture in New Mexico: Tourism, Mary Austin, and the Spanish Colonial Arts Society." Ph.D. diss., University of New Mexico, 2003.

Turner, Kay F. "Mexican American Women's Home Altars: The Art of Relationship." Ph.D. diss., University of Texas at Austin, 1990.

Valdez, Luis, and Stan Steiner, eds. *Aztlán: An Anthology of Mexican American Literature.* New York: Vintage Books, 1972.

Vanderwood, Paul J. *Juan Soldado: Rapist, Murderer, Martyr, Saint.* Durham: Duke University Press, 2004.

Walsh, Arlene M. Sánchez. *Latino Pentecostal Identity: Evangelical Faith, Self, and Society.* New York: Columbia University Press, 2003.

Weigle, Marta. *Brothers of Light, Brothers of Blood: The Penitentes of the Southwest.* Santa Fe: Ancient City Press, 1976.

————, and Peter White. *The Lore of New Mexico.* Albuquerque: University of New Mexico Press, 1988.

Whaley, Charlotte. *Nina Otero-Warren of Santa Fe.* Albuquerque: University of New Mexico Press, 1994.

Wolf, Eric R. "The Virgin of Guadalupe: A Mexican National Symbol." *Journal of American Folklore* 71 (January–March 1958): 34–39.

The WPA Guide to the 1930s New Mexico. 1940; reprint, Tucson: University of Arizona Press, 1989.

Wroth, William. *Images of Penance, Images of Mercy: Southwestern Santos in the Late Nineteenth Century.* Norman: University of Oklahoma Press, 1991.

Yielding, Kenneth Duane. "The Apostle of the Border: Cleofas Calleros." Seminar paper, Department of History, Texas Western College, May 1960, Southwest Collection, El Paso Public Library.

Index

CPSIA information can be obtained at www.ICGtesting.com
Printed in the USA
LVOW07s0022200114

370062LV00002B/181/P